William Morris and the Uses of Violence, 1856–1890

William Morris and the Uses of Violence, 1856–1890

Ingrid Hanson

ANTHEM PRESS
LONDON · NEW YORK · DELHI

Anthem Press
An imprint of Wimbledon Publishing Company
www.anthempress.com

This edition first published in UK and USA 2014
by ANTHEM PRESS
75–76 Blackfriars Road, London SE1 8HA, UK
or PO Box 9779, London SW19 7ZG, UK
and
244 Madison Ave. #116, New York, NY 10016, USA

First published in hardback by Anthem Press in 2013

Copyright © Ingrid Hanson 2014

The author asserts the moral right to be identified as the author of this work.

All rights reserved. Without limiting the rights under copyright reserved above, no part of this publication may be reproduced, stored or introduced into a retrieval system, or transmitted, in any form or by any means (electronic, mechanical, photocopying, recording or otherwise), without the prior written permission of both the copyright owner and the above publisher of this book.

British Library Cataloguing-in-Publication Data
A catalogue record for this book is available from the British Library.

Library of Congress Cataloging-in-Publication Data
The Library of Congress has catalogued the hardcover edition as follows:
Hanson, Ingrid.
William Morris and the uses of violence, 1856–1890 / Ingrid Hanson.
pages cm
Includes bibliographical references and index.
ISBN 978-0-85728-319-1 (hardcover : alk. paper)
1. Morris, William, 1834–1896–Criticism and interpretation. 2. Violence in literature. I. Title.
PR5084.H36 2013
821'.8–dc23
2012050569

ISBN-13: 978 1 78308 335 0 (Pbk)
ISBN-10: 1 78308 335 2 (Pbk)

Cover image: William Morris, *The Story of the Glittering Plain* (Hammersmith: Kelmscott Press, 1894). © The British Library Board. C.43.f.8, f.152

This title is also available as an ebook.

CONTENTS

Acknowledgements		vii
Introduction	Warriors Waiting for the Word	ix
Chapter One	The Early Romances and the Transformative Touch of Violence	1
Chapter Two	Knightly Women and the Imagination of Battle in *The Defence of Guenevere, and Other Poems*	31
Chapter Three	*Sigurd the Volsung* and the Parameters of Manliness	65
Chapter Four	Crossing the River of Violence: The Germanic Antiwars and the Uncivilized Uses of Work and Play	97
Chapter Five	'All for the Cause': Fellowship, Sacrifice and Fruitful War	131
Afterword	'Hopeful Strife and Blameless Peace'	167
Notes		173
Bibliography		203
Index		223

ACKNOWLEDGEMENTS

Parts of Chapter One have appeared, in an earlier form, in the *Review of English Studies* prize essay '"The Measured Music of our Meeting Swords": William Morris's Early Romances and the Transformative Touch of Violence', *Review of English Studies* 61 (2010): 435–54; parts of Chapter Two have been published, in an earlier form, in '"Bring me that Kiss": Incarnation and Truth in William Morris's *The Defence of Guenevere, and Other Poems*', *English* 59 (2010): 349–74. Part of Chapter Five has been published in *Reading Historical Fiction: The Revenant and Remembered Past*, edited by Kate Mitchell and Nicola Parsons (Basingstoke: Palgrave Macmillan, 2012). I am grateful to the publishers in each case for permission to reproduce the material here.

Much of the research for this book was facilitated by funding from the University of Sheffield and sundry research expenses were covered by the William Morris Society's Peter Floud Memorial Prize, 2008. I have also benefited from the intellectual enrichment and specific critiques of many colleagues and friends who have read parts of this work or discussed it with me at earlier stages, and to all of them I'm very grateful. Particular thanks are due to Marcus Waithe for careful reading, generous intellectual support and incisive comments over the years of my doctoral research and subsequently, and to Matthew Campbell, Daniel Karlin, Samantha Matthews and Tony Pinkney for their encouragement and advice at various points. I owe an enormous debt of gratitude to Richard, Jess and Isaac Hanson, whose love, support and various senses of humour sustain me always.

Introduction

WARRIORS WAITING FOR THE WORD

In an 1896 obituary, the socialist writer Edward Carpenter recalled the last time he had seen William Morris, at the Paris Congress in 1889. He described how he watched him, 'fighting furiously there on the platform with his own words (he was not feeling well that day), hacking and hewing the stubborn English phrases out.' His speeches, Carpenter averred, were 'a trump of battle', and he himself a 'brusque, hearty, bold and manly form'. He 'stood up from the first against the current of ugly, dirty commercialism [...] like a captain in the rout of his men withstanding the torrent of their flight and turning them back to the battle'.[1] Walter Crane uses similar metaphors in his 'Sonnet on the Death of William Morris', calling him a 'skilled craftsman' in both art and song, 'Whose voice by beating seas of hope and strife / Would lift the soul of Labour from the knife'. The poem laments that Morris should die 'while yet with battle-cries the air is rife'.[2] Both the language of battle and Crane's emphasis on the combination of craftsmanship, orality, hope and strife draw on Morris's own characteristic language, picking up images and ideas that run prominently through his writings and shape his personal, political and artistic vision.

They are ideas clearly articulated in Morris's poetic Prologue, 'Socialists at Play', written for a gathering of the Socialist League at South Place Institute in 1885, and recorded by May Morris in her memoir of her father:

> War, labour, freedom; noble words are these;
> But must we hymn them in our hours of ease?
> We must be men.[3]

In these few lines Morris draws together the important relationships that I examine in this book. The multiple interactions of war, labour and freedom, and the idea of the nobility of certain kinds of war and violence are central to his writings, from the earliest romances to the socialist works of the 1880s and 1890s. The question of what it means to be manly, or as Herbert Sussman puts it, how a man 'shapes the possibilities of manliness available to him within his cultural moment' intersects with these ideas, and I will consider the ways in which Morris's literary and political constructions of masculinity shape and are shaped by his understanding of violence.[4] Morris's work is representative of his age in its preoccupation with questions of masculinity, violence and identity in relation to society as a whole. However, it deals with them in ways that not only complicate well-established critical views of his work, but also undermine a simply stratified reading of political or artistic movements in the second half of the nineteenth century. His work tracks a trajectory in national life by its consistent, deliberate opposition to prevailing social, cultural and political narratives, but in order to oppose those narratives it draws on them and sometimes echoes them closely. This book suggests a way of rereading Morris but also, in doing so, gestures towards ways of rereading the breadth, complexity and range of uses of the idea of battle violence in Victorian literature and culture.

As J. Carter Wood points out, 'while we may always have violence, we do not always have the same violence: its meanings are continually fluctuating.'[5] This dual emphasis on the continuities of violence and the constructed nature of its meanings is an important one in the chapters that follow: I argue that the violence in Morris's writings reads, reflects, distorts and participates in discourses of violence and war that are historically contextualized but draw on the mythical and transhistorical. While the Victorian period has sometimes been seen as one which, as John Peck puts it, 'seemed to ignore the existence of war', at least until the 1880s, this book contributes to a growing body of work discussing, instead, the ways in which ideas of war and combat (different though these may be) as foundational elements of national and individual identity run through the literature and culture of the period. Morris's writings contribute to complex and conflicting understandings of violence and combat, identity and change across the second half of the nineteenth century, from the representations of chivalry in Pre-Raphaelite poetry and painting to the adventuring wars of fin-de-siècle romances.[6]

The Prologue goes on to urge its audience of socialists to join together in singing the 'Marseillaise', 'that glorious strain that long ago foretold / The hope now multiplied a thousand-fold' (626), highlighting, in the invocation of this song, the importance of the poetic rendering of the battles of the past and the potential for their ideological uses in the present. Finally, it calls up two pairings that are central to Morris's lexicon: work and play, which are often synonymous or complementary, but certainly not set in opposition to one another; and strife and peace, the latter consistently framed as the fruit of the former. Together they form an image of the life of the 'warrior' Morris presents to his listeners:

> So through our play, as in our work, we see
> The strife that is, the Peace that is to be.

We are as warriors waiting for the word
That breaks the truce and calls upon the sword:
Gay is their life and merry men they are,
But all about them savours of the war.

How far the image of 'warriors waiting for the word' is simply figurative, and how far it might cross over into personal or political reality, and what this might mean, is of central importance to this book. The very use of the word 'warrior' suggests, as Ruth Livesey points out, an immediate transposition of 'the eclectic crowd clad in fustian, serge suits, aesthetic drapery, and Jaeger woollens (with or without sandals) into a corps of armored yeomen, flashing steel amid the material of everyday life'.[7] The question of the effect of this transposition on both speaker and listeners, in terms of action as well as affect, is particularly significant in relation to the broader cultural ideas of work, play and manliness alongside which it stands. Is it a commonplace to view a gathering of political activists as warriors? Is Morris creating, evoking or disrupting a particular tradition?

This book suggests that from mid-Victorian Pre-Raphaelite medievalism or the 'old northernism' of writers and scholars on the Teutonic and Scandinavian past to the socialism of the fin de siècle, Morris works on the borderlines of traditions of culture, art or politics that interact specifically with ideas of violence and its purpose: a man of his time, however much he felt out of place in it.[8] Yet the use he makes of violence is peculiar to him; the imbrication of violent action, work and play, of self-sacrifice and stoicism combines old traditions in a way that complicates their meanings. Morris the medievalist romantic uses the past to suggest disorder, rather than order; Morris the socialist adapts ideas of racial and linguistic purity and continuity from the old northernists and Nordicists of his time and ideas of self-sacrifice from the religious aristocratic discourses of chivalry. He simultaneously exposes and utilizes concepts of historical and geographical contrasts between civilization and barbarism that underlie the rationalization of colonialism; he engages with the various concepts of progress, peace and economic success that drive the nineteenth-century peace movement.[9] His work spans the period between the end of the Crimean War and the years just before the second Boer War, a period of increasing political liberalism in which understandings of manliness and national identity are nonetheless closely bound up with shifting constructions of the meanings and uses of violence. Morris engages with developing cultural conversations about violence in relation to the body, the mind, the will and the nation, critiquing certain constructions of manliness, war and identity, but always fascinated with battle violence and its effects.

The term violence is used in a wide variety of ways, both philosophically and in relation to literature, as the *OED* shows. It is a word that needs definition: as Raymond Williams notes, 'its primary sense is of physical assault [...] yet it is also used more widely in ways that are difficult to define.'[10] The violence I am concerned with in this book is primarily physical, corporeal acts of destruction between people, or, as a by-product, by people against things. I do not generally mean, by violence, the more abstract textual acts inherent in the concept of linguistic and symbolic violence that Jean-Jacques Lecercle outlines in *The Violence of Language*, or the disruptive interactions between form, structure, content and historical context that Garrett Stewart highlights in *Novel Violence*. These ways of reading violence are not wholly excluded: the book does consider physical violence in relation to symbolic violence or the unseen violence of oppression and it does recognize the potentially violent and violating power of language alongside the 'jolt to expectation' it produces, its capacity to 'reformat' the representation of violence.[11] However, these considerations are always in the context of forceful acts of destruction and their effects on the individual human body and psyche, as well as the class or group or nation. At various points, most extensively in Chapter Two, I discuss the sonic, formal or performative qualities of violent language, but here too it is important that my argument relies on an exploration of the relationship between the verbalization of violence and its actual, enacted effects on the body. This latter relationship, central to the problematics of violence, has particular significance because Morris's own personal engagement with physical fighting or aggression was limited. While his brother Arthur was a solider, Morris himself was never in active combat. His representations of violence are drawn primarily from fictional tales, accounts of history or contemporary political affairs in England and abroad, and only a very little from his own experience.

This is not to say he never fought or handled weapons. In his youth he engaged in both the combative sport of singlestick and volunteer military training. He was an enthusiastic but clumsy player of singlestick during his student days at Oxford. His first biographer, J. W. Mackail, notes that 'a friend' described him as 'unskilful, vehement and iron-handed in attack', and that Maclaren, the owner of the gymnasium where Morris used to play, 'once said that Morris's bills for broken sticks and foils equalled those of all of the rest of his pupils put together.'[12] Similar lack of skill seems to have characterized his brief spell of soldiering. He was an early recruit to the Artists' Rifles, a volunteer corps formed in 1859 in response to fears of a French invasion. Many of his friends and acquaintances also joined up: Edward Burne-Jones, Dante Gabriel Rossetti, Val Prinsep, John Everett Millais and Holman Hunt.[13] The corps' drill corporal, William Richmond, described the routine of 'drill, route marches and sham skirmishing' as 'hard work' and 'by no means child's play'. He also recorded that 'William Morris [...] invariably turned to the "right" when the order was "left"; then, surprised at his mistake, he invariably begged pardon of the comrade to whom he found himself facing.'[14] Although no writings of Morris's own survive in relation to his experience of soldiering, this comic account of his inability on parade matches the accounts of contemporaries of his lack of skill and co-ordination at singlestick to suggest that the order and prowess he created and demonstrated in poetry and prose were not part of his own physical experience. Nonetheless in joining the Artists' Rifles, he signalled an early eagerness to engage in battle for the sake of a cause that was reflected in his later commitment to socialism.[15]

Morris's lack of experience of war was in part due to the time in which he lived, during which there was no major prolonged war involving British troops, although the army was active in a series of short wars abroad across the period of Victoria's reign. It is perhaps for this reason that discussions of Victorian literature of war and violence have tended to focus on a few key imperialist texts. However, there is a growing body of work paying attention to wider cultural constructions of violence, including domestic and criminal violence, as well as a number of subtle rereadings of Victorian writings on soldiering, war and the representation of imperialism.[16] The most compelling recent work on the war writings of the Victorians has been concerned to demonstrate the complexity of their response to war and to debunk the assumption, set up by the modernists, of the Victorians' unequivocal glorification of battle. Matthew Bevis offers close and careful rereadings of minor nineteenth-century war poets alongside a reappraisal of Tennyson, and Daniel Karlin highlights the subtleties, contrarieties and shifts in Kipling's war poetry from the 1880s until the end of the First World War, while in a more fully developed consideration, Stefanie Markovits examines the ways in which the Crimean War was represented in literature and the media.[17] This book's readings of Morris and violence participate in this movement towards a more nuanced understanding of the representation and reception of battle in the Victorian period.

In pursuit of this end, the book engages in a discussion of the interplay of fiction and reality, literary discourse and political propaganda, but also an analysis of the phenomenology and philosophy of violence by which Morris delineates a complicated ethical position. His work can be understood in its diachronic relation to the history of ideas as well as its synchronic relation to the preoccupations of its own time: it presents the physical acts of battle as a way of knowing the world, according primacy to the senses as a source of imagination and understanding; it partakes of the commitment to excess and expenditure that Georges Bataille identifies as crucial to war and sacrifice as part of an energy economy, and also, as I argue in Chapter Five, contributes to a history of writing about violence that invests faith in the transformative power of cyclical violence identified in René Girard's critiques of sacrificial violence.[18] This imaginative investment in violence is not an aspect of Morris's work that has been much discussed, perhaps because it conflicts with the issues of holism, community, beauty and social justice for which he so evidently stands.[19] In a tradition he himself vehemently rejected, Morris has suffered the critical fate of being a Great Man. The radical left-wing politics that many of his near-contemporaries suppressed in their accounts of his life has been thoroughly recovered as central to his art, particularly in the wake of key works on his politics by E. P. Thompson and Paul Meier.[20] The attention to, and on occasion celebration of, violence in his work, equally inconvenient to later readers, has not.

As Tony Pinkney points out, 'even Morrisians of a strongly theoretical bent are in the end held back by their political allegiances and often a well-nigh personal love for their text and author.'[21] While it would be difficult to imagine readings of literature entirely devoid of acknowledged or unacknowledged political allegiances or personal feelings, Pinkney highlights an issue of particular note in relation to Morris: he has been claimed as a Marxist, an anarchist and an environmentalist, as well as a key figure in the Aesthetic movement.[22] So powerful is the myth of his personality, strengthened by his daughter May Morris's affectionate anecdotes and explanations in the introductions to *The Collected Works of William Morris*, that readings of his work have tended to turn aside from his undoubted, and discomfiting, preoccupation with violence.[23] It has been noted, however, if rarely examined. Lyman Tower Sargent observes that 'the likelihood of a violent transition to the better society is always part of Morris's vision even though it is sometimes easy to miss in his pictures of a peaceful future'.[24] Indeed, extended considerations of violence, or of the interaction of this imaginative commitment with Morris's literary or political context have been few and limited. Florence Boos, who makes the most sustained examination of Morris's relation to war and violence, concludes that he became increasingly pacifist over the years, and leaves unexamined the conflict she discerns between his political commitment to peaceful change and the violence of his fiction, as I discuss in Chapter Five.[25]

Set against this prevailing view, it is the premise of this book that underlying all of Morris's work is the commitment to a myth of violence that has the potential to be translated into action of various kinds. His poems and tales of violence take their place in an ethically difficult tradition of war writing that offers the transformation of violence into beauty or affect or meaning through its representation in words. As part of the medievalism that formed so important an element of Morris's milieu, the early nineteenth century saw the republication of Jean Froissart's fourteenth-century French *Chronicles of the Hundred Years War* in English. Morris read both the reprinted sixteenth-century translation by Lord Berners, and the 1805 Thomas Johnes translation, extensively reviewed by Walter Scott in the *Edinburgh Review*.[26] Just as Morris would do later, Scott praises Froissart's engaging style, writing that:

> In Froissart, we hear the gallant knights, of whom he wrote, arrange the terms of combat and the manner of the onset; we hear their soldiers cry their war-cries; we see them strike their horses with the spur; and the liveliness of the narration hurries us along with them into the whirlwind of battle.[27]

It is this same ability to conjure with words the experiences of the senses, coupled with what Morris describes as a 'Gothic love of incident', that runs through his own works and their portrayal of battles past and future.[28]

The potential of violence to make a good story is surely one of the reasons for its use in the work of this writer who preferred the action-packed tales of Alexandre Dumas or *The Thousand and One Nights* to the novels of George Eliot or the 'dull' feminism of Elizabeth Barrett Browning's *Aurora Leigh*.[29] Stories work in the world, however. Tales of battle and enmity are not separate from the circumstances of their composition and reception; the world of imagination and the world of action feed each other and stories may wreak or sustain actual violence. Richard W. Kaeuper examines the crossover between tales of chivalry and its practice in the Middle Ages, offering evidence that knights of the Middle Ages themselves both read and enjoyed romances, and that their practice was affected by the stories they read: 'chivalric literature was an active social force, helping to shape attitudes about basic questions'.[30] Morris's stories both enact and create a similar cycle of telling and doing, in which violence engenders new identities and a new kind of embodied consciousness.

In his strangely equivocal 1910 essay, 'The Moral Equivalent of War', the American pragmatist and psychologist William James sets out to consider 'only the higher aspects of militaristic sentiment', turning away – 'pacifist though I am' – from the horrors of war and its 'bestial side'. He argues that 'patriotism no-one thinks discreditable; nor does anyone deny that war is the romance of history. But inordinate ambitions are the soul of any patriotism, and the possibility of violent death the soul of all romance'.[31] While Morris issues his own warnings about false patriotism and unjust war and is bitterly opposed to the principles underlying the wars of empire, he cannot avoid suggesting the alternative possibility of both true patriotism and just war. Certainly he embraces 'the romance of history' in the wars of the past: an ongoing story of struggle and heroism, told and retold. James's idea of finding a moral equivalent of the energy, struggle and manliness of war in 'work as an obligatory service to the state', in which the worker would be 'owned, as soldiers are by the army' would have been anathema to Morris, whose response to Edward Bellamy's novel of regimented socialism, *Looking Backward*, was that 'if they brigaded *him* into a regiment of workers, he'd just lie on his back and kick'.[32] Nonetheless the idea of war as work and work as war, beautiful, holistic and communal, runs through his writings, presented as part of a way of life that offers a version of James's 'manliness of type', along with 'strenuous honor and disinterestedness'.[33] After his early explorations of the meanings of violence and its capacity for both revealing and transforming the world, he turns to the communal violence of clearly defined wars of oppressed against oppressors, in *A Dream of John Ball*, *News from Nowhere* and *The Pilgrims of Hope*, or of communal, integral societies against individualistic, greed-oriented ones. Work is not an alternative to revolutionary war, but coextensive with it.

As Daniel Pick observes, the etymology of 'war' relates it to confusion, discord and strife.[34] Strife is productive of change for Morris, and change leads to hope. As he argued in his 1885 lecture, 'The Hopes of Civilization', 'times of change, disruption and revolution are naturally times of hope also, and not seldom the hopes of something better to come are the first tokens that tell people that revolution is at hand'.[35] The fruitful reciprocity between hope and disruption can be seen in the content of Morris's work and in its forms, in which rhythmic and formal disruption or fragmentation work in tension with the historically meaningful forms and archaic language that give his work shape. This is as much the case in his earliest writings as it is in his deliberately political later works.

In the 1850s, when as an Oxford student Morris first began to write and publish, his life was very much informed by a culture of romantic violence, from the battle tales of Malory, Scott and Kingsley that he so enjoyed, to the political context of the 1854–56 Crimean War, reported on by William Howard Russell and much debated by Morris and his student friends. At the same time he was deeply familiar with the ideas of the Oxford Movement, which influenced him in his later years at school and early days at Oxford, with its emphasis on mysticism, sacrament and sacrifice, brotherhood and community.[36] It was as an undergraduate that Morris first came across Ruskin's writings, which were to have an enduring influence on his life and thought. Ruskinian ideas as well as romantic ones are evident in his early, critically neglected short stories, with their dreamlike settings and distorted spiritual visions of combat, published in the *Oxford and Cambridge Magazine* in 1856. Ideas of manliness and identity that he would revisit and reformulate in later works were already in evidence in these stories, considered in Chapter One. I argue that Morris's portrayal of visceral, corporeal violence as a form of intimate, transformative touch goes beyond the interest in knighthood common to much nineteenth-century medievalism and engages with contemporary debates about mind and body, violence and war. It offers a disturbing and culturally disruptive vision of the relationship between battle, knowledge and selfhood. At the same time, the stories' detailed portrayal of committed, communal war and passionate hand-to-hand battles offers an imaginative world free from the industrial mechanization and materialistic individualism of Victorian society that Morris and his friends deplored in other articles in the *Oxford and Cambridge Magazine*.

Despite his early and enduring love for Malory's *Morte Darthur*, read in Robert Southey's 1817 edition, Morris's own literary foray into specifically Arthurian territory is brief and characteristically tangential.[37] The poems of *The Defence of Guenevere* have received a great deal of critical attention, and while work on the title poem in the twentieth century focused often on the question of how Morris viewed Guenevere's adultery, more recent criticism has examined the poems' form, their relationship to art and their impulse of dissent.[38] Jonathan Freedman draws attention to Morris's use of the idea of battle and knightly defence in 'The Defence of Guenevere'.[39] In Chapter Two I argue that it is not only the language of battle, or language as battle, but the use of the body and words in battle that forms the central focus of the title poem and offers a way of reading the violence, the passion and the pain of the other poems in the volume. 'The Defence of Guenevere' and other poems in the volume draw on Malory's emphasis on 'adventure', on battle as a means of proving worth and of the body in combat as the arbiter of questions of morality, as well as on his somewhat cursory dealings with religion as a backdrop for the lives of his knights, rather than a motivation. The volume also harnesses the writings of Froissart, reframing the violence of history in layers of retelling. It draws on a Romantic legacy to emphasize the interrelation of violence and erotic passion in a way that Morris does not return to until his late romances in the 1890s. More importantly, it offers violence as a means of painfully but potentially generatively disordering the moral boundary lines or abstract truths of the world by the interactions of the body.

While the influence of Ruskin's ideas on work, art and architecture was lifelong for Morris, the less formative but nonetheless significant influence of Thomas Carlyle, evident particularly in the *Oxford and Cambridge Magazine* romances, persisted into the 1870s, when Morris, his marriage floundering, turned to Iceland for solace and inspiration. He had used some Icelandic material in his long poem cycle of 1868–70, *The Earthly Paradise*, and in the late 1860s and 1870s he began to work seriously on learning Icelandic and translating its tales.[40] Carlyle's enthusiasm for Norse mythology was made evident in his 1840 lecture on Odin, 'The Hero as Divinity', the first of a series of lectures on heroes, published in 1841 as *On Heroes, Hero-Worship and the Heroic in History*. His focus is on the enduring qualities of heroism that have appeared in various guises in different men across successive eras: 'Universal History, the history of what man has accomplished in this world, is at bottom the History of the Great Men who have worked here'.[41] While Morris's interest is already in stories of whole tribes or races rather than on single heroes, the values of manliness and courage that Carlyle addresses run through Morris's epic hexameter poem of 1876, *Sigurd the Volsung and the Fall of the Niblungs* and his Icelandic short stories and translations; his longstanding commitment to tales of heroic self-sacrifice and valiant battle finds its natural expression in the Norse sagas and the traditional poems and prose tales known as the Eddas.[42]

At the same time, by the 1870s a specialist but growing interest in the Nordic origins of the English language had led to the publication of a number of Icelandic or Old Norse dictionaries, grammars and histories, as well as theoretical accounts of the national and linguistic characteristics inherited by the English from their Northern forbears, accounts which laid the foundations for a much more troubling discourse of racial superiority by the beginning of the twentieth century. This discourse ran alongside the burgeoning interest in Aryanism that emphasized England's Teutonic linguistic and cultural heritage. As Tony Ballantyne observes, by the mid-nineteenth century, 'John Kemble and Benjamin Thorpe had elaborated a strong Anglo-Saxonist tradition, which emphasized the linguistic connection between English and its Germanic and Indo-European ancestors. Within such a context, Aryanism fortified both nationalist and imperialist ideologies'.[43] Andrew Wawn notes that, in the context of this emerging comparative philology, 'European and British scholars of Icelandic were prominent in what became a heavily politicised scholarly field.'[44] The influence of the old North makes itself felt in literature as well as linguistic and anthropological study: it found its way into Matthew Arnold's poetry, in the form of *Balder Dead* (1854), into popular literature such as George Dasent's 1859 translation of Norse stories and later, into official national record, in his scholarly translations of Norse sagas for the magisterial Rolls project.[45] Through these varied writings, with their nuances of emphasis and interpretation, there runs a narrative of the courage and manliness of the Norse people and their language.

While the interpretation of the relationship between manliness and violence shifted significantly over the course of the nineteenth century, as John Tosh's careful examination of definitions and discourses or Graham Dawson's detailed examples demonstrate, the two remain key ideas in relation to both individual and national identity, not only for men but also, partially for women.[46] As his diaries of two trips to Iceland in 1871 and 1873 make clear, Morris's interest in Iceland became a personal quest for courage and manliness in the face of difficult circumstances, and these same characteristics inform the tales of battle, suicide and violence, as well as the distinctively archaic, quasi-Northern mode of telling them, that make up *Sigurd the Volsung*, which is the focus of

Chapter Three. Before embarking on *Sigurd*, Morris worked with Icelander Eiríkr Magnússon to translate its Icelandic original, the *Völsunga Saga*.[47] May Morris wrote of her father at this time: 'although after Morris had first read the translation Magnússon made for him of the *Völsunga* he showed by a rather disparaging remark his distaste for the violence of some of the legends in the grim brief statements of the Saga, we have seen that he changed his opinion.' She quotes a letter from Morris to Charles Eliot Norton in which he comments on the 'depth and intensity' of the Icelandic saga, and how much 'grander' it is than its German counterpart, the *Nibelungenlied*.[48] My reading of the poem in Chapter Three argues that Morris's representation of violence and the kind of manliness it sustains allows for a nuanced understanding of a community of violence that arises from the interaction of deed and tale, and is shaped by both men and women.

The idea of manliness in literature and in life runs alongside a developing discourse of civilization and barbarism in nineteenth-century culture which is reflected not only in the growing popularity of tales of the Viking past, but also, towards the end of the century, in the popular literature of imperial adventure. The twin concepts of barbarism and civilization, situated both temporally and geographically, had gathered force and complexity by the late 1880s, when Morris was writing his Germanic romances, *The House of the Wolfings* and *The Roots of the Mountains*, stories that pit the barbarian against, first, the forces of civilization and, next, the brutal savage.[49] By this stage Britain was at the height of its imperial expansion, gaining and maintaining territories through a series of small local wars, while an emerging discourse of evolution and degeneration theorized the relative states of development of colonized peoples. Morris's romances make use of some of the racial theories and stereotypes that fuel colonialism, even while his political writings of this period inveigh against the colonial project as a degrading and deceptive offshoot of capitalist injustice. The polyvalence of the ideas of civilization and barbarism in relation to Victorian culture and its empire as well as in relation to the European past and present makes them slippery concepts, as I argue in Chapter Four, so that Morris's archaic tales of the heroic battles of the ancient barbarian Goths resonate uncomfortably with the imperial romances of such writers as H. Rider Haggard or the racialized proclamations of Cecil Rhodes. At the same time they engage obliquely in a developing cultural debate, in which Marxism is only one strand, about the relative values of civilization and barbarism and its present as well as historical manifestations. In their intensely realized representation of war as work the romances embody Morris's commitment to the seamless continuity and holism of unalienated labour, but at the same time locate this holism in the physical destructiveness of war. The societies Morris depicts are partly socialist prototypes, then, but they also intersect with more conservative, imperialistic or even protofascist Victorian ideas of glorious war, racial cleansing and the pleasurable work of battle.

Chapter Five turns to the question of Morris's explicitly socialist writings, in which the idea of imaginary or idealized violence taking on flesh becomes more pressing than in any of his other works: in the political context of *A Dream of John Ball, News from Nowhere, Chants for Socialists* and *The Pilgrims of Hope*, Morris's works enter, more specifically, the field of political propaganda. Written, like the Germanic romances, in the busy and turbulent period between his 'conversion' to socialism in 1883 and his gradual reduction of political activity in the 1890s, they adumbrate, by looking both forward and back, an ideal of communal battle against injustice leading to a communal life without injustice. They draw into synthesis the ideals of chivalry, sacrifice and brotherhood that drove Morris's earliest work, the disruptive rereading of history that is evident in the poems of *The Defence* and the Germanic romances, the emphasis on manliness in battle developed in *Sigurd*, and the political imperatives of the Socialist League: education, agitation and organization.

A consideration of the original publication context of these stories in *Commonweal*, the journal of the Socialist League which Morris founded and edited, offers a fruitful way of reading them in the light of the wider narrative of socialist suffering and struggle that is given flesh in the pages of the journal. Key to my reading of Morris's socialist fiction and poetry is an exploration of his own frequently made distinction between the violence of open war and the hiddenness of capitalist violence against the working class. This distinction is important in order to understand how his ideas interact with other contemporary conceptions of violence, revolution, and social change. His short satirical play of 1887, *The Tables Turned Or, Nupkins Awakened*, greatly enjoyed by his socialist colleagues, relies for much of its humour on gentle mockery of the way in which fin-de-siècle anxieties about anarchist, Fenian and working-class violence led to a misinterpretation by the authorities of socialist language about revolution.[50] Morris himself is at pains to explain, in an early lecture, that revolution need not mean violence. Yet we do not need to read against the grain to suggest that Morris's works of the 1880s and 1890s evince a far greater investment in an ideal of actual political violence – albeit brought about by necessity – than has usually been acknowledged.

Back at the Socialist League's 'entertainment' of 1885, Morris concluded his Prologue with a nod to the idea of the combination of will and fate that drove the tale of *Sigurd the Volsung* and *The Earthly Paradise*'s 'The Lovers of Gudrun', and would, he believed, eventually bring about a socialist future:[51]

> There! Let the peddling world go staggering by,
> Propped up by lies and vain hypocrisy,

> While here we stand amidst the scorn and hate,
> Crying aloud the certain tale of fate,
> Biding the happy day when sword in hand,
> Shall greet the sun and bless the tortured land.[52]

The lies and hypocrisy that make up the 'peddling world', buying and selling in a stupor and scorning those who disagree, provides justification for the use of the sword, whose violence is nonetheless displaced onto the depersonified enemy who has already tortured not the people, but the land. The use of the sword in this image, rather than the muskets, rifles or handguns that were the primary weapons of the Victorian age, distances the image to a certain degree and mythologizes it; but at the same time it evokes a hands-on willingness to engage in the kind of hand-to-hand battle that continued to be seen as the most honest and manly form of combat by thousands of active soldiers.[53] As Joanna Bourke notes, well into the twentieth century, 'no one was prepared to detract from the glamour associated with the bayonet', and it continued to form a significant part of military training long after its usefulness in actual combat was in doubt.[54] It is this glamour, as well as warriorlike prowess, that Morris evokes in his image of the sword, and it is in this historical continuity as much as its own context that the significance of his engagement with the idea of battle lies.

At the same time this closing vision of the warrior-knight suggests the consonance of Morris's cause with nature and the inevitabilities of history. It evokes the sanctifying power of the sword to heal and bring prosperity, properly wielded: 'sword in hand', the people will 'bless the [...] land'. This book suggests that this sense of body, will and weapon being engaged in one enterprise on behalf of the land tortured by injustice or mismanagement runs through Morris's work, comprehending art, politics and personal relationships in its commitment to the generative, transformative, and even, paradoxically, healing power of combat. If in this it echoes many of the narratives of nationalism and imperialism that it opposes, it nonetheless reshapes them towards a different ideal, without cancelling out their troubling preoccupation with violence as means of establishing and expressing identity.

Chapter One

THE EARLY ROMANCES AND THE TRANSFORMATIVE TOUCH OF VIOLENCE

In 1856, the year following the publication of Alexander Bain's influential volume of psychophysiology, *The Senses and the Intellect*, Alfred Tennyson's controversial poem of war, excess and madness, *Maud*, and Charles Kingsley's historically transposed tale of valiant Elizabethan battle, *Westward Ho!*, as the much-criticized Crimean War limped to its equivocal end, the young William Morris published his first short stories. They appeared in the shortlived *Oxford and Cambridge Magazine*, which Morris wrote and edited with his university friends that year.[1] All but one of the eight dreamlike, fragmented tales are set in the heroic medieval past and are concerned with battle, courage, and a search for identity, expressed through the actions and reactions of the individual body.

In the March issue of the magazine was an unsigned article by fellow Oxford student, Richard Watson Dixon, defending the Crimean War and deploring the government's decision to pursue peace negotiations with Russia:

> To be summoned to lay down our arms, just at the time when we were becoming habituated to their use, and had nerved ourselves for a long and obstinate struggle; just at the time, moreover, when the tide of success seemed about to set steadily towards us, is in itself a baffling and irritating thing, sufficient to produce lassitude and disgust.[2]

Dixon laments that 'a war so splendidly begun' should be abandoned at this stage. It would be better, he argues, to see through the defeat of Russia and the overthrow of its influence across Europe than to leave the war apparently unfinished, 'the cause of freedom only half-asserted'.[3] The evils of tyranny and oppression could – and should – be overcome by a just and 'gallant' war courageously carried through to completion, which means, in this account, the absolute defeat of the enemy.[4] Yet Dixon goes beyond the use of lofty words or abstract ideals about the politics of war and hints at its fundamental connection with both character and body. The concept of becoming 'habituated' to the use of arms bears traces of the Aristotelian and Thomist idea of *habitus*, the development of character through repeated choices for good or evil.[5] At the same time it adumbrates a more direct relationship between the action of bearing arms and the nervous reactions of the body itself, resonating with the emerging discourse of Victorian psychology concerning the relationship between body and mind, action, habit and will. Bain's newly published work of psychology stresses the continuity of body and mind, the centrality of the nervous system as a means of communication between them, and the importance of 'muscular and nervous action' in 'confirming a physical habit' and 'forming an intellectual aggregate'; William Carpenter's *Principles of Mental Physiology*, published in the same year, devotes a whole chapter to the development of 'Intellectual and Moral character' through the habitual actions and thoughts.[6] Doing, knowing and being in the world are intrinsically linked here.

Dixon suggests that withdrawal from war leads to 'lassitude', and 'disgust', words with unavoidably corporeal and sensory implications, carrying the suggestion of a failure of bodily health, energy or pleasure. Bearing arms or ceasing to bear them is not simply a matter of martial obedience or political expedience, he suggests, but rather is able to effect change in the somatic reactions not only of the soldier but also of the society that supports him: this protest is made in the voice of a collective, vicarious 'we' who must 'lay down our arms'. The body and its actions are the locus of meaning here. It is this intimate corporeal understanding of both individual and communal being and identity through the violence of combat that Morris explores in his short stories. While the clarity and moral certainty of Dixon's impassioned defence of war as political strategy for the good of Europe is blurred and revised through the romantic medievalist prism of the stories, its commitment to an idealistic but materially grounded notion of the courageous and necessary work of bearing arms as a means of social renewal and personal transformation underlies their every oneiric twist and turn.

These early romances have received little critical attention, either at the time of their publication or subsequently.[7] Both E. P. Thompson and Fiona MacCarthy make only the briefest of mentions of the stories, linking them to the biographical details of Morris's life.[8] Carole Silver and Amanda Hodgson both consider the short stories in relation to the forms and traditions of romance. Hodgson concentrates on Morris's use of the past, observing that he 'wishes to demonstrate that the realities behind medieval romance were harsh and brutal'. She offers a perceptive discussion of the significance of judgement and revenge in 'The Hollow Land' but stops short of considering the specific uses of violence in any of the stories.⁹ Silver pays particular attention to Morris's sources and discusses literary, visual and mythic symbolism in the tales. She notes Morris's focus on violence and death, and gestures towards a central difficulty with his presentation of them: that 'often, his preoccupation with mutilation and decay becomes excessive'.¹⁰ Yet it is this very excess, a deliberate and disturbing extravagance of active violence, that gives meaning to the battles of the stories.

More than this, these romances celebrate the haptic and kinaesthetic development of self and identity through battle, challenging ideas of knowing or being that focus on the purely abstract or even the chromatic or visual, important though these are in the stories. My emphasis on Morris's absorption in and celebration of battle offers an alternative view to the recent brief consideration of the early stories in Eleonora Sasso's Freudian analysis of Morris's violence. Sasso argues that in these romances, 'lust for killing, hatred and destruction is somehow reduced by intense love for family and damozels.'¹¹ It is my argument, on the contrary, that love is not reduced by, but rather expressed through various kinds of battle. The stories are, for the most part, as Morris's biographer Mackail observes, set in a world of 'pure romance'; historical realities do not apparently impinge upon these often inexplicable fairytale worlds.¹² Their preoccupation with telling tales of deeds in relation to battle recalls the heroic sagas and chivalric romances whose influence is specifically acknowledged in epigraphs, quotations or direct references, while the emphasis on perception reflects a more subjective consciousness.

Yet their representations of just and unjust battle and their focus on courage and cowardice, leadership and honour, draw at least some of their power from the contemporary context of the Crimean War. They are, after all, stories written during that unsuccessful but well reported and publicly discussed war, for which Morris's close friend Edward Burne-Jones proposed joining up in 1855.¹³ Not only the war itself but also other writings on it feature repeatedly in the *Oxford and Cambridge Magazine*, from Dixon's opinion pieces early in the year to the review, in the December issue, of Sydney Dobell's 1856 volume *England in Time of War*.¹⁴ The romances' preoccupation with the geography and corporeality of violence, then, suggests an engagement, however displaced, with contemporary ideas of duty, war, conquest and social change. They are exploratory tales in which the various effects and manifestations of violence shape the lives and relationships of individuals, communities and the lands they live in. The lacerations of skin and flesh produced by violence open doorways to new kinds of perception and new, tactile understandings of the world, just as, in 'Golden Wings', the young Lionel's slaying of the unknown knight at his door opens a new understanding of his own identity and a new path into the world for him ('Golden Wings', 293).

The violence of battle is central to Morris's stories as a means of altering both reality and perception. The relationship between subject and object, self and the world is re-examined through the practice of violence; in the process the meaning of violence and the nature of human relations are redefined. Violence is not secondary or incidental, but physically detailed and essential. Like the knights of the *Morte Darthur*, which Morris read and reread in his university years and later, his characters come to an understanding of themselves and the world through the actions of their bodies in combat: as Jill Mann observes, 'the knight realizes himself and his destiny, the nature and events that chance has willed to him, in the long succession of physical engagements with his fellows'.[15] This emphasis on chance, so central to combat, runs alongside the emerging ideas of individual will and choice developed through physical action and habit that are important not only to Morris's developing thinking but also to wider social, religious and political concerns that converged in contemporary psychological discourses such as Bain's, as Rick Rylance points out.[16] Yet the tales turn away from the exploration of cause and effect on which such discourses rely, to portray instead the irrational relations between self and others forged through the physical contingencies of violence. The battles of his stories involve hands-on, close-up physical contact; in portraying them, Morris turns his back on the political complexities of his own age and its compromises in war to embrace the apparently simpler, blunter and more direct interactions of medieval times and tales.

Nonetheless his stance betrays its Victorian origins. His stories, like the writings of Ruskin, Carlyle, Tennyson and Kingsley, form part of what Edward Burne-Jones called 'this most godly crusade against falsehood, doubt, and wretched fashion, against hypocrisy and mammon, and lack of earnestness'.[17] Like Morris's and Burne-Jones's earlier, abandoned plans to found a monastic Brotherhood, this is a crusade that subscribes to an idealized vision of knightly manhood. Morris's contribution to the crusade offers certain kinds of violence as an antidote to others, bearers of falsehood and doubt, hypocrisy and mammon; it does not engage with individual or social alternatives to violence as a means of transformation. Neither the pacific economic values of mid-Victorian capitalism nor the anti-sacramentalism of the low church theology of Morris's childhood have any place in a world where meaning is expressed and honour gained through prowess in battle. The shedding of blood is physically brutal and immanently meaningful in these stories. Morris has no literary truck with the idealistic Free Trade pacifism of William Cobden, John Bright and the Peace Society, vocally opposed to the Crimean War; neither does he engage with the pragmatics of war. Instead, the temporally distanced chivalric combat in these narratives offers a different kind of touch from the Midas touch of greed that Carlyle identifies as characteristic of their times;

the world of dreams and tales which frames the battles offers an alternative to the spiritual enchantment of money that Carlyle describes; and the heroic values of courage, love and truth stand in contrast to the 'bourgeoisdom and philistinism' that Morris later identified as characteristic of the world of his youth.[18]

In his exploration of violence Morris wrestles with and reconceives both the Christian myth of redemption through blood and suffering and the medievalist representations of his contemporaries, with which he was deeply familiar. The stories' depiction of violence is more stylized, fragmented and gothically disorientating than the physically powerful, morally sanctioned and orderly violence evident in Kingsley's *Westward Ho!* (1855) and *Two Years Ago* (1857), and more intensely detailed than the allegorically pure violence of La Motte Fouqué's romantic tale, *Sintram*, a favourite with Morris and his university friends as a source text for Charlotte M. Yonge's 1853 tale of spiritualized knighthood, *The Heir of Redclyffe*. They offer the madness of violence as a state of transformation, going beyond the lyrical, if equivocal, aestheticization of violence in Tennyson's *Maud* (1855), favourably reviewed by William Fulford in the March edition of the *Oxford and Cambridge Magazine*.[19] The tales both acknowledge and question the Catholic idealization of knighthood as a code of behaviour outlined in Kenelm Digby's *The Broad Stone of Honour* (1822), a book which Georgiana Burne-Jones observed that her husband still liked to read in later life, because 'his youth lay enclosed' in it, despite his recognition that it was a 'sillyish' book.[20] They interrogate issues of love and power in relation to violence, but avoid the misogynistic gender implications inherent in Ruskin's later explication of the role of women in causing war.[21] Medievalism is the context of the stories and forms the grounds of their approach to violence. Yet their ambiguities also reflect many of the anxieties of Morris's own age in relation to war and violence.

That these anxieties are manifold is evident in the debate in mainstream periodicals in the mid-1850s over the tension between industrial capitalism, free trade and bourgeois moneymaking on the one hand and the necessity for war and its benefits for the nation on the other. Amid much public discussion about the Crimean War, an article by the poet W. E. Aytoun in *Blackwood's* in March 1854 hails the commitment to war with Russia as evidence of national character. It demonstrates, he writes, that 'we have not degenerated during the long period of peace which we have enjoyed. It shows that [...] the love of Mammon has not so occupied our souls as to render us insensible to the part which we are bound to take, as the freest and most advanced community in Europe'.[22] The identification of war with spiritual and physical health as well as with the more abstract idea of freedom is one that carries through into Dixon's article and Morris's stories. A more ambiguous and pragmatic narrative about the relationship between war and national identity runs through William Howard Russell's trenchant journalistic accounts of the Crimean War, published in the *Times*, which critique the conduct and organization of the war on the ground.[23] Beyond the immediate context of the war, concerns about the meanings and uses of violence and combat for individuals surface in the mid-century public discourse of civilization, which suggests the need for middle-class men to leave behind or suppress the impulse to violence; but they are also present in literary depictions of personal, historical and communal battle in which national character, manliness and identity are called into question, defined or affirmed by battle.[24]

Although, as John Peck argues, specific images of contemporary war are limited in the major novels of the mid-nineteenth century, discussions about the meaning and place of violence in its various forms nonetheless permeate the fiction and poetry of the period. War or combat and its meanings are present to readers in the 1840s and '50s not only in the realist novels of Kingsley, William Thackeray and Elizabeth Gaskell that Peck discusses, but also in the broader tradition of historical adventure and romance writing that informs Morris's work and on which he draws in his preoccupation with the generative effects of extreme, disorientating, physical violence, unusual in prose and poetry alike at this period.[25] Peck, noting the disturbing brutality of W. E. Henley's poetry later in the century, suggests that 'in the Crimean War, there is a far more traditional emphasis on heroism' in poetic engagements with the violence of battle. He highlights Morris's 1858 *Defence of Guenevere* poems and Tennyson's 1855 *Maud* as exceptions to this tradition.[26]

Yet recent rereadings of Crimean War poetry suggest that there may be more complex engagements with the heroism of war than has often been recognised, in poems such as those in Alexander Smith and Sydney Dobell's polyvocal *Sonnets on the War* (1855), which, as Stefanie Markovits notes, create 'confusion – even bewilderment' by their 'refractive diversity'. Even such apparently patriotic and unproblematic poems as Tennyson's 'The Charge of the Light Brigade' (1854) may reveal more ambivalence about war than has often been recognized, as Trudi Tate and Matthew Bevis have convincingly argued.[27] Morris's stories turn away from the idea of heroism and its complicated relationship to patriotism to focus instead on the excesses of battle and war, much as Peck suggests *Maud* does, as a response to 'social alienation'.[28] However, while *Maud* verbally recreates the disordered internal life and the psychological effects of both war and social alienation, Morris's stories, like his 1858 *Defence of Guenevere* poems, focus on the physical disorder and relational resolutions afforded by violence. The form of these stories, gothic, fragmented, haunted as they are, suggests both their own extreme alienation from their time, and their investment in fragmentation and dislocation as a way of understanding the world.

Even as contemporary representations of war, both literary and journalistic, engaged with ideas of violence as battle heroism or patriotic duty, its role in an increasingly liberal society became more and more marginal. The meaning, social implications, and legitimate parameters of violence came under political and cultural scrutiny over the course of the nineteenth century as war receded further from the shores of Britain.[29] At the same time, a cultural preoccupation with the medieval past led to representations of knightly violence that equated knightly chivalry with Victorian gentlemanliness, although not always as explicitly as Tennyson does in his poetic description of King Arthur as a 'selfless man and stainless gentleman'.[30] Morris's disorientating tales engage obliquely with the nuanced debates of his day but refuse to rationalize, mitigate or spiritualize acts of combat. Instead they insist on the intimate, one-to-one touch of violence and its effects on the body. Violence is not subsumed into a morally linear narrative, but confronted in its somatic immediacy.

Intimate Violations: The Touch of Hand and Sword

Violence is a form of touch. It takes the intimacy of touch beyond the tentative or exploratory into the forceful and transformative. It may be, in each act, as brief as the thrust and retreat of a sword or as prolonged as the grabbing and twisting of limbs or features. It may be the sanctioned destructive touch of combat, or the disallowed transgressive touch that violates the body beyond the needs of battle. Maurice Merleau-Ponty describes the mutuality of touch as a way of perceiving the world and the self, in his image of the right hand touching the left, so that 'both hands can alternate the rôles of "touching" and being "touched"'.[31] While violence partakes of this mutual tactility, it is not necessarily actively reciprocal. Whether reciprocated or endured, however, it defines relationships between people, things and the world. Aristotle claims, in *De Anima*, that 'the primary form of sense is touch' and that:

> Touch has for its object both what is tangible and what is intangible. Here by 'intangible' is meant a) what like air possesses some quality of tangible things in a very slight degree and b) what possesses it in an excessive degree, as destructive things do.[32]

For Morris's characters both the tangible and the intangible can be understood through the touch of violence, a kind of touch characterized by deliberate excess, and by the dissolution of boundaries.[33] The repeatedly re-embodied lovers in 'A Dream' (159–75) or the grotesque inhabitants of the enchanted castle in 'Lindenborg Pool' (245–53) are solid as well as ghostly, susceptible of wounds and embraces but at the same time evanescent or mutable. In story after story, the destructive certainties of battle, the deceptive physicality of dreams or visions, and the lingering spaces of transition between life and death are interpreted by touch. Morris's stories depict a world in which violence underlies all that is known and offers both meaning and a means of transformation. At the same time unambiguous acts of combat become implicated in the ambiguous process of understanding and defining moral values, yet without becoming merely symbolic.

The multivalent touch of violence is explored with a peculiar mixture of mysticism and materialism in one of the most fully developed and frequently republished of Morris's 1856 stories, 'The Hollow Land' (254–90). The tale begins with an address to the reader by the aged narrator and protagonist, Florian:

> Do you know where it is, the Hollow Land? I have been looking for it now so long, trying to find it again, the Hollow Land [...]. It is near our country: but what time have we to look for it or any good thing, with such biting carking cares hemming us in on every side? (254)

The elegiac tone of this opening casts its shadow of longing and loss over the rest of tale, establishing at the beginning the inaccessibility of the Hollow Land and the impermanence of what it offers. The story continues with a series of acts of transgressive violence, which call into question the purity of the perpetrators. Like the vengeful acts of the Northern heroes 'with spirit free and bold' evoked in the story's epigraph from Carlyle's 'Nibelungen Lied', bold violence sets in train a series of events that can only be resolved through more violence (254).[34]

After his opening lament, Florian describes his early life in the House of the Lilies, where he grows up with his older brother, Arnald. Following the death of their father, a feud develops between their household and that of their cousin, Harald, whose father has also died. It begins with an act of physical awkwardness at the remarriage of Harald's mother, Queen Swanhilda. Arnald stumbles while carrying her bridal canopy, so that its gold threads become entangled in the flowers of Swanhilda's crown. Her skin bears the signs of her sudden anger, graphically described by the watching Florian: 'she flushed up in her rage, and her smooth face went suddenly into the carven wrinkles of a wooden water-spout' (255). The skin, locus of interaction between the body and the world, is both real and symbolic: it simultaneously registers and foreshadows the effects of violence.[35] Emotion, stimulated by the somatic, creates a visible cutaneous response, first animated, then apparently inanimate.

Swanhilda, furious at her unseemly stumble, 'smote [Arnald] across the mouth with her gilded sceptre, and the red blood flowed all about his garments'. In a matching but opposite response to Swanhilda's, Florian's ruptured skin registers the violation: while the blood flowed, he 'turned exceeding pale' (255). Skin bears the marks of both violent touch and violent emotion; its laceration suggests the transgression of other, less tangible boundaries.

'The Hollow Land' insists on boundaries between legitimate and illegitimate uses of violence and crossing them serves not so much to illustrate the characters of the perpetrators as to form them. Florian and Arnald nurture their hatred for Swanhilda and, sixteen years later, take a cohort of knights to her castle, to murder her in revenge for this earlier slight. Once they have entered the castle and found the queen, it is her face that, once again, shows the first signs of her fury: 'the veins in her forehead swelled, her eyes grew round and flamed out', in anticipation of the violent touch that was to come (261). Later, just before her execution, Florian describes a curiously realistic detail, that as she kneels to him for mercy, she 'kissed my feet and prayed piteously, so that water ran out of her mouth'. Similarly, her tears 'lay on the oak floor' as she 'wept like a child' (262). The ability of the body to retain its fluids begins to break down as the horror of death comes on her, prefiguring the blood that will run when she is killed. Swanhilda's death is a clumsy, brutal and intensely tactile process. She shrieks, threatens and weeps; she rolls around on the floor; she dashes about the room. Finally she cuts one of Arnald's men across the shoulders with his own sword. Her wild activity and loud cries are contrasted with Arnald's silent, pale stillness. He touches her only once, with the stroke that kills her. The sweep of his sword is as true and clean as his vengeance appears to be: 'in no battlefield had Arnald struck truer blow' observes Florian (263). The narrative itself does not uphold this view. Instead, Florian and Arnald's knightly credentials, and with them the whole concept of knighthood, are tainted by their hatred. The humiliating bodily details of Swanhilda's murder, set against its careful planning, highlight the inadequacy of a social code that allows the brothers to carry out this act in defence of their honour. To do so means violating the boundaries of Swanhilda's home and body. This kind of violence is more akin to the common ill-treatment of women that both the code of chivalry and Morris's own society publicly condemned – although frequently countenanced – than to the heroic swordplay of idealized knighthood.[36] It hints disturbingly at the impossibility of containing violence once it is unleashed.

For Florian, the process of questioning the morality of his actions and gaining a new understanding of judgement and knighthood paradoxically comes about through a series of increasingly bizarre acts of violence and intense experiences of touch or its terrible absence. The two brothers and their men are forced into a battle with Swanhilda's son, Red Harald. It is full of intimate but casual brutality: one knight throws his helmet at Florian, who 'swung out, hitting him on the neck; his head flew right off, for the mail no more held than a piece of silk'. Another was 'run through the eye with a spear, and throwing his arms up fell dead with a shriek' (271). As the battle turns against them, most of the men surrender and the rest are killed. Arnald leaps into the crevasse that has mysteriously opened up beneath them. Florian is backed towards the edge of the precipice by Harald until he too falls into 'a great Hollow Land' (274) – 'and as I fell I fainted', he notes. The Hollow Land is not quite either heaven or purgatory, as Hodgson suggests, but rather an alternative mystical space where physical experiences reframe meanings and alter both Florian's and the reader's perception of judgement and reality.[37]

Like the Wasted Land of medieval tales, and indeed of Morris's own earlier, unpublished story fragment, it is a disorientating and mutable land arrived at, or perhaps created by, sinful or sacrilegious violence. In the much-told medieval romance, Balin's 'dolorous stroke' with the sacred sword that pierced Christ's side leads to devastation of the castle and lands around him, laying them waste; in Morris's unfinished story there are rumours of 'a land which men called the Wasted Land' from which no-one ever comes back until the antihero, Richard, returns from it to attack the priest and trample on the Eucharist at his friend's deathbed.[38] Closer to Morris's own time, images of hollows, hollowness and hollow places run through Tennyson's poetry; if, as Markovits suggests, the 'dreadful hollow' in *Maud* 'can be thought of as a grotesque reinterpretation of the stark valley of "The Charge", another hollow in which "death" echoes as the answer to every question posed', then Morris's Hollow Land might be seen to reframe both the hollow and its answers.[39] Rather than Tennyson's 'dreadful' hollow, or the destructive wastes of Morris's fragment, this Hollow Land is unspeakably beautiful, with 'reaches and reaches of loveliest country', a place of redemption and transformation (274).

It is a hollow, then, that is metaphysical as well as physical. In *Being and Nothingness*, Jean-Paul Sartre explores the development of the conscious self in terms of the desire to enter or fill physical holes. He suggests that 'the hole [...] presents itself to me as the empty image of myself. I have only to crawl into it to make myself exist in the world which awaits me'.[40] A fall, more violent and less volitional than crawling, propels Florian into the hollow world in which a new self will be formed. Rather than the absolute oppositional emptiness of Sartre's image of the hole of being, however, this hollow is more like Merleau-Ponty's concept of non-being which is already related and connected to 'the fold or hollow of Being', so that 'nothingness (or rather non being) is hollow and not hole': there is a reciprocity between the conscious development of the self and the life of the body in the world.⁴¹ The conventional language of falling in battle converges with a trope of spiritual falling, which is, in this case, also a kind of rebirth. Florian's fall is both somatic and topographical, a complete collapse of the landscape and the normal laws of nature. He gains a new identity, comes fully into being, not through filling the hole, as Sartre's psychosexual model suggests, but through tactile interactions with the world inside the hollow.

Gillian Beer identifies Morris's later use of a romantic 'kind of hyperaesthesia which allows the materials of the world to press directly upon the identity and intensify awareness'.⁴² In the Hollow Land, identity is intimately reliant on a two-way process, in which the materials of the world and the material of the body act upon one another. Florian, whose sense of touch has been disturbed by his guilt, so that he is unable, on first coming round from his faint, to touch the beautiful and erotically available Margaret, embarks on a journey of self-awareness through the interaction of the matter of the world and the sense of touch.⁴³ Later, inexplicably separated from Margaret, Florian finds both his identity and his sense of touch through the experience of their loss. As he walks in the grey November fog, the visual gives way to the somatic: he feels the fog in his bones, and in a rare moment of olfactory realism, smells it all about him. His clothes are heavy and the mist lies 'in great drops'. The repeated evocation of fog, mist and mud on this 'horrible grey November day' recalls the foggy, muddy opening of Charles Dickens' *Bleak House* (1853), a novel of misjudgement and misperception ('Hollow Land', 281).⁴⁴

A similarly indeterminate physical state of mud and muddy water provides the structuring motif of Morris's 'Lindenborg Pool' (245–53). An atmosphere of sensual disorder pervades the tale from its opening description of 'the leaden waters of that fearful pool', with its 'steep banks of dripping yellow clay' (245), to the horrifying confusion of human and animal, male and female, tangible and intangible that marks its climax. Only violent battle secures the protagonist's escape and restores the landscape to its discrete elements. In 'The Hollow Land', elemental dissolution leaves both Florian and the reader disorientated. At the same time it echoes widely publicized descriptions of the Crimea, in which fog and mud abound and solid outlines become blurred. The *Times* correspondent, Russell, reports in November 1854 that 'the fog and vapours of drifting rain were so thick as morning broke that one could scarcely see two yards before him'; the landscape around Sebastopol is 'a vast, black, dreary wilderness of mud'.⁴⁵ The primeval ooze echoes the increasingly chaotic progress of the war.

The loss of order, clarity and control that Russell highlights in his descriptions of Crimean sludge and fog is reflected in Morris's tale at this moment of breakdown and loss brought about by battle. The common experience of both chaos and physical dissolution carries through into later war writing: David Jones writes of the First World War, 'solid things dissolve, and vapours ape substantiality'.[46] Santanu Das's work on First World War poets draws on Sartre's phenomenological discussion of slime to suggest the potent association of mud with the fear of absorption, dissolution of boundaries and loss of meaning that occurs in war.[47] This offers a useful framework for interpreting the way landscape, body and meaning begin to coalesce for Florian: the moral chaos of vengeful war and violent wrongdoing finds its physical expression in the clinging viscosity of mud and the blurring, blinding insubstantiality of fog. His body and his garments begin to lose their solidity, to become elusive and ungraspable. His heightened sense of touch is all the more sensitive for its lack of solid object. His scanty, waterlogged clothing loses the texture of cloth: 'it draggled so (wretched, slimy, textureless thing!) in the brown mud.' This combination of slime and mud blurs the boundaries between subject and object, the body and the world. In Sartre's terms: 'to touch the slimy is to risk being dissolved in sliminess'.[48]

Florian's disorientation is palpably expressed as he reaches up to his head to take off his helmet:

> But when I touched it I stood still in my walk shuddering, I nearly fell to the earth with shame and horror; for I laid my hand on a lump of slimy earth with worms coiled up in it. I could scarce forbear from shrieking; but breathing such a prayer as I could think of, I raised my hand again and seized it firmly. Worse horror still! The rust had eaten it into holes and I gripped my own hair as well as the rotting steel, the sharp edge of which cut into my fingers. (281)

His misunderstanding of the true identity of a knight leads to a loss of physical integrity far greater than that suffered by the drooling, weeping Swanhilda in the fearful moments before her death. The slimy corrosion of his helmet, extending even to his own hair, is suggestive of a state of physical and moral decay akin to that which Carlyle attributes metaphorically to Europe before the coming of Luther: 'the European World was asking him: Am I to sink ever lower into falsehood, stagnant putrescence, loathsome accursed death; or, with whatever paroxysm, to cast the falsehoods out of me, and be cured and live?'. Luther's radical voice may have led to conflict and war, Carlyle admits, but it was necessary to prevent a slide into decay brought on by false values.[49] Florian faces a similar choice, physically represented; only violent rejection of all that is not solid can free him from moral degradation. Yet this rejection does not take the form of turning away from combat, but rather of embracing a different kind of violence.

While unjustified murder and misguided war have precipitated the slide into miry decay, it is nonetheless the physical symbols of martial courage that signify a realignment of proper boundaries. His helmet is almost corroded away, but it still has sharp edges, elements of solidity, as he pulls away the clumps of mud. Only when he has finally managed to pull off the slimy helmet is he able to feel properly again, morally and physically. Feeling, for Florian, means touching. The first thing he feels is the blade of his hard, clean sword, on touching which he reflects that 'it sent a thrill of joy to my heart to know that there was one friend left me yet' (282). As James J. Gibson observes, 'active exploratory touch permits both the grasping of an object and a grasp of its meaning'.[50] Florian has passed a preliminary test of understanding, and the evidence of it is the solid touch of his sword, the sign that he may yet be worthy to be a knight. The etymological relationship between the arms he bears and the arms in which he bears them is here extended into an ontological one.

Combat is not only a means to an end, then, but an end in itself, a kind of crucible for the forging of identity. Kaeuper observes that in medieval literature knights are pictured 'enjoying a privileged practice of violence; it suggests they found in their exhilarating and fulfilling fighting the key to identity.'[51] While Morris appropriates this medieval ontology of violence, his stories are nonetheless written in the light of mid nineteenth-century debates about the nature of manliness and the relationship between spirituality and the body, brought into sharp literary focus by the works of Charles Kingsley, Thomas Hughes and F. D. Maurice.[52] His emphasis on the physical and corporeal as a way of knowing draws on ideals of physical manliness with which he was familiar through Kingsley's works as well as on the conversely sacramental traditions of the Oxford Movement, by which he was fleetingly captivated.[53] At the same time, his focus on the body in battle resonates with contemporary cultural debates about the relationship between mind and body, evident not only in Bain's widely publicized *The Senses and the Intellect* but also reflected in broader public discussion in the periodical press on the relationship between body, soul and will, questions which, as Roger Smith points out, 'reflected on central moral questions of human identity and agency'.[54] In Morris's tales the identity forged in battle involves a breakdown of rational, socially prescribed ways of thinking as much as of abstract and rigid honour codes untempered by mercy or reality. While 'The Hollow Land' discriminates between right and wrong uses of violence, the form of the tale, as well as its content, suggests the necessity of furious disorder – both mental and physical – in the creation of a new identity.

Florian becomes a true knight through a wild, passionate swordfight. Freed from his slimy garments, wounded and naked, he meets Harald in the Hollow Land, in the guise of an unknown knight. They fight each other in a wild and joyous battle of equals that undoes the injustice between them. The battle is both frantic and erotic, but not entirely out of control. The knights strike and parry, merging and separating in a 'mad waltz', yet the touch of their meeting swords makes 'measured music.' There is a ritual beauty and rhythm to their battle, despite its suprarational fury. Their cries mingle, their swords meet, blood spatters flesh. Words themselves touch and separate rhythmically in the repetitions and alliterations of Morris's lyrical description. When Harald's sword falls 'flatlings' on Florian's head, so that his eyes pop, he 'remembered the old joy I used to have and the *swy, swy* of the sharp edge' (285). Touch awakens memory: consciousness, like conscience, resides in the body. As Malory's knights are made more knightly through their wounds, so here Florian and Harald find healing and restoration of true knighthood through their physical battle.

In the heat of battle the logic of the body takes over from the mind. It is a troublingly joyful madness admitted to not only by the imaginary warriors of medieval romance and Nordic myth, but by soldiers through the ages. Joanna Bourke gives numerous examples from the twentieth century, of soldiers confessing to the 'delight' and 'joy' of battle.[55] Morris captures, in the battle between Florian and Harald, the frightful abandon of combat, and frames it as a means of healing relationships and redressing past wrongs. Florian's body expresses his true feelings and overrides the restrictive practices of politeness or chivalric form. Madness, like dreaming, or being wounded, or fainting, is a liminal state. As the anthropologist Mary Douglas observes in her analysis of the role of boundaries and their transgression, this involves a 'venture into the disordered regions of the mind'. The person who comes back from these regions 'brings with him a power not available to those who have stayed in the control of themselves and of society.'[56] Disorder of the mind corresponds, in this battle, to the disordering of the body through the wounds and scars of combat. Both lead to powerful transformation, as did the biblical Jacob's dreamlike wrestle with the angel, the result of which he bore in his body.[57]

At the same time, in Florian's story the Christian narrative of healing through the wounds of Christ's body is reframed as the two knights come to a state of harmony through their mutual injuries. As Kenneth Hodges notes in relation to injuries acquired on the Arthurian grail quest, 'injuries are used to punish sin but also to point the way toward moral restoration'.[58] There is nothing here of the model of noncombative forgiveness suggested by Burne-Jones's 1863 painting, 'The Miracle of the Merciful Knight', in which Christ leans off the cross to bless a knight, who, Burne-Jones writes on the picture's frame, 'forgave his enemy when he might have destroyed him'.[59] Wounding leads not to destruction but to healing. At the same time, in a refutation of the code of justice enacted in a medieval trial by combat, neither knight wins, but both are wounded and their understanding of the world is changed.

Violence, then, breaks down relationships and heals them, dissolves identity and reconfigures it. It is exhilarating and unstable. It defiles the pure margins of the body and in so doing suggests a willingness to cross other boundary lines, moral or social. Douglas observes that 'the body can stand for any bounded system. Its boundaries can represent any boundaries which are threatened or precarious'.[60] In the Hollow Land the boundaries of the body are also the boundaries of the self and the contested moral boundaries of the chivalric code, realigned and affirmed through the intense interactions of violent touch.

The Unbalanced Balance Sheets of War

In his classic 1832 treatise on war, Carl von Clausewitz examines the purpose and meaning of martial combat, succinctly suggesting that 'war is nothing but a duel on an extensive scale'. While his emphasis is primarily on the calculations of politics and strategy, he repeatedly comes back to this idea of the individual one-to-one battles that make up war. He stresses the inevitable interactions of people and environment in warfare, and their contingent results: 'from the commencement, the absolute, the mathematical as it is called, nowhere finds any sure basis in the calculations in the Art of War.'[61] This element of the unpredictable, the incalculable and unbalanced, is central to Morris's portrayals of hand-to-hand violence, knightly and martial. While 'The Hollow Land' focuses on personal transgression and transformation through the individual touch of knightly violence, Morris's tales of warfare emphasize the communal and the contingent. They offer images of brutal, physical violence that draw on, yet destabilize the rhetoric of heroism and brotherhood that informs many medieval and medievalist stories of martial combat. The wild excess of loyal, committed, fiercely bloody battle offers a deliberate contrast to the practical political expediency that Dixon describes as the underlying force for peace in their own time.

In the warfare of 'Gertha's Lovers' (176–225), the brief final battle of 'Svend and his Brethren' (226–44), or the local skirmish that ends 'Golden Wings' (291–308), passionate communal acts of war are shaped by individual acts of combat. Bourke observes, in her study of the two world wars and the Vietnam War, that 'the characteristic act of men at war is not dying, it is killing. [...] Its peculiar importance derives from the fact that it is not murder, but sanctioned blood-letting'.[62] The centrality of legitimized killing in war is a fact easily obscured by heroic writing; yet Morris neither balks at describing it nor underplays its complex significance. Both killing and dying in battle are urgent acts of commitment here. They form part of what Georges Bataille describes as an 'energy economy' that focuses on expenditure, destruction and loss, rather than accumulation and calculation. Bataille suggests that sacrifice and war have less to do with gain than with loss, and that such loss 'must be as great as possible if the activity is to assume its true meaning'.[63] This paradigm requires a commitment – evident in Morris's romances – to the present moment of battle, and to the enduring significance of its physical acts rather than its strategic success. Morris explores the imaginary violence of battle as a wildly extravagant and meaningful corporeal transaction in which there is little of the careful calculation of political economy. Excess is not accidental to his stories, but essential. The experience of ancient warfare is glorious and transformative for Morris because it constitutes, in Bataille's terms, 'measureless expenditure of energy', which is 'beyond calculation'.[64] Warrior knights become sacrificial victims, not offered by society, but offering themselves for the sake of renewal.

Ancient, hand-to-hand combat functions as an antidote to the balanced accounts of utilitarian capitalism in which, Carlyle writes, 'all the Truth of this Universe is uncertain; only the profit and loss of it, the pudding and praise of it, are and remain very visible to the practical man'.[65] Morris's knights have no such practical view. Rather, for them, the truth of the universe is discovered through a particular kind of manly physical passion, which shows itself in thwarted caresses, accomplished killing and gruesome death.[66] If Bourke's formulation expresses a powerful truth about war, it is in part because only those who kill, rather than those who die, are able to tell the tale. In Morris's stories, however, the dead reassume some sort of bodily form, transcend the constraints of time, embrace their lovers and unreasonably live to tell the tale from beyond the grave.

War is personal and local in 'Golden Wings', whose epigraph reminds readers that it is a partial retelling of the tale of 'Sir Perceval of Galles'. Morris sets this knightly *Bildungsroman* of chivalric development and unequal but passionate battle between acts of vividly described killing. Lionel's first act, the stabbing of the unknown knight who comes to his door, is swift and final: he drives his sword through him 'so that it came out behind, and he fell, turned over on his face, and died' (293). After a series of trials and adventures, he wins his love, his castle and an army of knights to fight the brief war with which the tale finishes. Lionel ends his life in close combat. He describes his own death at the hands of enemy knights, in language both graphic and poetic:

> One thrust me through the breast with a spear, and another with his sword, which was three inches broad, gave me a stroke across the thighs that bit to the bone; and as I fell forward one cleft me to the teeth with his axe. (308)

Killing, like dying in this story, is both knowable and potentially noble; what happens afterwards is by no means as certain as the physical imperatives to defend land and honour and to live by physical courage.

Certain outcomes are not as important to Morris in these stories as physical interactions. As Wilfred Heeley writes in the first issue of the *Oxford and Cambridge Magazine*, 'We want to see men as they were and are; not with motives, but with impulses; not equations, with so many virtues minus so many vices, but men, with infinite possibilities of good and evil.'[67] These infinite possibilities are proved, for Morris, in the arena of combat. The imbalance in these stories is all physical, in contrast to the moral imbalances of wealth or power. The body retains autonomy: it is a flesh and blood entity, not a metaphor for the state or the church. The corporeal autonomy and integrity of the individual in community with others is asserted through the ultimate violence of killing in fair combat. There is a passion for honour and chivalry in the battles of these tales, yet it is not the kind of stately, formalized combat that medievalism offered to upper class men in the mid nineteenth-century: it bears no relation to the organized simulation of violence evident in the much-derided Eglinton tournament of 1839, in which thirteen participants jousted genteelly with real weapons, but at no risk of genuine wounding.[68] Morris, writing from the other side of the Crimean War, refuses this disconnection between the trappings of chivalry and its corporeal effects. He insists on the present reality of killing.

It is in 'Gertha's Lovers', a tale of fullscale war, that Morris deals most directly with the causes and effects of killing, rather than merely fighting or wounding. Combat and war make evident the connections between the body and the soul, the body and the earth, the body and things, that Morris and those he admired felt were lost in their society. Carlyle writes of England that:

> We call it a Society; and go about openly confessing the totalest separation, isolation. Our life is not a mutual helpfulness, but rather, cloaked under due laws-of-war, named 'fair competition' and so forth, it is a mutual hostility. We have profoundly forgotten everywhere that *Cash-payment* is not the sole relation of human beings.[69]

In this story, by contrast, cash-payment, drudgery, unwilling work is absent altogether from the lives of the protagonists, and only hinted at in the values and lives of their enemies. Violence, not money, is the currency: lands and honour are won by the transactions of combat. These are men with no time for what Kingsley's impetuous hero, Lancelot, terms the 'effeminate pursuit' of moneymaking.[70] Open war, or knightly combat, is the state in which they live, helping those who are with them and frankly fighting those who are not. Morris appears to accept Carlyle's dictum that 'Man is created to fight; he is perhaps best of all definable as a born soldier; his life "a battle and a march" under the right General.'[71] While Carlyle offers suggestions of both physical and metaphorical forms that battle might take, Morris focuses on the physical. Life and love take place in the explicit context of immanent violence.

In 'Gertha's Lovers', war and desire are inextricably mingled as Olaf, the king, and his right-hand man, Leuchnar, both fall in love with the same peasant woman, Gertha. Their desire for Gertha and their brotherly commitment to one another are given context by the war they fight together against a common enemy. Individual desire is sublimated in the communal action of war. The act of killing, for Olaf's people, is an act of love: for the land, for their regent, and for each other. It is in the extravagant imbalance of war – the sanctioned acts of killing it involves – that the identity of the people is forged. Leuchnar's doomed romantic passion for Gertha is merely one expression of the love and loyalty of the people. It is a passionate, wholehearted feeling that shows itself in action and grows stronger and purer through deeds of loyal combat, in an extension of Kenelm Digby's assertion that 'the violent amusements of ancient chivalry' generate 'the love of virtue'.[72] This association of combat with the expression and development of virtuous characteristics is one made even more dramatically by Ruskin.

'Gertha's Lovers' was published nine years before Ruskin gave his lecture on war at the Royal Military Academy, but the sentiments expressed by Morris's characters foreshadow those set out so clearly in that lecture. Ruskin suggests that 'the Muse of History' does not couple together 'peace and learning', 'peace and plenty', 'peace and civilisation', as people commonly do. Rather, he says:

> On her lips, the words were – peace, and sensuality – peace, and selfishness – peace, and death. I found, in brief, that all great nations learned their truth of word, and strength of thought, in war; that they were nourished in war, and wasted by peace; taught by war, and deceived by peace; trained by war, and betrayed by peace;– in a word, that they were born in war, and expired in peace.[73]

War is paradoxically associated with life and birth, rather than death. This can only pertain because Ruskin takes as his subject 'all great nations'. Individuals, inevitably, will kill and die in war, and what Ruskin's rhetoric glosses over – the individual acts of battle – Morris's tale makes explicit. Ruskin goes on to draw on the past for evidence of the powerful, invigorating force of war on the artistic and moral life of a people. He emphasizes, however, that only certain kinds of war achieve this invigoration: 'the creative, or foundational, war is that in which the natural restlessness and love of contest among men are disciplined, by consent, into modes of beautiful – though it may be fatal – play'.[74] It is this element of beautiful, freely chosen, manly play that Morris embraces. As the Crimean War comes to its unsatisfactory and, in Dixon's terms, politically craven end, Morris creates a war of his own in which heroism and boldness are beyond doubt, and in which the end for which it was fought is accomplished – although at the cost of individual life and love. If Victorian Britain is 'deceived by peace', this fictional war demonstrates how a people nourished by war instead of moneymaking deal with their enemies.

For the enemy, war is self-interested and its reward is material gain. King Borrace shows his immorality in his greed for slaughter as well as gold: 'clearly the fools will wait to be killed, and we shall kill them all, and then hurrah for plunder!' (201). Battle brings no redemption for them. Things are treasured but people are not. The greedy, depraved King Borrace is killed by a mace blow to the head. In a part-vampiric, part-necrophilic parody of the Eucharist, one of his aides, Sebald, gloats over his dead body and takes revenge in the most gruesome way for the king's mistreatment of his sister. He repeatedly grinds his foot into Borrace's mashed face, then 'stooped down and put his hands to the warm blood that flowed from the wounds, and raised them to his lips and drank, and the draught seemed to please him' (214). Unlike the wounded and wounding bodies of Florian and Harald in 'The Hollow Land', Borrace's already dead body offers no hope of redemption, and its desecration is therefore merely an empty act of revenge. It is not the spiritual sin of sacrilege that damns Sebald, however, but the greed and calculation of his people's relationships with each other and with the land. Their moral poverty is demonstrated, and violence against them justified, by this desecration of the body of their king, in contrast to Olaf's people, who lovingly tend and revere his corpse.

Susan Stewart notes that the 'war inside a war', of Book Ten of the *Iliad* 'illustrates the antinomy of atrocity and recognition. In the darkness all territory is without bound or name, all lines are crossed, all acts are improvisational in their means and ends, and every death is an animal's death.'[75] Here the recognition of meaning gained through violent touch is denied to the enemies of Gertha's people: Sebald's desecrating touch sets him apart from humanity. At the same time, his act of drinking blood highlights his moral and spiritual degradation. Aristotle suggests that 'tasting means a being affected by what can be tasted as such'.[76] There is not the reciprocity of touch here, but rather a shaping of the taster by the tasted. Borrace's evil lives on in Sebald's act in which a line between human and animal is crossed. Again and again in the stories, the idea of the Eucharist is interrogated and its myth of redemptive violence and spiritual renewal reframed. The extravagant violence of war is justified, in part, by the embodied violence at the heart of the Christian story. This cameo of debasement serves to highlight the removal of the enemy from the wholeness signalled by the heroic violence of Gertha's people as well as by the Eucharistic symbols of sacrificial suffering and willing death on behalf of others.

For Olaf's and then Gertha's people, it is the glory of dying bravely for a cause they believe in that drives their acts of battle; the old warrior, Barulf, cries:

> How glorious to die in a great battle, borne down by over-many foes, to lie, never dead, but a living terror for all time to God's enemies and ours, a living hope to the sons of God! And to die altogether, beholding, between the sword-strokes, the faces of dear friends all a-light with intensest longing – is not that glorious! (195)

The withdrawal from the Crimea that Dixon deplores in his article is not only a strategic mistake, he argues, but also, more importantly, a loss of the opportunity to demonstrate courage in the face of death, and to arouse courage in others. England could justly be accused, he suggests, of converting 'a war of principles into one of expediency'.[77] The war of Gertha's people, on the other hand, is one of passion. It does not partake of either the machinations of politics or the religious eschatology of ultimate war. Rather, in this intensely realized but antirealist tale, it offers the opportunity for a heroic people to engage in an act of war against evil as part of a progressive purification of the land.

Gertha feels the moral effects of long years of war on her people; they are 'so drawn together' that 'through the love they bore to one another sprung terrible deeds of heroism', and 'almost every man of that nation was a hero and a fit companion for the angels' (178). There is no narrative disorientation or distancing to undercut this assessment of morally purifying war. The confident voice of the third-person narrator affirms the martial exploits of Gertha's people. In order for their willing embrace of death to live on in memory as an act of righteous heroism, those who die bravely must also kill ferociously. The evidence of courage and honour is the ability to kill well, as much as to die well. Leuchnar sets fire to King Borrace's camp and then gallops into it with his thousand horsemen in a ruthless surprise attack: 'at first there was scarce any resistance; the men were cut down and speared as they ran half-armed from out of the burning tents' (211). The story relies on the distinction between good and evil that has been carefully made through the words of the two sides about the violence to come. Both sides will kill and die, but Gertha's people kill for land, honour and the beautiful commoner-queen who has succeeded Olaf, while Borrace's people kill from hatred and greed. As Kaeuper observes of medieval chivalric literature: 'belief in the right kind of violence carried out vigorously by the right people is a cornerstone of this literature.' The acts of war may be the same, but their meaning is quite different.[78]

The imaginary battles of 'Gertha's Lovers' accomplish what the Crimean War does not: the overthrow of tyranny and the purchase of freedom for a noble and courageous people. They urge on the imagination a realistic vision of violence in an antirealist story. Elaine Scarry discusses the difficulty of creating convincing images with words of things that are solid, and demonstrates the ways in which Hardy and Proust offer images of solid objects by depicting them in contrasting proximity to insubstantial, shadowy, falling ones.[79] In some of the 1856 tales, with their multiple shifts of place, perspective and narrative voice, the story itself functions as the filmy, impalpable backdrop against which the solid characters and their hard-edged weapons move. In 'Gertha's Lovers', Morris represents the solid by precisely imagining its destruction. He pays close but detached attention to the corporeal effects of violence. He details the bodies of the dead, 'who lay with ghastly breakings of the whole frame, torn by great stones, or slain by wounds that struck them haphazard in strange unlikely places'. Distorted syntax mirrors the bodies it describes. Others 'lay with their bodies twisted into unimaginable writhings brought about by pain and fear' (215). He refuses the simple glorification of violence as an idea, and demands that his reader confront the actual, specific acts of breaking and spearing, severing and wounding, that combat entails. The clean cleavings of violence are described with a precise brutality that demands acknowledgement of their solid reality. At the same time they undercut the dirty complications of war and killing by their mythic specificity. There is much separating and skewering of body parts, but little moaning or pain or drawn out death. Leuchnar, in 'Gertha's Lovers' is one of the few warriors depicted in the process of dying and, despite his many wounds, he is 'not in great pain, for his spirit was leaving his body gently, as if he were worn out merely' (221–2). Death may be brutal, embodied and dramatically realized, but it is still, in its own way, clean. Unlike the formless dissolutions that follow unjustified violence, just war retains its meaning, in Morris's tale.

The unsullied passion of this imaginary war stands as an idealistic condemnation of the political compromises of the Crimean War, with its practical failures and muddy disillusionment. Dixon's article in the *Oxford and Cambridge Magazine* mourns the loss of initial battle fervour:

> A month ago the terrible heat of the battle with the giant of fraud and violence was upon our faces, and in our hearts the sternest determination to do such a work as the world never witnessed; and now we are withdrawing from a half-finished contest.[80]

The sense of battle as an inspiration to the world recalls Barulf's image of the people dying gloriously in battle, yet living on in the memories of others: 'a living terror for all time to God's enemies and ours' (195). Dixon laments that the Crimean War has not yet 'succeeded in calling forth the national spirit of Germany', something he argues could have been accomplished had the war continued.[81] Morris's fictional war does just that for Gertha's people. It calls forth their national spirit, carrying all before it. War subsumes the rivalries of love. It offers opportunities for men to prove themselves and to die well. Most of all, it unites the people and gives them a new identity as a people of war. For the story's protagonists, battle ends in death, and the afterlife is not at all certain, as the equivocal final chapter, with its sudden shift in narrative voice, suggests: the reuniting of Olaf and Gertha, seen by Edith the handmaiden at some distance, and related second hand, allows glimpses of the afterlife and its rewards, but it is distanced by the manner of its telling. It has none of the immediacy of the war and its mutilated bodies. Life and afterlife do not necessarily balance out. The wrongs of the world may not be redressed in heaven.

For Morris, then, the economics of violence are necessarily unbalanced: life is not weighed up carefully, but thrown away extravagantly in the cause of love for the land and people. The 'preoccupation with mutilation and decay' that Silver observes in these stories is, as she suggests, 'excessive', but not in the sense of being more than is right or necessary. Rather, it deliberately calls attention to the processes and effects of violence, in an attempt to reconnect the imagination with the body. In so doing it overthrows linear conventions of writing, the balance-sheet expectations of political economy and the careful calculations of international affairs. The stories create a world whose centre is neither symbolic religious acts nor strategic economic ones, but rather tactile, physical interactions which locate meaning and truth in the body and its relation to the world.

Hand to Hand: Making, Writing and Making Right

Of all the body parts touched or twisted, cut or maimed or embraced, none is more important in these romances than the hand. Morris's knights demonstrate and interrogate ideas of manliness, brotherhood, identity and morality by the ways they use their hands. I suggest that acts of battle are equivalent in these stories to work, conceived as the process of making things by hand, and that both are ways of understanding and reshaping the world, making right through creative work what is wrong. The individual, active hands of the warriors are the antithesis of the mechanization of the Victorian age, when a 'hand' was no longer merely a body part, at the disposal of its owner's creativity, but a factory operative, working by rote and according to instruction rather than for pleasure and beauty.[82] Ruskin writes in *The Stones of Venice* that Victorian forms of labour 'unhumanize' people, separating the mechanical actions of the body from the human soul or thought so that a person becomes merely an 'animated tool'.[83] The prevalence of guns in the nineteenth century makes battle equally mechanical; the hand-to-hand duels or wars of the Middle Ages had long since been supplanted by less personal forms of fighting.[84] Through the motif of the hand, Morris rehumanizes people in relation to each other and the materials of the world. The hand is a sign of individuality and of the power of expressive action to understand and change the world.

Fighting and creating are both handwork in these stories. Carlyle, much read by Morris and his Oxford friends, makes the link between them: the battlefield is 'a kind of Quintessence of Labour', he writes.[85] At the same time, work done by hand is connected with spiritual meaning: 'all true Work is sacred; in all true Work, were it but true hand-labour, there is something of divineness.'[86] Despite the religious symbolism of the stories, Morris is less concerned with the immanent divine, and more with the human nobility of creation. None of the prose romances is without the element of manual creation, from the frenzied paintings of Harald and Florian in 'The Hollow Land' (284–7) to the emblem of golden wings on blue cloth that Lionel's mother works at each St Peter's day in 'Golden Wings' (292). Making things by hand brings new realities into being, just as violence and tales or dreams do.

In the late 1880s, lecturing on Gothic architecture, Morris linked the creative and harmonious work of Europeans of the past with their ability and courage on the battlefield. Gothic architecture reached its full potential, he says, in the hands of those 'gildsmen of the Free Cities':

> who on many a bloody field proved how dearly they valued their corporate life by the generous valour with which they risked their individual lives in its defence. But from the first, the tendency was towards this freedom of hand and mind subordinated to the co-operative harmony which made the freedom possible.[87]

The association of hand and mind is crucial. Violence is so powerful an emblem of freedom for Morris because it entails an action done by hand, just as craftwork, architecture, or writing does. It signifies a crucial link between hand and mind, the loss of which Carlyle laments in 'Signs of the Times': 'men are grown mechanical in head and in heart, as well as in hand. They have lost faith in individual endeavour, and in natural force, of any kind.'[88] Morris's own fondness, in the 1850s, for brass rubbing, was one of the earliest manifestations of his lifelong practice of bringing what he perceived as the artistic freedoms of the past into the present through the work of his own hands.[89] His awareness of his hands as expressions of his creative work is evident when, near the end of his life, suffering from gout, he writes to F. S. Ellis, 'my hand seems lead and my wrist string'.[90] This powerful image of ineffective weight draws attention, by contrast, to the hand's normal flexibility, mobility and usefulness.

Clausewitz's *On War* firmly refutes the idea of war as primarily a 'handicraft', or manual skill, series of duels though it may be, and concentrates instead on the politics and strategies of battle. In doing so, however, Clausewitz draws attention to the 'bodily exertion' and 'friction', created by a range of difficult circumstances, which contribute to the 'resistant medium' of war:

> Activity in war is movement in a resistant medium. Just as a man immersed in water is unable to perform with ease and regularity the most natural and simplest of movements, that of walking, so too in war, with ordinary powers, one cannot keep even the line of mediocrity.[91]

While Clausewitz's point is that those who have not experienced war for themselves cannot imagine the complexities brought about by 'friction', Morris's depictions draw on just such an idea, creating both realistic and romantic twists and turns of circumstance and environment against which the fighting of warriors is tested: the death of King Olaf in 'Gertha's Lovers'; the architectonic shifts of landscape in 'The Hollow Land'; the false accusations of the people in 'Svend and his Brethren'. Yet Morris's battles are always about handiwork or 'handicraft': the resistance that matters is primarily that of weapon against weapon. The triumph of war is the victory of solid weapons and individual courage against the resistant medium of armour. Each man brings about victory by working in harmony with his weapon, which may be sword or lance, or simply his own powerful hand. Imaginary war, like writing or carving, is honourable handwork.

Both the use of the hand and its appearance are important in the stories. The prominence of the hand in Morris's writing makes it not only an active agent of touch, but also a symbol of both character and will. In her wide-ranging study of the hand in early modern anatomical study, Katharine Rowe investigates the use of the hand as an image of agency, both human and divine, from ancient to early modern times: 'the hand becomes the prominent vehicle for integrating sacred mystery with corporeal mechanism [...] celebrated for its difficulty and beauty, it reveals God's intentions as no other part can.'[92] The Natural Theology of the early nineteenth century made similar claims for the hand as evidence of godly design. For Morris, the hand's meaning is less numinous. It is not evidence of divine design, but an agent and expression of human capacity.

The use of the hand as evidence of character and moral intention, expressed through battle, is particularly well established in the works of Morris's great favourite, Malory.⁹³ An English knight praises Tristram to King Mark as a knight 'of as grete worship as is now lyvyng', who 'hath wonne with his owne handes thyrtty Knyghtes that were men of grete honour', while Sir Launcelot brings Tristram and Isode to Joyous Gard 'that he had wonne with his owne handes'.⁹⁴ King Ban and King Bors are described as 'merveillous good men of her handes'; the unproved Sir Gareth is mockingly nicknamed 'Beaumayns that is fayre handes', and Sir Uwayne, 'le blaunche maynys'.⁹⁵ A man's strength and, by extension, his character, are shown by the way he uses his hands – and his arms, in both senses of the word – in battle. In 'Gertha's Lovers' the hopelessly unheroic death of the mincing, bejewelled 'fop', Erwelt, murdered by his fellow knight, is poignantly highlighted by his 'feeble nerveless hands' (215). Both murderer and murdered are rendered unmanly by the accusing evidence of those incapable hands. A similar connection between unmanned or unmanly hands and the activities in which they engage is made in Kingsley's *Yeast* (1851), in which Lancelot calls those who condemn the 'masculine' activity of fox-hunting 'cold-blooded, soft-handed religionists', who are themselves engaged in 'frantic Mammon-hunting', investing in the stock market and the railways. Morality and manliness, which includes both integrity and the capacity for combat, can be perceived in the hand and by the hand.⁹⁶ The violent grasp of hands on weapons or flesh is mirrored by the creative touch of hands on things: both kinds of touch change the material world and the relationship of people to the world. Both fashion something new, relying on the interaction of the hand with the weight and solidity of matter.

While much use has been made of Gaston Bachelard's concept of the 'material imagination' in recent studies of nineteenth-century literature, less attention has been paid to his emphasis on the hand rather than the eye as a means of knowing.⁹⁷ In the introduction to *Water and Dreams*, Bachelard writes that, 'speaking philosophically from the outset, we can distinguish two sorts of imagination – [...] a *formal imagination* and a *material imagination*.' He goes on to elaborate:

> Besides the images of form, so often evoked by psychologists of the imagination, there are – as I will show – images of matter, images that stem *directly from matter*. The eye assigns them names, but only the hand truly knows them. [...] These images of matter are dreamt substantially and intimately. They have weight.⁹⁸

While the visual is important in Morris's short stories as a way of interpreting the world, the tactile is equally so. In 'The Story of the Unknown Church' (149–58) – whose title and content strangely prefigure the war memorials of the future in the form of the Tomb of the Unknown Warrior – dreaming, making and violence come together in a tale in which acts of manual craftsmanship represent both the violence of war and the tenderness of homosexual desire.[99] Like Wilfred Owen, a later poet with 'an obsessively corporeal imagination', as Das observes, Morris uses hands as a polyvalent symbol, an agent of creation or destruction that may be both violent and sexual.[100]

Walter, the story's narrator, takes the reader back to the tale of his own work as master mason on a newly built church, six hundred years previously. He is carving bas-reliefs on the west front of the new building, helped by his sister Margaret, while they await the return of Walter's friend and Margaret's betrothed, Amyot, from the Crusades. As Walter works, he daydreams. His dreams of his friend focus on hands: Amyot's hand is 'white and small, like a woman's' (154); it is not a manly hand that fails to achieve manliness, but a womanly hand, and therefore an object of love and tenderness. Later, Walter remembers how 'I held his hand as we came together out of the cathedral' as Amyot prepared to go to war, and how 'his hand left mine at last' (156). In his reverie, Walter reaches out his arms to Amyot, and suddenly they are walking together in a beautiful garden, full of music and colour. As the dream fades, leaving Walter 'sad and sick at heart', he finds he has automatically restarted his carving: 'the chips were flying bravely from the stone under my chisel at last, and all my thoughts were now in my carving' (155). Hands – ancient symbols of procreation as well as power – become the means of expressing displaced desire, creating a new world to replace the inadequacies of the present.

Like madness and battle, doing and dreaming belong together, the mental and physical signs of the manipulation of reality by desire. Oscar Wilde argues that in keeping 'aloof from the social problems of the day', art 'more completely realises for us that which we desire'.[101] By turning away from the social issues of his own day, Morris creates a world where alternative values prevail, where desire is realized, but never satisfied. In a similar way, Walter turns away from the wars his friend is fighting and carves biblical stories of judgement and salvation on the church. The handwork of war is called into question by Amyot's gentle, womanly hands and by the storytelling work of Walter's hands. The strict divisions between sexual desire and friendship, between 'manly love' and homosexuality, are blurred in this fragmentary, disconnected narrative of touching, creating, caressing hands.[102] Morris refuses the spiritualization of friendship just as he refuses the spiritualization of war: both are corporeally felt and corporeally expressed. Kaeuper neutrally observes that 'those interested in psychological analyses might well think that some form of special bond is created between knights by the common element of violence in their lives, perhaps especially by their violence against each other.'[103] While such a bond can be seen between Harald and Florian in 'The Hollow Land', in this story Morris suggests a different kind of bond: one which is equally corporeally expressed, and equally exclusive of women, but which is broken, rather than forged, by battle. In Morris's gradation of war, the Crusades have little value; they are distant battles fought in another land over questionable principles, rather than a war of brotherhood at home. Walter can only respond to this kind of combat, and the concomitant loss of his friend, through the manual reframing of war in carving.

Amyot returns home, and inexplicably dies the following day, possibly from the wounds of the war he was evidently so ill equipped to fight. Margaret dies with him, and Walter carves their tomb, and 'could not yet leave carving it'. He becomes a monk in order to stay always near to the tomb. He goes on carving, painting, and carving again, 'with many flowers and histories', until he dies, still at work: 'they found me lying dead, with my chisel in my hand, underneath the last lily of the tomb' (158). Carving is the work of his hands, as battle and bearing arms is that of the knight, and like a good knight, he dies in action. The tale points to incompletion, without affirming a happy reconciliation after death. Hands, denied the touch of either violence or tenderness, cannot be sure of greater fulfilment in the future, but can only shape the world and the past through craftwork. The brotherhood of bearing arms is here replaced, and the story uses the tropes of battle and creation to suggest the possibility that the work of a man's hands may destabilize expected patterns of relationship and affirm different kinds of touch.

The work of writing, like the work of carving or bearing arms, is work that achieves something through its interaction with the material world. While Carlyle uses visual linguistic notation to give weight to abstract concepts, capitalizing, for emphasis, ideas like 'Mammon-Gospel', 'Cash-Gospel', 'Fight of Life', Morris uses the material world and its details to give weight to his words and solidity to the stories of courage and heroism on which he draws.[104] Eugene LeMire observes that 'by careful structuring of meaningful detail and action the stories suggest a coherence just beyond the reach of reason, but not therefore unreasonable'.[105] I suggest that Morris goes further than this. He uses a wealth of physical detail in dreamlike or selfconsciously constructed medieval settings to offer an alternative to nineteenth-century novelistic realism. Meaning resides not in an evocation of the real through the material, but of the imaginary and impossible – perhaps even the unreasonable – through the touch of the hand on the materials of the world. Reason and passion are not warring opposites, in these stories, but one and the same, residing in and expressed through the body. In Merleau-Ponty's evocative terms, 'to understand is to experience the harmony between what we aim at and what is given, between the intention and the performance – and the body is our anchorage in a world'.[106] Morris's use of the hand is both a metonym for the body as a way of understanding the material world, and a physical entity in its own right, stretching out to bridge the gap between 'what we aim at and what is given'. In hand-to-hand fighting both the milieu and the body's relation to it changes – the body's stance and grip on the world is altered. This kind of violence, as a way of reshaping the material world, reaches beyond the logic of Enlightenment rationalism to suggest a more interactive, embodied epistemology.

However, the ambiguity of the body as a way of knowing and being in the world is suggested by the motif of ambidexterity. The destabilizing effect of the stories is reinforced by a refusal to prioritize right over left. The formulaic Biblical and cultural equation of the right hand with power is overturned, and the division of labour Ruskin so deplored in *The Stones of Venice* is challenged by the equal use of both hands.[107] The body knows no such division. Medieval knights would have needed to use both hands for their weapons, and references to this are not uncommon in medieval romances or in contemporary Victorian literature, but Morris's insistence on the many uses of ambidexterity is unusual in its extent and in the particular link it creates between battle, work, and the shifting of power. In the *Morte Darthur* knights frequently use one hand for a shield and one for a sword, creating a safe circle around themselves by fighting on both sides. Tristram, fighting on foot, 'dressid his sheld with his swerd in his hand, and he smote on the ryght hand and on the lyfte hand passyng sore that wel nygh at every stroke he strake doun a knyght.'[108] Malory's Balyn is also known as the Knight with Two Swords, a champion fighter whose extraordinary prowess is shown by his ability to wield two weapons at the same time.[109] In Kingsley's medievalist tale of warrior courage, *Hereward the Wake* (1865), the hero, finding himself trapped on both sides, uses both hands: 'with his left hand he thrust aside the left hand lance, with his right he hurled his own with all his force at the right-hand foe'.[110] The use of both hands, then, is an indication of prowess, power and worthy knighthood.

However, for Morris it signifies a rather different interaction with the world. Knights use both their hands not merely to ward off enemies, but to touch and manipulate people, weapons and materials. Indications of ambidexterity in warfare and in creative activity suggest an undermining of fixed relations of power. In 'Svend and his Brethren', acquired ambidexterity signifies manliness and perseverance: Siur the smith demonstrates his skill, determination and love for Cissela by learning to use his left hand as well as his right in fashioning gifts of jewellery for her, a skill he later puts to good use as an armourer (238). His weapons of war, made in secret with both trained hands, undo the established order. In 'The Hollow Land', Florian, freed from the slimy morion, plunges into a river and as he struggles to stay afloat in the tangle of his garments, he sees an unknown man – later revealed to be his cousin and enemy, Harald – paddling a boat with his left hand, and in his right holding a spear, with which he stabs Florian in the shoulder ('Hollow Land', 282-3).

The Arthurian motifs of the Fisher King and the wounding of a sinful knight are combined in one person by this use of both hands: the Christlike, wronged knight provides the beginning of reconciliation and transformation through an act of deliberate wounding. In 'Golden Wings', Lionel proves his bravery by the ferocious use of both hands in combat, both in his first trial of strength and later. In his final battle, when an enemy catches his lover by the hair and calls her a whore, 'I turned and caught him by the ribs with my left hand, and with my right, by sheer strength, I tore off his helm and part of his nose with it' ('Golden Wings', 306). He is poor and powerless, but uses all the weapons at his disposal. The use of both right hand and left is a polyvalent visual and tactile sign, transferable into different situations, but suggestive of a redress of the balance of power through action in combat or through creative work.

The hand, as Michel Serres points out, is as versatile as 'inventive thinking': 'it is not an organ, it is a faculty, a capacity for doing, for becoming claw or paw, weapon or compendium'.[111] Both hand and thought are able to take on different shapes or explore different psychic or physical identities; their ability to interact with the world is not fixed and bounded. The hand's close association with invention and transformation, rather than automated obedience, is crucial to these early stories. Its capacity for violence as well as creation signifies the transformative possibilities of human agency. The stories present a world of dreams and uncertainty, in which all that is sure is the physical and corporeal. The body is accorded primacy and the severing of its parts recorded within a framework of honour and duty, where complex emotions are displaced into physical contortions and distortions. In this embodied world, hands touch the world and the things in it through violence, and in this way the individual and the world are changed.

§

Violence in the 1856 stories, then, suggests the ability to reconceive the world and to question dominant narratives through multilayered, multivalent stories of the body in conflict. The fragmented style of the romances, their multiple displacements of time and place, and their emphasis on the handwork associated with fighting, constitute an alternative to the dominant narrative of capitalism, the binary divisions of materialism and idealism, and the mechanization of work of mid nineteenth-century Britain. The unbalanced and unbalancing touch of violence alters the body and with it, the world, in ways that exceed both reason and calculation. The stories offer an image of violence that recognizes its intimacy and immanence, and the necessity of pain as part of the human condition. At the end of a decade that brought the multiple deaths of the Crimean War and a major cholera epidemic, as well as fear of a French invasion, Morris's stories refuse to mitigate the somatic or social effects of violence. They do not, like Tennyson's Crimean War poems or Kingsley's *Two Years Ago*, acknowledge the contemporary, but their publication in the *Oxford and Cambridge Magazine* sets them in the context of an ongoing debate about social and literary values in relation to heroism, identity and battle.[112] What distinguishes Morris's depiction of violence from that of many of his contemporaries is his espousal of an almost premodern attitude to pain as necessary, unavoidable and transformative, without being transcendent.

In Matthew Arnold's 1857 inaugural lecture at Oxford, 'On the Modern Element in Literature', he suggested that 'one of the most characteristic features of a modern age, of an age of advanced civilization, is the banishment of the ensigns of war and bloodshed from the intercourse of civil life.'[113] It is this kind of banishment that Morris refuses, in an instinctive revolt, which would in later years become a well-developed argument, against the 'advanced civilization' it betokens. Bevis persuasively argues that signs of war are not, in any case, as absent from modern life or literature as Arnold suggests. Even his own poem, 'Dover Beach', could be seen as a kind of war poem 'not only because the threat of war hovers in and around its edges, but also because war is part of the fabric of its most intimate human imaginings'.[114] Morris goes beyond the implied or the accepted, to make explicit the connections between violence and intimate human imaginings. His stories of violence offer the ensigns of past war and bloodshed as a means of turning readers away from the 'bourgeoisdom' and expedience of Victorian civil and military life. They make the violent and the corporeal central to an interrogation of notions of courage and cowardice, identity and action, knowing and doing. The violence of combat, like the tales themselves, is disturbingly unstable and its outcome uncertain, but it offers a passionate corporeal engagement with the world that contrasts with the social, political and religious mores of 'advanced civilization'. It suggests the power of the body in battle to effect change and mediate meaning. It is this power that Morris explores, idealizes, interrogates and troublingly affirms in most of the works that follow these first short stories.

Chapter Two

KNIGHTLY WOMEN AND THE IMAGINATION OF BATTLE IN *THE DEFENCE OF GUENEVERE, AND OTHER POEMS*

In Morris's 1858 poem, 'King Arthur's Tomb', the despairing Guenevere, meeting Launcelot after their betrayal of Arthur, recalls the common terms of praise used about him in times past, when he was known as the 'sword and shield of Arthur'. Instead, she cries, 'you are found a crooked sword, I think, that leaves a scar / On the bearer's arm'.[1] She extends the metonymic substitution of arms for the man into a metaphor for his effect on Arthur, drawing attention to the relationship between language, body and act in doing so. This is the central triangulated relationship of Morris's first volume of poems, *The Defence of Guenevere*, in which the interaction of imaginative language, confined or distorted bodies and acts of violence serves as a means of disrupting power relationships, gender roles and the moral consensus that sustains them. Published two years after the stories of the *Oxford and Cambridge Magazine*, still in the aftermath of the Crimean War, the poems dwell on medieval battle, the capture of prisoners and tales of their escape; written in the early days of Morris's friendship with Rossetti, they draw on intensities of feeling and distortions of form, both bodily and poetic, to disturb and disorient, working 'against the grain of contemporary orthodoxy' as J. B. Bullen notes in relation to the title poem.[2] Shaping the narrated bodily experience and corporeal poetics of the poems is the ambiguous power of physical violence in the relations between people, particularly between men and women.

Isobel Armstrong argues that *The Defence* 'could properly be seen as [...] a critique of a society which habitually goes to war', and John Peck, quoting Armstrong, goes on to add that, 'rather than setting the tragedy of war against the heroism of war, Morris could be said to venture some way towards seeking political alternatives to war.'[3] I argue, to the contrary, that Morris produces a volume that offers little critique of war, but rather uses the open violence of the medieval world to explore the disorderly – and potentially generative – effects of violence on both men and women, and in doing so to challenge prevailing views of proper femininity associated with the domestic and submissive.

Contemporary critics read the poems largely as escapist, their rhythmic and thematic focus on disorder a sign of poor art, poor taste and poor prosody.[4] Recent scholarship has attributed their style and content to a more deliberate dissent from social or artistic norms. Karen Herbert's Marcusean reading examines the tension between the private and public, personal and moral interpretations of past and present, arguing for the subversive uses of memory and imagination in framing truth, while Constance W. Hassett concludes that the volume is 'a sustained act of aesthetic non-compliance; its every artistic move is a sign of resistance'.[5] Other critics who have emphasized the role of dissent in the poems have dealt explicitly with the assumption that Morris's use of the medieval period constitutes a critique of its violence as well as of nineteenth-century society. While it is certainly the case, as Boos points out, that 'violence was endemic in this "lifeworld"', the poems surely do something rather more complicated with this violence than 'document[ing] the violence and degradation which flowed from feudal abuses of power'.[6] Indeed, Morris and his socialist colleague Ernest Belfort Bax would later defend medieval violence in contrast with Victorian violence because, 'in mediaeval times, the violence and suffering did not spare one class and fall wholly upon another, the most numerous in the community.'[7] The universality of violence in the Middle Ages modifies its effect, they argue. The poems, rooted in this view, use the violence of their world to imagine the possibilities of escape from convention, religion and social morality that a world predicated on physical interactions might allow.

In a more politically nuanced reading, further to her comments on the relation of war to the poems, Armstrong develops her analysis of Victorian poetry as both expressive and epistemological, to argue that the poems at once arise from and critique 'the condition of oppression' that pervades the medieval period and the nineteenth century alike. Her detailed reading of the poems in terms of Ruskinian grotesque raises crucial issues of the meanings of violence, dislocation and transgression, of gender relations and power that underlie the poems; yet she reads both the intensity of physical experience in the poems and their immersion in medieval violence as the 'representations' of 'the oppressed consciousness'. More particularly, she asserts that 'violence is the Grotesque's oversimplification of the complexities to which the numbed consciousness cannot respond'.[8] I suggest, rather, that the poems celebrate the intensity, the disorder, and even the violence of their medieval world. While the 'interrogation and uncertainty' of the 'double poem' is present in the volume, violence offers a physical, experiential basis for knowing that stands in contrast with uncertainty.[9]

The volume's emphasis on violence and disorder draws attention to the active, transformative imagination as it represents the embattled or imprisoned body. Written shortly after the publication of the first part of Coventry

Patmore's poetic vision of domestic felicity, *The Angel in the House* (1854), and Barrett Browning's conversely protofeminist and socially indignant *Aurora Leigh* (1856), the poems of *The Defence* turn to the past and its stories to explore the possible effects on both men and women of a society whose relationships and meaning are understood through the corporeal interactions of combat rather than through moral consensus.[10] If *The Angel in the House* is, as John Woolford and Daniel Karlin suggest, 'a celebration of domesticity as the place to which the war-weary male turns to recover bliss and reproduce himself', Morris depicts a world devoid of domesticity or reproduction in which the only alternative to action is imprisonment and ennui.[11] In doing so he undermines both the ideal of domesticity and the concept of female separation from the world of action, drawing on the inheritance of Romantic poetry and the late eighteenth-century gothic for his disjointed and fragmented, but sensually intense poems of disruption and escape. They are incarnations of the imagination in which violence is framed and reframed through the voices and bodies of the poems' personae and the people whose tales they tell.

The focus of the poems, to borrow Elaine Scarry's phrase, is on 'the body in pain', but also and equally on the body contorted by thwarted passion. Scarry suggests that the nineteenth century is one that anticipates the dominant societal drive of the twentieth century to produce 'out of its own physical well-being (or the well-being of its most articulate class) an endless fascination with the details of psychic distress and dislocation'.[12] Morris externalizes this kind of distress and dislocation in the physical reality of violence or in the movements of the body; but he draws attention to the act of externalizing, through the voices of the characters, narrators and poetic personae in these dramatic poems. The needs of the body in pain or passion are set against the requirements of abstract morality and socially constructed gender roles. The parity of men and women in matters of will and desire is suggested by the entry of women into the community of violence signified by war or knighthood. It is a dangerous community, however, in which physical force may be used for coercion as well as for freedom.

The representation of this liberating but imperfect community of knighthood, with all its failings, depends on an idea of the medieval past, not as 'an ordered yet organically vital universe', as Alice Chandler suggests the Middle Ages were for Victorians, but rather as a time in which disorder and imperfection, demonstrated in open and random violence, were a normal part of the 'organically vital' life of the people.[13] In his 1856 review of Robert Browning's *Men and Women*, Morris writes of 'Andrea del Sarto' and 'Fra Lippo Lippi':

> What a joy it is to have these men brought up before us, made alive again, though they have passed away from the earth so long ago; made alive, […] but rescued

from the judgment of the world, 'which charts us all in its broad blacks or whites', and shown to us as they really were.[14]

The Defence performs a similar kind of nonjudgemental reclamation, bringing before Morris's readers 'poor struggling, falling men' (and the women they imagine, or are imagined by) from the historical or mythical past, alongside his own poetic creations, set in an intensely sensory world of tangible things and touching bodies, fantasized and realized.[15]

Even the unseen world of heaven that impinges so much on the poems and represents the possibilities of the imagination rather than any more real guiding or ordering presence, is conceived as a place of bodies, things and war. In 'Rapunzel', the prince, coming on Rapunzel's tower, wonders:

> Whether my whole life long had been a dream,
> And I should wake up soon in some place, where
> The piled-up arms of the fighting angels gleam.
> ('Rapunzel', 65)

The numinous is denied in this image, which mortalizes the angels and gives solidity but not separateness to the sphere of heaven. The unseen world is not a realm of peace or holiness, but one continuous with the life of earth and accessible through the workings of the corporeal imagination: an imagination that is rooted in the body, that arises from the engagement of the body with the world.[16] It finds in the idea of violence the possibility of escape or transformation, which works in tension with the longing for physical consummation, community or satisfaction present in the intense and repeated acts of kissing that occur over and over in the volume.[17]

Morris follows his major medieval sources for the poems, Malory and Froissart, as well as the tales of the Grimm brothers, from which 'Rapunzel' derives, in his acceptance of violence and his portrayal of a society in which the disorderly and random prevail.[18] Equally important in my reading of these early poems are the traces of Barrett Browning's influence. Mackail records Morris commenting in later life that 'his first poems were imitations of Mrs Browning', and although Morris himself noted the influence of Robert Browning on this volume of a few years later, there is much that draws on the tone and themes of Barrett Browning's 1844 *Poems*, in its focus on medieval tales of love and war.[19] Most particularly, the motif of the woman as knight has its effect on Morris's work: the image of the betrothed of 'The Romaunt of the Page', going out to fight at her lover's side in disguise, is refracted again and again in the women of *The Defence*, who either take on the role of knight or imagine taking it on. Unlike Barrett Browning's page,

Morris's women retain their female identity and so their erotic potential while simultaneously taking on a male role: Jehane in 'Golden Wings' sets out to find her lover, armed with a sword, in her bare feet and undergarments, her name echoing that other 'martial maiden', Joan of Arc ('Golden Wings', 121–22); the long-dead woman whose skeleton the narrator comes upon in 'Geffray Teste Noire', appears at first to have been a knight ('Teste Noire', 77–8); Guenevere herself, 'glorious lady fair' though she is, nonetheless enters into verbal battle in her own defence ('The Defence', 2).[20] Morris draws on the Romantic tradition of the 'belle dame sans merci', but complicates it by the martial focus of the poems. He uses images of violence and battle in association with women to represent them both as independent agents and as erotic subjects of the male gaze.

While an atmosphere of violence shapes the whole volume only a minority of poems centre around an immediate act of violence: most of them rather offer violence imagined, awaited, or remembered. They work in tension with one another to destabilize the meanings of violence and suggest the possibility of its different uses. The volume affirms in one poem what it denies in another: in 'King Arthur's Tomb' the sexual freedom Guenevere has defended in 'The Defence' now becomes sin, subject to 'God's curses' ('Arthur's Tomb', 17); in 'The Haystack in the Floods' the contorted kiss of 'The Defence' becomes an abortive one; the escape of 'A Good Knight in Prison' is mirrored by the incarceration of 'In Prison', and refracted in the escaping heroine's sudden death in 'Golden Wings'; the absent knight whom the hemmed-in Jehane goes out to meet in 'Golden Wings' might be the enchanted knight imagining his beloved bringing him his sword in 'Spell-bound', while the mysterious magic of 'Spell-bound' is echoed in the 'The Blue Closet' and 'Rapunzel'. The title poem, one of the least overtly violent of the volume, sets up the possibility of female knighthood and explores the intersections of battle, sexuality and freedom that run through the rest of the volume. This chapter therefore begins with a close analysis of 'The Defence of Guenevere' and then goes on to consider the violence of the 'Other Poems' of the title in the context of this close reading.

'My Eyes May Bring Some Sword': The Performative Voice and Guenevere's Trial by Combat

Published in the same year that Augustus Egg's triptych 'Past and Present', depicting a woman's adulterous fall from comfortable home to watery destruction, highlighted the domestic imperatives of Victorian womanhood, Morris's title poem turns away from the present to the Arthurian past.

Yet its ambivalent narrative of female defiance speaks in its own moment, in conversation with history as well as with the many other poetic and artistic narratives of womanhood shaped by the Arthurian revival.[21] In its dramatization of Guenevere's response to the imminent threat of violent death, 'The Defence' offers the Queen's voice and her body as weapons of offence. Like the *Thousand and One Nights*' Scheherazade Guenevere tells stories to hold off death; but she also does more than this, attacking the very moral and political order that would condemn her.[22] The poem exposes the latent threat of violence and coercion inherent in a coherent, male-oriented social order: at the moment of Guenevere's trial for adultery, it challenges this threat through her own appropriation of the language, images and roles of battle. In doing so, it affirms the potential of open combat to disrupt and reconfigure social structures. A metaphor of battle runs through the poem, figuring it as a kind of disorienting disorder out of which a new morality based on the imperatives of the female as well as male body might arise. Guenevere refuses to accept the fate of a woman and acts instead as a knight, using her body and her words against her accusers. The poem itself represents the body in combat as arbiter of what is true.

The queen's monologue is framed by mirroring narrative interventions that offer her in the two separate guises of condemned adulteress and then skilled warrior. Her knightly stance at the end of the poem casts its shadow back over the rest of her monologue, as Jonathan Freedman persuasively argues.[23] As she comes to the close of her argument, Guenevere falls silent, listening for the sound of Launcelot's approaching charger, not like an adulteress awaiting rescue, but rather,

> Like a man who hears
> His brother's trumpet sounding through the wood
> Of his foes' lances.
> ('The Defence', 10)

She may be at the stake, waiting for rescue, but Guenevere is not, like Scott's well-known Rebecca, femininely submissive to the will of God.[24] Neither is her argument a reasoned defence, such as might be offered in a court of law. Instead, all that has gone before is a knightly act of battle, though it is more aggressive than Freedman's definition of 'knightly defense' as 'a parrying, by the use of language, of the thrusts of her accusers – a holding action'.[25] Guenevere's vivid tale does hold off the final moment of death, but it also mounts its own attack. Her voice mediates between her body and the world, the inner self and the unseen moral and social order.

This verbal defence is an act of battle, then, and for Morris battle has its own rules. His later defence of lying when it is a tactic of war suggests a way of reading the poem: 'it must be admitted that our Northmen were not above using the weapons of deceit in their struggles for life and fortune: but when they do so it is as an act of war.' Lying takes on a quality of honesty in this context; it is a means to an end, and one equivalent to, rather than opposite to, a physical act of battle. Morris goes on, 'in the Homeric literature and in the Norse, it was peace within the gens or tribe and war always outside it; a lie or deceit therefore was like an ambush in war'.[26] Guenevere's defence, then, is martial strategy rather than mortal sin: not perjury, but combat, in which both voice and body are weapons. By it she sets herself apart from Arthur's court and its rules and in doing so acknowledges the broken brotherhood of the Round Table.

Guenevere evokes the physical and visual again and again to draw attention to her body, which is both her plea and her protection. Armstrong suggests that Guenevere is 'forced into dishonesty and misrepresentation because of the contradictions in which she lives'.[27] Yet the poem endorses her skill in making her defence; it celebrates her somatic and linguistic prowess in the same way that Malory recounts the battles of the knights of the Round Table. Despite her tears and her burning cheek, 'still she stood right up, and never shrunk/ […] Spoke out at last with no more trace of shame' (2). Unlike Tennyson's Guinevere, whose postadulterous supine body, as she 'grovelled with her face against the floor', is evidence of her sinfulness, Morris's Guenevere is upright, articulate and deliberate in her use of her body to defend herself.[28]

The poem begins, as it ends, with Guenevere's unexpected silence, her speaking body and her burning cheek:

> But, knowing now that they would have her speak,
> She threw her wet hair backward from her brow,
> Her hand close to her mouth touching her cheek.
> ('The Defence', 1)

The moment of Guenevere's monologue is delayed by this description of her separate body parts, emphasized by the rhythmic stresses that fall on them, so that she appears first of all as the vulnerable sum of her parts. Knowing that she is expected to speak, she does not. Rather, attention is focused on both the body's beauty and its objective unreliability. Certainty and doubt, wholeness and separation work in tension with each other, the tightly ordered rhyme scheme and repetitions of word and sound countered by shifts in rhythm, from the martial beat of that last line into the uneven stresses that follow:

> As though she had had there a shameful blow
> And feeling it shameful to feel aught but shame
> All through her heart, yet felt her cheek burned so

> She must a little touch it.
> ('The Defence', 1)

Already, appearance may not tally with reality; perception may be deceptive as the shame her accusers cast on Guenevere is here transferred to the imaginary blow, and the burning at the stake that awaits her is prefigured and dismissed in the touching of her burning 'cheek of flame'. The body is the means of interpretation, but its reactions are not entirely contiguous with external events, so that it suggests the possibility of an intersubjective reality.

Eventually, unlike Malory's silent queen, she does begin to speak, but her words are quickly interrupted by a description of their sound:

> Her voice was low at first, being full of tears,
> But as it cleared, it grew full loud and shrill,
> Growing a windy shriek in all men's ears,
>
> A ringing in their startled brains.
> ('The Defence', 2)

The tone and pitch of Guenevere's voice startles, not merely her listeners, but specifically, their brains. The specificity of vocabulary here recalls Alexander Bain's near-contemporary analysis, in *The Senses and the Intellect*, of the intimate relationship between the actions and sensations of the body and the workings of the mind and will. He argues that 'the organ of mind is not the brain by itself: it is the brain, nerves, muscles, organs of sense and viscera'.[29] Considering the effects of sound in particular, Bain argues that 'according as the loudness of a sound increases, so does the stimulation. [...] A loud speaker is exciting.' He goes on to list various loud noises, including 'the ringing of bells close to the ear'. Once the sound rises to a pitch that can be defined as 'shrill', he suggests, 'the intensity [...] turns to pain'.[30] Guenevere uses the traditional female weapon of the voice to launch a direct attack on her judges' minds and bodies, not merely challenging their implied claims of moral truth or political commitment to order, but aurally disordering their nervous systems and responses. Bain concludes his explication of the effects of the varying intensity of sound by commenting on 'suddenness': 'if unexpected, they produce the discomposure usually attending a breach of expectation'.[31] Like the rhythms of the Spasmodic poets that so offended their contemporary listeners, like the rhythms of this poem itself, the very sound of Guenevere's voice challenges the expectations of her auditors. This is, to adapt Jason Rudy's term, 'physiological poetry'.[32]

For all the apparent fragility of the queen's halting appearance as the poem begins, her speech is characterized by a confident and hostile versatility with language that is increasingly reflected in the movements of her body. Her opening statement, 'God wot I ought to say, I have done ill', is surely not an admission of guilt, as W. David Shaw suggests.[33] Rather, it is an ironic dismissal of conventional forms, carried through in her subsequent refusal of the grounds on which she might admit to sin. There is none of the deceptive appearance of veracity evident, for instance, in Browning's 'Count Gismond', in which the narrator gives herself away by the gaps and slips in her own story.[34] Instead, Guenevere openly manipulates her audience: her monologue is a performance, in J. L. Austin's terms, and her language is performative: neither 'true' nor 'false', but designed to achieve specific results.[35] Cornelia Pearsall argues that Victorian dramatic monologues are not, as has most commonly been argued, 'unintentionally self-revealing'; instead, she suggests, they 'constitute efficacious, highly intentional articulations: something happens during the course of a dramatic monologue because of the deliberate operations of the dramatic monologue itself.'[36] Certainly Morris makes no pretence that Guenevere's monologue is unaware of its own disorderly complications and contradictions. Indeed, as Walter Pater noted approvingly, 'The Defence' itself is 'a thing tormented and awry with passion, like the body of Guenevere defending herself.'[37] Both the poem and the queen privilege imagination over reason and offer corporeal experience rather than abstract values as the basis of truth.

Guenevere asks her accusers to imagine lying on their deathbeds: an angel, whose commands 'seem', by a trick of the light, to be God's, asks them to choose between two cloths: one red, one blue; one for heaven, one for hell. The cloths themselves give no clues: 'no man could tell the better of the two' (2). The cameo's imaginary dying characters therefore make what seems the obvious choice to anyone familiar with the conventional meanings of colour: 'After a shivering half-hour you said: / "God's help! heaven's colour, the blue;" and he said, "hell"'.[38] In these echoing aspirants all difference is collapsed: instead of help from God the choice results in its orally shortened counterpart, hell. On imagining her listeners making the wrong choice, Guenevere has them writhing in regret, moaning, 'Ah Christ, if only I had known, known, known' (2). The plea for God's help is as ineffective as the appeal to Christ is routine.[39] God is more a rhetorical device than a numinous guiding presence, his name a curse as much as a prayer. Language, as well as aesthetic convention, is destabilized. God becomes a weapon in Guenevere's oral armoury rather than an external reality. What is vivid here is the shivering, writhing body of the imagined chooser, and the desolate, stalled repetition of 'known, known, known'. The body registers the uncertainties of the world in blushes, in tears, and in contortions or 'passionate twisting' (2), an image that suggests both violent emotion and corporeal suffering.

The poem demands an engagement with the body as much as with its words. Guenevere's argument arises from and relies on her body, much as Malory's knights resolve their quarrels or prove their worthiness by combat: 'so, ever must I dress me to the fight', she mutters (6).[40] Like a knight in combat, she uses a variety of approaches in this offensive, first offering her body as evidence of her unhappiness with Arthur:

> I grew
> Careless of most things, let the clock tick, tick,
>
> To my unhappy pulse, that beat right through
> My eager body.
> ('The Defence', 3)

Physiology embodies desire here. Kirstie Blair suggests that 'the rhythm of the heart stands in opposition to the will because it represents an alternative source of control'.[41] In Guenevere's account the rhythm of the pulse – irregular, as well as unhappy, if the rhythm of 'careless of most things, let the clock tick, tick', can be trusted – becomes the measure of her true feelings, its unhappiness in her 'eager body' contrasted with her laughter and her apparent coldness.

She goes on to give an account of meeting Launcelot in the walled garden that is not merely a description, but an erotic demonstration. Indeed Antony Harrison, tracing the stages of her self-presentation here, suggests that she 'performs onanistically' its rippling culmination and 'compels her auditors' awareness of their own irrepressible sexual urges'.[42] This is display, but it is also attack. She shows her listeners how, 'shouting', she:

> Loosed out, see now! all my hair,
> And trancedly stood watching the west wind run
>
> With faintest half-heard breathing sound.

Guenevere's shout contrasts with the faintness of the 'breathing sound', which might be both her own and the wind's, in an image of abandon that is physically startling. Having disoriented her listeners and at the same time evoked images of the loose-haired fallen woman for the poem's readers, she turns their expectations against them, making use of the medieval idea that physical beauty signifies moral purity: 'Say no rash word / Against me, being so beautiful'.⁴³ She couples this with a curious threat of violence, engendered by her weeping eyes, if they should doubt her:

> My eyes,
> Wept all away to grey, may bring some sword
>
> To drown you in your blood.
> ('The Defence', 8)

The body itself, in this image, marshals its resources against those who refuse its logic. Eyes themselves may command weapons. Guenevere counters the threat of death with her own threats of violence.

She goes on to exhibit and enumerate her own separate body parts in an invitation of the intense male gaze that evokes both pornography and blazon: 'see my breast rise / Like waves of purple sea, as here I stand'. (8). She draws attention to her arms, her hand, her long throat, in which words themselves rise 'in ripples', solidly material, as Hassett points out, but not thereby deprived of meaning; rather they highlight the mutually constitutive meanings of words and bodies.⁴⁴ Guenevere continues:

> Look you up,
>
> And wonder how the light is falling so
> Within my moving tresses: will you dare,
> When you have looked a little on my brow
>
> To say this thing is vile?
> ('The Defence', 8)

Although readers may have learned that such an association is not to be trusted, that beauty is not necessarily truth and truth, beauty, Guenevere insists upon the evidence of her body to back up her words, and on the imagination of her audience to see truth in her body. The poem recalls an idea elaborated by Keats in 1817: 'what the imagination seizes as Beauty must be truth – whether it existed before or not – for I have the same Idea of all our Passions as of Love they are all in their sublime, creative of essential Beauty.'⁴⁵ Truth is not an absolute, then. It is not based on fact but on the subjective interpretation of the physical.

Just as Guenevere turns her words and her body on her accusers, disordering expectation, the poem itself sets up a combative relationship with the traditions of Arthurian myth, disordering its tales of chivalric violence. Rather than making the treacherous Mordred and bitter Agravaine Guenevere's accusers, or facing her with Arthur, whose claims against her are more political than personal, Morris assigns the role of silent uncompromising judge to Gauwaine, who in Malory's tale is Guenevere's defender until almost the very end.[46] His status as judge recalls his own trial by a court of ladies convened by the queen, in the *Morte Darthur*: after the establishment of Arthur's court, Gauwaine sets off on a quest and, preparing to kill a knight who has begged him fruitlessly for mercy, accidentally strikes off the head of a lady who turns up by chance at that moment. When he returns to Arthur's court, 'by ordenaunce of the quene ther was set a quest of ladyes upon sir gavayn, and they juged hym for ever whyle he lyved to be with all ladyes and to fyghte for her quarels'. He is ordered to be 'curteys' and 'never to refuse mercy to hym, that asketh mercy'.[47] If Guenevere has undermined the moral code of Arthur's kingdom, and overstepped its boundaries, so too, the poem insistently reminds us, has Gauwaine, and he too has been on trial for it, though his life was never at risk. Male violence, it seems, is less reprehensible than female adultery, written as it is into the structure of Arthurian life. The poem offers an alternative judgement, without denying the fellowship of violence or the disruptive power of Guenevere's actions and voice.

Guenevere draws attention to Gauwaine's turning away from her and his refusal of mercy, calling into question the terms of his own sentence. She attributes to him a physical reaction that betokens pity, claiming the power of her own ocular authority as she had asserted the power of her judges': 'Do I not see how God's dear pity creeps / All through your frame, and trembles in your mouth?' (6). The abstract is rendered concrete by the body: 'God's dear pity' 'creeps' and 'trembles'; yet Guenevere's verbal construction of Gauwaine's corporeal emotion is not enough to make it real. His lack of response to her appeals and threats is suggested by her return to a more conventionally abstract use of language a few lines on: 'I pray your pity! [...] / Ah! God of mercy, how he turns away!' (6). Her imagination cannot create a lasting embodiment of 'God's dear pity' in Gauwaine.

His turning away from her is all the more powerful a gesture in the light of his own sexual betrayal in the *Morte Darthur*: promising to win the recalcitrant damsel Ettard for Pelleas, Gauwaine sets off for her castle, and there woos her for himself, abandoning Pelleas's suit. Ettard, discovering his treachery, cries that 'ye have deceyved me and bytrayd me falsly, that al ladyes and damoysels may beware by yow and me'.[48] Morris's Guenevere, then, is confronted with the lawful double standards of power and the treacherous expression of unfettered desire that Gauwaine represents. At the same time, her bodily defence recalls his own faith in proving goodness by physical combat: after the death of his brothers, Gauwaine tells Launcelot that, but for the Pope's command, 'I shold do bataille with myn owne body ageynst thy body, and preve it upon the, that thow hast ben [...] fals'.[49] Guenevere claims this same right, using her body against Gauwaine.

Where Malory's tale emphasizes the importance of Launcelot's prowess in Guenevere's deliverance – 'there myghte none withstande sir Launcelot'– in 'The Defence', Guenevere's own prowess sets the ambush for her accusers, so that Launcelot's arrival is a continuation of what she has begun to prove with her own body, in this trial by combat.[50] J. B. Bullen observes that 'the form of the poem is linked to the form of the confessional identified by Foucault as so important in defining human sexuality in this period' in which, in Foucault's words, 'the scope of the confession – the confession of the flesh – continually increased'. Bullen goes on to suggest that in this kind of confession desire meets fear of punishment 'and their interaction leads to the spontaneous overflow of powerful feelings in language'.[51] There is nothing of this Wordsworthian spontaneity in Guenevere's defence, however. The poem makes it clear that her language and her movements are calculated, however desperate. She remains in control of this monologue and undermines the power of confession as a means of accessing truth by acknowledging her actions but refusing common constructions of their meaning. This is not a conventional Augustinian confession leading to conversion, nor a forced confession to an authoritative auditor, but rather a subversion of these forms.

Conventional forms and old stories are used and disordered in the poem; words and the sound of words become weapons, celebrating the power of language and the body together to challenge accepted forms and conventions, artistic and moral. The freedom and autonomy Guenevere attains by the end of the poem, hard won though it is, does not secure her place in the fellowship, but rather dissolves it, and in the end, as 'King Arthur's Tomb' suggests, cannot be sustained. Nonetheless the poem celebrates the power of the imagination and the knightly body in action to create, however temporarily, a different set of social conditions. While the poem challenges nineteenth-century constructions of marriage, fidelity and adultery, it also expresses a broader protest against social conformity and religious certainty, evoking images of medieval battle as expressions of faith in the physical and embodied rather than the spiritual, legal or abstract. An 1858 *Spectator* reviewer of the poem observed with disapproval that Morris had introduced into his poems of chivalry 'touches of what modern research or judgment has shown to be its real coarseness and immorality'; it is precisely the terms of this 'modern research or judgment' that the poem refuses.[52]

The themes of 'The Defence' reverberate through the volume. The repetitions of names (Jehane, John, Giles, Alice), body parts (hands, fingers, lips, hair), and motifs universalize the poems, so that the experience of one

Jehane or Alice modifies the meaning of another's.[53] Poem after poem replays or reframes the relationships between men, women and violence set up by the opening poem, depicting a world of violence in which intimate relationships are mediated and understood by battle. Morris imagines violence for women as a way of undermining social or sexual boundaries, without ignoring its destructive power. The poems represent different kinds of violence with different effects: it is not sanitized or idealized, but it does become part of an imagination of the body in which pain is less damaging than imprisonment, injury less destructive than confinement. The privileging of the corporeal over the abstract and the questioning of gender roles made evident in the interplay of bodies, words and unexpected violence that underpin 'The Defence' form the basis for the rest of the volume.

From Violence to Stories: Retelling the Violent Past

A reviewer for the *Saturday Review* of 1858 who damned Morris's collection as 'decidedly unpleasant', and 'The Defence' in particular as 'a very tedious affair', also complained of Morris's commitment to a 'false principle of art. False principle we say, because a poet's work is with the living world of men. Mr Morris never thinks of depicting man or life later than the Crusades'.[54] This critic is only partly right; Morris's principle of engaging with the past signals his own judgement on, rather than simply escape from, the 'living world of men'. It offers a view of the past, in all its violence, as essential to the construction of the present through acts of creative retelling. Morris's poems do not turn to medieval violence in order to critique it. As he and Bax would write in the 1880s of the medieval period: 'the very roughness and adventure of life in those days made people less sensitive to bodily pain than they are now.' They go on to argue that 'history affords abundant evidence' that 'their nerves were not so high-strung as ours are, so that the apprehension of torture or death did not weigh heavily upon them.'[55] These are not poems that represent violence itself as a form of oppression. Rather, after the triumphant knightly defence that achieves freedom for Guenevere, Morris uses the other poems in the volume to explore the possibilities of pleasurably retelling and interpreting moments of violence as a means of understanding the essential human experiences of loss, death and consummation. In doing so, he combines a gothic investment in moments of excessive violence and horror with a Romantic emphasis on what Mario Praz describes as the 'mysterious bond between pleasure and suffering', which is evident in the experiences of the body and the experience of poetry.[56]

In turning to the past, he suggests the failures of the present. While his mode of doing so is less a critique of life shaped by 'conditions of labour', as Armstrong argues, than a refusal to acknowledge the present, it does obliquely reflect on the social, economic and spiritual conditions of life of his own time. The Froissartian and fairytale poems offer intense images of combat and pain as a way of turning aside from the failures of satisfactory narratives in the utilitarian or spiritual ethics of Morris's own time. There is no Gradgrindian emphasis on facts here, and no High Church emphasis on the sacramental presence of God, but rather the poems prioritize physical perception and imaginative reconstruction as a means of understanding the world. As Merleau-Ponty suggests, 'Being is what requires creation of us for us to experience it'.[57] Both Morris and his characters create their own tales, out of their experience, in order to feel the world and their place in it. They are tales above all of bodies, reconfiguring the life of the earth and the imagination of heaven through the lens of a romantic medievalism. The *Saturday Review* critic continues his assessment of the volume rather mockingly:

> It must have been a queer world to live in [...] there must have been a great deal of blood as well as lances and shields in those days; and though there was a great amount of kissing, both according to the chronicles and Mr Morris, it appears that the kissers and kissed had but little respect for the marriage service.[58]

It is in this 'queer' and socially subversive combination of blood, violence and kissing, alongside the absence of respect for established forms or rigid social structures, that the poems' celebration of the life of the body lies.

In 'Sir Peter Harpdon's End' (35–61), 'Concerning Geffray Teste Noire' (75–81), and 'The Haystack in the Floods' (124–8), imaginary violence and real violence interweave and overlap. Each poem tells a story of combat or disruption in which the reimagination of past or future is the means of mediating relationships and understanding reality. A review of Morris's work after his death notes that 'Sir Peter' and 'The Haystack' are 'vivid realisations of the kind of medieaval savagery which the old chronicler relates as if such deeds were a matter of course'.[59] Froissart's own take on the scenes of combat he describes may offer a clue to Morris's: over and over he praises even the most brutal of battles as the scene of 'noble deeds'. Describing Sir Robert Sale cutting down peasants in 1381, Froissart writes that he 'drew out a good sword, and began to fight with them, and cleared a great space about him, so that it was a pleasure to behold him. [...] At every stroke he gave he cut off either leg, head, or arm.'[60] Violence – witnessed in person by Froissart, but thoroughly removed from reality for Morris – may offer aesthetic pleasure and an affirmation of action, as well as an insight into the grounds of communal and individual morality.

The threat of violence and its execution underlie the structure, form and poetic voices of the verse drama of 'Sir Peter Harpdon's End'. The poem dramatizes the tale of Sir Peter, a Gascon knight loyal to England, holed up in his besieged castle in France during the Hundred Years' War, betrayed and eventually killed by his cousin, Lambert, who is fighting on the side of the French. Peter's violent death and the wider losses of battle that lie behind his tale are given meaning through his voice and that of his lover, Alice, imagining one another. The violence of the events the poem records is brutal and final, but also generative, at least of stories, which effect a kind of supracorporeal immortality. At the end of the poem Peter's lover, Alice, hears a song about Launcelot and muses that: 'yea, perhaps they will, / When many years are past, make songs of us' (60). The painful separation of Launcelot and Guenevere recounted in 'King Arthur's Tomb' is overwritten here by the song affirming Launcelot's prowess and 'mickle worth' (61). Alice, in imagining the same might be done for Peter and herself, performs a variation on what Andrea Henderson describes as the Romantic project of the 'reformulation of sacrifice as indulgence': in imagining her loss retold, she sees it given meaning through the longevity of the act; it becomes both instructive and admirable in the retelling.[61] Morris himself makes a similar transposition in the poem, turning violence into reading pleasure through poetry. Just as in the *Earthly Paradise*, the Elders of the city comment that 'scarce can we be grieved' at the troubles of the wanderers 'since it shall bring us wealth of happy hours' in storytelling, so here violent death is given context by its verbal and formal reconstruction.[62] Bare facts may be transformed by imagination, and loss turned into gain.

At the beginning of the poem, Sir Peter thinks of the lies that have been told about him to Alice, back at home. He reconstructs the scene in which he would put right those lies, beginning:

I like to think,
Although it hurts me, makes my head twist, what,
If I had seen her, what I should have said,
What she, my darling, would have said and done.
('Harpdon', 38)

Like the narrator in 'Spell-bound' (104–6), who is similarly, but magically, separated from his beloved, Sir Peter calls up the physical image of Alice. While the 'what if' of 'Spell-bound' (105) ensures that the vision of the embodied beloved is purely imaginary, Sir Peter's language slides from the subjunctive into the simple past, as his creative monologue constructs both encounter and dialogue, until it becomes, in his retelling, a simple past tense encounter:

She said: 'I love you'.
[…]

She kiss'd me all about
My face, and through the tangles of my beard
Her little fingers crept.
('Harpdon', 40)

Distance is crossed by the embodied imagination of Alice's kisses and caresses. The material deprivations and martial horrors of the present war are assuaged by the linguistic reconstruction of the past and by the sensual imagination of touch.

Later in the poem, before sending Peter to his execution, Lambert mockingly says, 'But, cousin Peter, while I stroke your beard / Let me say this', in a linguistic act of cruel mimicry whose performativity is assumed in the play script form of the poem (50). The imaginary touch in which Peter had found such solace now becomes a painful parody that only serves to remind him of what he does not have: 'I am Alice, am right like her now/ Will you not kiss me on the lips, my love?', Lambert taunts him (51). Kisses are both physical and affective, made meaningful by intention and by context. That the touch of Alice's hands and lips is as real for Peter as the present mockery of Lambert is affirmed by the grammar of his speech. Bain discusses the kind of 'revived sensation' that is at work here in a section of *The Senses and the Intellect* entitled, 'tendency of an idea to become reality'. He notes that 'when the revival is energetic it goes the length of exciting even the surface of sense itself by a sort of back-movement. We might think of a blow on the hand, until the skin were actually irritated and inflamed'.[63] In an insight central to trauma theory, Bain notes that the body registers both pleasure and pain or violence in ways that may be recreated without physical touch.[64] The poems themselves work as a kind of back-movement of this sort, reviving not just tales of the past, but also its bodily sensations and sufferings.

Sir Peter uses revived sensation, imagination and words to conjure corporeality and kisses, and so temporarily, subjectively, to alter reality. At the same time, this imaginative recreation of the kiss serves to heighten the disappointment of its absence, intensified by Lambert's mockery. The gap between desire and consummation is dwelt on by the imagination, and the image of Alice created in this gap suggests the possibility of relationships mediated not by lies but by mutual desire. Both violence and kisses represent the intimacy, the connection and the corporeal authenticity whose absence Morris laments in the nineteenth century, and tries to recapture through such tactile activities as brass-rubbing or fencing with singlesticks.[65] Telling tales of thwarted kisses and achieved violence forms part of a coherent narrative in which language and body work together to create meaning.

God, like absent lovers, is conjured by the imagination. He too may be spoken into tenuous bodily being, giving meaning to violent death. Alice, hearing of Peter's death by hanging, invokes the physical Jesus: 'to-day I wish to pray another way', she says. In an act that resembles the methods of Ignatian prayer, but strips them of transcendence, she imagines the incarnate Christ: 'come face to face, / O Christ, that I may clasp your knees and pray' ('Harpdon', 59).[66] Christ is given erotic human form through Alice's words. In a line whose cadence and sentiment is curiously echoed in the invitational opening of T. S. Eliot's 'The Love Song of J. Alfred Prufrock' – another deceptively dialogic poem concerned with the complicated interactions of language, love and truth – she urges Christ, 'Let us go, You and I, a long way off'.[67] She imagines going to 'the little damp, dark, Poitevin church', lying down at Christ's feet and chattering 'anything / I have heard long ago, what matters it', until he loves her,

> Well enough to speak,
> And give me comfort; yea, till o'er your chin,
> And cloven red beard the great tears roll down
> In pity for my misery, and I die,
> Kissed over by you.
> ('Harpdon', 59)

The relentless physicality of 'kissed over', with its undertone of violent eroticism, also evokes the tenderness of 'watched over' or the grief of 'wept over', along with the missing echo of 'and over', to suggest both the intensity of longing behind this embrace and the close connection between passion – both suffering and urgent desire – and violence. There is a longing for physical pain to match or submerge psychic pain, as well as for erotic comfort to assuage the loss of a lover.[68] What is missing here is the conventional mid-Victorian Christian idea of pain as punishment or purification.[69]

Both Jesus and the signs of his love and passion are conjured by Alice's words, the expression of her longings. The completeness of being that is expressed through Christ's imagined kiss is expressed in the moment of ontological consummation that accompanies it: 'I die'. Isolation is not emphasized but ended by this image of the final unity of the self with the source of all language and all flesh. Silver notes the loss of 'the kiss of parting', in the poem and suggests that the kiss 'is to be supplied by a fleshly Jesus, who will comfort her – as a lover would – and let her reunite with Peter in a physical lovers' heaven.'[70] However, unlike the kiss of Christ for which the lonely Rapunzel calls out, the kiss Alice imagines does not transform her. She does not achieve the consummation of death, as she herself notices with surprise: 'strange I do not die' (60). Christ, 'the blending in one of feeling and imagination', as Feuerbach suggests, is the creation of Alice's longings, rather than an external or transcendent being.[71]

While the kiss that Alice desires is one that would signify death, in 'Rapunzel' (62–74) the idea of the kiss converts the numinous into the material. In her first prayer Rapunzel prays, 'Give me a kiss, / Dear God, dwelling up in heaven!', and then immediately follows it with this:

> Also: *Send me a true knight,*
> *Lord Christ, with a steel sword, bright,*
> *Broad, and trenchant.*
> ('Rapunzel', 68)

The violence of Christ's kiss is more explicit here, linked as it is with the gleaming sword. Rapunzel prays for liberation in life rather than death. Just as Peter's and Alice's imaginary visions cross over into one another, so here Rapunzel's prayer imagines a crossover of violence between the seen world and the unseen, mirroring the Prince's vision of the angels' piled up arms (65):

> *Lord, give Mary a dear kiss,*
> *And let gold Michael, who looked down,*
> *When I was there, on Rouen town*
> *From the spire, bring me that kiss*
> *On a lily! Lord do this!*
> ('Rapunzel', 68)

Kirchhoff notes the connection here with Joan of Arc, suggesting that it adds to 'the Christian aura with which [Rapunzel] is now surrounded'.[72] It also does something rather different from this, however, bringing the imagination of the spiritual firmly into the physical realm. Unlike Joan or Guenevere, Rapunzel is not able to take action on her own behalf. Instead she waits for rescue, using imagination to figure her escape through a combination of passion and violence, represented by the kiss and the sword. 'That kiss' becomes something physical in itself, to be brought by the archangel Michael, rather than Gabriel, who more commonly appears to people in the Bible. In a rare moment of satisfaction in the volume, Rapunzel's words speak life into being, in the form of the Prince: this is not a martial angel but a questing lover whose sword is wrought 'with golden hair / Flowing about the hilts' (71). Her escape from the tower and the witch is achieved by both violence and kisses, conjured by her own martial and corporeal imagination.

Only in the fairytale world of 'Rapunzel' is this immediate transformation possible, however. In the historical poems of the volume, the imagination works with the body to create other possible outcomes, but they are not realized in the poems' present. Rather, in 'The Haystack in the Floods', in which Jehane and her English soldier lover, Robert, are ambushed by a French knight named Godmar, even the temporary comforts of the imagination are limited. The pattern of Jehane's story overlaps with that of Guenevere, but follows, in the end, a quite different trajectory. Threat and counterthreat form the basis of the narrative, the imagination of violence offered as a means of wielding power and undermining it. As in 'The Defence', abstract concepts of sin and goodness are challenged by a confrontation with physical, somatic and social realities, but Jehane is merely the subject of other people's stories, not in control of her own. Nonetheless this is not a narrative of despair. 'Pain itself quickens those that God will not have die while they seem to live', Morris writes in his unfinished novel of 1872.[73] His commitment to this idea of the hopeful, generative potential of pain and suffering is evident in the poem in Jehane's threat of liberating counterviolence.

The aching absence of kisses between the lovers shapes the poem and counterpoints its physical violence, from the opening lines: 'Had she come all the way for this, / To part at last without a kiss?' (124). Surprised by Godmar's ambush, Robert, his soldiers and Jehane wait in the rain as the cruelty of their captors works itself out. Faced with the threat of an ordeal of judgement in Paris, the murder of her lover, or rape, if she refuses to give herself willingly to the knight, the creative power of language all but fails Jehane. She nonetheless denies Godmar her body, and instead responds with all that is available to her, a verbal image of physical violence:

> 'You know that I should strangle you
> While you were sleeping; or bite through
> Your throat, by God's help – ah!' she said.
> ('Haystack', 126)

She challenges Godmar's power to control her body by turning her own imagination of violence against his. It is a vividly corporeal imagination; rather than calling up a sense memory through touch, this threat creates an as-yet unrealized sense image. It allows the possibility of future acts and future transformation. Merleau-Ponty suggests that in the interaction of ideas and words, 'it is as though the visibility that animates the sensible world were to emigrate, [...] into another less heavy, more transparent body, [...] abandoning the flesh of the body for that of language'.[74] Here Jehane enfleshes her threat in words in spite of the incapacity of her body. Countering the bleak evidence, she uses words to suggest that there may be an alternative narrative to the dominant one in which Godmar holds all the power.

There is no help to be had here from a transcendent God. God appears, rather, as an extension of her own faint hope, and as Godmar's intentions suggest, her own body.[75] She cannot escape Godmar, but she does refuse to acknowledge his power by recruiting the imagination, albeit in mimicry of his own violence. As Kenneth Hodges observes of the *Morte Darthur*, while both men and women are wounded or injured, 'heroic men agree to risk or suffer bodily injury, thereby showing their commitment and bravery'. Women, by contrast, usually have injury 'imposed upon them', most often in the form of rape. 'Because the woman rarely if ever knowingly risks rape in the pursuit of a good cause, the injuries she sustains do not testify to her bravery and commitment in the way that a knight's wounds do'.[76] In Morris's constructed history, Jehane does choose capture, potential rape and the death of her lover over the voluntary submission of her body to the enemy.

In making this choice, and in the threat of future violence in the cause of her own freedom or revenge, she affirms, however faintly, her right to act in knightly self-defence, and refuses the traditional female role of passive victim. In allowing the primacy of her own claims over Robert's as well as Godmar's, Jehane draws on both the anticipation of pain and the imagination of future pain she might cause. Scarry observes that pain and imagination are both 'boundary conditions', at the opposite edges of human experience. Pain turns the body in on itself, she argues: it is 'an intentional state without an intentional object'; the body, injured, does not feel the injuring object, but itself, hurting. Imagination creates an external object when no real object is available: it imagines something or someone.[77] The imagination of pain, then, brings together the body and the mind to create a new condition. Jehane counters the absorbing expectation of her own pain with the image of Godmar's pain. The possibility of escaping the limits of powerless womanhood finds its expression in the idea of violence.

Yet the poem does not turn away from the reality that this escape is in imagination only. While Guenevere starts off with wet hair, perhaps from a dunking, lifting her hands to touch her face, Jehane, tears and rain running down her face, water dripping on her 'heavy hair', imagines the dunking that will await her if she is returned to Paris:

> The swift Seine on some rainy day
> Like this, and people standing by,
> And laughing, while my weak hands try
> To recollect how strong men swim.
> ('Haystack', 125)

Like Guenevere, Jehane thinks of her body parts as active agents, separate from herself; unlike Guenevere's, they cannot take on male identity or power. While her hands may try to 'recollect how strong men swim', it is not a sensation they can revive, never having been parts of 'strong men': they remain weak. Jehane imagines the limits of her own ability to act, signified by her hands. The poem offers this defiant weakness to the readers, as Guenevere offered her own body. Like 'Golden Wings' or John Everett Millais's 1870 painting, *The Knight Errant*, it trains the reader's gaze on the vulnerable, trapped, female body in an act that may elicit sympathy but also invites a more complex response of pleasure.

The proximity of the two lovers throughout the poem only makes the impossibility of either unity or transcendence more painful: there can be no imaginative substitution for the absent kiss of this poem, as there is for Alice and Sir Peter. In a description that echoes Guenevere's recollection of her passionate embrace with Launcelot – 'both our mouths went wandering in one way, / And aching sorely, met among the leaves' ('The Defence', 5) – Jehane and Robert attempt a final kiss:

> He tried once more
> To touch her lips; she reached out, sore
> And vain desire so tortured them,
> The poor grey lips, and now the hem
> Of his sleeve brush'd them.
> ('Haystack', 128)

Unlike Launcelot and Guenevere's embrace, this one is thwarted. Godmar, seeing them, slits Robert's throat. Jehane, rather like Guenevere mad with beauty in the walled garden, gazes at her hands 'with a rueful smile, / As though this thing had made her mad' (128). Lips and hands already appear as discrete as though violence has been done to them. The poem finishes with the absent kiss and the outstretched hands. Unlike 'The Defence', it offers no final rescue. Yet Jehane's brief corporeal imagination of violence allows the possibility of a transformation in the future. Her threat of retaliation, grimly violent though it is, remains to destabilize the absolute power of Godmar's tale, and to suggest the possibility of change beyond the 'first fitte' (128).

'Concerning Geffray Teste Noire' offers a different perspective, from a male narrator's view. The woman in this tale is already dead and it falls to the narrator to give meaning to that death. The poem begins as an account of a knight setting out on ambush, but his purpose meets its own ambush in the form of dead bodies which recall to the narrator previous acts of slaughter and turn him aside into reverie. Like 'The Defence', it opens *in medias res* and conjures into being both speaker and audience. The narrator offers the individual oral history of violence as an alternative to the accepted record of Jean Froissart, the Canon of Chimay:

> And if you meet the Canon of Chimay,
> As going to Ortaise you may well do,
> Greet him from John of Castel Neuf, and say
> All that I tell you, for all this is true.
> ('Teste Noire', 75)

The conversational opening and extratextual referentiality of the poem suggest a connection with reality belied by the tightly closed rhyme scheme and the compact internal assonance of 'well', 'all', 'tell', 'all'. The illusion of dialogue with an unseen interlocutor, foregrounded early on in the poem, is soon lost in layers of telling, remembering and retelling, in this story of sensory interaction with the events of the past. The tale it tells is as ambiguous as Guenevere's, its male narrative voice as nonlinear as hers. Like 'The Defence', it suggests the deliberate distortion of recorded tales and the rereading of events through the senses. However, the affirmation of female agency that is most pronounced in 'The Defence' and that asserts itself in other poems of the volume is denied absolutely here: the woman in this poem is long dead, her presence entirely constructed out of male desire. The violence that women in other poems use for their defence is here only an erotic projection of the narrator.

The narrator relates how, setting out with his men to ambush the 'Gascon thief', Geffray Teste Noire, he came upon the skeleton of a woman. The fine bones remind him of going out with his father in his youth to fight the peasants of the Jacquerie, and coming across the burnt bones of women in a church that had been set on fire: enclosure is intensified by an act of violence here in an image of inescapable horror. It leaves the young boy retching, echoing with his 'groans' the suffering made evident in the smell of 'burnt bones':

> I being faint with smelling the burnt bones
> And very hot with fighting down the street,
> And sick of such a life, fell down, with groans,
> My head went weakly nodding to my feet.
> ('Teste Noire', 78)

This story of war and brutality forms a parenthesis to the tale of finding the skeleton, which is itself an interruption to the tale of the ambush of Teste Noire. The past, here, does not offer moral lessons or patterns of heroism, but rather glimpsed connections between the physical memory of the past and the interpretation of the present. Like Guenevere, the narrator privileges an intense focus on vividly realized moments of sensory interaction. The memory of the burning of the women directly affects Sir John's interpretation of the woman's skeleton he finds, and the contingent meanings it suggests.[78] Sir John's tale is as distorted by the memory of past acts of cruelty as his ambush is.

Like Sir Peter's lover, Alice, he deals with the horror by aestheticizing violence. To counteract the extreme violence of the women's death, the narrator develops an extreme erotic response to the skeleton in front of him, through sensual apprehension of the material. Sight and touch are the means of sensing the minute and the particular: the 'little skeleton', the white skull 'loose within the coif', the 'ancient rusted mail' (77). These material remains may be misinterpreted, however; they are only given meaning by the imagination. On first seeing them, Sir John says 'What have we lying here? [...]/ This was a knight too'. He begins to tell a story of battle: 'he fought a good fight, maybe', until he realizes the bones are those of a woman (77). The responses of the senses are not entirely to be trusted, then, but must be mediated by storytelling. He begins a new tale, speaking flesh onto the bones, creating a living woman with his imagination. He pores over the bones and falls in love with his own poetic creation. The aestheticized materialism of his passion transforms the woman from victim of violence to femme fatale, bearing violence in her very flesh:

> I saw you kissing once, like a curved sword
> That bites with all its edge, did your lips lie,
> Curled gently, slowly, long time could afford
> For caught-up breathings.
> ('Teste Noire', 80)

Patrick Brantlinger's suggestion that 'the beauty of love and of an imagined lady' is set in opposition to the 'ugly reality of Geffray Teste Noire, violence and death', is difficult to reconcile with this presentation of the lady. I suggest that, on the contrary, violence, beauty, and love, reality and imagination meet on the lips of this kiss, their disorderly conjunction signified by the disorientating syntax of these lines.[79] Objective reality resides in the bones and in the fate of those who died, but it can only be understood through the imagination, which, for Sir John, is bound up with violence. His language creates a woman and silences her, pities her and blames her. Even the kiss that might signal consummation or delight is figured as destructive.

The intention of the poem's speaker appears to dissipate in this reverie; his ambush with Teste Noire appears forgotten. Indeed, Armstrong argues that 'what is really "concerning" the narrator is not Teste Noire but a woman's skeleton and the power of the woman both to disrupt and to confirm masculinity'.[80] In a reversal of the movement of 'The Defence' or 'Golden Wings', the imagination here reformulates communal violence as individual eroticism. While other poems affirm the centrality of human creativity and female agency in shaping human affairs, 'Teste Noire' highlights the power of male violence to silence women. Sir John is eventually recalled to the ambush, the purpose of which is defeated, although many are killed. Teste Noire is not captured, and it is 'much bad living', rather than war, that finally kills him (81). Violence is neither effective nor transformative here.

However, the poem does not finish there. It goes on to Sir John's description of the tomb he had carved for the dead woman and her lover. Their deaths are reframed by this act of remembrance, just as Walter in 'The Story of the Unknown Church' makes sense of the death of his friend and sister through carving their tomb. Handwork, like storytelling, becomes a means of making sense of the past. Through the sight and touch of the bones of the dead woman, Sir John brings to life the dreadful memory of the women burned in the church, assigning them a memorial in history. In addressing himself to Froissart, whose history is full of atrocities and gender violence, he offers his own story of violence to be reshaped and given meaning. Read alongside the other poems in the volume, 'Geffray Teste Noire' becomes part of a communal narrative of generative change brought about because of or in spite of violence, in which the poems themselves retell the retellings of the past, setting failures of consummation or transcendence alongside moments of wholeness, hope or disruption that might eventually lead to new tales.

Blood, Death and the Epistemology of Violence

If 'The Defence' dramatizes the possibility of female knightly agency to challenge moral consensus and notions of abstract truth and the Froissartian poems examine the painful, potentially generative and disruptive role of violence retold by or about women, the volume's many poems of enclosure and escape dramatize the circular interaction of the imaginative mind and the sensing body to transgress social boundaries. Just as later Morris would urge the importance of 'the education of discontent' as a primary tool towards socialist revolution, so in the volume's poems of entrapment and imprisonment he represents the hopeful but unstable power of the imagination, realized in the violent acts of the body, as a means of escape, but not merely escapism.[81]

In an adaptation of the Romantic concept of imprisonment outlined by Victor Brombert, in which prison may be productive of new self-awareness and possibilities, Morris creates poems in which escape by violent means is the generative result of confinement or imprisonment.[82] It is not the experience of confinement, psychic or actual, on which the imprisonment poems focus, but the means of escape from them; not only 'the dream of freedom through transcendence' that Brombert identifies, but the embodied moment of escape through the confrontation and violent transgression of physical or social boundaries.[83] Set against Morris's scathing description, later, of public schools such as Marlborough as 'boy farms', and his repeated use of the language of constriction and enclosure in relation to Victorian marriage and society, they enact a refusal of the safety of confinement, or the 'dull level of mediocrity' of Victorian middle-class life, and an assumption that freedom of all kinds may come at a physical price.[84]

The focus of these poems is on a combination of the immediate senses, the memory and the imagination; as Pater comments in his review of Morris's poems, 'not the fruit of experience, but experience itself is the end'.[85] The escape poems focus on violence as an intense experience that curiously enables sensory awareness, which leads to an understanding of the self and the world. In a later lecture on art Morris would urge on his audience the 'use of the senses which nature has given us and joined in a strange way to that other part of us which we call the mind and soul […] as a means for curing that bored and anxious expression of the Anglo-Saxon countenance'. The countenance to which he referred, specifically, was that of a fellow passenger on a train, whose refusal to open a window signified to Morris that his 'landscape was bounded by his ledger and his mutton chop'.[86] The poems I discuss next insist on the joining of the senses and the soul as a way of transcending limitations. Pater's review goes on to argue:

> With this sense of the splendour of our experience and of its awful brevity, gathering all we are into one desperate effort to see and touch, we shall hardly have time to make theories about the things we see and touch.[87]

The anticipation or memory of violence works in the poems as a means of accessing the splendour of sensory experience and staying alive to it.

In these poems, prison, with its denial of freedom and community and its deprivation of the senses, is far worse than the pain or the disruptions of violence, as Morris was later to assert in his socialist writings.[88] Dick, the guide to Morris's socialist utopia of 1890, explains that 'medieval folk […] were ready to bear what they inflicted on others; whereas the nineteenth century ones […] pretended to be humane, and yet went on tormenting those whom they dared to treat so by shutting them up in prison'.[89] This same preference for medieval violence over imprisonment is evident throughout *The Defence*. The bloody violence of 'A Good Knight In Prison' (82–6) enacts freedom achieved by bodily, hand-to-hand, transgressive combat. Sir Guy, a crusader incarcerated in a pagan fortress, is released with the help of Launcelot and his knights, and returns home to marry Lady Mary. Yet in order to effect his escape and gain the moral centre of marriage, he must use the shocking violence of his bare hands, 'throttling without ruth / The hairy-throated castellan', until 'deep I trod / That evening in my own red blood' (86). His freedom and reintegration into society come at the price of acts not normally sanctioned. Nonetheless, in a reflection of the knightly code of Malory, evoked by the presence of Launcelot in the tale, he risks his body, and by success in that combat, proves himself 'a good knight'. The achievement of identity comes not through submission but through risky action.

'Spell-bound' (104–6) and 'In Prison' (145) offer less tangible modes of escape. If 'Spell-bound' represents a more tentative version of speaking the beloved into life than 'Sir Peter's Harpdon's End', 'In Prison' offers a grim ending to the volume that begins with the creative embodiment of the past and transformation of the present that is Guenevere's defence. 'In Prison' depicts escape as impossible, and the ineluctable appears to prevail:

> Wearily, drearily,
> Half the day long,
> Flap the great banners
> High over the stone.
> ('In Prison', 145)

The opening line recalls both Tennyson's enclosed Mariana's 'dreary' / 'aweary' refrain, and the opening of Edgar Allan Poe's poem of hopeless entrapment, 'The Raven', as well as the final weary dreariness of the sinning heroine in Elizabeth Barrett Browning's 'The Brown Rosary'.[90] Yet the sense of hopelessness that inheres in the end-stressed alternate lines, the internal rhymes and tightly ordered assonance is broken by changes in metre and rhyme scheme between the stanzas.

The predictable metrical stresses of the first stanza give way to the uneven stumble of the second:

> While, all alone,
> Watching the loophole's spark
> Lie I, with life all dark,
> Feet tether'd, hands fetter'd
> Fast to the stone.

After this glimpse of light and the change of rhythm, the final stanza returns to the despairing rhythmic regularity of the first. Despite the thoroughness of corporeal isolation and immobility the poem depicts, hope lies in the faint possibility of disorder. The 'loophole's spark', which offers a counteridea to 'all dark' as well as a sense of latent conflagration and a hint of the 'vital spark' so dear to vitalists and Romantics, works alongside the 'wind's song' that might realize the spark's potential, to suggest the possibility of freedom (145). At the same time imagination, or spirit, continues to sing like the wind, and to roam: it tells a different story from the mere material facts.

The means of securing freedom, in poem after poem, is the close interaction of the senses and an act of violence. The enclosure and entrapment of the 'The Wind' (107–10) is psychic rather than physical, the central persona trapped in his own hyperaesthetic, traumatized fear. The tale of his escape into the world of action is enclosed by a refrain that suggests both the randomness of violence and its possibility for generative change:

> *Wind, wind! thou art sad, art thou kind?*
> *Wind, wind, unhappy! thou art blind,*
> *Yet still thou wanderest the lily-seed to find.*
> ('The Wind', 107)

The self-reflexive repetition, assonance and archaic internal rhyme of 'wind', 'blind', 'kind' and 'find' contrasts with the unconstrained and undirected movement of the wind, much as the poem sets the physical stasis and tension of the narrator against the tale he tells. At the same time the etymological link between wind and spirit suggests the movement between the spiritual or soulful and the physical, in which the soul relies on the physical for its existence. In between the refrain is the story of Margaret's violent death, told with the kind of strange detachment Robert Browning's narrator brings to 'My Last Duchess' and framed with such an intensity of hyperaesthetic, displaced horror as to suggest the narrator himself might have been her murderer.[91] Its awkward, shifting rhythms work in tension with the simplicity of the story and its distorted murder-ballad theme.

Like other poems in the volume, 'The Wind' refuses to flinch from brutal death. At the beginning of the poem the narrator is imprisoned in his own imagination:

> If I move my chair it will scream, and the orange will roll out far,
> And the faint yellow juice ooze out like blood from a wizard's jar;
> And the dogs will howl for those who went last month to the war.
> ('The Wind', 107)

There is a suggestion of displacement in the terror of moving and of noise, a suggestion of guilt in the association of the 'faint yellow juice' of the orange with blood, so visually unlike it in reality. These intense perceptions, while corresponding in some ways to ideas of the effects of guilt only articulated after Morris's writings, also flesh out and dramatize the ideas of mind and emotions set forth by Bain in 1855. He argues that 'the emotion of Terror gives a character to all the ideas or notions formed under the influence of the feeling.'[92] The yellow daffodils and the blood of Margaret's wounds appear again to the dreamer as he recalls the day of her death, and this association of colour breaks the spell of hushed horror with which the poem begins:

> Alas! Alas! There was blood on the very quiet breast,
> Blood lay in the many folds of the loose ungirded vest,
> Blood lay upon her arm where the flower had been prest
>
> I shriek'd and leapt from my chair and the orange roll'd out far.
> ('The Wind', 109)

The traumatized repetition of 'blood' marks a moment of change: like the graphically described 'spout of blood on the hot land' when Launcelot kills Mellyagraunce in Guenevere's account ('The Defence', 8), blood is both a conventional sign of violence and a vivid visual memory that changes the trajectory of the poem's tale.

For the first time the narrator now sees 'the ghosts of those that had gone to the war', confronting the incorporeal bodies of the war dead through the memory of another bleeding body. These soldiers bear the faint banner of 'Olaf, king and saint'. Like Morris's early romance, 'Gertha's Lovers', in which Olaf, as king if not yet 'saint', also appears, the poem raises questions of perception and epistemology through displaced, dreamlike violence that turns away from the politics of the present.[93] David G. Riede suggests that 'far from enabling him to escape the prison of his madness the thought of chivalric warfare only bolts the door'. Yet this reading sits uneasily with the sense of change and movement that comes at the moment of realization and visualization in the poem.[94] Rather, the visual memory of his lover's death unlocks his capacity for beginning to interact with the world. The poem offers an alternative mode of anticonfession to that of 'The Defence', figuring not the liberation of a woman by the taking on of knightly roles, but the escape from sensualized stasis into a new perception of the world through the memory of a woman's violent death or murder. The poem suggests the power of the imagination to access the past and to change the future. Like Sir John in 'Teste Noire', the narrator understands the past through the imaginative interaction with a woman's silenced dead body. If this is a poem about trauma, it is not the trauma of war that is evoked but of personal loss; insofar as it is a social critique, it is not of war nor feudal violence but of the destructive possessiveness of gender relations.

A more physical moment of liberation comes with death as its price for Jehane, the heroine of 'Golden Wings' (116–23) and knightly counterpart of Guenevere. Unlike Lionel in Morris's 1856 short story, 'Golden Wings', who tells his own tale of setting out into the world for adventure and finding both battle and love before his early violent death, Jehane is given no voice to tell her story of lost love, failed adventure and death. Like Rapunzel, like Guenevere in Arthur's court, or like Tennyson's Mariana, she is closed up in her castle, set apart from the world of war and action. Her mental pain has an effect on her physical body; it leads not to surrender and lament, as it does for Mariana, but to action.[95] Her surroundings are well ordered and luxuriant, vibrant and verdant: 'little war that castle knew' (116). There is no battle, blood or death here. Yet the mere absence of war does not lead to harmony. All around her the other women are reunited with their lovers, but Jehane's knight does not return. Eventually, after a long night of weeping, she comes out into the castle grounds at dawn in just her smock, with a 'great sword in her hand' (121). Her physical act of defiance is framed by a narrative of hope, which has its roots in the interchangeability of body and soul:

> If ten years go by
> Before I meet him; if, indeed,
> Meanwhile both soul and body bleed,
> Yet there is an end of misery,
>
> And I have hope.
> ('Golden Wings', 122)

The abstract and the somatic are juxtaposed here so that soul and body are both imagined in terms of the tangible. 'Hope', so important and active a concept for Morris, is embodied in action.[96] Her moment of choice to step beyond the bounds of the castle wall, out of enclosure, is set against the bright specificity of nature. As she stands on the 'green lawn grass' (121):

> O Jehane! the red morning sun
> Changed her white feet to glowing gold,
> Upon her smock, on crease and fold,
> Changed that to gold which had been dun.
> ('Golden Wings', 122)

The colours have a beatific effect. The repetition of gold, and the internal rhyme, create a sense of harmony and aural as well as visual patterning, and recall Dante Gabriel Rossetti's 'The Blessed Damozel' (1850), in which the maiden leans out from 'the gold bar of heaven' to watch her lover on earth.[97] Catherine Gallagher aptly uses this moment in Rossetti's poem to illustrate a wider cultural movement 'away from disembodied transcendence and toward embodied immanence', in which 'the culture's imaginary creatures were sending up a lament for their missing bodies'.[98] Morris's Jehane needs no such lament, all physical as she is, beatified not in heaven but by nature and on earth at the moment of violent action. Perhaps the morning sun blesses with gold not only what had been 'dun' but what had been 'done', in Jehane's decision to act. She refuses simply to wait. 'He could not come, / But I can go to him' (122). Like Guenevere, she takes on the role of knight. Her act of physical defiance, her transgression of gender boundaries in setting out from the castle armed with a sword, becomes also an awakening of the senses: it celebrates human will over determined destiny or divine appointment.

The moment of success leads to death, however, as it does for Lionel in the earlier short story. Jehane's death, like that of Margaret in 'The Wind', is unexplained, although it appears she has died fighting. The knights who find her body give a clue to the means of her death:

This is Jehane by her face;

Why has she a broken sword?
Mary! She is slain outright.
('Golden Wings', 122)

The broken sword offers evidence of a chivalric death in hard battle, and galvanizes the rest of the castle to action: 'Ladies' Gard must meet the war; [...] Man the walls withouten fear!' (122). Although 'Ladies' Gard' is defeated and falls into decay, the poem celebrates the impulse to escape, the willingness to take on corporeal responsibility and agency, and the enduring potency of physical acts, told and retold for those who come after. The desire for change and the transgression of boundaries it entails becomes a somatic imperative, regardless of cost. The move out of the female world of enclosure and waiting is met with death for Jehane as it is met, ultimately, with incarceration and remorse for Guenevere. This poem, like 'The Defence', nonetheless imagines the female body at the moment of action and the potential of battle to bring about change, despite individual failure.

Morris offers a pattern of hope in women who refuse to accept restriction. The poems are too immersed in the worlds they present to suggest by it a critique of feudalism, or a repudiation of violence. Rather, they offer imaginative glimpses of alternative stories in which women's appropriation of male roles lead to freedom and the disruptive but generative dissolution of prevailing communal values that that entails. Morris's desire for these poems to work against 'conventional rules' in both art and society is clearly signalled by his dedication of *The Defence* to 'My friend, Dante Gabriel Rossetti, Painter'. In this way he aligns himself with a movement conceived in opposition to the artistic establishment and defined by its uncomfortable reimagining of the past and its often transgressive presentation of the female body.[99] Morris's women refuse the enclosure and contemplative stasis that Rossetti idealized in *Bocca Baciata* (1859) or *Lady Lilith* (1864), and their appropriation of knightly roles suggests a repudiation of conventional gender roles akin to that evoked by the androgyny of Burne-Jones's paintings.[100]

§

Morris does not simply celebrate violence in these poems, any more than he simply condemns it. Rather, he offers the imagination of violence as a tool of escape and generative transgression. If, as Elizabeth Helsinger argues in her focus on Morris's use of colour, these poems 'expand Rossetti's poetic acts of attention [...] reinterpreting his explorations of sensuous presence and imaginative projection', the idea of violence serves as a means of focusing that attention.[101] Morris turns to the past for stories of the male fellowship of violence which offers a corporeal, kinaesthetic epistemology and a morality that arises out of the needs of the body. He broadens the fellowship to include women, showing the ways in which the corporeal imagination rebels against injustice, inequality and inaction. Yet the idea of knightly battle is complicated by the uncomfortable erotic gaze of the poems and the cruelty of some of their personae. As in his later work, he privileges the disruptive and generative possibilities of violence, with all the pain and destruction it entails, over the stasis and certainty of confinement or the comforting idea of divine or chivalric order in the world.

For all their focus on women and their challenge to separate gendered spheres, these are not primarily poems about women; instead, they focus on the experiences of men imagining women and women imagining men, as a means of paying attention to the possibilities of disruption, transgression and change through acts of violence. In his 1856 essay on 'The Churches of North France', Morris writes that, 'thinking of their passed-away builders, I can see through them, very faintly, dimly, some little of the mediæval times, else dead and gone from me for ever; voiceless for ever.'[102] In *The Defence*, he uses his own art to give voices and bodies to those violent medieval times. The poems revivify the people of the real or fantasized past at moments of rupture, and suggest the power of this intense imaginative moment to alter the present; to this extent they bear out Keats's vision of the relationship between imagination and reality: 'the Imagination may be compared to Adam's dream – he awoke, and found it truth'.[103] The poems of *The Defence* dramatize both a response to the mid nineteenth century and the beginnings of an ideology of the power of open violence retold or experienced in imagination to change the world. They suggest the urgency of telling tales of the violent past or invoking threats of a violent future as a means of making communal stories out of individual experience, developing a morality that is immanent and corporeal, but also shared.

Chapter Three

SIGURD THE VOLSUNG AND THE PARAMETERS OF MANLINESS

In his 1841 essay on 'The Hero as Divinity', Carlyle praises the 'wild bloody valour' of the 'Old Norsemen' and affirms the truth of 'Odin's creed', that 'a man shall and must be valiant; he must march forward, and quit himself like a man, – trusting imperturbably in the appointment and choice of the upper Powers; and, on the whole, not fear at all.'[1] The conflation of the biblical exhortation to 'quit you like men, be strong', and the emphases of Norse mythology on physical courage and destiny offers a potent vision of manliness, a term much used and variously defined in the nineteenth century.[2] It is an idea that is closely linked to violence: the developing discourse of manliness across the nineteenth century entails a variety of shifts in understanding of the meanings and uses of violence, from the anxieties about its place in middle-class life early in the Victorian period to what John Tosh describes as 'the validation of violence' that accompanied imperialism later in the century.[3] Morris's engagement with the idea of violence also shifts across the century, but retains always a commitment to this Carlylean vision of the imaginative, if not actual, possibilities of 'wild, bloody valour' as a sign of vigour, health and the 'manliness' that underpins them both.

Neither violence nor manliness are the exclusive preserve of maleness in Morris's work, however, as the last chapter has suggested. While the pervasive Victorian discourse of manliness and the ideologies of masculinity that implicitly underpin it encompass a wide range of ideas and ideals, they have certain cohesive characteristics which persist throughout the century and across differing schools of thought; among these characteristics, which may be individual or national, are an emphasis on individual courage, will and self-control, and an opposition to the bestial and the feminine or effeminate.[4] These characteristics are evident not only in Carlyle's Old Norsemen, but in the many representations and manifestations of the Scandinavian and Teutonic past that came to stand for a heritage of linguistic and political freedom and purity for a surprising range of Victorian writers, thinkers and linguists. Andrew Wawn notes that by 1837 only a few Victorian scholars 'had begun to acquaint themselves with those Anglo-Saxon texts in which the term [Viking] had been recorded', but that 'within fifty years, the term Viking was to be found on dozens of title pages', as were its cognates, Norsemen and Northmen, and its representative figure, Odin.[5] Morris's own extensive engagement with the idea of the old North, from his first visit to Iceland in 1871, is evident in his Icelandic diaries, in lectures and letters, in his translations and collaborations with Eiríkr Magnússon, and in his Icelandic stories and short poems. Nowhere is his own vision of Iceland more fully developed, however, than in his long, saga-derived poem of 1876, *Sigurd the Volsung and the Fall of the Niblungs*, in which the competing demands of individual desire and communal good, individual will and historical determinism summon the 'wild, bloody valour' of violent men and women to body forth a particular kind of manliness.[6] Morris adapts his Norse saga sources to offer a poetic narrative of inclusive, communal masculinity that simultaneously draws on the familiar discourse of individual will and courage and extends its parameters. At the same time this poetic tale of betrayal and revenge problematically absorbs and neutralizes difference in an ideal of wholeness attained through violence.

Both Simon Dentith and Herbert Tucker have given significant consideration to the poem in the context of their appraisals of epic form and its uses: Tucker draws attention to the poem's narrative completeness as 'a tale that will be its own interpreter', while Dentith explores its strategies of alterity as a critique of contemporary society.[7] More recently, Dentith has identified the violence of *Sigurd* with masculinity, noting that 'an ethic of heroic masculine violence, so central to the meaning of primary epic, is also central to *Sigurd*'.[8] His argument, while important in insisting on the violence of *Sigurd*, leaves open the questions of how violence, maleness and masculinity interrelate, how the meanings of both shift between the saga world of *Sigurd* and the Victorian world of its publication and how the women of the saga fit into this ethic of manly violence. These are questions this chapter addresses, drawing on Herbert Sussman's definition of both 'masculinity' and 'manliness', as 'those multifarious social constructions of the male current within society', and examining their manifestations in the text and its reception.[9]

Carlyle's formulation allows for degrees of manliness: the ability to control emotion will show 'how much of a man he is'. Manliness, this suggests, is measured against an implied absolute. The essays in *On Heroes and Hero-Worship* address themselves to creating a set of possible absolutes, which have as their centre a single great man, in various guises, to be emulated or followed. For Christian exponents of manliness, like Charles Kingsley or Thomas Hughes, this absolute would be Christ, variously represented, as is suggested by the unambiguous title of Hughes's 1879 book, *The Manliness of Christ*. Meanwhile poems like Tennyson's 'The Princess' (1847) or *Idylls of the King* begin to interrogate the boundaries of absolute masculinity and its relationship to the feminine, the nation or the empire.[10] Morris's approach turns away from a single absolute to communal multiplicity. While his poem relies on what he describes as 'the worship of courage', a central tenet of Victorian constructions of masculinity associated with Norse tales and poems, he alters the social and political meanings of the manliness evinced by acts of courage, so that it may include – or, indeed, subsume – those characteristics traditionally opposed to it: cowardice, femininity, and bestial madness or lack of self-control.[11] In doing so, he undermines the common associations of manliness with political stability, social containment and an implicit endorsement of imperialism, in opposition to female characteristics of formlessness, dissolution and instability.[12] He affirms a world in which masculinity is normative, but destabilizes the conventional power relations associated with the expression of manly character.

That the meanings of manliness are interwoven with the interpretation and establishment of nationhood and therefore with relations within the nation and beyond it is evident in both the context and the reception of Morris's epic. Dentith discusses the range of constructions of nationhood implicit in nineteenth-century uses of epic, locating *Sigurd* as an attempt at 'national epic', or heroic and heroically told history, a designation borne out by its reception by contemporary critics.[13] His analysis of Morris's style and uses of epic form concentrates on its limitations as a 'pastiche of primary epic' that is therefore bound, in some sense, to fail, attempting as it does to recreate a past form and a past experience. Morris does something rather more than this, however: his poem is both celebratory and critical. As Dentith rightly notes, the poem's deliberate, defamiliarizing strangeness – which arises from its extreme violence as well as its archaizing form and diction – allows it to act as 'an implicit critique of the paltriness of modernity, a standing rebuke to the outcome of the national story whose beginning the poem recounts'.[14] He identifies the significance of Morris's choice of a Northern rather than a Celtic tale of origin as one that reaches for older roots, for a closer identification with barbarism and a greater capacity for alterity from contemporary society; this choice offers the possibility, then, not only of a racialized understanding of both past and present, but also, more importantly, of a closer identification with ideals of anticivilized manliness.[15]

For the contemporary readership of male critics who commented on *Sigurd* in national journals, the achievement of a certain degree of manliness, which signifies health, is at the forefront of the poem's virtues, both in content and style.[16] Journal after journal considered it more 'masculine', or 'virile', with greater 'healthfulness of tone', than his earlier poems – although 'much is still wanting to it in this respect', and the reviews are by no means unreservedly positive.[17] While none affirm its absolute manliness or healthiness, it is seen as an improvement in this regard on his earlier work; the serially published

Earthly Paradise (1868–70), while widely praised and much read, was nonetheless defined in terms distinctly associated with the feminine. The *Academy* reviewer Sidney Colvin described the tone of the fourth volume as one of 'tender and various pathos', while parts of it tended towards 'a certain vagueness and dreaminess of the senses'; G. A. Simcox, writing for *Academy* on the previous volume, described Morris as the poet 'of moods rather than of passions, of adventures rather than of actions'. According to the *Spectator*, volumes two and three occupied themselves too much with 'involved reluctations of the will, dreamy seizures of the spirit'.[18] Morris himself, Alfred Austin argues in the *Temple Bar*, is 'not a great poet, not a mighty maker, not a sublime seer, but [...] the wisely unresisting victim of a rude irreversible current'.[19] Issues of action and emotion, will and passivity, as well as social usefulness signal the difference between *The Earthly Paradise* and *Sigurd* in this critical discourse. Nonetheless, as the guarded tone of *Sigurd*'s critics suggests, there are continuities between their vision of the feminine and the kind of masculinity Morris explores in *Sigurd*, which both engages with and complicates accepted gender distinctions.

These distinctions bear on style and geographical setting. The identification of the North with masculinity, courage and independence of spirit is commonplace in Victorian discussions of the literature as well as the character of Northern Europe, frequently set in contrast either with orderly but constrained and delicate Southern Europe or with the East, figured as the region of softness and femininity.[20] In *The Earthly Paradise*, Morris includes stories from Northern, Eastern and ancient Greek literary traditions in the orderly, thoroughly closed structure of the poem. In *Sigurd*, by contrast, his focus is solely Icelandic, his source the Nordic sagas and eddas, his language firmly rooted in the structures and lexis of the North; yet the same project of allowing the feminine to shape the masculine action of the tale is evident in his redaction and retelling of the saga. It is 'deeds' – which in the heroic world of the poem mean acts of violence – rather than gender, that define the characters in Morris's poem, placing them inside or beyond the wide boundaries of valiant manliness. At the same time, while *The Earthly Paradise* tells individual tales from individual people, *Sigurd* is the story of a whole people, and the interconnection and continuity of their individual lives makes them part of the tale. Manliness, and the violence that attends it, is not merely individual, but also communal, intimately connected with history, and natural: the voice and heroic hexameter of the tale link it not only to Norse poetry, but also to a history of manly epic poetry.

The Northernness of the poem's language, themes and style commends it to his critics as both nationally significant and fundamentally healthy and healthgiving in its purity and containment.[21] The relationship between contained emotion and expressive action is central to Victorian discussions of mental and moral health and manliness, in art as well as life. The anxiety about depictions of extreme or irresolvable emotion is expressed in public discourse as a critique of unhealthy, inactive effeminacy. Its argument is formulated particularly clearly in Robert Buchanan's much-discussed antagonistic critical essay, 'The Fleshly School' of 1871, in which he accuses Rossetti, Morris and Swinburne of setting out to 'extol fleshliness'. He argues that their aim is:

> to aver that poetic expression is greater than poetic thought, and by inference that the body is greater than the soul, and sound superior to sense; and that the poet, properly to develop his poetic faculty, must be an intellectual hermaphrodite, to whom the very facts of day and night are lost in a whirl of æsthetic terminology.[22]

Buchanan's central criticism, then, is that the Pre-Raphaelites have unsettled hierarchies of difference, and failed to distinguish between masculine and feminine. This hermaphroditism suggests an aesthetic problem that reflects and stems from a social, personal and sexual one in a cycle of disease and degeneration.

Rossetti's poems, in particular, are 'namby pamby', Buchanan argues; he resembles 'an emasculated Mr Browning'. Effeminacy leads to disease: 'the fleshly school of verse-writers are, so to speak, public offenders, because they are diligently spreading the seeds of disease broadcast.' While Morris escapes with mild praise for his work as 'often pure, fresh and wholesome', Rossetti is further accused of 'morbid deviation from healthy forms of life'. His poetry contains 'nothing virile, nothing tender, nothing completely sane; a superfluity of extreme sensibility, [...] and a deep-seated indifference to all agitating forces and agencies, all tumultuous griefs and sorrows, all the thunderous stress of life'.[23] The association of stasis, emotion and ill health, both physical and mental, potently suggests a dangerous undermining of the qualities of manliness. It is at least in part, as Clive Wilmer points out, the 'raw sexual violence' and 'blunt physicality' of Morris's early poetry that sets it apart from Rossetti's; this is also, I suggest, why Morris largely escapes Buchanan's designations of effeminacy and disease.[24] Violence, which destroys or disrupts physical wholeness, rather strangely becomes a marker of health in the discourse of manliness.

However, the imbrication of masculinity, violence and wholeness in *Sigurd* shifts the meanings of manliness subtly away from an essentialist association with maleness. Rather, manliness in the life of both men and women comes in part through a recognition of the inadequacies of life, and the willingness both to endure them and to take action to change them. The theory that Morris would formulate in his 1886 lecture, 'The Aims of Art', is already evident in *Sigurd*, both in its narrative and in its artistic practice:

> The world's roughness, falseness, and injustice will bring about their natural consequences, and we and our lives are part of those consequences; but since we inherit also the consequences of old resistance to those curses, let us each look to it to have our fair share of that inheritance also, which [...] will at least bring us to courage and hope.

This courage and hope lead to an eager life, Morris argues, which contrasts with the loss of 'manliness' that would result from failure to resist or revolt.[25] In another lecture Morris would imagine for his listeners the beautiful and generously built communal hall of the future, 'alive with the noblest thoughts of our time, and the past, embodied in the best art which a free and manly people could produce.'[26] This ideal of communal manliness, arising from individual actions and expressed in beauty of life and art, is already beginning to take shape in the violently heroic world of *Sigurd*.

The varieties of potential meaning inherent in the phrase 'free and manly' is evident in A. P. Stanley's use of it in 1844 to describe Thomas Arnold's dislike of independent communal organization or companionship among the boys at Rugby School because it tended to interfere with his relationship with the boys and with 'free and manly feeling in individual boys'.[27] However, the politically inflected vision of egalitarian freedom and creative work that Morris evokes is a far different and more fluid one than the hierarchical, exclusively male community of self-disciplined individuals associated with Arnold. Morris's more holistic vision of manliness is already beginning to take shape in the 1870s as he both experiences and imagines Iceland, its people and its stories.[28] It is a manliness that finds its fullest expression in communities rather than individuals: *Sigurd* features a hero who does not appear at all until the second of the tale's four books, after the story of his ancestors has been fully recounted, and even then none of the names that serve as titles in the following books is his. Thomas Carlyle, quoting John Ruskin at the end of 'The Early Kings of Norway', writes that the question made evident in these violent tales of kingship is, '"Who is best man?" and the Fates forgive much, – forgive the wildest, fiercest, cruelest experiments, – if fairly made for the determination of that.'[29] While Morris, by 1876, is moving further and further away from the vision of heroic individual leadership that Carlyle espouses as a remedy for the ills of Victorian society, he nonetheless embraces a conception of manliness that rests on action and heroism expressed in deeds. They may either be deeds done in defiance of fate, or in compliance with it: Morris's inclusive manliness allows both the actions of individual will and a recognition of the exigencies of fate or history.

In 1883, looking back on what drew him to the sagas, he writes that it was 'the delightful freshness and independence of thought of them, the air of freedom which breathes through them, their worship of courage (the great virtue of the human race).'[30] With this worship of courage always in view, he adapts his source materials to produce a poem that negotiates a position between what Buchanan describes as the 'weary, wasting, yet exquisite sensuality' of Rossetti's painting, and what he would later describe as the 'brutality and latent baseness' of Kipling's work, with its populist imperialist certainties and its depictions of the British soldier as 'a drunken, swearing, coarse-minded Hooligan'.[31] Ideas of degeneracy begin to gather force in the 1860s and '70s after the 1857 publication in France of Bénédict Morel's *Traité des Dégénérescences*, so that, as Stephen Arata points out, by the 1870s Morel's definitions of degeneracy 'had long since passed into public usage on both sides of the Channel'.[32] In this emerging discourse, both sensuality and indulgence of physical appetites are identified as unhealthy and effeminate, while the martial violence of Morris's heroes, combined with the controlled hexameter and repetitive alliteration of his verse, suggest an ability to subjugate ragged emotion into the determined action that signifies manly health and derives from a commitment to courage.[33]

At the same time, however, Morris succeeds in redefining the parameters of healthy manliness by his portrayal not of gentlemanly action but of deliberate and passionate, sometimes even suprarational, violence that paradoxically humanizes his men and women and gives meaning to the society he portrays. While his poem is not concerned in any way with Victorian society, the issues it raises bear on both the social constructions of Victorian Britain and on the patriarchal activities of the empire. They suggest a communal, relational response to the forces of history rather than either the individual heroism or the stoical submission to earthly and heavenly authority that Carlyle highlights. The formulation of masculinity implicit in the poem arises from an aggressive, heroic ethos of performative desire and male power that nonetheless disrupts conventional gender boundaries and the political and ontological ideologies which they maintain.

The Madness of Manhood: Will, Desire and Act

The 'extraordinarily reinforced coherence' and 'nearly obsessive integrity' that Herbert F. Tucker argues inhere in the form and content of *Sigurd* are complicated by a willingness to accept inevitable conflicts in the unity of the tale and its telling.[34] While John Goode sees a pattern of gradual dissolution, arguing that Sigurd's story traces 'a transference from a race in whom desire and action are unified to one in whom desire can only be fulfilled through duplicity', I suggest that there is no such clear linear trajectory.[35] Rather, disjunction is present from the beginning of the tale in its affirmation of the interplay of individual will and communal need, self-control and surrender. The separation of desire from action or the distortion of desire and action in madness, shape the tale. They underpin its narrative of manly wholeness, which arises, not from essential maleness, but from a complex interaction between circumstance, character and will. Manliness, to borrow Judith Butler's terms, is performative here: a 'doing' rather than a being.[36] While the poem affirms masculinity as the basis of relationships and nationhood as well as individual character, it undermines the power relations based on essentialist and ideologically conservative gender constructions that fuelled the imperialistic fervour of the late-nineteenth century.[37]

Morris's saga source begins its tale of the Volsungs with a brief account of Sigi, said to be a son of Odin. Sigi murders his friend's slave for being more successful than he on a hunting expedition; he hides the slave's body, and returns home. However, others suspect foul play, the slave's body is discovered and Sigi driven out of the land. With the help of Odin he carries out successful raids on other lands and so wins himself a kingdom, finds a wife, and spawns a dynasty.[38] Morris begins his tale with the next major movement of the saga, the appearance of Odin at the wedding feast of Sigi's great-granddaughter, Signy, daughter of Volsung, to King Siggeir. By leaving out the meaningless violence and murderous deceit of Signy's forebears, Morris lessens both the randomness of the gods' choice and their complete power over the affairs of men. The wedding feast and all that happens there becomes the originary moment, setting what follows in the context of individual heroism and choice, as well as the broader movements of destiny. There is brutality in the unfolding of the tale, but it is not without purpose. Violence is not a random element of manhood to be controlled, but rather a legitimate expression of the 'animal life' of a man, evidence of his association with the material and the corporeal rather than the abstract.[39] In this way, it is neither wholly predetermined, nor wholly controlled by individual will, but rather the inevitable correlative of a history of developing manliness.

The fine distinction between entirely meaningless violence and the raging violence that plays a part in the achievement of manhood and freedom is evident in the episodes of the meeting of man and wolf in the poem. The first episode offers a model of manly rage, uncontrolled in act, but controlled in the retelling into an assertion of power against undue aggression. Sigmund and his brothers, lured to Siggeir's land by promises of friendship, have lost their father, Volsung, in battle. On Signy's pleading, they are spared immediate death and instead, with cruel glee, Siggeir orders them to be tied to a felled tree trunk in the forest. The brothers are killed one by one by a wolf on successive nights, until only Sigmund is left alive. At this point Morris significantly changes the effect of the violence of the original tale. In the saga Signy, watched by Siggeir's men and unable to go to her brother, sends a servant to him with instructions to smear his face and the inside of his mouth with honey. The she-wolf comes to attack him, licks his face for the honey and then puts her tongue inside his mouth:

> He [...] caught the she-wolf's tongue betwixt his teeth, and so hard she startled back thereat, and pulled herself away so mightily, setting her feet against the stocks, that all was riven asunder; but he ever held so fast that the tongue came away by the roots, and thereof she had her bane.[40]

This close interaction between man and beast is quick and decisive. Ravening, bestial violence is repaid with an equally brutal and calculated counterattack, in which Sigmund's strength is miraculous and his jaws as monstrously powerful as those of the wolf whose body and character he will later, briefly, assume.

Morris's poem eschews the taut immediacy of the saga description for a more crafted first-person account. Signy has no part in the planning of the event, and knows nothing of it until Sigmund recounts it to her, imposing order and symmetry on a disorderly and instinctive encounter by its retelling:

> The Gods helped not, but I helped; and I too grew wolfish then;
> Yea I, who have borne the sword-hilt high mid the kings of men,
> Must snarl to the she-wolf's snarling, and snap with greedy teeth,
> While my hands with the hand-bonds struggled; my teeth took hold the first
> And amid the mighty writhing the bonds that bound me burst,
> As with Fenrir's wolf shall it be.
> (*Sigurd*, 21)

With its tightly structured rhetorical repetitions and dramatic use of caesurae to suggest the pace of struggle, climaxing in the powerful plosives of 'bonds that bound me burst', this account closely identifies Sigmund himself with the wolf, and signals a metaphorical metamorphosis that foreshadows his later, actual transfiguration.

Contemporary critics comment approvingly on Morris's transformation of this scene of violence from the saga: *Sigurd*'s manliness, in their view, derives in part from its modification of the monstrous violence of the saga by a controlled and poetic retelling. Yet the identification of Sigmund with the wolf is far greater in Morris's account than in the original. The suggestion of equality in 'I [...] / Must snarl to the she-wolf's snarling' and 'my teeth took hold the first' offers a wild response to unpredictable circumstance that demonstrates a capacity for violence far more spontaneous than the planned, rapacious, mouth-to-mouth intimacy of the saga. Morris clearly separates out violence from sexual desire or interaction. There is nothing here of the kind of sexualized pleasure in murderous loss of control that Klaus Theweleit identifies in the twentieth-century protofascist soldiers whose leaders would draw strength from nationalistic Nordic myths.[41] This image of human-lupine interaction turns away both from the idea of the sexual domination of the primal feminine, and from the suggestion of clashing models of female power in the actions of Signy and the she-wolf. It focuses, instead, on an equal animal struggle that calls out all the desperation of manly courage. Muscular manliness is apparently expressed and contained in the relationship between the action and the poem's account of it.

Yet Morris allows his hero to go well beyond the boundaries of manly self-restraint. The will here is brought under the control of instinct, rather than the other way around. In an era increasingly anxious about the bestial side of human nature and the possibilities of its reassertion, Morris confidently allows his hero to identify with the wolf.[42] He draws into the nineteenth century, with its fears about degeneration and the incursion of the disruptive Other, the ancient folktale association of animals with wisdom and subversion. Clinton Machann argues that in Tennyson's *Idylls of the King*, 'manhood [...] implies virility but is not primarily an extension of biological maleness; it is rather a strategy for controlling or stifling man's natural bestiality as civilization advances.'[43] This is particularly evident in 'Balin and Balan', in *Idylls of the King*, first published nine years after *Sigurd*, in which mad violence signals the loss and destruction of manliness and honour, as shown in Balin's cry:

> Here I dwell
> Savage among the savage woods, here die –
> Die: let the wolves' black maws ensepulchre
> Their brother beast, whose anger was his lord.[44]

This analysis is upheld by the poem. It bears out the fear of 'a manhood ever less and lower' that will 'reel back into the beast, and be no more'.[45] The wild violence of Balin leads first to his fraternal identification with wolves rather than knights, and then to his brother's death and his own; it is a manifestation of the dissolution of Arthur's kingdom. In *Sigurd*, manhood, while not simply coextensive with bestiality, allows a far closer and more constructive engagement with the feral.

In a letter of 1894, Morris comments on the different versions of the tale in the Old Norse Eddas and the saga, noting that 'the terrible incestuously begotten Sinfjotli, is, I think, the original Sigurd (so to say)'.[46] There are hints of social Darwinism in the long time frame and the interplay of action and circumstance that Morris offers in the poem. Both biology and environment shape the people; manliness is associated with the animal rather than with the rational. In the poem's second encounter between heroes and wolves, Sigmund and his son Sinfiotli, living as outcasts in the forests of Siggeir's land, enter a house and find two men asleep with wolf heads lying above them. They try on the wolf heads and become enchanted, turning into werewolves. In this form they go on a killing spree, which ends with Sigmund, weary of fighting, tearing out Sinfiotli's throat in anger at his murderous attack on a group of sailors. Sinfiotli's unreasoning, instinctual violence is matched by Sigmund's half-reasoned response. Only when Sigmund has quite killed Sinfiotli and begins to come to his senses, does he chance to see a weasel bring back a dead mate by the use of a herb, and by copying this action, restore his son to life. Animal instinct offers a solution to animal violence.

However, unlike the isolated Fafnir, who is transformed through the overwhelming greed for gold, first into a parricide and then into a blind serpent, with a 'wan face [...] wrought in manlike wise', but with none of redeeming features of manliness (*Sigurd*, 110), Sigmund and Sinfiotli retain a manly companionship that sustains them even in temporary animal madness. Their descent into violence prepares them for acts of revenge. Once restored to himself, Sinfiotli says to his father:

> Thou hast taught me many things
> But the Gods have taught me more, and at last have abased us both,
> That of naught that lieth before us our hearts and our hands may be loath.
> (*Sigurd*, 34)

Here the linguistic mirroring links the men with each other and with the gods. Their sobering loss of the usual restraints of human interaction releases a level of courage and determination between them that allows them to fulfil their destiny. Restored to themselves, father and son look at each other. 'I am the sword of the Gods', says Sinfiotli, 'And thine hand shall hold the hilt' (35). There is a suggestion here that Sinfiotli's disconnection from his people means that he is only able to be the means of violence, not its meaningful perpetrator. He does not have the potential to be the heroic 'righter of wrongs' that Sigurd, his half-brother, born in peace, will have (255), nor does he demonstrate the instinctual but liberating passion that Sigmund showed in the struggle with the she-wolf.[47]

Unlike most Icelandic *hammramir*, or 'shapestrong', who, as George Dasent explains, could change into shapes of animals and 'work mischief', or, without changing shape, become strong with rage, Sigmund and Sinfiotli are not left weaker after the fit has passed; rather they are newly energized for their task.[48] The interaction between choice, character and unwilled circumstance determines their manliness, that is, their ability to act selflessly and courageously on behalf of their people. In 1867 Kingsley, using a term that suggests the achievement of an ideal form of manliness, argued that 'all true manhood consists in the defiance of circumstances; and if any man be the creature of circumstances, it is because he has become so, like the drunkard; because he has ceased to be a man, and sunk downward toward the brute.'[49] Morris resists such unequivocal definitions, allowing a little more breadth to the concept of manliness, which may involve abandonment to destiny rather than defiance of it. Kingsley's preoccupation with such manly defiance extends even to his imagination of heaven where 'I trust one's not going to be idle' in fighting 'a devil or devils, even an ass or asses.' This kind of fighting, Kingsley asserts, is necessary for the satisfaction of one's *thumos*, that is, '"rage" or "pluck" which Plato averreth (for why, he'd have been a wraxling man, and therefore was a philosopher and the king of 'em) to be the root of all virtue'.[50] David Rosen demonstrates that this idea of *thumos* is central to Kingsley's view of manliness, which consists of a volcanic, bestial natural force that must be expressed 'through sex, fighting and morality' in order for manhood to be fully achieved.[51] Morris draws on a similar idea of animal manliness, but turns aside from the emphasis on self-actualization and individual will, offering instead a communal vision of manliness in which unfettered excess and lack of self-control in one generation may be essential to the development of a 'free and manly' society: it is dangerous and destructive, but may also be generative and productive.[52]

Sigurd suggests that the unreasonable disorderliness of animal wildness may be accommodated in the long-term development of communal manliness. Already, some years before his discovery of Marxist dialectical materialism, Morris suggests a development of manliness that transcends the lifespan of one man, accepting the disorder and imperfection that may be attendant on its accomplishment over a number of generations. Politically, this acceptance of the rage, disorder and threat associated with unchecked masculinity, with the working class and with the feminine, prefigures his views of the 1880s that change may require a degree of upheaval and turmoil that goes well beyond the incremental changes of reform.[53] At the same time it allows for a temporary destabilizing and decentring of the self-controlled male and suggests a merging of the masculine and feminine as the basis of change, which I discuss further towards the end of this chapter.

Narratives of bestiality also resonate with fears of madness or disease, usually associated with the feminine or the colonial subject but equally evident in the signs of male hysteria that nineteenth-century critics both detected and deplored in Tennyson's *Maud*. In this construction uncontrolled or overwhelming emotions are closely associated with madness and bestiality: one springs from emotions not worked off in action, the other from emotions or desires expressed through excessive action.[54] They threaten stable, manly nationhood; at the same time, controlled, deliberate violence may be inflicted by the manly individual or state in order to control the formless, fearful unpredictability of the unmanly. In *Sigurd*, in whose sealed world there is no effeminate, frightening Other, animalism may signify a violent but fruitful loss of self-control that is akin to madness and allows the development of new perspectives.[55] In an elaboration of Carlyle's admiring exclamation about the Norse kings, Morris explores the extent of 'wild bloody valour; yet valour of its kind; better, I say, than none'.[56] While Sigurd himself demonstrates a more measured kind of martial courage than his forebears, he is only enabled to do so by their savage actions: not the suppression of all feeling, but its expression in action. The crossover into madness and loss of self-possession has the potential to generate both active, connected violence and the callous violence of irresponsible revenge. Morris allows Sigurd and his forebears to shape their destiny through a combination of intergenerational action and the fated train of events those actions set in motion. They are in control but sometimes choose to relinquish the possibility of self-determination; they exercise their wills, but they also submit to circumstance. In this way manly character is developed through the interaction of circumstance, will and deed, over generations.

The Permeable Boundaries of Manliness

The impulsive actions of temporary insanity are not nearly as destructive, in the poem, as the calculated dissociation of desire from responsibility and action, or individual desire from communal good. It is here that evil lies, I suggest, rather than in the temporary loss of self-control signified by animal instinct and madness, or in the failures of courage or sexual prowess that beset some of the heroic Volsung and Niblung people. Communal manliness is broad enough in the text to include individual failure. Silver argues that 'Morris sharpens moral distinctions which had been either unstressed or simply intimated in the saga. Like Wagner, he heightens the contrast between good and evil, between those heroes who are ideal warriors and their base opponents'.[57] This is only partly borne out by the text. While Morris certainly makes clear the nature of Siggeir or Atli's evil, as I go on to discuss, his telling of the tale equally importantly allows for significant blurring of moral boundaries among the tale's tribes; his heroes are not ideal warriors, but rather imperfect men and women through whose actions the life of the people is developed. His emphasis on action rather than internal reflection, so different from Wagner's, means that the focus of the poem's narrative is on the enacted and the embodied as markers of movement between moral positions within the broad scope of heroism and manliness.[58]

The poem itself crosses a boundary between past and present in its use of the language and forms of the old North. Morris's commitment to the Teutonic roots of language and nation is evident in the poem and in his own writings about the sagas, setting up an uncomfortable resonance with nineteenth- and twentieth-century Aryanism and racial purity theories, remote though they are in some ways from his own emphasis on the intersections of behaviour, environment and language. He draws on notions of individual heroism and national effeminacy when he writes that the saga hero, Grettir the Strong, endured his life 'in a kind of way that is a lesson I think to us effete folk of the old World'.[59] Yet the persistent broadening of boundaries and dissolution of difference within the parameters of manliness that *Sigurd* establishes means that his text is less sharply divided between good and evil than Silver suggests, less amenable to readings of national or individual manliness that rely on the clear boundaries Theweleit identifies as so important in the protofascist ideologies of twentieth-century Germany.[60] Undoubtedly, contemporary ideas about the linguistic distinctions between pure Northern language and corrupted nineteenth-century English or the ideological elevation of the manly North and its people inform the text. Yet the distinctions of the racially-oriented German nationalism of the twentieth century, between soldier and civilian, hardened masculine warrior and effeminate coward, are as difficult to trace in *Sigurd* as the more complex Victorian boundary lines between masculinity and its many opposites.

Boundaries and borders, both literal and metaphorical, are central to the maintenance of class and imperial order. In *Sigurd*, by contrast, the maintenance of strict boundaries – between responsibility and action, individual and community, domestic and public spaces, for instance – is a barrier to the development of a manly people, much as the alienation of a labourer from his work prevents the freedom, equality and manliness that Morris missed in nineteenth-century culture. The formal unity and epic coherence of the poem are destabilized by the elision of boundaries suggested by its content. Courage and cowardice, masculinity and effeminacy inhabit the same spaces – and indeed, sometimes the same people. There are clear distinctions between a manly people and its enemies, but they are not contiguous with the boundaries of maleness and femaleness. Yet while Morris allows a certain expansiveness to the idea of manliness, acts of violence are a necessary part of its achievement and maintenance. Violence on the part of the heroic, manly Volsung and Niblung people is justified in a slightly circular way within the world of the poem by their willingness to risk their own bodies and lives, which is itself evidence of their manliness.

In an avuncular letter of 1874 Morris writes to young Philip Burne-Jones, away at boarding school: 'alas I did not fight enough in my time, from want of hope let us say, not want of courage'. Morris goes on to give Philip advice on how best to fight, but also extols the virtues of feeling pain and sorrow as the necessary obverse of feeling joy: 'we may be well content to be alive and eager, and to bear pain sometimes rather than to grow like rotting cabbages and not to mind it.'[61] The word 'eager' appears over and over again in *Sigurd*, to describe hearts, eyes, swords, and faces. Eagerness goes side by side with courage, which is fed by hope, as Hogni asserts when faced with death in King Atli's hall: 'For tears beseem not king-folk, nor a heart made dull with dreams, / But to hope, if thou may'st, for ever, and to fear nought, well beseems' (266). Both hope and eagerness suggest a kind of active passion that stands in contrast to mental or emotional detachment as well as to the fundamental fragmentation of life and work that Morris deplored in his own society.[62]

It is a fragmentation adumbrated by the actions of the great enemies of the tale, 'smooth speeched' Siggeir, who 'came not into the battle/ Nor faced the Volsung sword', and Atli, 'the master of guile', who orders his 'thrall-folk' to kill Gudrun's brothers. These are men who refuse to do battle themselves, and delegate the cruel murder of their enemies to their underlings. Like the sinister narrator of Browning's 'My Last Duchess' who 'gave commands', they plot from afar.[63] For Morris, this refusal of personal involvement is not merely indicative of dishonesty or untrustworthiness; it suggests the fundamental disjunction between the needs and good of the community and individual action that he was beginning to see as central to the ills of Victorian society. It is the perception of this kind of disjunction that leads him, the year that *Sigurd* is published, towards active personal involvement in political agitation on the Eastern Question. Writing to the *Daily News*, he suggested that, had he heard that 'the English nation [had] been roused to a sense of injustice [...] by a story of horrors', and so gone to war against the Turks, 'though we have nothing to gain', he would have 'rejoiced in such a war'. This is not the case, however, and he goes on to lament that the government has ignored such protests as 'Mr Freeman's manly and closely-argued letters' and 'is determined to drag us into a shameful and unjust war' against Russia.[64] He presents the choice to go to war, then, as a refusal of responsibility for the common good, such as Atli and Siggeir also demonstrate: war itself is not shameful, but the motives of the government, which he comes to see as greed and self-interest, make it so. He urges other 'quiet men, who usually go about their own business' to 'break silence at last, if they in any wise can, and to be as little hopeless as may be'.[65] Personal courage and action born of hope exemplify the fusion of feeling and action that signify manliness.

This fusion is not always achieved by the tale's manly heroes. Even Sigurd himself fails to act on his desire for Brynhild when he is drugged by Grimhild. The tale suggests that 'when the day of Sigurd is done, / And the last of his deeds is accomplished, and his eyes are shut in the sun', those who look on him will think of the moment when he forgot his love and his promise to Brynhild: 'then perchance shall ye wonder and cry, / Twice over, King, are we smitten, and twice have we seen thee die' (167). In *Sigurd*'s story of communal manliness, temporary failures of courage or action may be accommodated, despite their destructive outcomes. This is particularly true in relation to sexual performance. By separating sexual prowess or domination from the achievement of manliness, Morris departs from his source material and from an increasingly audible Victorian discourse of effeminacy and emasculation in relation to race and degeneracy: in both of these contexts, anxieties about uncontrolled bestiality run alongside an idea of unmanly submissiveness associated with effeminacy and contrasting with sexual power.

Kingsley articulates a widely held view of racial inferiority in terms of morbidity and effeminacy: 'the races of Egypt and Syria were effeminate, over-civilised, exhausted by centuries during which no infusion of fresh blood had come to renew the stock. Morbid, self-conscious, physically indolent, incapable then, as now, of personal or political freedom'.[66] Morbidity signifies passivity, effeminacy and lack of both action and freedom. George Dasent claims that Europe at the beginning of the ninth century was in danger of a similar loss of energy: neither Frank nor Anglo-Saxon nation 'could arrive at perfection till it had been chastised by the Norsemen, and finally forced to admit an infusion of Norse blood into its sluggish veins'.[67] Ruskin asserts his continuing faith in this particular kind of infusion of manliness in 1873, when he supports his argument for colonization with the claim that 'we are still undegenerate in race; a race mingled of the best northern blood'.[68] By contrast, the opposite and equally subordinate positions of the wild, bestial menace and the powerless, feminized subject are frequently detected in colonized races.

Accusations of effeminacy or homosexuality, closely associated with cowardice, occur frequently in the sagas as both insult and spur to battle, reflecting the social mores of their day, as Icelandic scholar Preben Meulengracht Sørensen observes: 'in ancient Icelandic consciousness cowardice and effeminacy were two aspects of the same thing, and in the world of the sagas, nothing hits a man harder than the allegation that he is no man.'[69] Morris downplays this association. Cowardice associated with sexual performance is not damning. He leaves out altogether the saga's lengthy trading of sexual insults between Sinfiotli and Granmar, in which Sinfiotli counters Granmar's charge of bestiality and vampirism by taunting him with effeminacy: 'dim belike is grown thy memory now, of how thou wert a witch wife on Varinsey, and wouldst fain have a man to thee, and chosest me to that same office'; 'mindest thou not then, when thou wert stallion Grani's mare, and how I rode thee an amble on Bravoll'.[70] At the same time Morris offers a far more subtle handling of sexual failure than either the twelfth-century German version of the tale, the *Nibelungenlied*, with its blunt mockery of Gunther's inadequacy, or the *Völsunga Saga*, which has Brynhild and Gunnar sitting together 'in great game and glee', apparently quite happy until Brynhild's discovery that he has won her through deceit.[71]

Morris's poem, instead, explores the interactions of desire and agency that lead to the love triangle, without allowing them to erase the potential of his characters for manly action. Brynhild is 'cold and strange' and Gunnar jealous and ashamed from the very beginning of their marriage:

> But of Gunnar the Niblung they say it, that the bloom of his youth is o'er,
> And many are manhood's troubles, and they burden him oft and sore.
> [...]
> And the shame springs fresh in his heart at his brother Sigurd's might;
> And the wonder riseth within him, what deed did Sigurd there.
> (*Sigurd*, 204)

On the discovery that it was Sigurd who won her, in Gunnar's form, Brynhild reviles her husband as 'a faint-heart dastard' who 'loveth life, / And casteth his deeds to another, and the wooing of his wife' (211). While the connection between cowardice and sexual inadequacy is all too apparent in Gunnar's inability to win Brynhild or to keep her love, it is nonetheless a problem of 'manhood', rather than one that lies outside the boundaries of manhood or manliness. His unflinching acceptance of death, playing his harp to the end in the pit of snakes, shows him to be a brave man. Sexual dominance or prowess is not always necessary to manliness, and there may be slippage between courageous and cowardly behaviour within the broad parameters of communal manliness.

Both wild fighting and a bold embrace of death or failure may be expressions of will, through which manliness is honed. This may mean, however, the abandonment of individual will to destiny or the will of the people. Morris is less concerned with the internal moral nexus of traits and attitudes that might be perceived to define character, and more with the actions by which individuals either become part of a unified whole, or break down that wholeness. There is a tension between fate, individual will and community in the poem which Hartley S. Spatt suggests is resolved by an affirmation of the power of the individual over the ordering of destiny – the transformation of man into god. It is precisely this Nietzschean transformation that Morris avoids, I suggest.

Spatt argues that 'Morris has attempted to exorcise the spectre of Odin and his deterministic "wird", making from the saga's central action a new myth dedicated to the heroism of self-determination'.[72] There are echoes not only of Carlyle, but also of both Samuel Smiles and John Stuart Mill in this verdict: Smiles argues that 'it is will – force of purpose – that enables a man to do or be whatever he sets his mind on doing or being.'[73] Mill acknowledges the importance of circumstance in shaping character and action, but adds that the 'desire to mould [one's own character] in a certain way is one of those circumstances. [...] We, when our habits are not too inveterate can, by [...] willing the requisite means, make ourselves different'.[74] However, *Sigurd*, in a more complex way than Spatt allows, shows the acceptance of fate itself to be an act of individual will and communal commitment, evident in the determination to fight and in the willingness to allow a temporary loss of control.

Morris sidesteps the concern of both Mill and Smiles with self-improvement, and focuses instead on the ability or desire of his characters to change the world around them: it is in the ways that they do this that manly character is made manifest. Violence is not necessarily dehumanizing in the mythic world of *Sigurd*, but may be a necessary means of intervening in circumstances in order to bring about change. On first reading the *Völsunga Saga*, Morris wrote to Philip Webb that it was 'rather of the monstrous order'; the same could not be said of his poem, because he significantly shifts the uses of violence in the tale so that they become purposeful expressions of character, rather than fated acts of monstrous horror.[75] Violence is neither dehumanizing nor free of evil consequences; rather it humanizes those who carry it out passionately and at the same time deepens their human experience of pain by bringing with it a train of consequences and complications that must be faced and transformed.

Far more damaging to masculinity, and to the freedoms of male society in the poem, than femininity or wild energy out of control are the dissociations between body and deed or desire and act that deny the animal side of human nature and refuse its necessary connection with the physical world and the exigencies of circumstance. It is here that Morris locates true cowardice in the poem. It is not merely an absence of physical courage, but involves an unwillingness to suffer or bear what Morris describes as 'mental pain' or take emotional risk.[76] In the *Völsunga Saga*, Signy sends her son by Siggeir to be a helper to Sigmund in his exile in the forest; when he fails a crucial test of courage, Signy instructs Sigmund to kill him: he is not man enough to live. Morris transmutes this scene, so that the son is returned to his mother and behaves honourably in keeping Sigmund's existence a secret. He is not a coward, as those are who use violence without personal involvement and whose greed for both gold and women dehumanizes them: not only Siggeir and Atli, but Fafnir, the gold-hoarding dragon and Borghild's cheating brother, Gudrod, 'king of the greedy heart, [...] king of the thievish grip' (44). Greed and the cowardly separation of action and desire that accompanies it deny the possibility for direct and honest violence, and in this way they destroy the unity of a people.

The association of greed with cowardly unmanliness is neither politically radical nor contextually surprising. In Kingsley's thinking the distaste for greed or 'money-making' takes the form of an opposition to middle-class pursuits as 'effeminate', in contrast to an upper class way of life. It is thus brought into the service of Christian Socialism, which sees hope for the poor in the actions of the upper classes.[77] Tennyson makes a similar association of greed with unmanly qualities in his address to the Queen in the 1873 edition of *Idylls of the King*: 'cowardice, the child of lust for gold'. While this dedication suggests that Tennyson sees order and empire as an antidote to cowardice, Morris's opposition to the foreign wars of the 1870s sets the stage for his imminent turn to socialism, and suggests the beginning of a different understanding of the roots and effects of this kind of cowardice. He identifies greed, laziness and a separation of the upper classes from meaningful labour or meaningful battle as the cause of imperialist aggression against foreign nations. His manifesto of 1877 is addressed, 'To the Working Men of England', a form of address that echoes the 'English Folk' he addresses in his prologue to the *Völsunga Saga*.[78] In it he draws attention to the sources of illegitimate war in the separation of responsibility and action. Responding to the Eastern Question, Morris writes, 'Who are they that are leading us into war? Greedy gamblers on the stock exchange, idle officers of the army and navy (poor-fellows!), worn-out mockers of the clubs'.[79] There is both avarice and a refusal to work or act personally here, vividly evoked by the accumulation of adjectives, and heightened by the biblical inflection of 'mockers'.[80]

Morris refuses categorization by internal essentialism: cowardice and even greed, like courage and manliness, are performative. While he acknowledges that in many of the tales, 'a hard and grasping side to the character of the heroes is not uncommon', only the enemies of the Volsungs and Niblungs are entirely consumed by it.[81] As Silver notes, he downplays the desire for gold as a motive for Sigurd's actions, departing from the crude goldlust of the *Nibelungenlied* or the subtler, but nonetheless apparent, longing to see the gold hoard that drives the hero of the saga.[82] Momentary desire for gold may play a part in the development of manliness, but it cannot endure in manly society. Although Sigurd's acquisition of wealth through the courageous slaying of Fafnir is presented as unproblematic, the curse of the gold hoard underlies the action of the poem. Courageous manliness eventually both triumphs over individual moments of greed and overcomes, through death, the intergenerational curse of the gold hoard.

Despite his protestation that he had not changed it at all, Morris alters quite significantly the tone of the saga by his presentation of violent courage and its relationship to deceit and cowardice. He offers violence as a finely graded means of understanding the character of an individual or a people, while at the same making character less an individual expression of fixed internal traits and more the outcome of actions. Manliness does not consist in suppressing violence in Morris's version of the tale, but rather in acknowledging and accepting its primal power. He broadens the concepts of manliness and courage to allow them to encompass both failure and loss of control in varying degrees, judging manliness by the response to suffering rather than the ability to avoid or inflict it. In his lecture on the literature of Iceland, Morris points out that 'in all stories of the north, failure is never reckoned as a disgrace, but it is reckoned a disgrace not to bear it with equanimity'.[83] It is in this willingness to embrace failure, if not always with equanimity, that his poem stays closest to the spirit of the sagas.

Contradictions and complications run side by side in *Sigurd*, so that manliness is not the orderly, ordering characteristic of the naturally ruling race or class, but rather a broad spectrum of behaviours that arise from and shape circumstance and will, and are connected with freedom rather than success. The range of masculinities evident in the poem through the different meanings and uses of violence undercuts the very supposition of fixed and identifiable qualities of manliness on which Morris's critics draw. The things that manly society cannot be – consumed with greed, isolated, self-interested, power grabbing – are far clearer than the things it may include. Madness, individual lack of self-control and failures of prowess or courage may all be accommodated within its parameters. Neither masculinity nor violence is as stable as might be imagined, and it is this ontological instability that is particularly evident in the poem's treatment of women.

Sex, Violence and the Ontology of Manliness

Joseph Valente suggests that the 'honorific title' of manliness in Victorian Britain is 'an instrument of masculine hegemony' and as such, it 'has to remain ontologically affixed to the masculine gender position; otherwise, it could not serve to secure and advance an exclusively male dominion.'[84] This is not borne out in Morris's works, however: rather, he destabilizes both the ontology of masculinity and the ethics of self-restraint to which it is anchored while upholding an ideology of courageous, inclusive manliness, expressed through personal engagement in violent action. Women as well as men may be manly. Yet the very inclusivity of this vision becomes, in relation to the feminine, a problematic absorption. In undercutting the prevailing binaries between men and women, Morris suggests a kind of manliness that is not tied to maleness and that is rather based on circumstances and behaviour: the opposition that pertains is manliness versus isolated domination, overweening greed and self-interested cowardice in which personal action is separated from desire. The distinction between masculine and feminine is subsumed into this larger basis of distinction, in a way that prefigures the absorption of feminist concerns as merely a subset of class issues in the ideology of Marxism that Morris would soon espouse.[85]

Despite the manliness that Morris's contemporaries identify in *Sigurd*, it nonetheless embodies a longing for social structures in which the clear divisions between male and female roles may be overridden. George Marsh, prefacing his 1848 dictionary that draws on the work of the language scholar Rasmus Rask, ascribes to Icelandic a range of characteristics that resonate with nineteenth-century ideas of both masculinity and femininity: it is 'strikingly characterized by copiousness, flexibility and force, and in the power of enlarging its stock of words from its own resources, it yields to no language, the Greek itself not excepted.'[86] It is this flexibility and capacity for expansion and inclusion, often seen as feminine characteristics in contrast to masculine force and firmness, that characterize Morris's presentation of manliness and its potential for the inclusion of women. The combination of flexibility, force and a communal capacity for regeneration allows for the presentation of the female characters of *Sigurd* choosing active death by suicide – the destruction of the body in order to preserve both the soul and the story of the people.

The inclusion of women in manliness is not evinced in the sensuous, 'hermaphrodite' emphasis on enclosure and intense emotion that Buchanan deplores in Rossetti's poetry, neither does it lead to the kind of conscious exploration of androgyny evident in Burne-Jones's paintings; the women of the saga do not bring Victorian 'feminine' elements of inwardness or purity to the saga's men. Yet *Sigurd* does not evoke the all-male world of Haggard's saga-based *Eric Brighteyes*, in which women remain at home, plotting and manipulating or passively waiting. Rather, Morris's active women participate in and moderate or dramatically change the predominantly male world of the story. The seepage between conventionally separate male and female worlds works to erode essentialist differences between them, so that people are defined by their actions rather than by their biological sex or socially prescribed gender. In this way, the socially accepted and apparently hegemonic discourse of manliness, health and vigour to which *Sigurd*'s critics subscribe is open to more nuance than its proponents suggest.

The potential for nuance within ideas of manliness is present in the Norse saga sources themselves. Morris draws on an element of fluidity in gender constructions of Norse saga that most of his contemporary critics contrive to ignore, downplay, or translate into Victorian categories of gendered meaning.

Carol Clover highlights considerable slippage between conventionally male and female roles in Icelandic literature, law and life. She points to a 'gender continuum' in which men and women are not necessarily defined by the characteristics or actions commonly associated with them, 'and each can, and does, slip into the territory of the other'.[87] Drawing on Thomas Laqueur's explication of the Galenic idea of male and female as an inversion of each other, as essentially one sex, she suggests that the Old Norse world of the sagas is one in which 'maleness and femaleness were always negotiable, always up for grabs, always susceptible to "conditions"'.[88] The valour and courage that make up manliness, then, are not determined by sex or gender, but by action and circumstance together.

This offers an illuminating model for reading the awakening of Brynhild by Sigurd, a brief event in the saga, but dwelt on at length by Morris. Led to the top of the mountain by his horse, affirmed in his choice to venture forward on foot, because his sword, named 'the Wrath', 'cried out in answer as Sigurd leapt adown', Sigurd comes upon 'the shape of a man', apparently asleep. The inert body is:

> shapen fair,
> And clad from head to foot-sole in pale grey-glittering gear
> In a hauberk wrought as straitly as though to the flesh it were grown.
> (*Sigurd*, 122–3)

However, 'a great helm hideth the head and is girt with a glittering crown' (123). Once he takes off the helmet and sees from her face that she is a woman, he falls in love with Brynhild. In contrast with the more conventional sleeping beauty legends, she is outside in a scene of stark sublimity, dressed in armour, like a man slain in battle, rather than enclosed in a house – although that will come later, when the separation of desire and action has set in, and the manliness of the people is in decline. This moment recalls Sir John's discovery of the dead woman in 'Concerning Geffray Teste Noire', but here, she is not dead and permanently silenced, only temporarily enchanted.[89] The intimations of gender-crossing and social challenge that are evident in the earlier poem are more developed here in a world where women are able to partake freely of the warrior society. Sigurd's erotic use of his sword to slit open her armour and her clothes and so free her from the spell leads to an immediate exchange of passionate embraces and vows of love. She is beautiful and active, warrior and woman, but not in any way domestic. The setting and the context of their fulfilment of desire are not expressed in sexual or gender opposites.

Brynhild takes on the role of prophet, claimed by Carlyle for the male hero figure, but, while she foretells the future and shows wisdom, she conspicuously does not fit the image of woman as spiritual guide and moral compass for man, popular in nineteenth-century renditions of Nordic literature.[90] Dasent articulates this view of women, suggesting that the wild prophetic Norns of Iceland are the forebears of English 'witches and "wise women" whose charms are still potent in many an English village', and that 'the respect paid to both [is] that feature of our society which proves that it has outrun older civilizations by raising woman to her true position in the social scale'. In contrast to 'the Greek', 'the East' or 'the Roman', Western civilization, drawing on its Icelandic inheritance, has uncovered woman's true mission, he argues: 'she has risen to be a really worthy helpmeet for man, with a clearer insight into things divine than is vouchsafed to her shortsighted yoke-fellow'.[91] In Dasent's hands the descendant of the Norns bears a strong resemblance to Ruskin's ideal woman, cut to a pattern he discerns in Shakespeare, who 'represents [women] as infallibly faithful and wise counsellors, – incorruptibly just and pure examples – strong always to sanctify, even when they cannot save'; his best women, Ruskin asserts, offer wisdom, counsel and guidance to calm the passions of men. The wild Nordic prophet has become a Victorian angel. Her role may be no more limited than a male one, but it is distinctly separate from the turbulent realm of battle and action.[92]

Brynhild, on the contrary, is the active, desiring and desirable avenging warrior Valkyrie, the designated 'Victory-Wafter' who goes into battles and leads men to Valhalla: her role in war defines her, just as Sigurd's defines him. She is masculine and feminine at once and in his unity with her, Sigurd stakes out new territory for manliness, in which man and woman are equal in action. It is battle readiness and courage demonstrated in action that denote manliness here, rather than gender or sex. Brynhild's separation from Sigurd, after their first meeting, leads to a destruction of her internal integrity, which highlights difference, sets male and female against each other, and results in his death. Only when she then takes her own life with her sword and orders that she be laid on Sigurd's funeral pyre with both their swords are they once again united. What is broken may not be fixed by restraint or even by endurance or inner courage, but only by action. The unity of the masculine world can accommodate the feminine, but only at the cost of its separate identity.

Morris is not alone in allowing that women may be partakers of the qualities of manliness, particularly in times past. John Stuart Mill argues, in *The Subjection of Women* (1869), that, in feudal times 'it seemed natural that women of the privileged classes should be of manly character', demonstrated by their involvement in politics and war. In his own times, however, social conditioning has made them otherwise: 'their ideal of character is the very opposite to that of men; not self-will, and government by self-control, but submission, and yielding to the control of others.'[93] Other contemporary writers allow a more limited inclusion of women in the characteristics of manliness: Samuel Smiles reportedly began a letter to Eliza Lynn Linton: 'beloved woman, most manly of your sex'.[94] Thomas Hughes' treatise on Christian manliness frames it in spiritual terms, warning that both men and women may encounter 'trials of courage and manliness' in which they must choose to 'stand by what approves itself to their consciences as true'; women may be manly when they demonstrate integrity or hold to their beliefs.[95] Morris's designation of manliness is closer to Mill's, but more expansive. He refuses the moral, internal characterization of manliness and locates it instead in the actions of each person. The inclusion of women within the parameters of manliness, then, must result from their martial or violent actions in this warrior society. However, 'submission' and 'yielding' to fate may also be part of the manliness of the people. Morris reconfigures manliness so that it is able to accommodate both male and female, and to suggest the power and healing potential of a merging or blurring of boundaries rather than a clearer defining of them. The feminine is not opposed or defeated but accommodated, and its power of disruption utilized – or even neutralized – in the masculine narrative of battle.

Jan Marsh's comment about Morris's early work has some resonance with *Sigurd*: that he 'was striving to resist the excessive masculinity of his time, producing what is as yet an inchoate search for a wholeness to encompass both aggression and harmony, both the masculine and the feminine'.[96] Marsh's insistence on 'binary opposition' does not seem entirely justified, even in Morris's early work, and I suggest that Morris, rather than resisting an established 'excessive masculinity', reformulates its already unstable construction for his own ends. Nonetheless Marsh highlights the paradoxical commitment to coherence and unity that underlies Morris's portrayal of violence and its uses in identifying and defining a manly people. Fragmentation and destruction, however, are inevitable. For the central women of the poem, forced by fate into sexual relationships based on duplicity and at odds with desire, only in suicide – violence directed against themselves, finally, rather than against others – is their struggle between what they long for and the deceit with which it is achieved resolved. This act of suicide also seals their place as part of a masculine world, in which they are able to use weapons of violence rather than the cunning still associated in nineteenth-century discourse with women. The Edinburgh doctor, Thomas Laycock, writing in 1840 about reproduction and sexual desire, compares the 'propensity to fight' among male animals, with the 'artfulness', 'timidity' and 'cunning' characteristic of 'females of the higher class of animals', most particularly of women; 'and this seems to be given them in place of those weapons of offence and defence with which the men are generally provided.'[97] The poem enacts the repudiation of this formulation. Women may be largely excluded, even in this heroic world, from the battlefield, but given the opportunity, they too, like men, will demonstrate the courage, willingness to bear arms and commitment to violent revenge that characterizes the manliness of their men. While deceit is neither an essential characteristic of women, nor reserved for them alone, suicide is evidence of the absorption of the female into the manly ethic of violent courage.

Like the modernists after him who would draw on ancient myths, Morris uses the idea of sacrifice and renewal, giving meaning to violence and death through the framework of a story. Violent suicide does not accomplish its end in the world of the tale, but only after it, in the retelling. Nonetheless the suicides of Signy, Brynhild and Gudrun are acts of will that signal the character of those who perform them, and inscribe them in the history of their people. Signy's self-chosen death by immolation in the burning house of her hated husband, Siggeir, is clearly framed as the completion of an act of willed self-sacrifice for the sake of the people: she chooses communal wholeness and honour over individual life. Early on in the saga, desperate to find a way of perpetuating the Volsung line, Signy swaps bodies with a beautiful young witch and sleeps with her brother Sigmund in order to conceive a suitably heroic son. The blunt account of the saga is sharpened in the poem into a subjective portrayal of an active choice of self-sacrifice: 'And she thought: "Alone will I bear it; alone will I take the crime; / On me alone be the shaming, and the cry of the coming time"' (27). Morris focuses on her choice of incest for the sake of Sigmund and his children, knowing it is taboo: 'Yea, and he for the life is fated and the help of many a folk, / And I for the death and the rest, and deliverance from the yoke' (28). The result is the birth of Sinfiotli, which leads, eventually, to Signy's suicide: 'the day my grief hath won' (40). The omission of the scenes of Signy sewing her sons' shirts to their arms, or casually telling Sigmund to kill her son for want of courage makes this scene of violence against herself more potent: she is not callously or carelessly violent, but rather, willing to use violence to bring about change. Female desire here is subservient to the needs of male power and the system of patriarchy, but it is neither passive nor dormant; rather, it is expressed in deliberate acts of calm violence and finally in suicide. Like Brynhild and Gudrun after her, Signy becomes not merely one of the 'irreplaceable, or almost irreplaceable goods' of exchange between men, in Lévi-Strauss's terms, but an active, desiring subject.[98] Her death, like her marriage, is an act of manly will that exposes evil even as it embraces it.

Nonetheless the manliness of the people continues to absorb its women. Simone de Beauvoir proposes, in terms that echo Mill's, that 'one is not born, but rather becomes, a woman' and that a woman 'is indoctrinated with her vocation from her earliest years'.[99] Morris's poem traces a somewhat different process. Where de Beauvoir's account, like Mill's, emphasizes a suspect 'becoming' through social conditioning, Morris's poem posits manliness as something earned. It is a process open to both men and women. While this may suggest, like Edward Carpenter's *The Intermediate Sex*, that men and women are not fundamentally opposed, but 'they rather represent the two poles of one group – which is the human race', the language and orientation of that one group in *Sigurd* is masculine; to attain full humanity is to be manly.[100] Feminist psychoanalytic criticism examines the effects of this all-encompassing model of masculinity. Luce Irigaray, attributing a monolithic singleness to the masculine, suggests that Western language and philosophical discourse are marked by 'phallocentrism', and 'phallocratism', so that the masculine is 'everything', and 'the feminine finds itself defined as lack, deficiency, or as imitation and negative image of the subject'.[101] However broad the parameters of its manliness, *Sigurd* bears out, to a certain extent, this problematic writing out of the feminine, evident in the suicides of all the poem's women.

Yet this dynamic of negation or neutralization is, at least in part, challenged by a countervailing dynamic of internal transformation. While femininity or femaleness largely becomes absorbed into performative masculinity, it is not entirely contained by it. Its recalcitrant presence underlies the novelistic psychological realism of the poem, which in turn undermines its capacity to function as an epic of national heroism. It allows a focus on turmoil and subjectivity which suggests the inadequacy of self-control as a measure of manliness or, by extension, a mode of national life. As Eve Kosofsky Sedgwick suggests, 'the loose ends and crossed ends of identity are more fecund than the places where identity, desire, analysis, and need can all be aligned and centred'.[102] The disruptions of identity and desire in the poem originate from the female characters, who shape the masculine world of the tale.

The transformation of Gudrun, Sigurd's unloved wife, from clinging lover to avenging heroine involves a repudiation of the Ruskinian female role of moral guide and a decisive, destructive reconciliation of desire and agency in acts of manly violence. While Brynhild, Sigurd's counterpart as a figure of integration in the poem, is both desirably feminine and courageously, actively manly at the same time, Gudrun begins as a figure of loving, girlish dependence, awakening feelings of protective tenderness in Sigurd, who married her out of pity while drugged into forgetfulness of Brynhild:

> But Sigurd sitteth by Gudrun, and his heart is soft and kind,
> And pity swelleth within it for the days when he was blind;
> And with yet another pity, lest his sorrow seen o'erweigh
> Her fond desire's fulfilment, and her fair soul's blooming-day.
> (179)

The dim sense of gentle loss and grief caused by the deceit at the heart of their marriage is finally brought into focus by Brynhild's arrival at the court. Then for the first time Gudrun sees the past clearly, 'And the shadowy wings of the Lie, that the hand unwitting led / To the love and the heart of Gudrun, brood over board and bed' (205). 'The Lie' cannot coexist with manliness. It is Gudrun's awakening to the realization of her misplaced desire with no hope of satisfaction that sets in motion the events that lead to Sigurd's death and then the death of the women, who are, emotionally if not materially, dependent on him. Only after the deceit that underlies her marriage becomes evident to Gudrun does she develop into a figure of cold fury and vengeful violence, taking responsibility for her actions, and preferring the destruction of herself and others to the compromise of 'the Lie', which is the separation of desire and action that Goode identifies in the poem.

Truth and lies, concepts that occur repeatedly in Morris's poetry, fiction and political lectures, are key determinants of manliness or unmanliness in Victorian writings.[103] For Morris, they are not about words or abstract ideals but about actions. Both Gudrun and Brynhild partake of the manly life of the people by refusing passive submission to the circumstantial lie brought about by deceit. In this refusal, their actions become in themselves a submission to the inevitable unfolding story of their people. Within the violent heroic ethos of the poem, Byrnhild and Gudrun's willingness to murder and commit suicide in order to bring about change does not signify destructive despair, but hope. As Morris would later urge in his lecture on 'The Aims of Art':

> I ask you to think with me that the worst which can happen to us is to endure tamely the evils that we see; that no trouble or turmoil is so bad as that; that the necessary destruction which reconstruction bears with it must be taken calmly; that everywhere – in State, in Church, in the household – we must be resolute to endure no tyranny, accept no lie, quail before no fear, although they may come before us disguised as piety, duty, or affection, as useful opportunity and good-nature, as prudence or kindness.[104]

The poem itself surely enacts this appeal: it urges its listeners to think with Morris that to take violent action, to destroy in order to reconstruct, is better than to endure the lie. Morris goes on to argue that recognizing an inheritance of resistance to evil leads to 'courage and hope; that is, eager life while we live'.[105] This may not be a life of satisfaction, but it will be one of integrity, he suggests.

Gudrun, at first a character of conventional femininity, becomes the final emblem of both manly courage and female disruption in the poem. After the deaths of Sigurd and Brynhild, she accepts a proposal of marriage from King Atli.

He later lures her brothers to his land with promises of gold. Gudrun sits impassively throughout their battle with the treacherous Atli and later watches, 'a white queen crowned, and silent as the ancient shapen stone' (276), with 'deedless hands and cold' (280), while her husband orchestrates their murder. Once they have shown their manliness in the unflinching contemplation of their painful deaths, her silent stillness, described as feminine and queenly, is transformed into action and loud cries. As she burns down Atli's hall and all his nobles in it, her act is figured as one of war: 'as the battle-horn is dreadful, as the winter wind is wild / So dread and shrill was her crying and the cry none heeded or heard' (304). After this awakening of emotion, her murder of Atli is swift and triumphant and her final act of suicide is a calm assertion of individual will in response to implacable fate.

Morris's vision of female suicide draws on the kind of careless courage depicted in Paul Henri Mallet's popular *Northern Antiquities*, which includes a description of the Nordic warriors' joyful embrace of death:

> To die with his arms in his hand was the vow of every free man; and the pleasing idea they had of this kind of death would naturally lead them to dread such as proceeded from disease or old age. In the joy therefore which they testified at the approach of a violent death, they might frequently express no more than their real sentiments.[106]

Yet Morris complicates this picture too, not least by exploring the range of emotion of his heroes and suicides. While neither women nor men hesitate in the face of death, they do not revel in it.[107] Nor is it a sign of victory or success. Rather, like Arnold's Byron, 'in anguish, doubt, desire' their 'fiery courage' enables them to choose an unfaltering act of finality.[108] Women, like men, take part in the life of the people and become partners and equals in both the courageous endurance of suffering and the unflinching infliction of violent death.

Violence against one's own body, in this poem, becomes a means of self-definition, of choosing to contribute to the ending of the tale. Tucker's analysis of the poem demonstrates the interaction of content and form, and the significance of deeds done for the sake of tales told: he observes that 'heroes of the fiber Morris found in the sagas crave the end not as release but as completion'.[109] Completion, rather than perfection, is important: it is not primarily a tale of progress towards a better world, but rather one of courageous action, first for vengeance but finally for wholeness. Gudrun, about to throw herself into the sea to her death, cries out,

> O Sea I stand before thee; and I who was Sigurd's wife!
> By his brightness unforgotten I bid thee deliver my life

From the deeds and the longing of days, and the lack I have won of the earth,
And the wrong amended by wrong, and the bitter wrong of my birth!
(306)

The lacks and lacunae left in the tale will finally be amended by the fullness of death and inscribed in the telling of the tale. Gudrun's act is neither resignation nor celebration. Rather, like Sinfiotli's willing acceptance of poisoning, her death is a final act of choice, after a series of carefully calculated wrongs set in place for the amendment of 'wrong'. The parallels with Sinfiotli are evident in Gudrun's language. Signy, turning back into the flames of Siggeir's house, says to Sinfiotli: 'meseemeth, thy day shall not be long, / To weary thee with labour and mingle wrong with wrong' (40). Briefly like Sinfiotli, Gudrun becomes an instrument of revenge, acting out an inevitable fate. Yet she does not wholly surrender her will as Sinfiotli does, and her murderous violence arises from her own desperate passion. She becomes, through killing and dying, part of the manly story of her people, a character who acts and chooses and uses the weapons of violence available to her.[110]

While Spatt's contention that 'forced to articulate the conditions of their own lives, the protagonists of *Sigurd* find themselves articulating the formula for transcendence of the individual life', holds true in relation to the sense of a wider story of which each character is a part, it is the recognition of individual desire that drives the story in these last two books of the poem. There is a tension between fate, individual will and community that Spatt does not wholly acknowledge. Morris's tale allows for both to exist side by side rather than offering the triumph of one over the other.[111] As Barbara T. Gates points out, while nineteenth-century journalists and the writers of popular novels distanced contemporary suicide by sensationalizing it, poets from Arnold and Tennyson to Meredith and Browning grappled with issues of will, courage and health through depictions of ancient suicide.[112] Morris joins this chorus of male poets, yet he resists a single representation of suicide as evidence of valour and manliness, as is common in Victorian representations of Viking death, or of female weakness, as is common in contemporary sensational reports.[113] Instead, the female suicides of the poem represent the merging of the individual and the communal. Through acts of will, the women of the poem sacrifice themselves to the tale of the people and are integrated into a history of manliness.

The poem, itself part of the tale, is the bearer of the broad and multistranded manliness it represents. It offers, in language and style, an invitation to partake of the manliness of a contiguous but alien past. It blurs, without entirely erasing, conventional gender boundaries and the political and ontological ideologies which they maintain. It proposes, as its reception suggests, a means, rather than a model, of renewal of the English nation, through what James Fitzjames Stephen termed 'the great cognate virtues – truth and courage', virtues translated by Morris into epic, ancient violence.[114] As Morris writes in the introduction to his translation, with Magnússon, of the *Völsunga Saga*, it is:

> The Great Story of the North, which should be to all our race what the Tale of Troy was to the Greeks – to all our race first, and afterwards, when the change of the world has made our race nothing more than a name of what has been – a story too – then it should be to those that come after us no less than the Tale of Troy has been to us.[115]

This suggestion of the transhistorical meanings and uses of the poem links it to the historical circumstance of the 'change of the world', past and future. It suggests that despite the healthgiving links with the Teutonic or Old Norse past, the English people of the nineteenth century may have to go through the kind of complete annihilation that befalls the Volsungs and the Niblungs; degeneration may lead to extinction. It is an idea to which Morris recurs again, and more fully, in his Germanic romances of the 1880s, as the next chapter suggests.

In the meantime, the tale itself offers an intimation of an ongoing community of transnational Northern manliness. This is achieved not only through content but also through language. Magnússon recalls Morris denouncing it 'as something intolerable to have to read an Icelandic saga rendered into the dominant literary dialect of the day – the English newspaper language', because the saga's 'dignity of style cannot be reached by the Romance element in English. If it is to be reached at all – and then only approximately – it must be by means of the Teutonic element in our speech'.[116] Yet this very immersion in the stories and language of the past, this refusal to comment on the present in the poem itself, sets Morris's appeal to the past apart from the strident pro-Germanic nationalism of Carlyle, or the 'urgent need to win back the old North for the Anglo-Scandinavians' that drove George Stephens or Mary and William Howitt.[117] Morris trusts in the language itself to confront his readers with the powerful alterity of the saga world. He does not offer a vision of manliness that upholds imperial or class domination. Rather, he chooses the tale of an annihilated people, in part as a warning or prophecy, but also as a demonstration of martial values that cross the boundaries of gender and time.

§

W. H. Smith, reviewing *Past and Present* in 1843, suggests that Carlyle's work produces in his readers a 'tone of mind' that is 'manly, energetic, enduring, with high resolves and self-forgetting effort'.[118] Over twenty years later, Alfred Austin lists the 'masculine' qualities lacking in Swinburne's poetry: men, he writes, are 'brave, muscular, bold, upright, chivalrous, [...] daring, enduring, short of speech and terrible in action'.[119] Morris's vision of manliness draws on both these conceptions, setting them firmly in a martial Northern society, but broadening the parameters of their enactment. He offers the possibility that manliness resides in a lack of restraint, and celebrates a wild use of energy, careless of danger or pain, evoked in the 'copiousness' and 'flexibility' of the poem as well as its content.[120] In the sacrificial or self-denying suicides of his female heroines, he depicts a different use of energy and violence: an energetic submission to the demands of both the masculine world and the continuing tale of which it is a part.

Sigurd dramatizes the idea that violence, used well or ill in Morris's terms, is not merely an individual act of bravery or an expression of essential maleness, but rather a complex expression of the character of a people, their will to act and their ability to respond with courage and hope to the world around them. Women, like men, are differentiated, and their individuality is demonstrated in the ways they use violence. While these women are not yet the fully formed warriors of the Germanic romances of the next decade, Morris is already drawn to tales in which women work, fight and suffer alongside men for the good of the people. Their emotional complexity shapes the poem and makes its tale of heroism more than a simple expression of active manhood. Female courage is neither denied nor demoted. It contributes to the world of the tale and helps to shape a manliness that challenges ideals of godlike individual will and racial superiority. Yet, ultimately, the female and the feminine are subsumed into the manliness of the tale, which is all that remains of the acts of the people.

Chapter Four

CROSSING THE RIVER OF VIOLENCE: THE GERMANIC ANTIWARS AND THE UNCIVILIZED USES OF WORK AND PLAY

In *The House of the Wolfings* (1888) and *The Roots of the Mountains* (1889) Morris tells stories of the victorious battles of the ancient Goths, in archaic language that is vivid and celebratory, evoking not only the communalism and harmony of Teutonic society but also its commitment to martial violence.[1] The burgeoning civilization of the Romans, in *Wolfings*, and the rapacious cruelty of the fictional Dusky Men, in *Roots*, are set in contrast to the committed harmonious warfare of the Goths. Just as the Marxist socialism that Morris embraced from 1883 onwards sought not to modify capitalism, but to overthrow it, so in these texts the Romans and the Dusky Men must be utterly defeated by the barbarians – temporarily, at least. As Face-of-god says in *Roots*, 'There can be no two words concerning what we have to aim at; these Dusky Men we must slay everyone, though we be fewer than they be' (*Roots*, 248). Five years before *Roots* was published, Morris had said in a lecture, 'Misery and the Way Out': 'this earthly hell is not the ordinance of nature but the manufacture of man [...] and it is your business to destroy it: to destroy it, I say, [...] to make an end of it so that no one henceforth can ever fall into it'.[2] This chapter will suggest that the romances, written more than ten years after *Sigurd* and at a time when Morris's political activism was fervent but beset by difficulties, demonstrate his literary commitment to absolute war, and to the imaginative annihilation of a thoroughly evil enemy. This is a position fraught with ethical perils. While *Sigurd* drew on ideologies of racial and linguistic purity and superior Nordic manliness, but modified the elements of those theories that would develop in the twentieth century into virulent fascism, the Germanic romances' literary commitments intersect with later contemporary political ideologies of violence and racial difference, particularly with representations of the imperial violence Morris so abhorred. The imaginary violence that shapes the tales spills over into a problematic justification of certain kinds of war.

In one of the few developed considerations of Morris's response to violence, Boos pays careful attention to Morris's active political opposition to the violence of empire and to unjust war, but acknowledges that 'the most obvious question these convictions pose for those who are familiar with Morris's literary work is one of consistency.' She goes on to suggest that 'many of his writings [...] focus on elaborately stylized forms of allegorical combat', and that his 'literary representations of the conflicting moral claims of *eros* and *thanatos*' are 'ambivalent'. About the Germanic romances, she writes simply that, in comparison with *Sigurd*, they 'offered less stylized accounts of struggle against predatory invaders.'[3] However, the violence of the romances bears a closer relation both to Morris's political context and to the rhetoric of imperialism against which he writes and campaigns than this allows. His political writings show a more enduring commitment to particular kinds of violence than Boos suggests, as I argue in the next chapter, while the violence of his fiction merits more searching readings than are suggested by its consignment to a representation of competing psychological drives. It is visceral, detailed, not entirely allegorical violence against carefully described enemies.

In order to consider the uses of violence in the Germanic romances, I will borrow from Brantlinger's neat formulation of *News from Nowhere* as an 'anti-novel', a kind of writing that refuses the context and conventions of novels, and indeed largely banishes them from the world it depicts.[4] I suggest that Morris's wars in these romances are antiwars, in the sense that they stand in deliberate, stark and evident contrast to the kinds of organization, purpose and division of labour of Victorian warfare abroad, as well as to Victorian civilization at home, which Morris suggests is based on 'a state of perpetual war [...]. War, or competition, whichever you please to call it'.[5] This is not to say they are 'antiwar' in the commonly understood sense; far from it. These are tales that celebrate certain kinds of war. They propound a militant notion of noble war whose demands supersede the milder concerns of peace; their implied critique of contemporary war rests on the assumption, made clear in the text, that there are different kinds of war, and moral differences between types of killing. As other critics have noted, the tales combine a focus on personal heroism with a history of dialectical materialism, in which war is a necessary and inevitable force of change, recurring at various points in history.[6] Yet the romances cannot escape the necessity inherent in heroic war stories of legitimizing violence as a means of bringing about peace.

Despite Morris's declaration in 1883 that, 'I have a religious hatred to all war and violence', he repeatedly displays a willingness to countenance both fictional and actual violence as a means of bringing about social change.[7] In *Socialism, Its Growth and Outcome*, an account of the historical development of socialism, Morris and Bax conclude their argument about the necessity and means of avoiding war with this proviso: 'armed revolt or civil war may be an incident of the struggle, and in some form or another probably will be, especially in the latter phases of the revolution'.[8] This admission of the likely inevitability of violence echoes a letter of 1884 from Morris to a young socialist recruit: 'I mean that we must not say "we will drop our purpose rather than carry it across this river of violence". To say that means casting the whole thing into the hands of chance, and we *cant* [*sic*] do that' (Morris's emphasis).[9] Social change, like conversion or death, involves a temporary immersion in pain that will lead to a better outcome. Violence is a natural force, a river that can be forded; to cross it is more certain than to turn away from it – a willed choice rather than the uncertainty Morris suggests will result from a refusal to confront violence with violence. In both the political treatise and the personal letter, Morris goes on to talk about violence as a necessary part of 'the evolution of history'. While Bax is more committed to this language of evolution than Morris, it does appear elsewhere in Morris's own writings, and here it suggests a willingness to countenance violence as the natural biproduct of the development of a better society.[10] Violence is not something to be sought, but must be readily embraced when thrust upon the people by history or progress.

Morris's political writings make clear that the idea of war was central to his thinking about capitalism and socialism. Contemporary capitalist civilization is inseparable from violence, he asserts. In 1888, he writes in the Socialist League journal, *Commonweal*, that 'the march of commerce […] is *itself* war, and violence is of its essence'.[11] The romances therefore offer exemplary stories of people living in conditions of actual war, whose willingness to engage in fighting is both the means of saving themselves and of changing their way of life. Brantlinger argues that the later romance, *News from Nowhere*, 'stands in opposition to the literature and art produced in the context of industrial capitalism'.[12] This is not entirely the case: just as the Germanic romances rather problematically engage with war stories to make fine distinctions between forms of war, *News from Nowhere* engages with a popular form of writing to make its critique of contemporary art and the realist novel. The romance form that Morris uses for all three tales was becoming increasingly popular in the late nineteenth century, and as Nicholas Daly observes, was beginning to be seen by some as both more virile and more particularly English than the novel.[13] Anna Vaninskaya argues that Morris's romances can be firmly located in the romance revival of the fin de siècle and notes that the reading public 'would have been aware of the critical consensus on a number of generic features, such as the opposition of purity to immoral filthiness, the improving nature of the subject matter, and the focus on plot as opposed to analysis and introspection'.[14] Just as important, the romance is a form popularly associated with rousing tales of action, heroism and battle.

While the tales offer a vision of ancient battle as necessary and productive communal work that is pleasurable and productive of change, the exigency of creating credible enemies in a tale of war reveals currents of thought that mirror, rather than oppose, some of the ideologies of nineteenth-century imperialism.[15] The creation of credible enemies is a political necessity as well as a literary one: a tale of war can only be effective if the reader's sympathies can reasonably be expected to be with the heroes and against the enemy. In order to ensure this, Morris makes use of the immediacy of battle violence while distancing the tale through archaic language and heroic style. In 1888, writing in *Commonweal*, he compares news coverage of the death or injury of four hundred Tibetans at the hands of British troops, 'the killing *all* on one side', to the much-reported Whitechapel murders of prostitutes in East London. In relation to the Tibetan deaths, he writes; 'if the history of this slaughter had been given Homerically – i.e., with abundance of realistic detail – it would have made a pretty good multiplication of a Whitechapel murder.'[16] Morris's own tales describe their wars 'Homerically' – with abundance of realistic detail; yet they are not presented as one-sided mass murder to be condemned, but epic battles between clearly marked good and evil. The stories so demonize the enemy that their 'slaughter' is not questioned. It is not killing itself to which Morris objects, the stories suggest. The fervour of war may be justified if the enemy can be shown to be sufficiently evil.

The fluid boundaries of manliness that characterized *Sigurd* still pertain within the tribes: Thiodolf's struggle in *Wolfings* is to surrender his personal desires to the good of the people; the complications of love threaten the communal continuity of tribes in *Roots*. But the focus in these tales is far more on battle lines between the tribes and their enemies, their differences a matter of essential, even racial characteristics rather than simply behaviour. There is little of the mythic sense of fate that drives the narrative of *Sigurd*. These are vividly imagined, unshrinking and absolute tales of battle that evoke contemporary as well as ancient struggles against evil in ways that destabilize their ideological function. They eschew realism for a more deliberately stylized evocation of violence, but combat is neither simplified nor neutralized by this. Rather, it appears as the corporeal expression of a set of values developed in opposition to, but unavoidably intertwined with, the prevailing culture of late Victorian Britain and its preoccupation with the conflict between civilization and barbarism. Even in genre, the tales' celebration of ancient barbarian violence resonates with more politically complicit stories of imperial derring-do.

The Romance of Barbaric Violence

Morris's use of the romance form offers a way of engaging with ancient stories of victorious violence over absolute evil, while working in tension with an emerging tradition of adventure romance in his own time. As he argued in 1889, 'what romance means is the capacity for a true conception of history, a power of making the past part of the present'.[17] What is evident in the Germanic romances is that what is 'true' in history does not mean what actually happened, but rather what meaning underlies the events of the past and how it might both illuminate and transform the present.[18] *Roots* and *Wolfings* offer an imaginative exploration and reformulation of abiding socialist concerns about 'modern civilization', yet they draw on ideas of the wild manliness of barbarian people and the excitement of a remote and exotic world that are common elements of the contemporary adventure fiction that celebrates empire. They turn to the past, but arise from the Victorian context in which they were first read; in this way they draw the past into an implicit critique of the present but also suggest aspects of a possible future. In doing so, they resonate variously with the language, style and assumptions of contemporary romance writing, anthropology and journalism in their handling of the concepts of barbarism and civilization, which suggest both temporal and geographical oppositions. Arising from the same broad old northernism as *Sigurd*, the Germanic romances engage with their cultural moment in a very different form and style. Along with Morris's political journalism and propaganda of the 1880s, they make an investment in the idea of glorious violence as a bearer of alterity and change that draws as much on the context of nineteenth-century literary and cultural depictions of imperial barbarism as on Marxist historiography.

While Morris's avowal that 'apart from the desire to produce beautiful things, the leading passion of my life has been and is hatred of modern civilization' is well known and susceptible of different interpretations, his elaboration of this sentiment in a lecture in Manchester in 1888 offers further insight into the nature of this hatred. 'There has been amongst people of different minds abundant discussion as to whether civilization is a good thing or an evil […]. I must tell you that my *special* leading motive as a Socialist is hatred of civilization; my ideal of the new Society would not be satisfied unless that Society destroyed civilization' (Morris's emphasis).[19] While neither Morris nor his fellow socialists were alone in critiquing modern civilization – as Morris notes here – nor in offering a form of barbarism as an alternative to it, this usefully indicates the particular vehemence of Morris's opposition to civilization and sets it in the context of an ongoing cultural debate. Alongside the growing culture of ultracivilized aestheticism in Britain towards the fin-de-siècle, an alternative ideal of barbarian manliness that emphasized brutality and violence – the 'Hooliganism' that Buchanan decried – was largely expressed in relation to empire.[20] Bradley Deane argues that between 1871 and 1914, 'Victorian popular culture became engrossed as never before in charting vectors of convergence between the British and those they regarded as primitive, and in imagining the ways in which barbarians might make the best imperialists of all'.[21] What this meant, however, was allowing an element of barbarism into civilized society, or allowing civilized, nineteenth-century white men to experience the liberation of temporary barbarism, away from centres of civilization. Deane goes on to suggest that 'this transvaluation of savagery found its most striking expression in the emergence of a wildly popular genre of fiction: stories of lost worlds.'[22] While Morris's ideas of barbarianism, imperialism and civilization are significantly different from those described by Deane, his Germanic romances nonetheless reflect this subgenre of adventure fiction in their presentation of a society entirely unlike the present, committed to the celebration of barbarism made evident in unrestrained warfare.

However, while Haggard or Doyle or Kipling retain the civilizing, imperial white man in the form of the adventurer who travels to a lost world and is changed by the wild violence he encounters there, Morris has no such envoy from the present, so that the reader becomes the adventurer to be changed by the encounter with violence.[23] The verse introduction to each tale reaches into the present, and invites the reader into the story world, breaching its epic completeness. Like the 'epic past' that M. M. Bakhtin describes, the language of the tales works seamlessly with the subject matter to create closed worlds in which the boundary between the time portrayed in each story and the present 'is immanent in the form of the epic itself and is felt and heard in its every word.'[24] The reader enters the lost world of the past. Yet Morris undermines the totalizing assumptions of epic, both by the contemporary language and references of the verse introductions, and by his use of allusive intertextual language that borrows from contemporary narratives, which, in Bakhtin's terms, brings an element of formal novelistic dialogism into the work, so that the boundaries of epic are breached and neither its form nor its values are closed and complete.[25] In entering the fantastic past, the reader brings it into the present.

Morris himself is such a reader in relation to Richard Jefferies's fantasy of a dystopian future, *After London* (1885). In it the cataclysmic destruction of England's cities has reduced the country to a series of disparate, primitive communities in a state of permanent and vicious small-scale warfare. The hero, Felix, travels among them, making his way by skill, craftsmanship and cunning on a quest to prove himself to his beloved and find a new way of life. 'Absurd hopes curled round my heart as I read it', Morris wrote to Georgiana Burne-Jones; 'I rather wish I were thirty years younger: I want to see the game played out'.[26] While Vaninskaya argues that 'if anything in *After London* could have given sufficient cause for Morris's excited reaction it could only have been [the] brief concluding episode of the Shepherds', there is much in Morris's own writing to suggest, instead, that the idea of the complete destruction of current civilization and all its trappings is appealing to him, emotionally if not pragmatically. It is surely this, rather than the brief moment of communal life offered by Jefferies's description of the shepherds, that gives the story enduring significance for Morris. Another letter, written the following month, again suggests just this: that he imagines with pleasure the imminent ruin of his society. He writes that civilization is 'doomed to destruction, and probably before very long':

> What a joy it is to think of! And how often it consoles me to think of barbarism once more flooding the world, and real feelings and passions, however rudimentary, taking the place of our wretched hypocrisies. With this thought in my mind, all the history of the past is lighted up and lives again to me.[27]

The idea that civilization may contain within itself the seeds of its own destruction is not a new one. Indeed Jefferies's novel could be read as a fictional exploration of the image of a future society painted by Thomas Babington Macaulay in his famous 1829 attack on James Mill's utilitarianism in the *Edinburgh Review*. Taking issue with Mill's principles, he asks, 'is it possible that in the bosom of civilisation itself may be engendered the malady which shall destroy it?' He goes on: 'is it possible that, in two or three hundred years, a few lean and half-naked fishermen may divide with owls and foxes the ruins of the greatest European cities – may wash their nets amidst the relics of her gigantic docks, and build their huts out of the capitals of her stately cathedrals?'[28] Babington concludes that under Mill's system of government, if his principles were right, this would inevitably be the case. He deplores Mill's ideas and therefore this vision. For Morris, however, such a vision is suggestive of a revitalized and revitalizing barbarism that signals the beginning of something new and better. What is evident in this response to Jefferies is a commitment to the revolutionary idea that society can begin to be healed by the annihilation of all that is, coupled with a willingness to accept the 'rudimentary' feelings and passions which that new beginning will entail.

While Jefferies leaves unspecified the means of the destruction of English society, and begins his story with an account of its results, Morris's tales are directly concerned with the acts of battle and physical destruction that lead to social change. They draw on historical models of ancient societies, as well as on the distancing and generalizing techniques of romance. Morris was familiar with the anthropological history of Friedrich Engels and the American Lewis Morgan, who describe the historical stage of barbarism as a state in which warfare takes place primarily to protect the gens or tribe from those outside it.[29] In Morris and Bax's descriptions of early society they make use of this idea to suggest that 'people, tribe or gens were essentially exclusive; within their limits peace and community of property was the rule – without, a state of war was assumed; it was not war that had to be declared, but peace'.[30] War, then, is a natural state of affairs, and paradoxically essential for the preservation of the peace and community of the society. As Morris's Marxist history suggested was necessary, it also resulted in the evolution of the exclusive peaceful society out of which it arose. In the midst of his socialist activity to bring about political change, Morris turns his imagination to this distant barbarian past, in which open war – rather than the 'competition' of his own society – is as normal as any other kind of work.[31]

In doing so he brings into play ideas that straddle the fields of political theory and fantasy fiction, and engage with questions of the emergence of national identity and the relationship between society and the individual. As early as the 1830s John Stuart Mill was arguing that some important qualities of barbarism, including energy and heroism, were in danger of being lost in civilized England, although such losses would be minor in comparison with the advances of modern, co-operative civilization. He shares both with contemporary Whig historians and with Marx the conviction that history is a story of progress.[32] So too does the pioneering evolutionary anthropologist of the 1870s, Edward Burnett Tylor. Committed as he was to the idea of progress through the evolution of societies, Tylor nonetheless noted what might be lost, at least temporarily, in the transition from barbarism, observing that despite the gains of civilization, 'courage, honesty, generosity are virtues which may suffer' as cultures evolve.[33] By the 1880s, alongside a widespread commitment to the concept of European racial superiority and progress, an image of tamed masculine barbarity as a counter to the degeneracy and effeteness that threatened Western civilization was emerging in public discourse. This is evident not only in the revival of interest in the violence of the old North, demonstrated in the representation of berserker warriors in novels such as Kingsley's *Hereward the Wake* (1865) or Haggard's *Eric Brighteyes* (1890), but also in the broader discourse of imperialism.

As Deane notes, the archimperialist Cecil Rhodes curiously asserted his appreciation for certain qualities of strength and honesty that he identified as barbarian, buying furniture that was 'big and simple, barbaric if you like', even while he asserted his racial superiority over Africans, who were, he claimed dismissively, 'children, [...] just emerging from barbarism'.[34] Drawing on the common language of evolutionary anthropology that saw the development of races as analogous to the development of individuals, Rhodes viewed barbarism as a stage of racial development, in which Europeans figure as adults and Africans as children. Yet he also presents barbarism as a current and desirable aspect of manliness, evidence of grandeur, honesty and force. Morris, despite his own commitment to Marxist history in which barbarism is a necessary dialectical stage of development, nonetheless frames it, in a way that goes well beyond Rhodes' vision of barbaric qualities in the 'civilized' man, as a more desirable moment than modern civilization, both in itself and for the sake of the new beginning it heralds.

In the year that Morris wrote of his hopes for the end of civilization, the death of General Charles Gordon in Sudan caused a ripple of public debate about imperialism and heroism that would spread out over the rest of the century. He came to exemplify, in different ways for his admirers and his detractors, the spirit of imperial heroic soldiery, a complicated blend of masculinity and civilization, barbarism and chivalry. Against a background of the popular colonial adventure stories of Rider Haggard or G. A. Henty, the 1884 deployment of Gordon, already famous for his exploits in China, occupied a prominent place in the pages of newspapers and journals such as the *Pall Mall Gazette* and became the focus of political debate and manoeuvring.[35] After his death he was immortalized in newspaper articles and cartoons, in George Joy's famous painting, 'General Gordon's Last Stand' (1885), in boys' magazines and hastily written hagiographies.[36] Tennyson produced an epitaph hailing him as a 'warrior of God, man's friend' and claiming that 'this earth hath borne no simpler, nobler man.'[37] *Blackwood's* lauded the 'knightly name' of this 'hero', and described his firm but fair dealings with the 'half-savage' soldiers he had previously commanded in China, as well as with the 'savages' he encountered in Egypt; the article affirms that 'he was all that the popular imagination desires as a hero. And the requirements of the popular imagination, when truly inspired, are great'. He was 'a Bohemian, yet a fervent Christian', a model of selfless devotion to his country and his God to the end.[38]

The posthumous lionizing of General Gordon and the sympathetic portrayal of his actions was attacked again and again in *Commonweal*, of which Morris was founder and coeditor. The March 1885 issue opens with an unsigned editorial condemning Gordon's actions and the society that admires him. It is immediately followed by an article by Bax, which concludes by urging 'the working classes of England' to 'remember that this organised brigandage was deliberately *planned* from the beginning and that Gordon's "pacific mission" was only too obviously a blind'.[39] In a letter of 3 March of the same year, Morris writes that, 'I hope by this time most people know what we Socialists think of the Khartoum-stealers and the spreaders of the blessings of shoddy civiliation [sic]'.[40] As late as 1889, Morris used Gordon's actions as a touchstone for all that was wrong with colonialism as an expression of capitalism: 'slaughter and destruction carried on wholesale in a bad cause is murder of the worst kind: murder, the evil consequences of which are hard to foresee or measure.'[41] The qualifications here are important: the value of the cause has a bearing on the morality of killing, and 'the worst kind' allows for degrees of murder. Earlier, in 1888, still finishing writing *Wolfings*, Morris had made clear the problem with Gordon. A memorial statue of him had recently been unveiled in Trafalgar Square, and Morris, reporting on this, describes him as a 'soldier of fortune [...] that most dangerous tool of capitalistic oppression, the "God-fearing soldier"', who allowed himself to be used to 'drive the wedge of profit-mongering into barbarous Africa'.[42] He breaks the link between the chivalric representation of Gordon and his actions and draws attention instead to his battle skills as mechanistic soldiering rather than knightly gallantry or courage, thereby also reversing the class stereotype of the obedient working-class soldier versus the heroic, aristocratic officer. His is not a heroic body, but a mere tool of capitalism, in this account. That it is the exported combination of God, war and financial greed that Morris abhors here, is clear. Barbarous Africa is better without them.

However, there is an alternative tale of the 'civilizing mission' to barbarous Africa that comes much closer to Morris's own romances, and illuminates something of the literary context in which these tales were written and read. Haggard's *King Solomon's Mines* (1885) suggests a level of reciprocity between civilization and barbarism in the rejuvenating encounter of the white adventurer with the primitive people of Africa. Morris read the novel in November 1885, shortly after its publication, and wrote to his daughter, May, that it is 'amusing if a good deal made of Poe and C. Read'.[43] Ideas of fellowship in battle, courage in fighting, and leadership by force represent an alternative, in this tale, to what had begun to be seen by some in the late 1880s as effete British civilization. The adventurous manliness of the tale's narrator, Allan Quatermain, the slightly foppish but brave Captain Good, and their aristocratic companion, Sir Henry Curtis, is enhanced by their encounter with the fictional Kukuana tribespeople (identified by Haggard as the Matabele), in a hybrid exchange which allows them to admire and learn from the Kukuanas' courage and ferocity, while maintaining their superiority over them.

Earlier, in his first published short story, 'A Zulu War-Dance' in the *Gentleman's Magazine* (1877), Haggard positions himself as mediator between the 'highly-civilised reader' and 'the barbarian', as he describes a Zulu war dance.[44] He is already preoccupied with issues that he will develop further in *King Solomon's Mines* (1885), already mourning, to an extent, what he sees as the necessary destruction of the Zulu culture with its 'system of chieftainship and its attendant law'. He writes that 'surely even the most uncompromising of those marching under the banner of civilisation must hesitate before they condemn this deep-rooted system to instant uprootal.' He is committed to the 'march of progress', but at the same time is attracted by the idea of the savage and wild warrior as 'an emblem and a type of the times and the things which are passing away'. This savage stands in contrast to the British traders who have, he avers in terms similar to Morris's own, 'supplied the natives with those two great modern elements of danger and destruction, the gin-bottle and the rifle.'[45] While Morris's political stance and purpose is quite different from Haggard's, his literary depiction of exotic, primitive cultures in contrast with the corrupt Victorian present draws on similar conventions of battle and adventure in a barbaric lost world.

In *King Solomon's Mines*, the tale itself is mediated by the colonial adventurer, Allan Quatermain, whose status sets him on the edge of English civilization. It is a tale to titillate and shock, an investigation of alternative models of manliness in the uncivilized spaces of empire. As John Tosh points out, 'the empire was inscribed in British masculinities not only as a source of imagined "others", but as a space where redundant masculinities could flourish.'[46] Adventures with the Kukuanas are a brief, though exciting, contrast to civilization for the maverick Quatermain, an invigorating brush with the colonial Other, not a viable alternative to the societal norms of the colonizers. In entering their world, Quatermain and his companions are able to enjoy, temporarily, the sanctioned violence and lack of restraint offered by immersion in the barbarian world.

Morris's tales offer his readers a similar, but rather more demanding opportunity. Like Quatermain in Africa, the readers of the Germanic romances are invited to enter, in imagination, the lost worlds of the ancient barbarian people and throw off the trammels and hypocrisies of civilization for a simpler and more warlike way of life. The tale itself offers no possibility even of Haggard's attenuated version of what Homi Bhabha terms 'hybridity': 'strategies of subversion that turn the gaze of the discriminated back upon the eye of power'.[47] *King Solomon's Mines* allows the values of the Kukuanas, as Haggard perceives them, to reflect on those of the colonists and their home country, albeit without relinquishing the power of the colonist. Morris's are romances of absolute war, with no possibility of compromise between his barbarian heroes and civilization. The Roman civilization in *Wolfings* is not able to benefit from barbarism, but is utterly degraded and corrupt. There is a kind of grudging respect for aspects of the Romans' warcraft, but this is cancelled out by scorn at their venality and cowardice. The reader is expected to learn from the tale or at least to benefit from immersion in it, as the verse introductions suggest, but cannot influence it by intervention as Haggard's heroes do.

Nonetheless there is a kind of reciprocity in the interaction between the tales and their Victorian context, as well as with what Gérard Genette terms 'paratexts': other writing by the author or publisher, beyond the main body of the text itself, from titles and epigrams to interviews and related articles.⁴⁸ In the last of a series of five articles on 'The Development of Modern Society' published in *Commonweal* in 1890, Morris makes the connection between past and present explicit by comparing contemporary society to Roman civilization and urging his readers to 'throw off' the fear of death that runs alongside tolerance of capitalist oppression: 'so shall we be our own Goths, and at whatever cost break up again the new tyrannous Empire of Capitalism.'⁴⁹ The Dusky Men also represent aspects of this tyranny, uncivilized though they are, and must be utterly destroyed. Yet the romances rely for their imaginative and persuasive power on one of the pervasive fictions that props up the wars of empire Morris so vehemently opposes: that violence begets peace.⁵⁰ In 'The Hopes of Civilization', Morris writes that 'after all brave men never die for nothing, when they die for principle'.⁵¹ However, the tales do not tell of individual heroes bravely accepting death, but of communities of people fighting to the bitter end: these are not only tales of dying for a cause, but killing for it; not primarily stories of individual sacrifice, but of wars to renew the earth. They are more fully realized and politicized evocations of the righteous communal warfare Morris had so early evoked in his 1856 *Oxford and Cambridge Magazine* tale, 'Gertha's Lovers'.⁵²

The lives of the barbarians Morris imagines in his various socialist writings are shaped by a willingness both to bear and to inflict pain, in marked contrast to the model Victorian gentleman John Henry Newman had evoked in 1852, noting that 'it is almost a definition of a gentleman, to say he is one who never inflicts pain.'⁵³ Morris concurs with a contemporary consensus in suggesting that pain and violence came more naturally to people of past times and caused them less anxiety, but he aligns himself with an emerging late Victorian view of national and individual manliness that works in tension with his anti-imperialist politics in applauding rather than denigrating this capacity for both giving and bearing pain. The ability of the barbarians to endure pain is suggested again and again in the Germanic romances. As the Wolfings battle the Romans, not only are they 'eager to smite', but they do not 'crave peace' if they are wounded, 'for to the Goths it was but a little thing to fall in hot blood in that hour for love of the kindred' (*Wolfings*, 189). This insistence on the ability of ancient or 'primitive' people to endure pain better than civilized moderns is echoed in Victorian historical and imperial romances as well as in the old northernism discussed in the previous chapter.

This idea formed one element of John Stuart Mill's writings earlier in the century on barbarism and civilization. That Morris was familiar with Mill is not only suggested by his deliberate location of his own critique of civilization in the context of a wider public debate, but is also confirmed in his specific avowal that it was Mill's writings on Saint-Simon, Fourier and Owen that persuaded him, against their intent, that socialism was necessary.[54] Contrasting barbarism with civilization, Mill writes:

> The state of perpetual personal conflict, rendered necessary by the circumstances of all former times, [...] necessarily habituated everyone to the spectacle of harshness, rudeness and violence, to the struggle of one indomitable will against another, and to the alternate suffering and infliction of pain.[55]

Mill, like Morris and Bax after him, draws on the language of habit to suggest that violence and pain had a different effect on the barbarians of old than on the people of Victorian Britain: 'these things, consequently, were not as revolting even to the best and most actively benevolent men of former days, as they are to our own. [...] They, however, thought less of the infliction of pain, because they thought less of pain altogether.' Mill suggests that the life of the barbarians fostered heroism and a readiness for suffering absent among 'the whole class of gentlemen in England' over whom 'there has crept [...] a moral effeminacy, an inaptitude for every kind of struggle'.[56] While Mill nonetheless vindicates civilization as superior to barbarism, he does not applaud the gentlemanly refusal to inflict pain, as Newman does. Rather, he sets out the idea, picked up by romance writers at the end of the century, that both bearing and, on occasion, inflicting pain might be markers of manliness and heroism from which civilization would do well to learn.

A more definitely celebratory approach to the violence of barbarism is evident by the end of the century in Andrew Lang's writings about romance as a vehicle for the primitive. As Julia Reid points out, Haggard 'figures repeatedly in [Lang's monthly *Longman's Magazine* column] "At the Sign of the Ship" as a touchstone of romance's primitive, regenerative powers'.[57] Lang's 1887 article, 'Realism and Romance', hails the delight of a 'mixed condition', of being 'civilized at the top with the old barbarian under our clothes'.[58] While the civilized part enjoys realism, he writes, romance appeals to the barbarian. 'Are we to be told that we love the "Odyssey" because the barbaric element has not died out of our blood? [...] Very well. "Public opinion" in Boston may condemn us, but we will get all the fun we can out of the ancestral barbarism of our natures'. Part of that 'fun' is reading adventure stories, and it is clear from Lang's article that adventure stories, by and large, mean war stories: 'the savage within us calls out for more news of the fight with the Apache'.[59] Morris's tales of violence cannot have been read without an awareness of this context and its inevitable effect is to draw his romances into this discourse, however much their intent is to keep it out. He too wants to awaken the 'ancestral barbarism' of his readers, not simply that they might enjoy the tale, but that they might reclaim its heritage. At the same time, through the completeness of their archaic language, they reach back to older romances and epic tales of conflict and dissolution.

The blunt language of battle and the detailed description of acts of war in the tales evoke both Malory's *Morte Darthur* and *Beowulf*, which Morris was to translate in 1895. His use of archaisms here signifies a link not with the past but with the tales of the past. The completeness of the archaic language and its refusal of modernization or development creates a world in which war is interwoven seamlessly with the everyday, material lives of the people. In a linguistic act of connection with *Beowulf* and its tale of the overcoming of an unspeakable evil, *Wolfings*, in particular, makes extensive use of kennings, drawing on the material to convey the life of the people: 'evening-farer' (11); 'cot-carle' (22); 'hall-glee' (202).[60] Morris signals the importance of fighting, and its many associations, by the *Beowulf*-like multiplication of war-related compound nouns and adjectives: 'battle-wrath' (22); 'war-sea' (128); 'steel-spray' (128); 'war-learned' (128); 'sword-hardened' (129); 'war-fit' (129).[61] Like the world of the older epic, this world is defined by the concrete and the corporeal, by events and actions.

At the end of *Roots*, Sun-Beam, lover of the hero Face-of-god, comments, with great satisfaction, that 'there is no better man of his hands than my man' (*Roots*, 409–10), a phrase whose archaic syntax links it directly to the *Morte Darthur*, in which the damsel from the Lady Avilion swears that she may only be delivered of her troublesome sword by a knight, who must be 'a passyng good man of his handes and of his dedes'.[62] In the final battle in *Roots*, Face-of-god 'drave the point of Dale-warden amidst the tangle of weapons through the open mouth of a captain of the felons and slashed a cheek with a backstroke and smote off a blue-eyed snub-nosed head' (*Roots*, 336). In similar style, Malory's King Arthur 'smote syr mordred under the shelde wyth a foyne of hys spere, thorughoute the body more than a fadom.'[63] The matter-of-fact openness about wounding stands in contrast to the pretences that cloak the Victorian 'civilized soldiering' of competitive commerce which has 'an outside look of quiet wonderful order about it' while it wreaks destruction; Morris's language distances his wars from this kind of quiet order and forces on the reader their physical intensity and disorderly fervour.[64]

Nowhere are the similarities between Morris and Haggard so marked as in their descriptions of this kind of passionate, personal fighting. In *King Solomon's Mines*, the battle between 'the great Englishman', Sir Henry, who fights 'like his Beserkir forefathers', and the African leader Twala, over the leadership of rival (and rightful) chief, Ignosi/Umbopa, leads to a decapitation as vividly described as anything in Morris or Malory:

> Once more Twala came on, and as he came our great Englishman gathered himself together, and, swinging the heavy axe round his head, hit at him with all

his force. There was a shriek of excitement from a thousand throats, and behold! Twala's head seemed to spring from his shoulders and then fell and came rolling and bounding along the ground. [...] For a second the corpse stood upright, the blood spouting in fountains from the severed arteries; then with a dull crash it fell to the earth.[65]

Andrew Lang, in his review of *King Solomon's Mines*, writes of this scene that 'the slaying is Homeric'.[66] What could better answer Morris's own prescription? The story itself stands awkwardly between the vision of colonial slaughter Morris condemns in Tibet, and the wild, Gothic brotherhood of barbarism he celebrates in the romances. The barbarism and manliness of Haggard's Kukuanas require the temporary barbarism of the colonialist, with his own Northern barbarian heritage, to bring their battle to completion. The political stance implied in this is very different from Morris's, as is its aim and outcome, but the view of violence it represents bears much resemblance to his own. Hand-to-hand combat is at once the means and the expression of renewal. It is here that Haggard's thought converges with Morris's: both imagine individual and social transformation through a temporary engagement with barbaric violence.

In order for the romances to function as aesthetic antiwars, as creative propaganda against capitalist civilization and its results, they must offer a convincing vision of heroic communal war that leads ultimately to a new way of life. Ideas about the nature of evolution as well as revolution, and the details of Marxist materialist history, are subsumed under this political and aesthetic imperative. It is an imperative that requires warfare to be brutal as well as beautiful, productive as well as expressive. A reviewer of *Roots* in 1889 suggests, in tones that resemble those of Haggard's reviewers, that the warfare constitutes the primary pleasure of the novel. 'But as of fighting in this way or that way and love-making in that way or this, there is no end in any life while that life is worth living, so the extensive faculties of the romance which is, or ought to be, nearly all fighting and love-making are almost infinite.' The reviewer goes on: 'from another point of view, the chief charm of the book may seem to lie in the fighting, which is abundant and of the very best.'[67] What makes the fighting 'of the very best' is not elucidated by the review; but it articulates a view that fighting may be of varying moral, and perhaps fictional, value, which underlies the romances themselves.

The Ugliness of the Enemy

In a *Commonweal* article of May 1885, entitled 'Unattractive Labour', Morris argues that 'everything made by man must be either ugly or beautiful. Neutrality is impossible in man's handiwork.' He goes on to deplore the routine ugliness of the present, suggesting that 'an ordinary house, or piece of furniture or of attire, is not only not beautiful, it is aggressively and actively ugly, and we assume as a matter of course that it must be so.'[68] The assumption that ugliness can be in itself aggressive perhaps offers the internal justification for Morris's extraordinarily vehement response: 'for my part, having regard to the general happiness of the race, I say without shrinking that the bloodiest of violent revolutions would be a light price to pay for the righting of this wrong.'[69] The insertion of 'I say without shrinking' acknowledges the hyperbole of such of a comment, but at the same time invests its underlying premise with at least a degree of defiant seriousness: ugliness, Morris suggests, is an intrinsic part of the capitalist economic system, and as such must be destroyed when capitalism is destroyed.

In the romances the leap is made from the ugliness of things to the ugliness of people as a signifier of intrinsic aggression against all that is beautiful and good and whole in life. In either case, bloody revolution is capable of entirely wiping out what is ugly – a term that carries far more implications than merely unpleasant appearance, in Morris's lexicon – in order to produce beauty of life and of things. Ernst Bloch's somewhat dismissive suggestion that 'capitalism is fought by Morris not so much because of its inhumanity as because of its ugliness' misses the vital connection for Morris between ugliness and disease, inhumanity, or even subhumanness.[70] This elimination of ugliness is not a matter of otherworldly artistic concern but of pressing political ideology: he makes an explicit connection between ugliness and the 'slavery of the many' in poverty and servitude.[71] Yet in making the enemy in *Roots* as ugly and inhuman as the Goths are beautiful and wholly alive, the tales begin to carry an emotional and national charge that is at odds with their ostensible preoccupation with the past, and resonates awkwardly with contemporary racial theories of ugliness and degeneration. That violence is capable of wiping out what is ugly and securing the 'general happiness of the race' is not questioned here. Between revolution to wipe out ugliness and 'commercial war' for the gains of empire, Morris allows no connection. The difference between them lies, in part, in their relationship to beauty and the life of the body.

The wars of the tribes take place in the context of a physical life that suggests a fundamental connection between warfare and the fulfilment of a desire for beauty, love and community. The identity of the people in *Roots*, far more than in *Wolfings*, draws not only on the legendary ferocity of the Goths or the old Norse people but also on the emotional expressiveness of Homeric heroes.[72] Morris's people of the Mark weep, shout, laugh and sing, and they kiss and caress both lovers and friends equally freely. Like Homer's heroes, men as well as women weep frequently and openly. After the final victory song in *Roots*, 'there was many a man wept as the song ended', in sorrow for the dead (*Roots*, 360). In a more personal expression of sorrow, Face-of-god weeps over his broken relationship with the Bride, and when she is injured in battle he 'wept as a child that would not be comforted; nor had he any shame of all those bystanders' (*Roots*, 94; 246). Expressions of emotion are not confined to a private, domestic sphere, but are part of the integrated life of the people. At the same time there is no realistic complexity about these emotions, or investigation of subtlety; rather, the physical stands in for the emotional.

Beauty of life requires the free satisfaction of the desires of the body. In a lecture contemporaneous with the writing of *Roots*, Morris argues that the existence of a 'free and unfettered animal life for man' is essential to the socialist future: 'I demand the utter extinction of all asceticism. If we feel the least degradation in being amorous, or merry, or hungry or sleepy, we are so far bad animals, and therefore miserable men.'[73] His words closely echo those of Marx, who argued that:

> If you live only as an economic being, you must stint the gratification of your immediate senses, as by stinting yourself on food etc: you must also spare yourself all sharing of general interest, all sympathy, all trust etc if you want to be economical, if you do not want to be ruined by illusion.[74]

Marx spells out what is implicit in Morris's statement: that to deny the sensuous needs of the body is also to deny community, imagination, and trust. The stories of the Wolfings and the people who follow them in *Roots*, then, are stories of people whose connection to their animal nature is made explicit through the totemic emblem of the Wolf, and contrasted with those who are either primarily concerned with economy, and therefore disconnected from their animal nature, or deeply enmired in sensual gratification without any regard for community, trust or beauty. A distinction is apparent in Morris's work between the healthy attention to animal needs and instincts, and the degradation of monstrous bestiality: between the occasional unreasoning savageness of the wolf evident in *Sigurd*, and the relentless ravening brutishness of *Beowulf*'s Grendel. People may be animal without being bestial. In ancient society, unlike Victorian Britain, the enmity between those with regard for the connection between body, earth and community and those with none manifests itself in war.

In *Wolfings*, the connection between the story and the present is made evident in the similarities between the Roman and Victorian civilizations, both of which allow luxury without work to some and work without the free satisfaction of animal needs to others. One of the Elking men reports of the Romans, that 'mighty men among them ordain where they shall dwell, and what shall be their meat, and how long they shall labour after they are weary' (*Wolfings*, 45). The Wood-Sun describes the Romans in terms that evoke the inequalities of rapidly urbanizing Victorian Britain:

> For these are the folk of the cities, and in wondrous wise they dwell,
> Mid confusion of heaped houses, dim and black as the face of hell;
> Though therefrom rise roofs most goodly, where their captains and their kings
> Dwell amidst the walls of marble in abundance of fair things.
> (*Wolfings*, 21)

Morris comments on this aspect of Roman civilization in 'The Development of Modern Society', arguing that it is 'founded on the corruption of the society of the tribes by the institution of private property' and characterized by 'worship of the city'.[75] The Dusky Men in *Roots* are not so easily identified with modern civilization, and could be seen to represent, as Waithe suggests, 'the opposite extreme, a communism at once demeaning and hostile to expressions of individuality'.[76] Certainly Morris had no time for such faceless communism, as is clear in his vehement criticism of the mechanical state socialism portrayed in Edward Bellamy's *Looking Backward* (1888).[77] However, this aspect of the Dusky Men's social organization is less threatening than their blatantly imperialist and expansionist theft of land and people, which precipitates the war with the people of Burgdale and Silverdale. They begin their terrorization of the people of Silverdale by demanding a tribute and 'houses to dwell in and lands to live by' (*Roots*, 194). Their society, even more explicitly than the Romans', is built on theft, so that by degrees they steal all the people's land and possessions, and finally enthrall the people themselves. While there may be hints of the dangers of ugly uniform communism, the context of war and the insistence on utter annihilation of the enemy suggest comparisons with a far more urgent and immanent threat, for Morris and his socialist contemporaries: nineteenth-century colonialism.

This is not a wholly satisfactory parallel, however. The Dusky Men whose colonizing desire to amass the land and goods of other tribes and take their people captive bear a striking resemblance, at the same time, to the fearful 'savage horde' of 'dusky' colonial subjects the empire is designed to subdue. Boos notes Morris's debt to Gibbon's portrayal of the Huns and their well-documented atrocities, and observes that his insistence on the dark skin and small stature of the Dusky Men is surprisingly consistent with long-held European prejudices that Morris is usually at pains to reject.[78] Yet the tale relies heavily on mobilizing the worst of those prejudices: this is not a story of a battle of equals, or even of the battle of a heroic people against an evil but at least partially worthy enemy, as is *Wolfings*. In *Roots*, only if the Dusky

Men are demonstrably, unalterably and therefore physically inferior to the fair, beautiful people of the Dale, can their complete annihilation be justified. Morris's earlier investment in the idea of a 'dominant' Northern race from whom the English are descended, with its necessary correlative of inferior races, surfaces in the accounts of the people of the Dale and their enemies.[79] Before turning to the descriptions of the Dusky Men and their behaviour, a brief contextual consideration of their name and characteristics suggests that, unpalatable as it may be, Morris also undoubtedly, if not straightforwardly, draws on contemporary colonialist uses of language. Not only is the word 'dusky' routinely used at this time in newspaper articles, magazines, poems and novels to describe the people of Africa, India, Afghanistan or other parts of the empire, but it is used specifically in contexts that conjure frightening, undifferentiated masses of dark people.[80]

Most strikingly it is used to describe the enemy in accounts of the Anglo–Zulu War of 1879, frequently coupled with the idea of 'hordes' and images of swarming animals. Emily Pfeiffer's 1879 poem, 'The Fight at Rorke's Drift', describes the Zulus as a 'dusky host', 'dusky ranks' and a 'swarthy wave'.[81] The *Times* describes the Zulus as the 'dusky enemy', and gives an account of them 'swarming over the ridge like bees'; the *Daily News* describes 'hordes' of Zulu 'savages'.[82] While accounts of battle like those of the *Times* or *Daily News* register admiration for the Zulus' soldiering skills, as well as horror at their 'savageness', popular retellings of the resounding defeat of the British at Isandlwana focus on the enemy's colour, numbers and bestiality. 'T'sandula', a patriotic poem by Harding Lawrence, printed in *Chambers's Journal*, closely prefigures Morris's language with its evocation of 'legions' of 'dusky foes':

> Now, with swift suddenness, from right, from left,
> From o'er the hills, from ev'ry rocky cleft –
> In countless hordes – the dusky warriors swarm.[83]

This enemy is animal-like too, in its attack: 'stealthy as a tiger from his lair – and just as pitiless'; the 'gallant British' mow them down but as each row falls, others step over them, 'and still they come, like locusts o'er the plain'.[84] In startlingly similar language, the Sun-Beam warns Face-of-god that the Dusky Men are increasing 'in numbers and insolence' and soon they 'will gather in numbers that we may not meet and then will they swarm into the Dale' (*Roots*, 126–7). Her brother, Folk-Might, adds that the Dusky Men might easily 'overrun you unless ye deal with them betimes'; for 'they are like the winter wolves that swarm on and on, how many soever ye slay' (*Roots*, 130). There can be little doubt that these descriptions would have raised the ghosts of Isandlwana in the minds of his readers.[85] He mobilizes racial fear of the colonial subject in this tale to suggest the rapacity, ferocity and potential for evil of the enemy of the people. If in doing so he makes a complicated and powerful connection between the actions of the British Empire and the potential violence of the subjects of the empire, he nonetheless uses prejudice and fear of the dark-skinned Other to do so.

The war that occurs in *Roots* is one that is thrust upon the people of the Dale, and it is their response to it that is Morris's primary focus in the tale. A reading of the Dusky Men as a direct reversal of the common use of the image might suggest that the horror Morris's readers feel for the dusky hordes ought properly to be felt for the imperial expansionism and inherent cruelty of British commerce and government. Yet the identification of the Dusky Men with expansionism is not quite enough to align them unequivocally with the new imperialists, as they bear no traces of civilization, but are wholly savage and monstrously Other. Rather, they seem to be a useful and easily identifiable enemy, unimportant in themselves except as representatives of all that is evil, against which the people of the Dale must fight. They are, to some extent, simply a foil for the people of the Dale and a justification for their battles: more Old English monster than Victorian imperial subject. The killing of the Dusky Men then becomes the equivalent of the killing of Grendel – mythic, necessary violence against subhuman monsters.

Nonetheless the contradictory contemporary resonances remain. Like H. G. Wells in the next decade, Morris draws on contemporary discourse about the dangers of decadence as well as degeneracy. The pale-skinned, free people of Silverdale are enthralled by the Dusky Men because of their own enfeeblement and luxurious living. The escaped slave, Dallach, explains: 'we were a happy folk there; but soft and delicate: for the Dale is exceeding fertile, and beareth wealth in abundance, both corn and oil and wine and fruit, and of beasts for man's service the best that may be' (*Roots*, 194). They became so accustomed to wealth and ease that when the Dusky Men first demanded tribute, 'then had we weapons in our hands, but had not hearts to use them' (*Roots*, 194). Salmon notes the resonances here with social Darwinism and rightly observes that Morris believed that 'the health of a society could be gauged by the appearance of its people.'[86] More than this, Morris makes a connection here between work, leisure and physical condition, and specifically between physical struggle and communal health. It is the people of Silverdale's detachment from physical work and consequent unwillingness or inability to fight that has led directly to their enslavement, as the lack of battle and struggle leads to the emasculation and infantilism of Wells's future people, the Eloi. Simon James suggests the Eloi are descended from 'the inhabitants of William Morris's Nowhere without the need to work'; but they surely bear far greater resemblance to the people of Silverdale who, unlike the Nowhereans – whose beauty is closely associated with their creative, satisfying work – do not work.[87]

Although Morris had little time for Herbert Spencer's political philosophy and commitment to individualism, his picture of the people of Silverdale nonetheless resonates with Spencer's evolutionary claim with regard to the uses of human faculties: 'Take away the demand for exertion, and you will ensure inactivity. Induce inactivity, and you will soon have degradation.'[88] Such is the fate of the people of Silverdale. Morris is as concerned with the dangers of luxury and ease as he is with the horrors of faceless mechanical lack of individuality. Both dangers are met and vanquished by the war his tale evokes.

The exceptional cruelty and willingness to inflict horrible pain on their slaves evinced by the Dusky Men and the Romans goes beyond the simple barbarian willingness to give and receive pain described by Morris and Bax or by Mill, and instead resonates with the racially stratified corporeal consciousness suggested by social evolutionary race theory. Spencer's influential critique of Bain's 1859 psychophysiological study, *The Emotions and the Will*, argues that 'the lowest savages have not even the ideas of justice or mercy: they have neither words for them nor can they be made to conceive them'; Darwin suggests that 'most savages are utterly indifferent to the sufferings of strangers […] humanity is an unknown virtue'. He adds that 'the greatest intemperance is not reproach with savages. Utter licentiousness, and unnatural crimes, prevail to an astounding extent.'[89] The Dusky Men are not Morrisian barbarians, but fictionalized savages, historically at an earlier stage of development, but they are savages with colonizing aims: the worst of old and new evil combined. The tightly repetitive and evocative vocabulary used to describe them affirms their status as an unindividuated mass of bestial evil. Their destruction is justified by their misuse of beauty, physicality and desire.

In an extension of their irresponsible seeking of the sensual, the 'foul' and 'filthy' Dusky Men trample down all that is beautiful, like 'hogs in a garden of lilies' (*Roots*, 355, 363). They are not only ugly and cruel, but unable to create or appreciate beauty:

> Whatsoever is fair there have they defiled and deflowered, and they wallow in our fair halls as swine strayed from the dunghill. No delight in life, no sweet days do they have for themselves, and they begrudge the delight of others therein. (*Roots*, 135)

There is a literary tradition here: like the monstrous and 'foul' Grendel, or his 'poisonous' mother, they are aliens who defile what is lovely, which is also what is precious to the people.[90] Their complete annihilation is justified within the text by their bestiality and disregard for both life and beauty, as well as by the threat posed by their expansionism. Even the Romans, a more complex enemy, show a similar monstrous insatiability:

> Our tree would they spoil with destruction if its fruit they may never possess,
> For their lust is without a limit, and nought may satiate
> Their ravening maw. (*Wolfings*, 60)

Again, these words bear traces of the descriptions of Grendel, who comes upon a warrior 'a-sleeping', and 'unaware slit him'. Lust without limit is evident in the way the monster 'bit his bone-coffer, drank blood a-streaming, / Great gobbets swallow'd in'.[91] The satisfaction of the needs of the body is here divorced from community or thought or appreciation of natural beauty. It is greedy, selfish and opportunistic – qualities Morris repeatedly associates with capitalists – but also physically uncontrolled, arising from voracious appetites, qualities evident in current discourse about degeneration.

Fears of the bestial and justification of absolute war are further evident in the anxiety the tale evinces about miscegenation. The child of a forced union between a Dusky Carle and his Dale-born thrall has no redeeming features, but either resembles the Dusky Men altogether, rather than the slave, or turns out to be 'witless, a fool natural', as Salmon notes.[92] The Dusky Men keep the children of male slaves, or kill them, as they choose, 'as they would with whelps or calves' (*Roots*, 136). Attempts at interbreeding with this brutish, undeveloped people lead only to disaster, further evidence that they are neither fully human nor able to feel as humans do. They are brutes, 'long-armed like apes' (*Roots*, 339), yet incapable of even instinctive love for their children. Their physical ugliness reflects their characters. They are 'as venomous as adders, as fierce as bears and as foul as swine'; the people of the Dale and the Wolf must 'destroy them as lads a hornet's nest' (*Roots*, 152). This destruction must be complete and without compunction.

There is no evidence here of pacifism and not much of the more attenuated pacificism, to borrow Martin Ceadel's term, that crops up in some of Morris's explicitly political writings.[93] Morris departs significantly from the traditional stance of the Peace Society, set out by Richard Cobden, that war itself brutalizes and bestializes people; rather the destructive, bestial inhumanity is inherent in the enemy.[94] Morris made common cause from time to time with the Peace Society and spoke on occasion at meetings they organized, but he referred to them with a slightly scornful weariness, in public and private writings, as not prepared to go far enough in their aims.[95] His views converged with theirs in anti-imperialism, but his primary goal was the accomplishment of socialism and he disagreed with many in the Peace Society on the lines of connection between commerce, peace and war. There is no suggestion in Morris's work that war itself damages the identity or humanity of the kindred; rather it ennobles them. The bestiality of the Dusky Men is innate and therefore not susceptible of amelioration. Further, in language that not only harks back to *Beowulf*, but also recalls the more recent imagery of the 'Marseillaise' and anomalously anticipates the vocabulary of twentieth-century fascism and ethnic cleansing, they are described as 'devils', 'pests of the earth', to be cleansed, just as the hall is cleansed of their filth after the war (*Roots*, 190, 363). They pollute the land, and the act of war against them not only frees the people, but renews the land on which they depend: 'the land, when it was cured, was sweet and good' (*Roots*, 394). Yet this desperate battle of annihilation leaves the people of the Dale strangely untouched by bloodlust or damaged by their own acts of killing.

Roots, to a greater extent than *Wolfings*, relies for its narrative integrity on the absolute conflict of an entirely ugly enemy and a heroic people whose very heroism is predicated on their essential beauty of body, environment and action. The romances, informed by political ideology as well as Morris's artistic ideal of telling 'a tale of the world's history', in a time of 'cramped and ignoble' civilization, offer barbarian warfare as a model for restoring the beauty of life.[96] Yet Morris's commitment to the ideal of beauty is not enough to ensure the distance between his romances and more malign notions of the cleansing possibilities of violence, possibilities further suggested by his evocation of battle as work.

War, Work and the 'Hard Hand-Play'

A Canadian second lieutenant, F. R. Darrow, wrote of bayoneting Prussians in the First World War that it was 'beautiful work'. H. Hesketh Pritchard wrote of sniping that it was 'a labour of love.'[97] The image of work both these soldiers draw upon is neither of efficiency nor drudgery: rather, it suggests a loving and well-executed craft, a personal and committed act of workmanship. It reaches back to the concept of useful, manly work so passionately developed by Morris: work in which the workers find both hope and pleasure, in 'the exercise of their energies' as well as 'the hope of pleasure in [...] daily creative skill' and 'the hope of pleasure in rest'.[98] Work occurs over and over again in the romances to describe individual acts of combat and the wider battle of which they are part; more specifically, particular battles or moments of battle are described using compound words with 'play' in the manner of Anglo-Saxon epic. Playful work like this suggests the seamless interaction of battle with the land and with everyday life, as well its pleasurable productiveness and inherent beauty; the tales rely on the impossible paradox that not only can hope and beauty arise out of death and destruction, they may even be present in it. Acts of battle, and even the complete destruction of a people, are rendered beautiful in themselves and productive of fellowship and harmony. Morris's commitment to the idea of work and play complicates the ethics of battle in the tales and shapes their celebration of violence. Despite his fundamental opposition to Victorian warfare, his tales of communal courage take their place in a history of the fictionalization of heroic martial violence. The continuities of his language with that of ancient epic subtly distinguish it from the aristocratic idea of glamorous, individual battle leadership that runs through contemporary imperial poetry and fiction. Nonetheless he develops a particular conception of war as skilled and enjoyable work carried out honourably and lovingly in the interests of land and community that would carry through into the First World War and beyond.

Ruth Livesey argues for a gendered understanding of work among the socialist writers of the fin de siècle: 'Morris and other socialist writers attempted to resist the effeminate aesthetic of consumption associated with the aesthetes and reintegrate the material and corporeal into a productive aesthetic ideal'.[99] It is not only the aesthetic of consumption that Morris resists, but the capitalist civilization that nurtures that aesthetic and is the antithesis of 'free and manly' society.[100] In doing so in the romances, however, he co-opts the acts of killing, wounding and maiming that constitute war into his own 'productive aesthetic ideal'. By focusing on the physical, Morris transforms war into work or even play, making battle itself pleasurable, an imaginative act only possible where the enemy represents absolute, nonhuman evil. Goode argues that *Roots*, in particular, enacts 'the discovery of the potential for transformation of vision into collective action'.[101] Yet it cannot be ignored that collective action, here, means complete annihilation of an enemy, and an investment in the communal act of war. In the fantasy worlds of the romances, political complexities are overridden by corporeal problems that can be solved by committed corporeal work.

Work and play go together in these texts; they are not opposites, like leisure and work in nineteenth-century common usage. Rather, both are continuous aspects of the same thing: the application of physical labour and the use of skill for the accomplishment of an end, whose biproduct is physical pleasure.[102] War is as natural to the people of the romances as any kind of work. In answer to the war leader Thiodolf's question in *Wolfings*, 'What do ye sons of the War-shield? what tale is there to tell? / Is the Kindred fallen tangled in the grasp of the fallow Hell?', the warrior Geirbald replies:

Still cold with dew in the morning the Shielding Roof-ridge stands,
Nor yet hath grey Hell bounden the Shielding warriors' hands
But lo, the swords, O War-duke, how thick in the wind they shake,

Because we bear the message that the battle road you take.
(*Wolfings*, 124)

Life means the ability still to grasp a sword, while the implication of 'thick in the wind they shake' seems to be that while it is hands that hold the swords, they are as natural as trees or crops, shaken not by human volition, but by the wind. Language relates to the material. It is, in this sense, what Marx termed 'the language of real life', that is, language arising from material realities and the necessity of relationships between people and the world rather than from abstract ideas.[103] Even names and titles reflect a relationship to the natural and physical world: in *Wolfings*, the people's prophet is the Hall-Sun, their leader is Thiodolf, meaning Folkwolf, and his sword is named 'Throng-plough', while the warrior Geirmund has an axe named 'War-babe'. In *Roots*, the maiden Bow-may is a skilled archer and markswoman, the hero, Face-of-god, belongs to the people of the Face, his betrothed is the Bride, and his new lover at first is only known as 'the Friend'.

The seamlessness of people, language and the material world is evident in the manner in which the people fight. It is brutally specific, and, in *Wolfings*, technically detailed. The formation of the Roman army is described at some length at several different points in the narrative, as is the 'wedge-array' of the Goths. Early on in one of the battles, when 'fierce was the fight about the wedge-array', this arrangement of the warriors enables them to hold their own:

> The men of Otter [...] stormed on so fiercely that they cleft their way through all and joined themselves to their kindred, and the battle was renewed in the Wolfing meadow. But the Romans had this gain, that Thiodolf's men had let go their occasion for falling on the Romans with their line spread out so that every man might use his weapons; yet were the Goths strong both in valiancy and in numbers, nor might the Romans break into their array.
> (*Wolfings*, 148)

Careful attention is paid to the physical arrangement of the warriors. Later in the battle, the Goths crowd in on their enemies so closely that 'scarce could any man raise his hand for a stroke.' They hem in the homegrown enemy 'Roman-Goths', with the Roman army behind them, 'whose ranks were closely serried, shield nigh touching shield, and their faces turned toward the foe; and so arrayed, though they might die, they scarce knew how to flee' (*Wolfings*, 180). While the orderliness of the Roman army was a matter admiringly commented on by historians such as Edward Gibbon, Morris makes it into a weakness in comparison with the less regimented, more organic movements of the Goths.[104] The detailed description of the array of both armies suggests different modes of work; the Romans work by rote, using one technique and using it well, whereas the Goths learn from experience and modify their technique accordingly.

Roots, in which the fictional enemy is not ordered like the Romans, but bloodthirsty and unpredictable, is less concerned with accurate descriptions of battle formation but nonetheless offers minute, realistic engagement with war as work in its descriptions of battle and preparation for battle. The weapons of war are handmade works of art in this tale, to be admired as well as used; each one is named and personal to its user, an 'expression of his joy in labour', as Morris elsewhere describes art.[105] A whole chapter of *Roots* is devoted to describing the weapons the different gentes bear and the clothes they wear for war: there is a pre-battle 'weapon-show', in which 'many wore gay surcoats over their armour, and the women were clad in all their bravery, and the Houses mostly of a suit' (*Roots*, 224). These accoutrements of battle go well beyond the functional into the decorative, so that combat appears to be part ritual, part game, part work.

The war work of these barbarian people is equated neither with terror and horror, nor with extravagant heroic feats such as the protagonists of *Sigurd* perform, but with the quotidian satisfaction of labour. More than that, both preparation for combat and combat itself is described in terms of somatic pleasure. In *Wolfings*, an old warrior rides along with the young men, and the description of his experience of the ride into battle is one of beauty, harmony and heightened senses:

> But while they were all jingling and clashing on together, the dust arising from the sun-dried turf, the earth shaking with the thunder of the horse-hoofs, then the heart of the long-hoary one stirred within him as he bethought him of the days of his youth, and to his old nostrils came the smell of the horse and the savour of the sweat of warriors riding close together knee to knee adown the meadow. (*Wolfings*, 127–8)

The work of war, then, awakens and delights the senses. Morris draws attention here to one of the most troubling aspects of war. Thirty-five years later, in her searing critique of the intervening First World War, Vera Brittain was to write: 'it is, I think, this glamour, this magic, this incomparable keying up of the spirit in a time of mortal conflict, which constitutes the pacifist's real problem – a problem still incompletely imagined, and still quite unsolved.' The imagination of war in Morris's romances may highlight the evils of greedy, selfish, mechanistic societies, but it does nothing to diminish the 'magic' of war itself. Brittain continues: 'the causes of war are always falsely represented; its honour is dishonest and its glory meretricious' – a comment foreshadowed over and over again by Morris in his public and private judgements on the wars of empire. However, he seems not to have been able to escape the allure of battle itself that Brittain goes on to set against the evils of its false causes: 'the challenge to spiritual endurance, the intense sharpening of all the senses, the vitalising consciousness of common peril for a common end.'[106] It goes beyond the reflective or the conscious and touches the senses, creating emotional bonds between warriors old and young.

In battle itself, the sensory awakening of the Wolfings gives way to an unrestrained intensity of experience and expression. The men were 'merry with the restless joy of battle'; Thiodolf 'led forth joyously' into the attack and 'terrible rang the long refrained gathered shout of his battle as his folk rushed on together devouring the little space between their ambush and the hazel-beset green-sward' (*Wolfings*, 180). The headlong rush of the sentence carries the energy of the moment. The realism of this portrayal of the feeling of combat, if not its outcomes, is borne out by later testimony. Bourke records the accounts of servicemen in the twentieth century feeling, in their own words, 'joy unspeakable' or 'exultant satisfaction' in the act of killing in war. One soldier, Henry de Man, saw his mortar bomb blow up the enemy camp, and watched the body parts fly. He writes that he yelled aloud 'with delight' and 'could have wept with joy' in this 'ecstatic minute'.[107] While Morris would not recognize the distanced action of a mortar bomb as akin to the hand-to-hand war of his ancient Goths, the feelings he ascribes to his committed warriors closely mirror these later descriptions of mortal combat. 'The glamour may be the mere delirium of fever,' Brittain writes, 'which as soon as war is over dies out and shows itself for the will-o'-the-wisp that it is, but while it lasts no emotion known to man seems as yet to have quite the compelling power of this enlarged vitality.'[108] This 'enlarged vitality' in battle is precisely what Morris's romances portray and celebrate, drawing readers' attention to the intense, sensuous physicality of the people and their harmony, expressed in sound and action. The close of each romance at or just after the ending of the war allows for no dying out of the glamour. *Roots* offers an afterword of a kind, but it entails no disillusion with the purpose or conduct of war.

Rather, the romances focus intensely on the preparation for battle and the moments of battle themselves. Battle is effortful, energetic and productive work: 'in the acre of battle the work is to win' (*Wolfings*, 129). What it means to win is made evident in the following lines, which draw an analogy between labour and harvest, with all the implications of productivity that carries. Thiodolf calls out to his men:

> Let us live by the labour, sheaf-smiting therein;
> And as oft o'er the sickle we sang in time past
> […]

> So sing o'er the sword, and the sword-hardened hand
> Bearing down to the reaping the wrath of the land.
> (*Wolfings*, 129)

War is not compared to, nor contrasted with harvest, but is itself a kind of harvest; after the battle is over, the fatally wounded Thiodolf frees the men the Romans have held captive, and asks one of them for a drink of water, 'for this morning men have forgotten the mead of the reapers!', he says (*Wolfings*, 192). Morris takes the ancient trope of war as a field of harvest, and makes of it a scene of satisfying physical work. Like the war of the Greeks and Trojans in the *Aeneid*, this is a 'harvest-tide that bristles with the sword'.[109] Yet he underplays the horror of this association: the reaping is not grim but joyful and determined; the hand, 'sword-hardened', is well prepared for its work. There is nothing here of 'battle's fruitless harvest', conjured by Siegfried Sassoon, nor of the 'half-hushed sobbing' John McCrae would associate with the harvest of war.[110]

This association with harvest insists instead on the corporeal and environmental imperatives of war: its effects are located in the body, as are its causes. There is a refusal to look beyond the immediate context of war that removes it from the realm of the moral. Here the recurring images of harvest, like the frequent images of war as a storm, suggest that it is carried out in harmony with nature, restoring balance not only to human lives but to the earth itself, described in *Roots* as 'our Mother, the cherishing Dale'.[111] The prophetic Hall-Sun, in *Wolfings*, suggests that the harvest of war is a natural part of a cycle of destruction and rebirth:

> The deeds that make the summer make too the winter's death
> That summer-tides unceasing from out the grave may grow
> And the spring rise up unblemished from the bosom of the snow.
> (*Wolfings*, 87)

Rather than disrupting the fruitful abundance signified by harvest, or contrasting with the peaceful harvest of crops, war is figured as the necessary instrument of change and regeneration.[112] Ancient Nordic ideas of regenerative battle, Marxist dialectics and Morris's own growing willingness to entertain the idea of purposeful violence converge in a redemptive, historicized version of fin-de-siècle apocalypse. Ultimately the tales depend upon the problematic idea, echoed by heroes and enemies alike, that the result of war is both death and peace. Agni cries that 'midst the toil and the turmoil shall we sow seeds of peace' (*Wolfings*, 71). The earth itself is implicated in the battle, and the people work with the earth to sow at the same time as reaping: the harvest of death is justified by the crop of peace.

As such, it requires wholehearted work for an intense period of time. Thiodolf calls to his men in Wolfings, 'not to weary in their work, but to fulfil all the hours of their day' (*Wolfings*, 56). If this is a call to action, it also bears the signs of Morris's political determination not to allow 'palliative measures'.[113] Thiodolf goes on to urge his men:

> Let us rest tomorrow, fellows, since to-day we have fought amain!
> Let not these men we have smitten come aback on our hands again,
> And say, ye Wolfing warriors, ye have done your work but ill,
> Fall to now and do it again, like the craftsman who learneth his skill.
> (*Wolfings*, 56)

There is a rather chilling note in this hearty call to war. While the reference to the 'craftsman' may carry hints of the obsolete usage of *craft*, meaning strength or power, its obvious meaning is clearly a more contemporary one. The act of killing here is skilful, creative manual work, and to be done well, it must be done thoroughly. There is no horror of death or violence here, no acknowledgement of the shock of severing and wounding the flesh of another person. It is merely the accomplishment of an end, and will yield the satisfaction of a job well done. There is a mythical association: Athene, the goddess of war, is also the goddess of craft work. Yet it is an idea with the potential for a less benign interpretation, an idea that lurks behind the methodical work of the Nazi death camps, or the enthusiastic thoroughness of the Hutu *génocidaires* in Rwanda.[114] Given Morris's extensive theorizing of work as an expression of both personhood and environment, this idea of war normalizes and indeed celebrates killing. Similarly, in *Roots*, Dale-warden says, 'never have men gone forth more joyously to a merry-making than all men of us shall wend to this war' (*Roots*, 249). Combat is as pleasurable as a holiday. This image reveals a commitment to warfare as part of Morris's own imaginative landscape that ties into – and perhaps goes beyond – an underlying narrative of the very society his tales so insistently ignore: a binary tale in which good triumphs by force over evil.[115] The pleasure of this battle derives from the justice of its cause as well as from the skill and communal work it entails.

The tale and its people are seamless; there is no expectation of dissent and so no moral nuance in these depictions of war. In *Wolfings*, Thiodolf's magic hauberk that prevents him from fighting serves to illustrate his struggle between personal desire and community, but it does not call into question the necessity for war. In *Roots*, Folk-might's pronouncement on the need for war against the Dusky Men bears echoes of Tennyson's 'Charge of the Light Brigade': 'now at last is come the time either to do or to die' (*Roots*, 136).[116] Doing and dying are not necessarily the same thing for the people of the Dale, as they are for Tennyson's soldiers. This is not a call to the 'self-abnegation' or 'duty' that Christopher Ricks observes in Tennyson's formulation, 'to do and die'.[117] As the use of 'either' and 'or' along with the infinitive form of both verbs in *Roots* suggests, they are alternatives here rather than equivalents: doing is not simply fighting, which might lead to death, but killing. The aim of Folk-might's people is not primarily to die or even to fight as valiantly as they can, but to kill, to 'slay them everyone' (*Roots*, 248). It is an act of cleansing rather than one of self-sacrifice. Yet while Tennyson's poem raises the possibility that men might want to 'reason why', in its declaration of their duty not to do so, Morris allows no such questioning: there are no dissident voices in the tale's call to war, which is, in the trajectory of the narrative, a clear physical imperative to save the land from the Dusky Men.

However, this is not man as machine, an image conjured by Clausewitz to describe the army and by Cobden in relation to contemporary war.[118] The people of the tales are not obedient or under command, not alienated from the work of war, but mutually responsible, the tales suggest, because the war is their own. It is figured as the responsible handiwork of a tribe of equals for the sake of their land and people. In *Roots*, the people of the Dale welcome the chance to do or to die as a long-awaited event: 'now at last is come the time'. When the call to war comes in *Wolfings*, it is for 'all men, both thralls and free, / 'Twixt twenty winters and sixty' (*Wolfings*, 13). This is a communal act for which they are well prepared. More than that, in an organic image that stands in opposition to the idea of a machine, they have themselves become war. 'Now no longer can it be said that we are going to war, but rather that war is on our borders, and we are blended with it' (*Roots*, 227). Like Morris's ideal of work and play, war and the people are one and the same.

The idea of 'play' is perhaps most tellingly used later in the century by Henry Newbolt in his popular, imperialist 1897 poem, 'Vitaï Lampada', with its much-quoted refrain: 'Play up! play up! and play the game!'.[119] This draws into a compelling formula the ideas of sportsmanship and gentlemanliness that ran through much later nineteenth-century discourse on war in upper-class writings. It captures in tone, as Robert H. MacDonald notes, 'the ethic of the playing field' which 'dictated that what mattered was not winning, but rather playing chivalrously and with spirit; rendered in terms of war this meant fighting with "dash"'.[120] Newbolt's poem uses the metaphor of the gentlemanly or public school game of cricket to reformulate the violence and physical suffering of war. It has the tone of a commanding officer buoying up his men and relies on images of cultural superiority and well-known rules to minimize the blood and gore of actual warfare. It suggests both contest and limits, as well as the fairness – or fair play – implicit in the idea of the game.

Yet this idea of war is a temporary state of affairs, in which people take roles and know where the boundary lines lie. Morris's 'play', 'handplay' and 'hard hand-play', by contrast, are not limited or separated from the life of the people. This is not 'playing the game' but 'play'; it draws on the idea of fair play only to convert it into something much more visceral. Instead of the airy 'insouciance' MacDonald highlights in the upper class idea of play in relation to war, the linguistic archaism of the text evokes the primal contests of ancient warrior epic, offering a particularly seamless connection between life and language.[121] The generic term 'handplay' occurs eight times in *Wolfings* and five in *Roots*. It resonates with older works of battle and heroism, closely echoing 'the play of the battle', 'battle-play', and 'edge-play', which crop up in Morris's own translation of *Beowulf*, as well as suggesting the many kennings associated with hands and war in *Beowulf*, to whom these Wolfing, or Wulfing people are related: 'hand-grip', 'hand-spur', 'battle-hand', 'hand-bane', 'hand-fellows'.[122] 'Handplay' occurs in the Anglo-Saxon epic, *Brunanburh* – published in verse translation by Tennyson in 1880 – in a stock phrase that Morris directly borrows for his 'hard hand-play' (*Wolfings*, 196; *Roots*, 344, 383): 'heardes hand-plegan'.[123] There is nothing chivalric or elegant about this kind of battle. Nor does it have the distance implied in much writing about imperialist wars on foreign soil. Rather it is seamlessly connected with everyday life. When the Wolfing warriors go off to war at the beginning of the tale those left behind 'fell to doing whatso of work or play came to their hands' (*Wolfings*, 31). There are neither rules nor boundaries in this everyday work and play, which is intimately related to its environment.

Nonetheless the substitution of 'play' for battle is not an uncomplicated one. Morris's 'play' also carries connotations of pleasure and creativity. The image of a people for whom slaughtering the enemy is as free of negative consequences as creative play is disturbing. After the war with the Dusky Men, the kindreds sing together:

Fell many a man
'Neath the edges wan,
In the heat of the play
That fashioned the day.
(*Roots*, 360)

Combat as play shapes events here, in much the same way as a writer fashions a poem or story, or as a craft worker creates an article of use or beauty by hand. The sinister simplicity of the acts evoked is emphasized by the short monosyllabic lines with their emphatic rhyming couplets, while the horror of death is disguised by word substitutions: 'fell' instead of 'died'; 'edges' instead of 'swords'; 'play' instead of 'battle'. There is none of the competitiveness or finite duration of 'the game' here. Instead, the organicism of the people's battle means that the distinctions between the work of war and the work of peace are eroded. War and peace themselves are not simply conflated, however. Rather, the work and play of the people cross seamlessly between the domestic and the martial, so that war seeps into all areas of life, just as the domestic carries over into war. These are wars that affect the very life of all the people, not the far-off battles of Morris's time, fought on behalf of the empire by the beleaguered working-class soldiers Kipling represents.[124] Women as well as men participate in the fighting, although not to the same extent. In the final confrontation between the people of the Dale and the Dusky Men, Bow-may carries out her chosen work as a markswoman as though it were any other handicraft: 'even as she was speaking, she had notched and loosed another shaft, speaking as folk do who turn from busy work at loom and bench' (*Roots*, 334). Bow-may's natural affinity for her work challenges the domestic ideal of womanhood and at the same time removes the possibility of a safe sphere, without war.

The idea of war has long worked on the basis of gendered oppositions in which the female domestic sphere of the home serves as an alternative to the male, active sphere of war. However problematic this equation, it means that war is not all there is: it is a temporary state, and the domestic and feminine is an alternative to it. This is not to say that women have always opposed war, or remained separate from it. While Virginia Woolf could argue in 1938 that 'scarcely a human being in history has fallen to a woman's rifle', women have been assigned, or have taken on, other crucial roles in the story of warfare, from the mythical Helen of Troy to the flesh and blood Nazi women who supported, inspired and encouraged Hitler's armies, or indeed the women who fought in the two World Wars.[125] Nonetheless the sense of an alternative female or domestic sphere has made war an abnormal state. In the world of the romances, war is normalized; all the people and every aspect of their lives are 'blended' with it, and while war lasts there is no alternative, no other possibility. Like work and play, it is the responsibility and the burden of all the people.

§

The seamless holism that Morris posits as so desirable in relation to work and play takes on a more malign character in relation to war. The equation of war with everyday work and play raises difficult questions about the nature of killing and its effects. Morris allows Thiodolf's death in battle, in *Wolfings*, to be fittingly heroic. *Roots* ends with all its central characters alive and whole, peaceful and happy. War has taken no more toll than the temporary tiredness or minor injuries that might come after a long day's work. Killing, the romances suggest, is simply an extension of communal life, and the extermination of the enemy requires a refusal of their personhood. Ugliness becomes a dangerously unstable concept in the stories; while they carry the romance tradition of external features reflecting internal characteristics, the context of their writing and publication renders this simple equation more politically complex.

How, then, do these stories function as antiwars? Their language, style and presentation of organic, communal battle sets them in imaginative opposition to nineteenth-century wars of empire; to that degree they are not only antiwars, but vehemently antiwar. Yet their commitment to a notion of absolute war, and war that is able to herald historical change, personal transformation, and the promise of a purer future sets them up as myths of racial cleansing that look forward to far less benign evocations and incarnations of the Jamesian 'romance of history'. They celebrate heroism, courage, and commitment to community, but in order to so convincingly they must present a mythically dehumanized enemy and elevate killing to a necessary and even pleasurable job of work. They are, of course, romances: beautiful lies whose interaction with the politics and ideologies of Victorian England is complicated by the implications of their genre.[126] Beautiful, timeless and fantastical though they are, however, they do not entirely escape complicity in what Tim O'Brien describes as 'a very old and very terrible lie', which is the possibility of virtuous and redemptive warfare. [127]

Chapter Five

'ALL FOR THE CAUSE': FELLOWSHIP, SACRIFICE AND FRUITFUL WAR

In 1885, Morris wrote an editorial response in *Commonweal* to some comments made by 'a friend', who had written in, 'deprecating a forcible revolution; it would be better, he says, to obtain justice without violence, lest we should have violence without justice.' Morris does not wholly accept this view:

> True; yet surely, whatever may be in the future, we have not far to seek to find violence without justice in the present. Do men *choose* a miserable life, or are they *forced* into it? No one wants violence if a decent life for everyone can be obtained without it. But it is to be feared that the natural sequence of enforced misery will be violent revolution. We ask our friend, is that the fault of the wretched, or of the system which has made them wretched?[1]

Morris makes an important distinction here, between the hidden, coercive violence of 'the system' and the reactive violence of revolution. 'The system' that has made the poor miserable exercises what Pierre Bourdieu describes as 'symbolic violence', which is concerned with the social outcomes of coercive ideology, and results in both class inequality and physical suffering.[2] Morris is willing to countenance violent revolution if necessary as both an inevitable result of and a necessary end to the misery and symbolic violence that he elsewhere attributes to 'modern civilization'. This is a willingness borne out repeatedly in letters of the 1880s and 1890s, as well as in his fiction, poetry and political writing of this period.

Florence Boos suggests that Morris's views 'gradually converged towards pacifism as he gained in wariness and political sophistication' in his later years, while acknowledging that his creative writing continued to evince a commitment to the beauty and power of warfare. She suggests that after the Germanic romances the violence of the imaginative works is subsumed into Morris's wider political vision of peace. This is expressed in a 'fundamental opposition to militarism' and an '"obstinate refusal" of organized violence and its infinite capacity to obliterate and corrupt'.[3]

While this formulation captures part of Morris's vision, it is not only insufficient to explain the role of violence in his fiction, but also ignores a significant strand of his political writings. David Latham, who suggests that Morris was 'a pacifist by nature' – a claim difficult to substantiate – goes on to allow that 'Morris was forced by his analysis of capitalism to recognize with heart-wrenching reluctance that a violent revolution was inevitable'.[4] Yet Latham, like other critics who acknowledge Morris's commitment to violence, however unconventional it may be, stops short of examining the implications of that commitment.

I propose that his imaginative and political vision of a peaceful communal future is inseparable from his continuing commitment to the inevitability of organized revolutionary violence. At the same time, detailed but distanced representations of violence form a potent image of the physical, mental and communal transformation Morris sees as essential to the success of future revolution. His late creative works engage with wider cultural and political narratives through the depiction of active and reactive violence in relation to the past and future.[5] Metaphors of violence drive the content, form and structure of his propaganda poems, while more acutely realized scenes of active violence underlie the vision of fellowship that is central to *John Ball*, and offer a countervailing tension to the idea of tolerance in his 'epoch of rest' in *News from Nowhere*.

The violence of resistance, as Morris describes it, involves an end to passive acceptance of symbolic violence; it is the expression of a spirit of 'fruitful discontent, or rebellion; that is to say, of hope'.[6] Revolutionary battle is an act of hope in that it represents the physical eruption of a struggle that Morris sees as already taking place: violence brings the enemy into the open. He wrote in 1884 that in his own lifetime he expected to see no end to his society's inequality and alienation, but that rather he might simply hope to see the struggle between capitalism and its enemies become 'sharper and bitterer', until it 'breaks out openly at last into the slaughter of men by actual warfare instead of by the slower and crueller methods of "peaceful" commerce.'[7] The necessities of commerce undercut the possibility of open warfare, while nonetheless leading to death and destruction. Commerce itself is a kind of war, then, as Richard Cobden had long since avowed. In 1836 Cobden had decried any attempt at the 'unnatural union' between 'that daughter of Peace, Commerce, whose path has ever been strewed with the choicest gifts of religion, civilization, and the arts', and 'the demon of carnage, War'.[8] Yet Morris's phrase, 'slower and crueller methods' suggests that the apparent peacefulness of commerce is deceptive, and its effects more devastating than violent combat. Its outcome is not only misery at home, he argues in *Commonweal* in 1889, but also 'commercial war' in the colonies, which 'has made England so "great" and so unhappy'. He continues the analogy, adding religion to it:

> One day it is rum-and-bible, another sword-and-bible, but cheap wares and sweating are what both these instruments are used for alike; and horrible as the slaughter of the bullet is, it is not more horrible than the slower process of the sweater if we could only see the latter as plainly.[9]

Commerce pretends to be peaceful while making war on those it oppresses. And while 'commercial war' is clearly a metaphor, it runs alongside, or slides into, the actual 'sword-and-bible' violence that Morris identifies as its concomitant. The anticolonialist psychiatrist and activist Frantz Fanon, concerned with injustice, violence and colonization in the twentieth century, makes similar use of the concept of apparent peace in an unjust system, with his oxymoronic description of 'peaceful violence'. He suggests that 'between the violence of the colonies and that peaceful violence that the world is steeped in, there is a kind of complicit agreement, a sort of homogeneity'.[10] Oppression, both Morris and Fanon argue, is sustained by disguised violence, and may only be overthrown by unmasking this figurative violence, by recognizing its affinity with – but also, for Morris, its difference from – actual, physical violence.

'Slaughter' – a word also used later by Fanon to describe the actions of the colonizers against the colonized – vividly suggests the dehumanizing brutality of war: its etymology reaches back to the Old Norse word for killing livestock for food. Yet it is this that Morris looks for; better the hideous violence of slaughter, that will show the unequal relations between the classes for what they are, he suggests, than the ongoing exploitative violence of commerce.[11] Provoking the violence of the ruling class would be a significant step towards true peace, in Morris's formulation: 'for it will mean the rich classes grown conscious of their own wrong and robbery, and consciously defending them by open violence; and then the end will be drawing near'.[12] There is a commitment here to an idea of violence as representing an awakening to consciousness, and perhaps conscience, as well as a final resolution beyond which new hope can be glimpsed. It is, perhaps, an antidote to the 'dullness', or mental and emotional deadening of civilization that Morris deplores elsewhere.[13] He does not underplay the significance of violence: 'slaughter' allows of no softening. Nonetheless it is evidence of reality and honesty about the struggle, a 'sharper, shorter remedy' to the evils of capitalism than a long, slow process of reform.[14] Like Herbert Marcuse after him, Morris distinguishes between different kinds of physical violence. The oppressive violence of the state – both active and passive – is opposed to the active revolutionary violence of the workers, which signals an end to toleration of inequality.[15]

An 1886 letter to the *Daily News* has Morris correcting a story that implies his own condemnation of a riot following a public meeting of the unemployed, called by the Fair Trade League and taken over by the Social Democratic Federation: 'it is not Socialist agitators who are responsible for the wreck and pillage committed by the crowd on Monday, but that society which has forced these unfortunates to be what they are.'[16] In a private letter Morris comments that 'as to Mondays [*sic*] riot, of course I look at it as a mistake to go in for a policy of riot, all the more as I feel pretty certain that the Socialists will one day have to fight seriously'.[17] Violence here appears as both a solemn duty and a historical inevitability rather than a spontaneous expression of anger. The working classes are 'doomed' to make an end of 'the capitalist', Morris argues in an 1885 lecture, in terms that similarly combine dialectical history with personal responsibility, and which recall the underlying argument of William Godwin's *Caleb Williams*: the individual may be forced into action by the relentless injustice of the state.[18]

In this view of violence Morris is closer to the anarchists of his day, such as his friend Peter Kropotkin, or the poet and writer Louisa Sarah Bevington, than to many of his fellow socialists, particularly those interested in pursuing change through parliament. Indeed, in a review of his collection of essays, *Signs of Change*, the gradualist socialist journal *To-day*, edited by Morris's old comrades Ernest Belfort Bax and James Leigh Joynes, comments that his views make a mockery of socialism and will turn away the unconverted, not least because, 'we gather from the little volume before us [...] that the author *desires* to bring about a civil war'. The *Saturday Review* accuses the same volume of mingling 'bloodthirsty aspirations' with 'dreams of a land flowing, not so much with milk and honey as with milk and water'.[19] It is both violent and unrealistically romantic, the article suggests, and in this sense irresponsible. What both these reviews identify is that Morris does not see violence as an absolute wrong, or to be avoided at all costs.

However, war can only be of use as a communal act, for Morris. Bevington, in her posthumously published pamphlet, *Anarchism and Violence*, argues that although 'anarchism is not bomb throwing, violence, incendiarism, destruction', there may be circumstances in which violence is a valid option:

> Can a real Anarchist – a man whose creed is Anarchism – be at the same time a person who deliberately injures, or tries to injure, persons or property. I, for one, have no hesitation in saying that, if destitute because of monopoly, he can.[20]

While Morris is convinced that injustice may lead to justifiable violent insurrection, he repeatedly distances himself from this anarchist emphasis on individual action. His objection is not on moral or absolute grounds, as his support for the Chicago Anarchists charged with police murders in 1887 demonstrates, but is an instrumental one.[21] His commitment to long-term peace leads him to believe that short-term war may be necessary, but sporadic individual acts of violence are counterproductive.[22]

That Morris's own personal views on political violence changed over time is evident, but his commitment to an idea of redemptive violence remains firm. Although he was actively opposed to some imperial wars and always to the jingoistic patriotism or capitalist values that drove them, his objection was not to physical acts of violence themselves, as I have argued in the previous chapter.[23] While still a supporter of the Liberal party in 1880, he condemned the impulse to war arising from 'false patriotism' and 'National Vain-glory' and acknowledged the terrible human cost of war.[24] 'Real patriotism', however, will not necessarily prevent war but only certain kinds of war:

> Real patriotism bids us to be keen-eyed to note whether at any time the public opinion of our country sways towards justice or injustice, and to resist both in ourselves and in others blind and ignorant impulses that drive men on to grasp at phantoms of gain and glory created long ago by follies dead or half dead.

This kind of patriotism may also, in the end, lead to war, in accordance with the demands of 'irrepressible *justice*, or the hard need of self defence', but it is war with a very different outcome: 'we should then cleave our way through it with the well-assured hope of coming to better days beyond it'.[25] Motivation, in this account, affects both the conduct of the war and its outcome. Much later, in 'Why I am a Communist' (1894), Morris explicitly writes that 'I do not believe that our end will be gained by open war'.[26] In between these two statements his letters and lectures reveal many shifts of position with regard to the necessity or probability of actual violence in relation to revolution.

Nonetheless he continues, to the end of his life, to write imaginative works in which peace and social harmony are inextricably linked to violence. This might in part be explained by a consideration of the paradox Brantlinger identifies in his examination of the role of literature in the future world of *News from Nowhere*: 'most literature is structured around conflict, and if you could eliminate conflict from life, then you would also eliminate literature.'[27] However, Morris's socialist works reveal an investment in the idea of transformational revolutionary violence that goes beyond the necessities of art. This is not the spontaneous violence of chivalric adventure that characterized his earliest works, but a more instrumental violence, deliberately chosen and planned for the accomplishment of a particular purpose. It is not an end in itself, a trial of strength, or a means of vengeance, but rather a last resort to bring about long-term social change. Yet Morris's stories and poems insist on the responsiveness and expressiveness of battle: it may be planned and organized, but it is never cold or passionless in its execution; it is, rather, co-operative and committed. It arises in reaction to unbearable circumstances. The battles of these political writings of Morris's later years are characterized by the motivational use of metaphors and images of violence. They highlight the centrality of affect in bringing about revolutionary battle or political action, as well as the uses and limitations of imagined violence in transforming a readership into a political force.

'I Saw the Battle Awake': The Rhythms of Conversion

In Morris's long narrative poem, *The Pilgrims of Hope* (1885–86), the working-class hero, Richard, is taken to a socialist meeting, where he listens to the speaker talking 'of man without a master and earth without a strife / And every soul rejoicing in the sweet and bitter of life.' Richard responds to this idyllic vision of the harmony of the generic 'man' and the earth in these terms: 'his words were my very thoughts, and I saw the battle awake, / And I followed from end to end, and triumph grew in my heart'.[28] The idea of future peace generates an image of personified battle that is central to individual conversion; in seeing the sleeping battle awake, Richard is changed. Morris's socialist vision of the communal future, laid out in *The Pilgrims of Hope* and the propaganda poems of the 1880s, *Chants for Socialists*, is inseparable from the individual, physically experienced idea of battle and indeed cannot be achieved or even imagined without it.[29] This present, corporeal imagination of battle changes both body and mind in preparation for sacrificial action.

While Anne Janowitz convincingly locates the socialist poems in the revolutionary, 'interventionist' tradition of Romantic poetry, and notes their echoes of both Shelley and Blake, I suggest that they draw equally on a contemporary tradition of religious conversion that invites individuals into a community of struggle and validates their own sufferings.[30] In the poems, however, this conversion is rooted in present physical experience as much as future hope. While the language of battle in these late poems is expressly framed in opposition to Victorian capitalism and nineteenth-century wars, it nonetheless contributes to wider cultural and religious myths of the glorious possibilities of transformational violence that run through the late nineteenth century and into the twentieth, bolstered by a discourse of battle that crisscrosses a line between the metaphorical and the actual.

Pilgrims and three of the *Chants* were published in *Commonweal*, whose statement of intent on its launch in February 1885 was 'to awaken the sluggish, to strengthen the waverers, to instruct the seekers after truth', for the ultimate end of 'the propagation of socialism.'[31] Reading this journal is not to be merely a cerebral or rational experience, but one that engages mind and body in a holistic experience that transcends reason. The senses, the mind and the idea of battle are brought together in the poems published in its pages to suggest a vital connection between the transformation of the body now and the transformation of society that is to come. While socialists such as Edward Carpenter or George Bernard Shaw demonstrated their commitment to the healing of society through attention to the health of the body by taking up vegetarianism, clothing reform or meditation, Morris demonstrates his commitment to the transhistorical, despiritualized sacrificial body by the sensual evocation of battle and its effects on the body and mind.[32] In the socialist poems, he evokes the corporeal and mimetic qualities of violence as a way of internalizing the values of revolution and inciting personal renewal that may eventually lead to communal action.[33] The poems hold in uneasy tension the idea of the future redeemed society and the present political conversion of the individual through their focus on the body itself as the centre of violent transformation.

Morris goes beyond the metaphorical in his willingness to use myths of violence in poetry and song. His poems reflect the revolutionary sentiments of the German poet Ferdinand Freiligrath, frequently translated in *Commonweal* at this time, and the communal appeal of songs of the French Revolution, popular at socialist meetings.[34] With equal potency, they reformulate the ideas of commitment to a cause and internalization of a battle mentality central to such staple nineteenth-century hymns interpreting scriptural tradition as 'Onward Christian Soldiers', 'Stand Up! – Stand Up for Jesus!' or 'We Are Soldiers of Christ'.[35] As in these hymns, battle is presented in Morris's poems as an urgent necessity for a better end: 'Fair the crown the Cause hath for you, well to die or well to live / Through the battle, through the tangle, peace to gain or peace to give'.[36] While Morris holds up the common socialist ideal of the 'coming day' as the hymns evoke an afterlife with God, the rewards in his chants are not only after the battle, but also in the fighting itself: the 'crown' may be found in dying well or gaining future peace for others just as much as in surviving or finding peace after the battle. There is no heavenly reward to be won and ordinary people may be sacrificial offerings on behalf of their fellows. The only transcendence to be found here is in the sense of community with a cause larger than the personal.

The rhythms and settings of these late poems make use of both popular and literary traditions of more physically immediate battle or revolution. *Pilgrims* employs a mixture of the tetrameter of popular song, in the first two poems, and the classical hexameter of epic poetry in the later ones, as Janowitz points out, while the *Chants* are set to what May Morris describes as 'well-known tunes'.[37] Many have heroic associations of struggle against the odds: 'The March of the Workers' is set to the tune of 'John Brown's Body', which is also the tune for 'The Battle Hymn of the Republic', and so has religious intimations of heaven as escape from slavery as well as powerful associations with the battles of the American Civil War, manifested in its marching rhythm.[38] 'The Hardy Norseman', a tune Morris used for 'No Master' and had earlier used for his first protest song, 'Wake, London Lads' (1878), was well known and associated with rousing patriotism.[39] As Birmingham Congregationalist R. W. Dale commented on the popular hymns of Moody and Sankey, who visited Britain in the 1880s, 'people want to sing not what they think but what they feel.'[40] Morris stirs up emotion by making use of tunes and rhythms familiar and well used, but with heroic overtones, turning the religious or conservatively patriotic uses to which they might be put to his own revolutionary ends.[41]

Chris Waters suggests that Morris's poems and chants stand out in the fin-de-siècle socialist movement for their 'historical analysis of those forms of oppression that would ultimately be overthrown'.[42] This is not entirely borne out by a comparison of the *Chants* with, for instance, Carpenter's 'England Arise', well known among political radicals of the time, which poetically but specifically details the causes of poverty and their outcomes, including unjust labour practices and starvation wages. Where Morris's poems do stand out, as Waters goes on to point out, is in their focus on 'the struggle that would be necessary to bring the new society about'.[43] It is here that the emotive charge of the poems is located, as well as in their rhythms. A *Commonweal* article of August 1885 records Morris saying that the Socialist League must have 'music as a power in their organisation. It roused the spirits often apt to be depressed with the hardness of the work. Sentiment and the passions must be appealed to.'[44] He is less concerned with fostering literary excellence in his readers or developing good poetry from within the working class, as Mike Sanders shows was part of the Chartist project, and more with stirring their passions to bring about personal change and eventual action.[45] The account of his speech continues: 'further, all must be prepared to sacrifice. He longed to see yet more of the revolutionary fervour. Then [...] instead of accepting everything dolefully, of lying down to die, all would be up and doing'.[46] There is a domesticity about the colloquial 'up and doing', alongside 'revolutionary fervour' that converts the power of music not into immediate battle but into fervent quotidian activity. These are not songs designed to inspire random street fighting, but rather a longer-term programme of revolutionary action.

As always, however, Morris appeals to the passions by evoking battle, and specifically in the *Chants*, the sounds of battle. 'The March of the Workers' begins:

> What is this, the sound and rumour? What is this that all men hear,
> Like the wind in hollow valleys when the storm is drawing near,

Like the rolling on of ocean in the eventide of fear?
'Tis the people marching on.
(*Chants*, 11)

The sound of the people in action is 'the blended sound of battle and deliv'rance drawing near' (12). War means not destruction, but deliverance. The chant is performative: it brings into being what it describes. Physical marching is suggested by the song's rhythm, and itself stands for other kinds of action. The revelatory hollow of Morris's earlier short story ('The Hollow Land') and the wandering wind of his earlier poem ('The Wind') here merge in an image of purposeful transformation. The wind, normally evanescent and shifting, is instead rushing through 'hollow valleys when the storm is drawing near', and so becomes something unidirectional and forceful, reminiscent of Tennyson's call to 'Let [...] the war roll down like a wind'.[47] Its sound is a sign of worse to come, just as the sound of the song itself in the mouths of the workers is intended to be.

That what these songs aim at is nothing less than the conversion and physical transformation of the workers is signalled by their focus less on rousing hatred for the enemy than on the process of preparation for battle, which takes place both in the mind and the body. The intense focus on the senses precludes the virulent demonizing of the enemy that is common to battle songs: the *Chants'* calls to action include few of the emotive descriptions of the composite, dehumanized enemies that inform Morris's Germanic romances and that are central to the 'Marseillaise' of the French Revolution, which identified the enemy as 'mercenaries', 'foreign troops', 'tyrants' and 'pitiless tigers' – designations toned down in the popular versions of the 'Marseillaise' used by fin-de-siècle socialists in Britain.[48] Morris's chants rely instead on a combination of the Christian imagery of spiritual battle and the metaphors of natural power that ran through Chartist poetry.[49] The battle is directed towards present personal and material change, rather than against the enemy. Violence, when it comes, is to spring less from animosity than from hope.

This is not to say, however, that no enemy is identified: 'the rich man' or the more individualized 'rich men' appear again and again in the chants as the oppressor: not an individual, but a type. John Plotz notes that in Morris's late romances, 'like his late socialist "chants", enemies are defined only positionally: triumph comes not in conquest but in the transformation that makes opposition between persons only the result of a semantic mistake'.[50] There is no possibility of semantic mistake here, but the opposition is circumstantial rather than necessary. It is the condition and actions of 'rich men' that make them the enemy, rather than innate evil. 'The March of the

Workers' apostrophizes them like this:

> O ye rich men hear and tremble! For with words the sound is rife:
> 'Once for you and death we laboured; changed henceforward is the strife.
> We are men, and we shall battle for the world of men and life.
> (*Chants*, 12)

The curious image of a sound 'rife' with words suggests that the battle is a communicative rather than an oppositional one. It is positive, aiming to bring life out of strife, as the end-rhymes emphasize. In a strategy that functions like a tale of spiritual battle for the salvation of a soul, in which the possibility of conversion is always present, Morris lays out the future damnation facing the rich man and invites him, in the voice of the worker, to switch sides in the battle:

> 'Is it war, then? Will ye perish as the dry wood in the fire?
> Is it peace? Then be ye of us, let your hope be our desire.
> Come and live! for life awaketh, and the world shall never tire,
> And hope is marching on.'
> (*Chants*, 12)

Just as later, in *News from Nowhere*, Morris will depict some of the soldiers set against the people changing sides and joining in the struggle, so here he makes clear that people are only the enemy as long as they continue to support the capitalist system.

Like hymns of the period, then, Morris's songs aim not merely to mobilize and transform the committed workers, but to convert the unconverted. Victorian socialism invested a great deal in the unifying, motivating and memorializing power of song.[51] An admiring fellow socialist, John Bruce Glasier, records an instance of a meeting in Glasgow where French refugee Leo Melliet 'sang the "Carmagnole" with such dramatic effect that we were roused to our feet and danced the chorus with him round the room'. This was followed by a German workers' song and a Yiddish revolutionary song, interspersed with short speeches. As Morris returned to his hotel after the meeting, he was accompanied by local socialists, 'chorusing along the streets his own "March of the Workers" and feeling almost persuaded we were destined to foregather some not far distant day at the barricades!'.[52] There is a coyness about that 'almost': this is about affect, not practical effect. It works on the emotions. This is not to downplay its significance, however. As Sanders notes, 'poetry's affective capacity helps to generate the emotional bonds, the common feelings, which are as necessary a part of any movement's infrastructure as its organisational forms.'[53] The aim of stirring these 'common feelings' is, in Morris's poems, to produce concerted action: to move the people on from being 'deedless', a state of apathy and unmanliness, into readiness for confrontational action. As the word itself relies on what is missing for its meaning, so Morris suggests that 'deeds' are the basis of community and their absence suggests not a different way of being but a distinct and specific lack.[54]

It is a lack represented rhythmically in the pause of the midline caesura so common in the hexameter poems that make up most of the long narrative *Pilgrims of Hope*.[55] *Pilgrims* dramatizes more concretely than the *Chants* the scenario of preparation for change through an appeal to the passions and the somatic response to sound. The poem's primary narrator, Richard, goes to London to look for work and there witnesses a parade of soldiers setting off for war. It is a war Richard has heard of in his village, one in which there is neither reason nor commitment: 'no cause for a man to choose; / Nothing to curse or to bless – just a game to win or to lose' (374). This negative construction again draws attention to the values Morris espouses: better to curse or bless than to be without commitment or passion. What is desirable is evoked by what is missing. Waiting with the crowd to see the soldiers, Richard hears, 'faint and a long way off, the music's measured voice' (376). This is not the sound of the people's battle, but the war of the capitalists. Its 'measured voice' is double-edged: on the one hand it partakes of the oppressive orderliness and control evident in the previous stanza where Richard bitterly describes this war as 'the ordered anger of England'. It is a phrase that calls up the idea of 'order' attacked again and again in *Commonweal*'s news reports and poems such as Glasier's 'Ballade of "Law and Order"', with its mockery of the 'peerless apothegm / Of long live law and order'.[56] Yet, just as violence may be put to different uses, so apparently may the sounds that herald it. This 'measured voice' is at the same time rousing, stirring and transformative, like the 'measured music' of the knights' swords in 'The Hollow Land', discussed in Chapter One.[57] It combines both rhythm and a personal call – this is not just music, but music's voice – in a way that stirs the passions and in doing so brings about a change in both the body and the will.

To demonstrate this change in body and will, Morris mobilizes and then reframes an idea of measure and form as a means of shaping what is naturally formless and therefore threatening. This 'music's measured voice' brings into the political and communal realm the kind of ordering that Tennyson calls on in *In Memoriam* as a means of dealing with unruly feelings:

> But, for the unquiet heart and brain,
> A use in measured language lies;
> The sad mechanic exercise,
> Like dull narcotics, numbing pain.[58]

The measured music of battle offers a contrast to the sprawling formlessness of London, whose downtrodden working people form 'a stream of every day', 'a street flood' that 'ebbed and flowed' (374–5). This language of flooding and formlessness draws upon the 1880s middle-class fears of the sprawling working class, fears that after 1871 combined with horror at the Paris Commune to create anxiety about a comparable working-class uprising by the 'amoebic Populace', as Matthew Beaumont argues.[59] Morris draws on the idea of formlessness, only later to combat it with a vision, not of the mechanical march of an army, but of an organically unified, working-class uprising that both utilizes this fear and challenges its basis. The rhythmic poem itself shapes the formlessness of its matter into a focused tale of purposeful, revolutionary will.

As in the 'March of the Workers', communal battle is blended with the promise of liberation. Richard, hearing the music, says, 'somehow, I knew not why, / A dream came into my heart of deliverance drawing anigh.' Eventually the music comes closer:

> Then clamour of shouts rose upward, as bright and glittering gay
> Came the voiceful brass of the band, and my heart beat fast and fast,
> For the river of steel came on, and the wrath of England passed
> Through the want and the woe of the town, and strange and wild was my thought,
> And my clenched hands wandered about as though a weapon they sought.
> (*Pilgrims*, 376)

The sounds of war have a physical effect on his body that leads to an instinctive somatic response: 'my clenched hands wandered about as though a weapon they sought.' The body itself is spurred by the sound of battle into a longing for action. The movement of Richard's hands suggests the aimlessness of his individual desire, however: this corporeal longing can only be fulfilled purposefully in communal action.

The poem charts the transformation of unfocused physical desire into the selfless communal action that drives Morris's chant, 'The Day is Coming': 'Why, then, and for what are we waiting? There are three words to speak: / WE WILL IT' (*Chants*, 4). As he does in *Sigurd*, Morris draws on the Victorian preoccupation with individual will as a sign of character and manliness, evident not only in the writings of Mill, Carlyle and Smiles discussed in the previous chapter, but also, as Matthew Campbell suggests, in the potent rhythmic wrestling between individual will and the shaping will of God evident in Gerard Manley Hopkins' poetry.[60] In the *Chants*, as in *Pilgrims*, Morris turns this central tenet of individualist expression, religious self-understanding and capitalist activity into an anti-individualist, communal, corporeal transformation, activated and effected by voice and word. The declaration of communal will in 'The Day is Coming' leads to the call: 'Come, join in the only battle wherein no man can fail, / Where whoso fadeth and dieth, yet his deed shall still prevail' (*Chants*, 5). As C. Wright Mills observes of Marxism more broadly, 'ideal and agency are closely combined, even confused'. E. P. Thompson formulates this pairing rather differently in his suggestion that Morris's work is a combination of 'necessity and desire'.[61] Wright Mills more usefully draws attention to the emphasis not merely on longing but on doing that inheres in Morris's work. What brings together the desiring individual, the desired future and the determined course of history is communal will expressed in acts of battle that lead ultimately to success: failure is only ever temporary, in this model.

As the 'shouts and the rhythmic noise' fade away, Richard dreams of 'the deeds of another day':

Far and far was I borne, away o'er the years to come,
And again was the ordered march, and the thunder of the drum,
And the bickering points of steel, and the horses shifting about.
(*Pilgrims*, 376)

The relentless rhythm of the poetry here, with its repetitive piling up of clauses, and the 'far and far' echoing the 'fast and fast' of Richard's heart, makes corporeal the sound of battle and the vision of the future, linked as they are by the assonance of 'come', 'thunder', 'drum'. As the sound of the army dies away, a change has occurred: 'woe had grown into will, and wrath was bared of its sheath'. The longing of Richard's hands for a weapon now becomes a complete physical transformation, in which familiar things are 'made clear, / Made strange by the breathless waiting for the deeds that are drawing anear' (376). As he stands in the street, Richard imagines that the people are no longer a formless, flowing mass, but upright and unified: 'here and here by my side, shoulder to shoulder of man'. The amorphous 'street flood' becomes an organic, fighting body, self-controlled and coherent. Collective will changes not only the people's minds and feelings but their very bodies, preparing them for 'the people's war' (376) that, like fate or God, will draw 'anear' and guide them through deeds to peace.

The commonplace anticipation of a new dawn is coupled with concrete action and quasidivine force here, in a way that sets it in contrast with the wars of the imperialist and capitalist. This section ends with a denunciation of such fighting:

War in the world abroad a thousand leagues away,
While custom's wheel goes round and day devoureth day.

> Peace at home! – what peace, while the rich man's mill is strife
> And the poor is the grist that he grindeth, and life devoureth life?
> (376–7)

The linear productivity of the 'people's war' is quite different from the destructive cyclical futility of imperial war in this stanza. Although Boos suggests that 'Morris's hope for a "people's war" and "new peace" contrasts pointedly with the sentiments of Tennyson's *Maud*', the resonances with that poem are unavoidable.[62] In a meter recalled by Morris's, Tennyson's speaker conjures a vision of injustice in which, among other horrors, 'chalk and alum and plaster are sold to the poor for bread', and concludes: 'Is it peace or war? better, war! loud war by land and by sea, / War with a thousand battles, and shaking a hundred thrones'.[63] These are sentiments that suggest not only the 'imperial adventure' that Boos highlights, but also a commitment to war as a means of social transformation, a commitment that Morris, however problematically, also evinces. Tennyson's later phrase, 'peace, that I deemed no peace', picks up on an Old Testament sentiment and is echoed here in Morris's poem.[64] War is justified, in both works – as in the Bible passages – by the exposure of peace as a sham.

Spurred on by this moment of transformation, Richard does eventually take up arms. He converts to communism, loses his job because of his outspoken political views and makes a close communist friend, Arthur, who also, in a complicated personal touch, becomes his wife's lover. All three of them, 'craved some work for the cause' and 'what work was there indeed, / But to learn the business of battle and the manner of dying at need' (403). In a strange conflation of political moments that serves to give urgency to the cause, the tale has these socialists of the 1880s setting off for Paris to fight in the last days of the Commune. Richard, motivated both by frustrated love and by political faith, cries that 'for me I know my part, / In Paris to do my utmost, and there in Paris to die!' (400). His words echo those of the Communard Edouard Vaillant, writing in *Commonweal* in April 1885 that:

> The fighting, the struggle for existence and power, was everything, the rest only an accident. Of what value were words, of what value ephemeral reforms, when it was a question of conquering or dying? The people of Paris, rising to the height of the task they had undertaken, knew how to fight and die.[65]

To know how to fight and die is a corporeal kind of knowing, not a mental exercise. Like singing or chanting, it transcends the cerebral and involves the body; paradoxically, it is a way of allowing hope to become embodied.

Pilgrims, having dwelt at length on the build-up to battle, passes quickly over the fighting in Paris and the death, not of Richard, but of his wife and friend.

What matters is not primarily the immediate outcome but the transformation that the sound and story of battle might effect, within the poem's narrative and in Morris's readers. *Pilgrims* is, in Georges Sorel's terms, a series of 'warmly-coloured and clearly-defined images, which absorb the whole of our attention', without which, Sorel observes, 'we do nothing great'.[66] The later sections, telling of the days in Paris, are also powerfully rhythmic sound texts whose regular hexameter coerces the experience of death and sacrifice into an oral pattern of order, purpose and certainty that contrasts with the disorder and failure of the Commune. Richard returns home, bereaved but emotionally untrammelled, to continue the fight by other means: 'I came to look to my son, and myself to get stout and strong/ That two men there might be hereafter to battle against the wrong' (408). The deaths of the Paris Commune leave a legacy for those left behind, in a motif of sacrifice that reconfigures that of the Christian narrative of death and rebirth that runs through the poem and is further reframed in *A Dream of John Ball*.

This tale of conversion and transformation, which celebrates the moment when Richard is 'born again' (384) and ends with the aftermath of sacrificial death, eschews the spiritual and trusts to the interaction of the individual senses and the communal will. Both *Chants* and *Pilgrims* draw heavily on the rhetoric of war, character, will and sacrifice that underlay much Victorian evangelical discourse and hymnody, as well as contemporary political and economic thinking about individuals and the state. They counter ideas of spiritual sacrifice and a future heavenly hope with an embodied, aurally stirring narrative of physical conversion from apathy and inertia to brotherly commitment. They hold out a vision of war that only waits for the present transformation of individuals into a community able to take part in it. The desired result of that preordained 'battle against the wrong', which may be physical or symbolic, is a change in the material conditions and relationships on which society is based.

A Dream of John Ball: The Fellowship of Violence

In Morris's historical tale of 1886–87, *A Dream of John Ball*, the motifs of martial sacrifice and brotherhood that emerge in *Chants* and *Pilgrims* are put to the service of a more fully developed myth of transhistorical community. An 1888 review of *John Ball* in *To-day*, the journal that objected to the political violence of Morris's essay collection, *Signs of Change*, sees nothing of that reprehensible desire for war in this work. The reviewer suggests that after reading it, 'one has a heart-deep sense of satisfaction at knowing that at last, after centuries of neglect and scorn and derision, something like justice has been done to the loyal priest and martyr in the people's cause.' He goes on to claim that 'this reverent memorialising of the true heroes is surely an earnest of the near triumph of the true cause'.[67] While Morris's tale certainly works to elide the space between the battles of the past and the struggle of the nineteenth-century working class, his commitment to an ideal of the efficacy and beauty of sacrificial violence nonetheless serves rather to remove 'the true cause' from the realms of the real into the ideal. *John Ball*, first published serially in *Commonweal*, serves less as 'reverent memorialising' and more as an invitation to an active, transformative reading of past battles.[68] Yet its very intensity of realization and the completeness of its vision risks leaving readers with 'heart-deep [...] satisfaction' rather than an urgent desire for present political action.

Commonweal promises, in its opening number, 'a series on historical revolutions' and later issues include articles on the Paris Commune, the 'English Revolutionary Movement, 1815–1817' and the fourteenth-century Revolt of Ghent, as well as a regular 'Revolutionary Calendar', which notes key figures and events over the ages. Only Morris's tale of revolution, however, takes the form of a sustained fiction. History is both mythologized and reclaimed as present experience: reading this story becomes a way of participating in the battle, harvesting both meaning and pleasure out of its failure. Morris's preoccupation with failure has been noted by many critics: Waithe and Goode have paid particular attention, from different perspectives, to the ways in which Marxist dialectical materialism competes with individual agency in the tension between immediate failure and ultimate success presented in *John Ball*.[69] While this political argument clearly has a role to play in Morris's work, the tale ensures that failure and success are both subsumed into the quasi-chivalric ideal of the redemptive, sacrificial fellowship of war. As Vaninskaya points out, Morris's focus on 'fellowship' has been noted in many critical analyses of *John Ball*, and her own work traces the relationship between the 'ethical message' of fellowship and Victorian socialist models of historical development.[70] My interest, however, is in the ways in which Morris uses the far more ethically problematic idea of sacrificial violence to elaborate the concept of fellowship. *John Ball* draws on a beguiling myth of sacrifice played out again and again through history, in which violence is the necessary means of social transformation and the paradoxical price of equal and harmonious community.

Jean Paul Sartre, in his preface to Fanon's *The Wretched of the Earth*, suggests that 'violence, like Achilles' lance, can heal the wounds that it has inflicted'.[71] Sartre writes in the context of colonialism and the struggles for independence of colonized people, suggesting that 'the settler has only recourse to one thing: brute force, when he can command it; the native has only one choice, between servitude or supremacy'.[72] Morris, writing in the context of class war and aiming to stir both discontent with the present and hope for the future, offers a similar view of the violence of the oppressed in *John Ball*. In the struggle against oppression violence not only heals the wounds it has inflicted, but in the act of inflicting wounds offers a kind of healing. Those who take up arms against injustice bear the seeds of a new, harmonious and violence-free society in the very act of communal battle, validating the lives of those who went before them and passing on a legacy to those who follow. The dreamer-narrator in *John Ball*, taken back in time to the Peasants' Revolt of 1381, muses on the effects of failed revolution:

> Men fight and lose the battle, and the thing that they fought for comes about in spite of their defeat, and when it comes it turns out not to be what they meant, and other men have to fight for what they meant under another name.
> (231–2)

In the context of *John Ball*, this cycle of violence is not a metaphorical but a literal one. The fellowship of the people is expressed in violent action, and further fellowship results. At the same time, in the very telling of violence, both act and actors are mythologized and the malleable matter of history reformulated.

That the story of the Peasants' Revolt was widely known in the late nineteenth century and was used for different ideological purposes has been well established by recent critics.[73] It featured as a pivotal event in the accounts of well-established historians such as William Stubbs, John Richard Green, and James Thorold Rogers, and was fictionalized from different points of view.[74] John Ball himself merits only a dismissive note in Stubbs's 1875 history of the uprising, a brief mention in Rogers's (1884), and a more substantial role in what is nonetheless a very succinct account of 'Wat Tyler's rising' by the prominent socialist H. M. Hyndman, in 1883.[75] However he is a significant and vocal figure in Jean Froissart's fourteenth-century aristocratic account, and in Green's liberal Victorian one, while the radical C. Edmund Maurice dwells on him at length as 'the moving spirit in the insurrection'.[76] Morris was familiar with all these writers and his narrative draws particularly on the dramatic tones of Froissart and details of interpretation offered by Green.[77] It differs from the accounts of most contemporary historians, not in its estimate of the event's significance in terms of results, on which all agree – the eventual disintegration of feudalism – but in its sensual and mythical presentation of the enduring significance of the battle itself.

It is important, therefore, that Morris does not choose rebel leader Wat Tyler as the focus of his story, but rather his 'worthier associate', the 'hedge priest', John Ball, whose powerful words to the people, passed down and adapted from writer to writer, urge the peasants into battle and attribute enduring meaning to their acts.[78] Morris's view of Ball's role is suggested by an October 1884 letter to the *Manchester Guardian*: 'John Ball was murdered by the fleecers of the people many hundred years ago, but indeed in a sense he lives still, though I am but a part of him, and not the whole of him'. It is not only his story that lives on, but he himself, in the lives of the people: 'nor will he quite die as long as he has work to do'.[79] The implied comparison with Christ is not accidental, but central to the story's mythmaking purpose. *John Ball* enacts what it offers, which is a tale of ritual battle that invites those who read it and those who hear it to enter into communion with the martyrs of the past and in this way validate their sacrifice.

The body and the senses are involved in apprehending this story. Glasier's account of Morris's visit to Glasgow includes a description of how Morris 'read, or rather chanted' John Ball's call to action in the marketplace to the assembled socialists, 'as one whose own heart and soul were in every word.' He goes on:

> And such was the effect of the recital that we all felt as though it were John Ball himself who was speaking to us and we were the yeomen assembled round him and were being consecrated with him to the Cause 'even unto life or death'.[80]

Like the experience of singing 'The March of the Workers' on this same occasion, hearing *John Ball*, in this account, forms a rite of intensification: a shared ritual experience that unites and motivates a community in the face of crisis or difficulty.[81] While Morris's reading and recitation skills were legendary, the transposition suggested by Glasier's 'as though' is one that the original publication context of the tale itself invites.[82] It offers nineteenth-century socialists a close identification with the peasants of John Ball's time, clustered as they were for those first readers in the closely printed pages of *Commonweal*, among reports of the sufferings and sacrifices of the working classes across the world. At the same time it maintains the separation from reality that is essential to ritual.

The vicarious experience of the fellowship of preparation for battle, and then battle itself, is offered not as a practical means of effecting the ends of 'the Cause', but as a catalyst for communal, almost spiritual, change. Morris's readers identify with the peasants and thereby begin to see that they go into battle not just for themselves, but for the sake of the future. Goode's compelling concept of the 'experiencing mind', alongside his analysis of Morris's affirmation of 'the revolutionary mind' and the 'creative mind' recalls Sorel's notion of myth, which emphasizes the role of imagination: 'men who are participating in a great social movement always picture their coming action as a battle in which their cause is certain to triumph. These constructions, knowledge of which is so important for historians, I propose to call myths'. For Sorel, this kind of myth is a means of galvanizing people to communal action: 'the myth must be judged as a means of acting on the present'.[83] *John Ball* does not only 'bring knowledge about their situation and its history to "the poor"', as Michael Holzman suggests, but more actively works to draw readers and listeners into an experience, both immanent and transcendent, of the fellowship of battle: the stories offer readers a vision of 'hopeful strife and blameless peace, which is to say in one word, life', in Ball's own words (286).[84] Yet it is not founded, as Sorel suggests myth must be, on either the experience or the promise of imminent success. Instead Morris frames his analysis of social problems with a story of deferred reward that elevates violence to a form of unattainably beautiful work and sanctifies it as part of a sacrificial inheritance.

René Girard argues that there is 'hardly any form of violence that cannot be described in terms of sacrifice'.[85] Certainly for Morris the idea of violence is closely associated with sacrifice. The interaction of mimesis, desire and reciprocal violence he identifies as part of the pattern of self-perpetuating sacrifice illuminates Morris's vivid but ritualistic telling of *John Ball* and its representation of battle. Girard suggests that a ritual sacrificial victim, peripheral to the community in some way, is offered up to violence as an alternative to, or means of preventing 'internal violence'. He argues that 'the purpose of the sacrifice is to restore harmony to the community, to reinforce the social fabric'.[86] Nonetheless sacrificial violence repeats itself cyclically in order to ensure this harmony or renewal; bloodshed leads to new life. Morris's preacher urges the peasants to offer themselves as willing sacrifices to the violence of their society in order to secure social change. To do this, they must also be prepared to fight and kill. They are both victims and warriors, choosing to fight as well as die, and so making available to those who hear their tale participation in a fellowship of heroism that sanctifies violent revolt.[87]

In reading about these deaths, then, Morris's contemporaries are invited into a bond of what Girard describes as 'mimetic desire', that is, a longing for what these model medieval men desire.[88] What Morris's readers are invited to desire is not primarily the freedom for which their forebears fought, but their fellowship, attainable only through battle and sacrifice. While the ideal of fellowship has been much commented on by critics, its continuity with violence has not. Because success is not possible in the tale, the focus is on the act of rebellion itself, and in Morris's account, this act takes the form of organized battle. Waithe argues that the 'philosophy of continuity, of transhistorical fellowship' enables Morris to hold in tension the historical inevitabilities of dialectical materialism and a personal commitment to a depiction of 'the historically compromised individual' battling for freedom and failing to achieve it. John Ball's 'Fellowship of Men', then, 'stands as [...] a transhistorical standard offering the consolation of future success'.[89] Between future success and present suffering, however, is the equally significant ideal of mimetic self-sacrifice. Ball, hearing from the dreamer about the lives of workers in the nineteenth century, cries out that having shaken off villeinage, people will surely not submit to this 'worser tyranny' without battle: rather, he says, in an image of shocking violence, 'maids and little lads shall take the sword and the spear, and in many a field men's blood and not water shall turn the grist-mills of England' (273). This transforms the image of degradation and coercion conjured by the 'rich man's mill' of strife in *Pilgrims*, in which the poor are 'grist', into one of agency and attack.[90] Violent self-sacrifice is essential for the long-term success of Ball's dream, and Morris's, and therefore becomes the means of both expressing and attaining fellowship. It includes, rather than precludes, deliberate infliction of pain and injury.

Allen J. Frantzen persuasively traces Girardian mimetic desire leading to sacrificial violence in the chivalric culture of medieval knighthood. He argues that 'self-sacrifice means that the knight voluntarily offers himself, but it does not mean that others, his enemies, will not die'.[91] Morris, deeply influenced by the chivalric tradition, as his earlier works demonstrate, moves distinctly away from the aristocratic knightly ideal in *John Ball*, but nonetheless, in quite specifically reconfiguring familiar spiritual motifs, offers a vision of both the fellowship of holy warfare and the power of self-sacrifice. The working-class fellowship of the living and the dead that he posits offers an alternative direction for the idea of brotherhood inherent in Christian chivalric warfare. At a period when Morris's own vigorous campaigning in the cause of socialism was met with varying degrees of answering fervour, his readers are offered a humanist tale of class war and sacrifice to stir them to commitment.[92]

Yet there is little realism in this mythic tale: its tone is numinous rather than practical. It is, as May Morris avers, 'a Confession of Faith [...], faith in the power and purpose of human life and its majestic continuity throughout the ages'.[93] This continuity is bought by death. Ball tells the gathered men at the cross, in words that stretch across the years to include Morris's readers:

> The deeds that ye do upon the earth, it is for fellowship's sake that ye do them, and the life that is in it, that shall live on and on for ever, and each one of you a part of it, while many a man's life upon the earth from the earth shall wane. (230)

In this prebattle speech, violence is justified by its alliance with an ideal of fellowship, even though it involves sacrificing the lives of others: 'cruel are these, and headstrong, yea thieves and fools in one – and ye shall lay their heads in the dust' (237). Killing in a good cause is countenanced as a means of bringing social transformation and eventually freeing future generations from the necessity of war. Ball reminds his listeners that 'in these days ye are building a house that shall not be overthrown' (254). This recalls not only the quotation's direct source in Proverbs (14.11), but also Jesus's triumphant assertion to his disciples that, 'I will build my church and the gates of Hades shall not prevail against it'.[94] There is absolute good versus absolute evil at stake here. The mundane battles of the nineteenth century are given meaning as part of a cosmic struggle. Morris's readers, who know, as John Ball at first does not, that his sacrifice did not bring about what it aimed at, become inheritors of his mantle.

As the people gather to listen to the words of the preacher, newly released from prison, the 'tall cross of stone' where they meet and beneath which the preacher stands, becomes a symbolic as well as a geographical focus, taking on new meaning in the light of the revolutionary struggle. Morris's Ball inverts the cry of present injustice attributed to the historical preacher, who compares the rich clothing and fine houses of the wealthy with the rags and poverty of the peasants.[95] This priest offers instead a prophecy about the postrevolutionary future, a fleshed-out version of the 'religious socialism' that Rogers attributes to 'Wiklif's poor priests':[96]

> What else shall ye lack when ye lack masters? Ye shall not lack for the fields ye have tilled, nor the houses ye have built, nor the clothes ye have woven. [...] He that soweth shall reap, and the reaper shall eat in fellowship the harvest he hath won. [...] And all shall be without money and without price. (237)

If Morris evokes the fourteenth century as forerunner to the nineteenth, his preacher looks back to older, biblical myths of sacrifice, justice and restoration.[97] In this way the story, language, and motifs of Christianity become the story of the people: Christianity is swallowed up in Marxist dialectics, as 'an historical phase through which the world of civilization has passed, or, if you will, is passing', as Morris wrote in 1888. Yet *John Ball* replaces one set of myths with another, in accordance with Morris's idea that 'the aim of Socialists should be the founding of a religion'. While he conceives of religion as 'a habit of responsibility to something outside myself', his depiction of it in this tale relies equally on a far less practical notion of the efficacy of violent death.[98] The dreamer counters Ball's faith in a Christian heaven by saying, 'though I die and end, yet mankind yet liveth, therefore I end not, though I am a man' (265). He may have a different view of heaven from Ball's, but their commitment to an ongoing fellowship, in one form or another, represents the faith of both in the continuity of the cause through martyrdom. Hannah Arendt notes the enduring power of this idea, in her observation that the experience of facing death collectively transforms the way death is viewed, so that 'it is as though life itself, [...] nourished, as it were, by the sempiternal dying of its individual members, is "surging upward", is actualized in the practice of violence'.[99] In *John Ball*, this collective process is represented as one that unites the working classes across history.

The comparatively minor sacrifices of the present are made in the light of the sacrificial deaths of the distant and recent past, those of the working people whose lives were laid down in the cause of freedom. In the light of historical determinism, these deaths in the struggle are inevitable, but they are also deliberate, and so store up historical debt for those for whom the sacrifice was made. As Morris argued in an 1884 lecture, in relation to the sufferings and sacrifices of international socialists, 'my friends, it is but a poor tribute to offer on the tombs of the martyrs of liberty, this refusal to take the torch from their dying hands!'.[100] Violence, both perpetrated and suffered in the past, is not merely an example or an education, but a legacy. The violence of the past is productive even in its failure. Waithe argues that 'the immediate defeat is redeemed by the ultimate, cumulative, victory'.[101] More than this, the very violence of past battles and the deaths they bring about are strangely generative: they engender change, fellowship and tales, which give meaning to the present as well as the past.

This generative legacy of active death is reflected in the detailed attention paid to the aftermath of the battle, which casts its meaning back over the fighting itself. When the skirmish is over, Ball takes the dreamer into the church to view the bodies of the dead, laid out in the chancel, surrounded by the beauty their age has created: 'everywhere was rich and fair colour and delicate and dainty form' (264). The thousands of deaths recorded by historians are metonymically represented by these bodies, but they are bodies made beautiful in death: fashioned into usefulness and coherence, like the rest of the tale.[102] In keeping with his propaganda purpose, Morris allows nothing of the ugliness and disorder of brutal death here. Neither is there anything mystical about the dead bodies themselves, however. The dreamer observes of the corpse of a young man that:

> this is an empty house, and the master has gone from it. [...] Here is no life nor semblance of life, and I am not moved by it; nay, I am more moved by the man's clothes and war-gear – there is more life in them than in him. (264–5)

Yet the viewing of the dead forms the prelude to a discussion first of the meaning of fellowship and then of the nineteenth century and the failure of the uprising to achieve its ends. The 'empty' dead bodies and their still-living weapons both animate and are animated by what follows, which is the ongoing tale of the people: the dissolution of villeinage and the rise of capitalism.

In contrast with the martyrdom of the body in willing, active death, capitalism means that 'a man who hath nought save his own body (and such men shall be far the most of men) must needs pawn his labour for leave to labour', the dreamer tells John Ball (282). For the tale's first readers, these battle corpses lie alongside the bodies of dead or wounded or imprisoned socialists across Europe, martyrs to the cause represented weekly in the pages of *Commonweal*. In September 1885, the journal reports a violent sabre attack by police on mourners at the funeral of a German socialist and the seizure of the corpse of another German activist by the authorities.[103] In the 1886 and 1887 numbers in which *John Ball* appears there are news reports, variously, of the unprovoked shooting of a child prisoner in Lille by a soldier, the solitary confinement of a Dutch Socialist and the dismissal of an entire striking workforce from a factory in Yorkshire.[104] The fourteenth-century battle dead offer a contrast, in the very dignity of their self-chosen, active death, to these 'enthralled' bodies of the nineteenth-century poor.

In a discussion of the language of sacrifice in the twenty-first century 'war on terror', Alex Houen, drawing on Girard's concept of the mimetic desire that leads to violent sacrifice, discusses the powerful role of what he terms *necromimesis* in the perpetuation of sacrifice: 'the intimate exchanges that take place between death and representation'. Death cannot be known or appropriated by those who are still living, but only understood through its representation, which, like sacrifice itself, draws in those who see or hear about it, but also 'turns death into something it is not'.[105] Necromimetic 'productions', such as books, not only represent sacrifice, but also carry on 'the work of sacrifice', Houen argues: 'necromimetic productions ensure that sacrificial deaths can circulate hauntingly and indefinitely as virtual afterlives while accruing indebtedness as social capital'.[106] The review from *To-day*, quoted at the beginning of this section, suggests that Morris's tale has something of this effect. It creates out of an increasingly well-known story a tale of heroism and martyrdom, converting death into fellowship and communal violence into a legacy of hope. The form of this representation holds together two effects that Houen identifies as characteristic of necromimetic productions: with its archaic language, popular subject matter and dream-narrative antecedents, *John Ball* works to 'deaden death's impact' to some extent, even while allowing the tale of battle itself to be experienced as 'all-too-real'.[107] It invites readers into a vivid and stirring vicarious experience that at the same time self-consciously proclaims its own unreality: once fighting commences, the dreamer is referred to as 'the ballad-maker', and in the final throes of battle he 'looked as on a picture' (245; 252).

What kind of action, then, might *John Ball* inspire? The answer lies in part in the way it presents the action of battle itself, in contrast with Ball's rousing words about it. The disapproving accounts of Stubbs and Froissart highlight the peasants' rising as a series of random lawless acts of murder and pillage.[108] Morris's tale, by contrast, emphasizes the orderliness, harmony and unity of the revolutionaries. The action of the tale all takes place in one village, and as soon as the peasants hear of men-at-arms approaching, 'the whole throng set off without noise or hurry, soberly and steadily in outward seeming'; preparing for battle, they 'got into their places leisurely and coolly enough' (242; 244). Written as it is during a time of tension between the anarchists, the parliamentarians and Morris's own revolutionary faction of the Socialist League, *John Ball* offers neither palliation nor random acts of violence, but rather emphasizes the need for concerted, organized battle.

There are traces of the chivalric ideal here, but it is the organized, heroically spiritualized violence of the Crusades, rather than the violence of happenstance that characterizes Malory's fellowship.[109] Yet there is nothing of the machine about this organization, nothing hierarchical or imposed. It is orchestrated but organic. While the instruments of violence and the words and actions of the warriors are vividly described there is none of the detailed, intimate stabbing and hewing characteristic of Morris's other battle tales. After the first skirmish, the faces of the dead are covered, because 'some of them had been sore smitten and hacked in the fray' (264), but the tale itself does not represent this smiting and hacking. Instead, the story's focus on weapons, surroundings, and movements through the field of battle suggests the continuity of revolutionary warfare with the lives of the people, which in turn are continuous both with their environment and with each other. War is not a large-scale event, but is understood and experienced, by reader as by warrior, through its stylized, beautiful detail, not only as communal work, but also as play. The dreamer says to Will Green, 'I would see the play'; while Will in turn tells his daughter, 'this play is but little', and Ball begins his discussion with the dreamer by saying: 'I do not ask thee if thou thinkest we are right to play the play like men, but whether playing like men we shall fail like men' (244–5; 267). This 'play', does not mean merely the individual battles, then, but also the wider class war that Ball brings out into the open and Morris's readers might continue: the emphasis is not on winning, but on acting 'like men'. Battle is purposeful, even ritualized, at least in the retelling.

Ritual, as Mary Douglas observes, 'focusses attention by framing; it enlivens the memory and links the present with the relevant past.' It does not always arise as a formulation of experience. Rather, 'it can come first. [...] It does not merely externalise experience [...] but it modifies experience in so expressing it'.[110] For the peasants in *John Ball* this ritual of battle is energized by their faith in the meaning and power of the sacrificial encounter. For Morris's readers and listeners, the tale itself forms part of a ritual of identification with the struggles of the past. Morris's evocation of the fighting of 1381 invites an act of engagement with those struggles, not by rationally illuminating the justice of the peasants' cause, but by eliciting an emotional and ideological commitment to a myth of redemptive violence. Yet the very ritualized retelling of this tale insulates readers against the possibility of long-term, nonviolent action. Its tale of battle is so harmonious and well conducted, its religious myth of sacrificial death so familiar, that the experience of reading may be enough to inure readers to the expectation of vicarious violence and emotional satisfaction rather than planned political action.

News from Nowhere: Organic War and the Postviolent 'Errors of Friends'

Morris's 1890 futuristic utopia, *News from Nowhere*, makes much more explicit links than *John Ball* does between the politics of the present, the battles of the future, and the outcomes of both, violating, as does its subtitle's indication of incompleteness, the sealed wholeness of a typical utopia.[111] Nonetheless it maintains an imaginative separation from reality in the absolutism of its vision of the effects of political violence. In *Political Justice* Godwin argues that 'the injustice and violence of men in a state of society, produced the demand for government'.[112] *News from Nowhere* invites its readers to consider a future in which the end of government coincides with the end of history, the erasure of boundaries between people and the end of combat, all brought about by a willingness to engage in organized sacrificial violence for the elimination of injustice.[113] Matthew Beaumont argues that Morris's story is 'an attempt to imagine a communist society in which it is possible to grasp history as the present, that is, in which history is simply being.'[114] Morris goes further than this, however, and imagines in detail the processes by which the evolution of society, the necessity for storytelling, and the combat he consistently understands to drive these two related forces, might come to an end. In affirming the violence of this process, however, he destabilizes the completeness of his vision.

Violence plays a central role in *News from Nowhere*, first in creating the future and then in maintaining and defining its freedom from coercion and state control. Tony Pinkney argues of *News from Nowhere*, that 'to read ourselves reading it as such, is to open new angles on this excessively familiar work, to make it speak beyond its avowed political intentions, to have it read us just as busily and challengingly as we read it.'[115] This approach yields a cogent and appealing reading of the text and allows him to highlight its 'inner warrings of signification', suggesting further possible directions for new readings.

However, like many other critics, while registering the significance of the struggle described in 'How the Change Came', he passes over its violence, noting instead its commitment to the modernist project of 'strenuous jolting into Adamic renewal'.[116] Applying Pinkney's principle to the violence of this text, I suggest a reading of *News from Nowhere* that allows it to speak 'beyond its avowed political intentions': a reading that examines both the enduring significance of the violence by which Morris's beautiful, harmonious new world is won and the postviolent uses of violence in Nowhere, in the light of contemporary and subsequent political narratives of social upheaval.

The idea that violence can bring about peace is more fully developed in *News from Nowhere* than in any of Morris's other works. His alterego, William Guest, arrives in the postrevolutionary world of the future to find everything cleansed, renewed and healed: London, and indeed England, is restored to an idyllic rural state of harmony without the need for laws, prisons or coercion of any kind. The class system has vanished and hostility between people is reduced to good-tempered teasing or grumbling, except for occasional but significant murders. The story works beyond its own context, and reflects on later narratives as well as earlier ones, but it is firmly rooted in the circumstances of its composition and publication. By 1890, British socialism was driven by factionalism, based on conflicting ideas of how to bring about the new society. Morris stood between the increasingly active anarchist wing of the Socialist League, determined that acts of violence could bring about change, and the parliamentary wing, committed to standing for election. Before the serialization of *News from Nowhere* in *Commonweal* was complete, Morris had stood down from its editorship and left the Socialist League to form the Hammersmith Socialist Society. In its own time, then, this was an imaginative contribution to arguments not only about the shape and feeling of the future society, but also about how it might best be achieved: the lengthy description of the civil war in the chapter entitled, 'How the Change Came', is essential as a contribution to that debate, and in that context it upholds a commitment both to organized violent resistance as against anarchist 'propaganda by deed' and to absolute war and destruction as against what Morris saw as the counterproductive 'palliatives' of parliamentary politics.[117] While it encompasses Marxist principles of change, it functions at the same time as a passionate presentation of the renewing power of physical violence acting on the bodies and minds of the working class to bring about transformation.

As Morris makes clear in his evocative subtitle, 'Being Some Chapters of a Utopian Romance', this is an antirealist fiction of adventure and incompletion: both romance and utopia. Nonetheless it functions in dialogue with the world of politics. It is not, as Paul Meier argues, an orthodox Marxist account of revolution and the 'withering-away of the State', but an emotive image of the future: much detail is omitted.[118] It does present a point of convergence between Morris's political beliefs and his storytelling impulse, and it is significant that what is not left out is the certainty of battle, killing and wounding. The story echoes not only the Christian and Nordic religious myths of death and new birth, but also the belief of Hegel and Marx in dialectical progression and transformation through the interaction of opposing forces. It insists on this conflict and draws specific attention to the physical details of its enactment. Social change is kicked into action by a bloody massacre, in which 'the dead and dying covered the ground, and the shrieks and wails and cries of horror filled all the air, till it seemed as if there was nothing else in the world but murder and death' (116). There can be no mitigation of the effects of violence, the story suggests. It can only be overcome by more violence.

Beyond his own time, Morris's ideas find resonances in more applied political thinking on the possibilities of violence. The novel enacts the enduring myth that violence carried out by the right people can overcome oppression and lead to happiness, because, as Hannah Arendt characterizes the idea, 'evil is but a temporary manifestation of a still-hidden good.'[119] Violence is not conceived, in this view, as something with intrinsically corrosive effects on those who carry it out; neither is it simply a means to an end. Rather, in the exercise of violence, social and individual good is released. In an argument that rests on a belief akin to Morris's in the creative and transformative power of the violence of the oppressed, Fanon argues that violence is a kind of creative work, which binds the people together and forms their characters, 'since each individual forms a violent link in the great chain, a part of the great organism of violence which has surged upwards in reaction to the settler's violence'.[120] Fanon's comments highlight the enduring appeal of the idea of generative and transformative violence not merely as a Sorelian myth, but as revolutionary praxis.

At the same time, history – not least that of Fanon's Algeria – demonstrates that while the forging of identity may be possible through violence, it is less effective in the creation of long-term peace and social transformation.[121] Morris's contemporary, the poet Lionel Johnson, invokes both the French and the American revolutions in his review of *News from Nowhere*. He argues that:

> No man, however inclined to fight side by side with Mr Morris, could risk the terrors and the horrors of civil war, unless he had a greater certainty, than this book could give him, that all the misery and the blood-shed would end in peace and happiness.[122]

Johnson brings the real wars of the European past to bear on Morris's tale. He draws attention to a cavalier dismissal of the effects of extreme violence that has given curiously little pause to later critics of Morris's utopia.[123] Morris's own conviction that the right kind of violence is efficacious, despite the evidence of history, means that there is little to bridge the gap between the war and the much later ideal society encountered by Guest. This commitment to the idea of war without ill consequences is particularly evident in his account of 'How the Change Came', a strangely passive euphemism used throughout the text, which works to obscure the relationship between this kind of ideal war and the wars of the nineteenth century.

The key to the effectiveness of the revolution is a combination of organization and physical courage: the individual and communal manifestations of will, demonstrated in a willingness to fight.[124] Violence may be a bearer of meaning but it is not intrinsically morally charged. It is capable in the right circumstances of setting in train a kind of peaceable evolution, more Lamarckian than Darwinian in its emphasis on modification of inherited characteristics through need, communal desire, or the broader social good rather than aggressive competition.[125] The tale is not entirely without hints of eugenics or compulsion in Dick's account of ridding this new world of lazy, ugly people, who 'produced such ugly children if their disease was not treated sharply that the neighbours couldn't stand it' (39). Yet there is little need for the coercion and control of Bellamy's utopia of state socialism, *Looking Backward* (1888), because war itself changes people's desires, habits and even bodily responses.[126] Morris's commitment to the detailed presentation of cataclysmic 'change', rather than the vague description of gradual organic destruction given in William Hudson's *A Crystal Age* (1887) or the unspecified pretextual disaster of Jefferies's *After London* (1885) demonstrates his commitment to acts of war. His focus on the process of battle as the bearer of change suggests that it forms part of the essential physical transformation of the people from dull and quiescent to active and capable of establishing a new world.[127] Before the war is over, the 'revolutionary instinct' has so worked on the government's soldiers and the ordinary working people that most of them have switched sides and joined 'the rebels' (129). Instinct is on the side of the working-class revolutionaries, and is shaped by the conditions of battle. Violence functions as an agent of both revolution and evolution and its acts are idealized as the means of transformation of the individual and the society.

After Morris's death, John C. Kenworthy wrote that 'Morris was of the opinion (and who can escape it?) that fighting, bloodshed, must yet be gone through before the better society comes'. He went on to comment that 'I do not know that he has anywhere clearly written his own conviction as to the use of force in determining social relations.'[128] Morris did write of this, however, and quite clearly, shortly before the publication of *News from Nowhere*. In 1889, unable to attend the regular socialist celebration of the Paris Commune due to gout and rheumatism, he wrote to the leader of the celebrations, arguing that transformation of power relations between workers and masters could not be brought about by persuasion, but only 'by the threat of force, or, if it must be, by its action'. While this use of 'force' carries the sense of organized action, it is difficult to imagine what 'the threat of force' or 'its action' might mean, apart from violence of the kind that results from the clashes between workers and government in *News from Nowhere*. Morris goes on to argue that the workers must organize themselves 'into an irresistible power'; whoever does not contribute to the effort of doing this, 'need hardly call himself a Socialist':

> He really falls back into the ranks of those who have not learned the principles of action as he has, and who, being ignorant, can only wait for the impulsion of that *force*, which it is the Socialists' business to help to fashion for the realisation of the Society of Equality.[129]

Knowledge and action go hand in hand here. Force itself appears to be the creation of hard work, something that may be fashioned into a means of realizing a communal dream.

It is fashioned in part by the action of socialists themselves but also by the actions of the government. There is a symbiosis about the move towards war, despite the differences between government and people. The will and physical strength of the people is shaped by the government's violence, so that in the end, 'all ideas of peace on a basis of compromise had disappeared on either side' (128). War is presented as necessary because the people can only become a unified body through it. They see, as Morris sees, no alternatives but compromise or battle, and so equality can only be born out of violence. 'The end, it was seen clearly, must be either absolute slavery for all but the privileged, or a system of life founded on equality and Communism'. Despite the government's superior weapons and power, the people triumph through waging war because 'the sloth, the hopelessness, and […] the cowardice of the last century, had given place to the restless, eager heroism of a declared revolutionary period' (128). The war is created and shaped by the oppressive violence of the state: the manliness of the people is brought into being through opposition. Their own acts of violence, in this account, do them no moral or spiritual harm; instead a physically understood oppression is solved by a physical means – heroic war.

At a time when the newspapers of the day are full of stories of anarchist plots and socialists are understood by many to be rabble-rousers, Morris describes the government of his tale in words commonly applied to his own comrades. Old Hammond, in telling Guest about 'the change', characterizes the violent acts of the government as 'slaughter', 'massacre' and 'atrocity' (123; 118), which cause 'terror' and 'horror' (116). He describes how, during the civil war, 'the reactionist plot exploded probably before it was ripe' (120). These terms offer a parody of the fear of bombs and explosions associated in the press of the 1880s and 1890s with anarchists and Fenians, which Old Hammond mentions as a cause of army brutality in the period leading up to the revolution in Nowhere (126).[130] The transferral of this language to the government may well be a sly joke on Morris's part, but also makes a more serious point: as at the time of the Paris Commune, under the apparently ordered actions of the government lies the true terror, begetter of revolutionary violence. More recently, in the wake of the 9/11 attacks Jean Baudrillard has argued that 'current terrorism is not the descendant of a traditional history of anarchy, nihilism and fanaticism' because it is the mirror image of the state, the necessary result of globalization: an enemy generated 'from within'.[131] Yet Morris's parodic use of the language popularly used about revolutionaries suggests that they too were partners of the violent, universalizing state, their activities, if not their ideologies, only the product of its own.

Central to the story of the future revolution is an account by Old Hammond of a massacre in Trafalgar Square. This recalls the infamous Peterloo Massacre of 1819, but also draws on the actions of the government on Bloody Sunday, 13 November 1887, in which a demonstration by unemployed workers, socialists and other radicals was brutally broken up by the police, hundreds were injured, and the law-writer Alfred Linnell received injuries of which he died a month later. In an account of the day published shortly afterwards in *Commonweal*, Morris writes of the Metropolitan Commissioner of Police, that:

> Sir Charles [...] made his military dispositions admirably, and revolutionists should study them, since they have had a little piece of real war suddenly brought to their notice. [...] Sir Charles Warren has thus given us a lesson in street fighting, the first point of which is that mere numbers without organisation or drill are useless.[132]

In a curiously detached contemplation of the conflation of reality and fiction, May Morris comments that 'in all the excitement of the moment he had noted the strategical arrangement of the forces against the people with the keen precision which characterized the descriptions of the combats in his tales of the past.'[133] Fiction and reality are interchangeable as sources for imaginative constructions of the future: even in the midst of a police attack on the people, Morris is watching the way the violence is organized. This 'keen precision' suggests an interest in the strategic rather than the personal that underlies Morris's willingness to countenance battle as a means to an end, as well as his unwillingness to allow that violence might itself have any lasting effect beyond the physical.

As Old Hammond describes the attack on the people by the government of 1952, Guest supposes that 'this massacre put an end to the whole revolution for that time?' (117). The story suggests the inadequacy of this response to sacrificial violence. The old man assures him that, on the contrary, this began the revolution, and he drinks to the memory of those who died that day, 'for indeed it would be a long tale to tell how much we owe them' (117). Like John Ball, who cannot imagine the workers of Victorian times not rising in battle against their masters, Dick is shocked at Guest's own brief account of Bloody Sunday, when 'there was no fighting, merely unarmed and peaceable people attacked by ruffians armed with bludgeons' (42). In describing Dick's reaction from the vantage point of postviolent peace, Morris invites his readers to reconsider their own response to police violence. Dick's reply – 'and they put up with that?' – is accompanied by 'the first unpleasant expression I had seen on his good-tempered face' (42). Over a hundred years of peace and freedom have left this utopian man with no possibility of imagining the downtrodden workers of the nineteenth century; both body and mind have evolved in this society, in which, Old Hammond tells Guest, 'we live amidst beauty without any fear of becoming effeminate' (72). The very achievement of complete manliness and wholeness through battle undermines the possibility of the recurrence of oppression, the story suggests. This is in part because it has no place in this holistic new world, but also because the instinct for fighting it, developed through the now distant period of the war, remains.

The initial outcome of the revolution is complete destruction of the old world and all it stands for. Bloch observes that Morris 'welcomes the revolution, though only as an act of annihilation'; while this reductionist view of Morris's commitment to revolution ignores his investment in the process of combat and its values, it does highlight the significance of his commitment to the idea of the complete obliteration of his own nineteenth-century world necessary to social transformation.[134] This is not only 'the forcible overthrow of all existing social conditions' required of Communists by Marx and Engels, but a concomitant destruction of the very material fabric of that society: 'all historians are agreed that there never was a war in which there was so much destruction of wares, and instruments for making them as in this civil war', says Old Hammond (130).[135] Values inhere in things, this suggests, more than in abstract codes: physical destruction will lead, therefore, to social renewal. There can be no independent, inexplicable natural force that changes the world, for Morris; rather, in keeping with the story's role as a serial in *Commonweal*, he insists on the personal responsibility of each person for the revolution that will overthrow capitalism.

There is a pleasure in the idea of complete destruction: 'in that fighting time [...] all was hope; "the rebels" at least felt themselves strong enough to build up the world again from its dry bones' (131). In the light of later Year Zero experiments, this passion for complete destruction of the past, both material and intellectual, looks less hopeful than it may have done at the time.[136] It is, however, a characteristically Morrisian response to ideas of progress like those of the capitalist Darwinian, Spencer, who, like Cobden, saw industrial society and commercial activity as the centre of all that is good in society and inimical to war: 'a long peace is likely to be accompanied by so vast an increase of manufacturing and commercial activity [...] that hostilities will be more and more resisted and the organization adapted for the carrying them on will decay.'[137] Morris's ferocious insistence, instead, on the exact correlation between capitalism and unjust war is reflected in the commitment to complete destruction of that society. What is noticeable here is that this new world is figured in human terms. Like the biblical Ezekiel in the valley of dry bones, the people of the future flesh out their social world into a living body.[138] This new world will be as organically interdependent as a single human being on its separate parts.

The holism of Morris's future society entails an erasure of the sharp demarcation or boundaries between self and other, the body and the world, that is partially achieved in his earlier works by moments or acts of violence that transgress, and in doing so, affirm such identity-forming boundaries. In Hegelian terms, violence is a way of recognizing being and identity; both a physical and a metaphysical event. War itself is an 'ethical moment', in Hegel's terms, in which individuals overcome their selfish desires, and are preserved from 'that stagnation which a lasting, not to say perpetual peace, would [...] produce among nations'.[139] In *News from Nowhere* Morris posits the end of this romantic vision of violence in affirming an enduring, peaceful, communal identity achieved through the completion of violence, the utter destruction of all the institutions of the state as well as its economic structures. In doing so he necessarily accepts violence as a means of bringing this about, legitimating it until such an end is achieved, indeed as the only means by which such an end – and it is clearly a far-distant one in 1890 – may be achieved.

What then, of the postrevolutionary state of society? In the politically suggestive postviolence of Nowhere, there is no need for either punishment or coercion, although as I have suggested, there are hints of processes of corporeal violence or coercion in the postwar development of the society. Nonetheless violence does occur. The permanent erasure of demarcations that has been brought about by the revolution leads to a widespread homogenization of desire that is only occasionally disrupted by a brief resurgence of violent individualism by those whose desires do not broadly coincide with the rest of the community. This is not to say Morris's utopia is uniform in landscape, work or personal expression: clearly one of its bases is the potential for the expression of individuality in work and relationships. Dissenters are tolerated in this liberal utopia, but it is important that they are regarded as anomalies and not allowed to disrupt either the ethical consensus or the communal sensory interactions of society. The amazed or uncomprehending response of Nowhereans to Guest's frequent social or moral faux-pas serve, as Waithe observes, to 'impress on him the need to recognize and adapt to a distinct culture, a new set of rules'.[140] Dissent is not actively suppressed, but organically or communally eliminated.

In this social body, 'working for the whole' becomes a habit. As Fredric Jameson argues in relation to utopias more broadly, the new system demands 'a libidinal dissociation from the consumption of individual objects or works, and a projection of these impulses onto social and collective relations generally'.[141] This applies not only to works or objects, however, but also to people. In losing the need for strife, and the expression of communal commitment through violence, Morris loses at the same time the intense sense of male comradeship and homosocial desire that runs through his work. The brotherhood of violence that comes about through battle in other works has become in Nowhere a permanent state, but an attenuated one. The intensity of relationship that characterizes the earliest romances, or the latest ones, is absent here. Rather, violence has accomplished its dissolution of boundaries to such an extent that people and earth are one, and desire is general rather than specific.[142] As Old Hammond explains, the spirit of his age is 'intense and overweening love of the very skin and surface of the earth on which man dwells, such as a lover has in the fair flesh of the woman he loves' (132). Murders resulting from overwhelming passion remain as a kind of somatic expression of a trace; the actions of violence contain within them all that has gone before and serve to highlight the difference between nineteenth-century responses to crime and the responses of the Nowhereans.[143] Yet in themselves, they are also expressions of the kind of excessive desire Nowhere has largely eliminated and evidence of the instability of its fulfilment.

Despite the emphasis in *News from Nowhere*, highlighted by Holzman, on 'reasonableness' in solving disputes, this is not a rationalist's utopia, nor a pacifist's; its peaceful society is not brought about by reason, but by urgent physical interaction.[144] The communal violence of 'the Change' creates physical manliness and evolves into communal interidentification. Karl Popper, arguing against the political effectiveness of utopian thought, and for the centrality of reasonableness as the opposite of violence, writes that 'some people [...] love and venerate violence. For them a life without violence would be shallow and trivial. Many others, of whom I am one, hate violence.'[145]

While utopian thinking appears to stem from a certain kind of rationalism, Popper suggests, its focus on ends always leads to violence. Although Morris's open-ended, deliberately incomplete utopia largely – although not wholly – operates by reasonableness, toleration and discussion rather than coercion, it is nonetheless only achievable by violence. Its harmonious vision demands catastrophic rather than gradual change. Morris, I suggest, unreasonably holds both the positions Popper posits, of loving and hating violence, and the outcome of peace that his utopia envisages is destabilized and compromised by his investment in violence as an antirational bodily expression of communal or individual desire.

The only remaining violence in the postviolent, 'phallocratic' society of Nowhere is attributable to women.[146] It is not only Ellen who has 'troubled men's minds disastrously'; all women have the potential to do so (188).[147] 'Tis is a good job there are so many of them that every Jack may have his Jill: else I fear that we should get fighting for them', Dick comments to Guest, before going on to tell the tale of one such recent 'mishap', which 'in the end cost the lives of two men and a woman'. This is figured as a slightly unpleasant but passing disruption: it 'put out the sunlight for us for a while', Dick says (35). There is no room for individual grief over the victims or anger at the perpetrators. Like Dick, Old Hammond considers any occasional 'transgressions' against the 'habit' of good fellowship as 'the errors of friends, not the habitual actions of persons driven into enmity against society' (80). Just as men might habituate themselves to bearing arms and so become manly, so now the language of habit is placed at the service of social harmony. The occasional violence that occurs in Nowhere is the unfortunate but natural result of the individual heterosexual desire that persists in this communal fellowship.

The practice of fellowship, then, leads to a gradual physical elimination of personal or dissident desire so that the individual is absorbed into the communal, the female remaining as the one potentially disruptive force in this world of contentment. There is a level of symbolic violence here, particularly against women, who are the objects of passionate mishaps – murders – and who are required by the text to be complicit in the constant male desire that pervades Nowhere.[148] If *News from Nowhere* is, as Beaumont argues, a 'fantasy of effortless self-fulfilment', it only comes at the price of a relinquishment of the boundaries of that self. Counterbalancing that, Morris returns, as he goes on to do more fully in the late romances, to the acceptance of the inevitability of violence in gender relations which relies on a narrative of the destructiveness of heterosexual desire that functions as partner to the narrative of sacrifice.[149] Laziness and ugliness have been thoroughly eliminated in Nowhere, but passionate violence, anomalous without being unduly reprehensible, remains as a paradoxical sign of freedom.

Like *John Ball* and *Pilgrims*, *News from Nowhere* offers a tale of transformation through battle that relies on the simultaneous affirmation of the body and refusal of the individual over the communal. It asks readers to engage with the politics of the present while refusing its limitations for the duration of the tale. It is, in this sense, rather than an end of history, a parenthesis, as David Jones describes his poetic tale of the First World War: 'this writing is called "In Parenthesis" because I have written it in a kind of space between – I don't know between quite what – but as you turn aside to do something.'[150] Morris similarly turns aside, offering *News from Nowhere* as an unfinished vision of the future, standing between the struggles of the present and their anticipated success as an affirmation of their value. Like Jameson's vision of utopia as a moment of suspension, this suggests not the accomplishment of political action but the transformation of the imagination.[151] Yet for contemporary readers, no less than for those coming to *News from Nowhere* in the aftermath of the failure of totalizing ideologies in the West, and in the midst of an international political climate shaped by charged competing ideologies of sacrifice in the twenty-first century, this utopia fails to offer readers a compelling alternative to violence. It invites us to consider the political struggles of the present as negligible in the light of future rewards, but in doing so it powerfully suggests the necessity of violence in engendering and enjoying peace and wholeness. The tale's commitment to morally malleable violence and the cleansing potential of absolute destruction undermines the power of Morris's political vision of equality and freedom, predicated as it is on what Popper describes as 'a distant ideal of a society which is wholly good', yet only attainable by cataclysmic violence.[152]

§

Metaphors of violence and battle inform Morris's writing and thinking. In 1885, he writes to Georgiana Burne-Jones that the early struggles of socialism are merely 'the petty skirmish of outposts, the fight of a corporal's guard'; he tells James Frederick Henderson that now he has joined the socialists, he has become 'a soldier of the Cause'.[153] At the same time, he affirms the possibility that actual violence may be necessary for political change. The writings discussed in this chapter work both as extended metaphors and as matter for political incitement, to change minds if not to lead to action. These metaphors, like myths, both shape reality and are shaped by it. They are not confined to the spiritual or imaginary, but draw on actual events and experiences, urging on their readers and listeners a view of the world shaped by ideas of battle and sacrifice. They detail acts of violence and their political outcomes with precision and passion, inviting readers to see violence as a means of attaining harmonious community as well as social change. They reflect an imagination that is willing to countenance actual violence as a means to an end, but unwilling to conceive of it less than mythically.

If *John Ball* invites readers or listeners into a community shaped by the violence of the past, and the *Chants* and *Pilgrims* offer an invitation into a community of present struggle, *News from Nowhere* offers the ultimate battle of the future as an inspiration for the more mundane struggles of the present. While the corporeal imagination at work in these texts makes them immediate and sensuous, their espousal of battle as a means of transformation leaves little room for the imperfections of political change. They work to elevate the idea of active violence and at the same time to set it in the distant realm of myth. Yet this is not the same as disavowing it. By refusing to allow the possibility of moral evil inherent in physical violence, Morris creates a corporeal, antirationalist myth of absolute good arising from evil through a willingness to achieve sacrificial death in combat. Rather than inspiring action in the present, this vision of beautiful battle suggests the limitations of anything less than absolute war and total self-sacrifice, and so works to further the potent, stirring but politically ineffective myth of redemptive corporeal violence.

Afterword

'HOPEFUL STRIFE AND BLAMELESS PEACE'

In 1885, the popular adventure novelist, G. A. Henty, urged his young readership to take pleasure in tales of war: 'It is sometimes said that there is no good to be obtained from tales of fighting and bloodshed [...]. Believe it not. War has its lessons as well as Peace'.[1] This acknowledges the existence of a counterargument, that stories of war may not be 'good', while affirming the basis of his own writing and preparing boys for the willingness to sacrifice that would lead them into the First World War. This comment is made in the preface to Henty's *St George for England*, a novel that draws, as Morris does, on Froissart's stories of the Hundred Years' War. Henty goes on to praise the courage, chivalry and martial spirit of the fourteenth century and to lament their loss in the present. While the ideologies Henty espouses may be very different from Morris's, the underlying emphasis on the important qualities engendered by fighting and indeed, specifically, by tales of ancient fighting runs across such imperialist narratives as Henty's and the anticapitalism of Morris's work. Morris himself delights in tales of war and offers them in turn to his readers as a means both of pleasure and of personal and social transformation, as this book has argued.

Morris was committed to the idea of violence not merely as a literary device, but as a marker of identity and manliness, as well as a fundamental ingredient of storytelling or propaganda. Not only this, but he frequently presents it in his public writings and private letters as a regrettable but unavoidable political necessity that will secure a lasting and fruitful peace. Morris's work is not war writing like the poems of David Jones or Wilfred Owen with whose work I have at points compared it. It does not arise out of personal experience of war, but only from the imagination of it. In this sense his tales and poems are idealizing ones, in which war is both itself and a sign of other things: manliness, brotherly love, class solidarity, commitment to a cause. Certainly these are not stories that critique physical violence itself: rather, they make fine distinctions between different kinds of fighting by different kinds of people, in the interests of narrative, propaganda and ethics.

While Morris's socialist writings went on to be read by succeeding generations of socialists, including Beatrice and Sidney Webb, R. H. Tawney and G. D. H. Cole, it is not my purpose here to trace the obvious political interest in his work by left-wing politicians or activists.[2] Rather, I want briefly to suggest that the romance of his tales of violence has also formed part of a different set of cultural influences, bolstering a language of mingled chivalry, sacrifice and manly violence alongside a celebration of the brutal work of war as a way of winning peace that sustained young men into the First World War and well beyond it, even drawing some of the adherents of socialist ideals of beauty, health and historical Teutonic manhood into an admiration for fascism and giving others a rationale for war.[3] That the ideals I have identified in Morris's work did not die with the First World War has been abundantly demonstrated by subsequent history and is made evident in such critical works of testimony such as Bourke's *Intimate History* or Houen's 'Sacrificial Militancy', as well as in reflective works such as the recent memoir by American war correspondent Chris Hedges, *War is a Force that Gives Us Meaning*.[4] Reading about chivalric or revolutionary or redemptive violence may take on new resonances in the light of the sacrificial rhetoric of today's 'war on terror' or the events of the Arab Spring. However, the immediate impact of Morris's work is evident in the writings of the generation that followed him. A brief consideration of these writings suggests some of the enduring uses of Morris's readings of violence.

Paul Fussell's much-criticized account of the influence of Morris's romances and others like them on the generation that fought in the First World War offers a rather broad sweep, but it does usefully highlight the ways in which Morris's work formed part of an intertextual cultural understanding of battle constructed in relation to ideas of chivalry, self-sacrifice and manliness, ideas which could be understood separately from his socialist politics and which shaped the cultural environment of the early twentieth century as much as they were shaped by the environment of the nineteenth.[5] His immediate legacy can be seen in the significance of his works for the idealist, medievalist warrior figure of T. E. Lawrence, later known popularly as Lawrence of Arabia, who had a copy of *The Hollow Land, and Other Contributions to the Oxford and Cambridge Magazine* bound especially for himself on his graduation from Oxford. He copied out several poems from *The Defence*, as well as the short verse fragment, 'Christ keep the Hollow Land', from the 'The Hollow Land' into the commonplace book, later titled *Minorities*, that he took with him to the First World War.[6] Alongside his own commonplace book, he took Malory's *Morte Darthur* into the Arabian desert with him, registering a commitment to the idea of medieval heroism that runs through Morris's work, while his own accounts of battle engage with the importance of imperfection and contingency in war.[7]

Morris's influence is evident in the writings of First World War poets as well as later modernist writers. George Thomas's footnotes to Edward Thomas's poems suggest that traces of Morris's 'The Hollow Land' may be seen in Thomas's 'The Hollow Wood', written on the eve of war, and after a review of Morris's early prose romances.[8] In Edmund Blunden's 1931 book of essays, *Votive Tablets*, he notes of Leight Hunt's poem, 'Sir Edgar, Sir Graham, and Sir Gray-Steel', that 'in it we recognise the golden tongue of romance, with those sharp contrasts of strange battle and beauty, expressed in significance and in music, that made William Morris famous'.[9] It seems reasonable to assume Blunden was aware of Morris's work before the First World War as well as after it. At the beginning of the twentieth century, a period that sees the proliferation of boys' books of adventure, including the publication of a newly selected *Boys' Froissart* in 1913, Morris's work forms part of a long history of the celebration of battle in literature, and offers both sustenance and literary models to young men going into actual war.[10] What his immediate successors draw from his work is not its particular political charge, but its commitment to mythologizing violence, especially the violence of the past, as a way of interpreting and interrupting the present. This approach can be seen in David Jones's long prose poem of 1917, *In Parenthesis*, and, as Chris Jones has demonstrated, in the old northernism of Auden's 'Paid on Both Sides' and the archaicism of Ezra Pound's 'The Seafarer', both poems concerned with exploring and aestheticizing brutal violence through experimental use of language.[11]

A different kind of emphasis on the imagination of war is evident in the fantasy writing of C. S. Lewis and, more significantly, J. R. R. Tolkien, whose mythical worlds are places where only a combination of war and self-sacrifice can bring about the salvation of the world. In a 1960 letter, Tolkien writes, perhaps disingenuously, that the World Wars had little influence on his writing of *The Lord of the Rings*, except 'perhaps in landscape. The Dead Marshes and the approaches to the Morannon owe something to Northern France after the Battle of the Somme'. He goes on to note that 'they owe more to William Morris and his Huns and Romans'.[12] Morris's work, then, feeds various strands of thinking about war in ways that links it to ancient ideals and mythic struggles in the face of present experience of brutality and carnage. Nonetheless his emphasis not just on handwork but on the handwork of war makes uncomfortable links between art, beauty and war, or perhaps, 'war, labour, freedom', that resonate not only into the two World Wars but solidly into the present, in the preference still expressed in recent years by soldiers for hands-on warfare.

This book has argued for a new reading of Morris that foregrounds his interest in and engagement with both literary and political violence. Morris's writing and politics offer a reading of his society, its ills and cures, that is more ideologically disturbing and occasionally complicit with ideals to which he was explicitly opposed than has often been allowed: they demonstrate continuities with ideals of war that carry over into the twentieth century and the post-1918 world, and form part of an ongoing history of ideas that continues to shape both British domestic politics and attitudes to war and international relations. Kate McLoughlin, arguing that 'while war literature may dazzle with its technique and resourcefulness, its subject matter can – and should – sadden and horrify', goes on to suggest that 'the two parts of this proposition are bound in an ethical-aesthetical nexus. The dazzlement's *raison d'être* is to keep the horror in view'.[13] Representing war from a distance, Morris's work sometimes loses sight of the horror in his depiction of the dazzlement, brutal though it may be, and the necessary, transformative potential of one-to-one combat and larger scale battle.

It is important that Morris writes without the personal experience of the devastating violence of war that would beget both war writing and historical reflection on violence in the generations that followed him. Yet the faith he evinces in the beneficial legacies of sacrificial violence and the healing potential of war carry over undiminished into the twenty-first century. In her passionate narrative polemic against war, Brittain asserted her belief that no international organization, pact or conference would be effective in preventing further war and destruction, 'until we can somehow impart to the rational processes of constructive thought and experiment that element of sanctified loveliness which, like superb sunshine breaking through thunder-clouds, from time to time justifies war'.[14] Hedges draws on the same kind of language in his reflective account of witnessing twenty-first century wars: 'war is an enticing elixir. It gives us resolve, a cause. It allows us to be noble'.[15] It is the combination of 'sanctified loveliness' and 'resolve, a cause' that runs through Morris's portrayals of war and becomes increasingly insistent until the brief, rejuvenating war of *News from Nowhere*. After the political romances and poetry of the 1880s, with their purposeful battles, his gothic romances of the 1890s return to an idea of random violence between small, discrete, embattled communities, and to violence as a way of proving identity. Even as he modifies his political thinking to accept the inevitability of parliamentary socialism, his imagination retains its commitment to the idea of violence as a way of exploring and understanding the world.[16] The enduring appeal of this idea as an imaginative trope perhaps suggests the necessity of other kinds of opposition to war than the 'rational processes of constructive thought and experiment', despite Brittain's faith in these, which resonates with Popper's emphasis on reasonableness and rationality. Imagination, myth and the suprarational have as important a role as 'rational thought' to play in the construction of an alternative model of 'loveliness' and meaning, deeply implicated as they often are in the representation and the experience of the joys of battle.

Brittain's point, like Brantlinger's about fiction, highlights an important question on which this book has touched. It concerns the complex relationship between reading about violence and the ways in which identity – personal, political or national – is constructed or imagined. It is a question that has been much discussed in relation to twenty-first century representations of violence, but much less so in relation to the nineteenth, although Morris and many of his contemporaries were acutely aware of the effect of reading about the past and its wars on national and class identity. In the introduction to this book I discussed William James's essay on war as 'the romance of history'. In a 2005 article in the journal *Poetry*, James's namesake, an American army officer, Lt General William James Lennox Jr, offers a new take on the reading of poetry and the conduct of war, implicating literature in the discipline of mind and body that constitutes preparation for battle. He writes of the importance of literature for cadets at the United States' top military institution:

> In the small classrooms of West Point, young cadets consider war through the eyes of Rudyard Kipling, Carl Sandburg, and John McCrae. During his or her plebe year, every West Point cadet takes a semester of English literature, reading and discussing poetry from Ovid to Owen, Spenser to Springsteen.[17]

He goes on to report that 'cadets must also recite poems from memory, a challenge that many graduates recall years later as one of their toughest hurdles'. Reading and reciting is figured here as an act of exertion, equivalent to the more conventional rigours of combat training. Reading about war offers not merely recreation, pleasure or instruction, but psychological preparation for the actual acts of battle that will follow. It figures as a form of discipline, and while the emphasis is perhaps on the mental training rather than the content of the recitation, it is of course no accident that the poets Lennox names are all concerned with the experience, meaning and representation of war. War and literature work together here to give meaning and cultural validation to the violence of battle.

Morris's persistent belief in the moral neutrality of physical violence *per se* leads him to embrace the idea that violence may achieve its end and lead to peace. Running alongside this is his belief that under the right conditions, both symbolic violence and actual violence can be overcome by violence on the part of the oppressed. In his lecture 'Useful Work *versus* Useless Toil', he argued that 'it is Peace [...] which we need in order that we may live and work in hope and with pleasure. Peace so much desired, if we may trust men's words, but which has been so continually and steadily rejected by them in deeds.' He goes on to urge his listeners, 'but for us, let us set our hearts on it and win it at whatever cost.' That cost may involve the violence of battle: 'will it be possible to win peace peaceably? Alas, how can it be? We are so hemmed in by wrong and folly, that in one way or other we must always be fighting against them.'[18] It is evidence of Morris's long-term wrestling with this relationship between fighting and freedom from wrong that the language of this lecture closely echoes the mournful cry of his earliest fictional narrator, Florian, in his lament for the Hollow Land: 'it is near our country: but what time have we to look for it or any good thing, with such biting carking cares hemming us in on every side?'[19] While the fight to escape this hemming in was often – though not always – metaphorical in Morris's thinking, his vivid, evocative writings draw on an idea of renewing, transformative violence that makes a far more enduring and troubling contribution to the cultural formation of ideas of just war and righteous battle than to social or political discourses of peace.

NOTES

Introduction   Warriors Waiting for the Word

1. Carpenter, 'William Morris', 118.
2. Crane, *An Artist's Reminiscences*, 439–40.
3. '"Socialists at Play": Prologue spoken at the Entertainment of the Socialist League at South Place Institute, 11 June 1885', in Morris, *Artist Writer Socialist*, II: 625.
4. Sussman, *Victorian Masculinities*, 14.
5. Carter Wood, *Violence and Crime*, 2.
6. Peck, Preface to *War*, ix.
7. Livesey, 'Morris, Carpenter, Wilde', 601.
8. I borrow the term 'old northernism' from Andrew Wawn, who examines the wide range of Victorian imaginative, historical and philological engagements with the 'old north', a term which encompasses both Germanic and Icelandic or Scandinavian literature, culture and heritage. He refers to Morris as a 'Victorian old northernist'. Wawn, *The Vikings and the Victorians*, 249, 337.
9. For a detailed analysis of the peace movement and its various proponents and ideologies, see Laity, *The British Peace Movement* and Ceadel, *Semi-Detached Idealists*.
10. Williams, *Keywords*, 329.
11. 'Language […] is an institution […]. It is pervaded not only by the violence of affects but by the symbolic violence of institutional struggle'. Lecercle, *Violence of Language*, 107; Stewart, *Novel Violence*, xxxii–xxxiii.
12. Mackail, *Life*, I: 67.
13. Mackail, *Life*, I: 166. See also Gregory, *History of the Artists* [sic] *Rifles*, 1–3.
14. William Richmond, quoted in Stirling, *The Richmond Papers*, 165.
15. As I discuss in Chapter Five, he did experience police violence in the 1880s as well as seeing the effects of state violence on many socialists around the world.
16. For social histories of interpersonal or criminal violence, see Carter Wood, *Violence and Crime*, and Wiener, *Men of Blood*; on military and imperial violence in literature, see Attridge, *Nationalism, Imperialism and Identity*, MacDonald, *The Language of Empire*, Peck, *War* and Franey, *Victorian Travel Writing*.
17. Bevis, 'Fighting Talk', 7–33; Karlin, 'From Dark Defile to Gethsemane', 51–72; Markovits, *Crimean War*.
18. Bataille, *The Accursed Share*; Girard, *Violence and the Sacred*.
19. For the coinage of holism, see Smuts, *Holism and Evolution*. Although his theory was not published until 1926, a form of his concept of the fundamental continuity of body, mind and world, and the centrality of the senses in forming reality is evident in Morris's

work, so that it seems appropriate to borrow the term, without suggesting absolute congruence between his ideas and Morris's.
20 Thompson, *Romantic to Revolutionary*; Meier, *Marxist Dreamer*.
21 Pinkney, '*News from Nowhere*, Modernism, Postmodernism', para. 17 of 29.
22 See Meier, *Marxist Dreamer* for orthodox Marxist Morris; for Morris's anarchism, see Kropotkin, 'In Memory of William Morris', and Sargent, 'William Morris and the Anarchist Tradition'. For the environmentalist Morris, see O'Sullivan, 'The Ending of the Journey'; for a reclaimed aestheticism, see Miller, 'William Morris, Print Culture, and the Politics of Aestheticism'.
23 Morris, *Collected Works*, 24 vols. Each volume includes a substantial introduction by May Morris.
24 Sargent, 'William Morris', 66.
25 Boos, 'Dystopian Violence', 9–48.
26 Froissart, *Antient Chronicles*, trans. John Bourchier, Lord Berners; Froissart, *Chronicles of England*, trans. Thomas Johnes.
27 Scott, 'Johnes's Translation of Froissart', 347.
28 Morris, 'The Lord Mayor's Show', 2.
29 For Morris's pleasure in Dumas and the *Thousand and One Nights*, see his list of favourite books for the *Pall Mall Gazette* in 1885, reproduced in May Morris, Introduction to *Collected Works*, XXII: xiii–xvi. Comparing Morris's list with Swinburne's and Ruskin's, she comments that only Swinburne 'will have Thackeray among his friends, or George Eliot ([…] the latter severely crossed out on Ruskin's list)' (xi–xii). On *Aurora Leigh*, see MacCarthy, *A Life*, 147.
30 Kaeuper, *Chivalry*, 32.
31 James, 'Moral Equivalent', 663.
32 May Morris, Introduction to *Collected Works*, XVI: xxviii.
33 James, 'Moral Equivalent', 670; 669.
34 Pick, Introduction to *War Machine*, 7.
35 Morris, *Collected Works*, XXIII: 59.
36 Morris later described himself as briefly under the influence of 'the High Church or Puseyite School' in the mid-1850s, in a letter to Andreas Scheu, in *Letters*, II: 228.
37 Thomas Malory, *Morte Darthur*.
38 Morris, *The Defence of Guenevere*, in *Collected Works* I: 1–145. See Armstrong, *Victorian Poetry*, 232–51; Herbert, 'Dissident Language'; Hassett, 'The Style of Evasion'; Helsinger, *Poetry and the Pre-Raphaelite Arts*, 55–86.
39 Kirchhoff, *Construction of a Male Self*, 58–81; Freedman, 'Ideological Battleground', 235–48.
40 Morris, *The Earthly Paradise*, 4 parts, vols III–VI of *Collected Works*.
41 Carlyle, 'The Hero as Divinity', in *Works*, V: *On Heroes, Hero-Worship and the Heroic in History*, 1–41 (1).
42 Morris, *Sigurd the Volsung and the Fall of the Niblungs*, vol. XII of *Collected Works*.
43 Ballantyne, *Orientalism and Race*, 6.
44 Wawn, *The Vikings*, 31.
45 Arnold, *Balder Dead*, in *Poems*, 376–421; Dasent, *Popular Tales from the Norse*; Dasent, *Icelandic Sagas*.
46 Tosh, *Manliness and Masculinities*; Dawson, *Soldier Heroes*.
47 Morris, *Journals of Travel in Iceland*, vol. VIII of *Collected Works*; Morris and Eiríkr Magnússon, trans. *Völsunga Saga: The Story of the Volsungs and the Niblungs*, in Morris, *Collected Works*, VII: 283–396.

48 Morris, 'The Influence of the North', *Artist Writer Socialist*, I: 471–2.
49 Morris, *The House of the Wolfings*, in *Collected Works*, XIV: 2–208; *The Roots of the Mountains*, vol. XV of *Collected Works*.
50 Morris, *The Tables Turned*. See *Letters*, II: 696: 'there was a good rehearsal yesterday and 'tis thought the play will be a success'; Mackail notes of the courtroom scene that it was received 'with uncontrolled amusement' and 'gave the ludicrous side of a bitter truth.' Mackail, *Life*, II: 200.
51 Morris, 'The Lovers of Gudrun', in *Collected Works*, V: *The Earthly Paradise*, III, 251–395.
52 Morris, 'Socialists at Play', 627.
53 Swords and cavalry lances were still used in the Victorian period, even in the Boer war of 1899–1902, but were much less significant war weapons than guns.
54 Bourke, *Intimate History*, 54.

Chapter One The Early Romances and the Transformative Touch of Violence

1 All further references to Morris's 1856 romances are taken from *Collected Works*, I: 149–325.
2 Dixon, 'Prospects of Peace', 185. The article is unsigned, but all lists of attributions for the magazine agree it was written by Dixon. See Buxton Forman, *The Works of William Morris*, 29, and Georgiana Burne-Jones, *Memorials*, I: 122. See also Lemire, *A Bibliography*, 3–5, on *Oxford and Cambridge Magazine* attributions.
3 Dixon, 'Prospects of Peace', 189.
4 'We are very far from any desire to disparage the achievements of the last two gallant years.' Dixon, 'Prospects of Peace', 186.
5 Aristotle, *Ethica Nichomachea*, 9.2.1103a–1105b. Thomas Aquinas draws on Aristotle for his lengthy explication of *habitus*, in Aquinas, *Summa Theologiae*, 1a2ae.49–54.
6 Bain, *The Senses*, 458; Carpenter, *Principles of Mental Physiology*, 338–75; Rick Rylance's detailed comparative study situates Bain's work in the context of Victorian psychology and notes his debts, acknowledged in his own work, to other contemporary thinkers. Rylance, *Victorian Psychology*, 148–202. The connection between habit and character permeates some of Morris's favourite contemporary reading, the novels of Dickens, as Athena Vrettos argues in 'Defining Habits', 399–426.
7 At the time of publication, *The Oxford and Cambridge Magazine* was reviewed substantially only once, in Anon., 'Undergraduate Literature', 196–7. The review offers evidence of the magazine's youthful passion, certainty and 'grand air', in tones of world-weary amusement and mild commendation (196). For listings of other notices and brief reviews, see Hosman, '*The Oxford and Cambridge Magazine*', 294–302. For later critiques, see Hollow, 'William Morris and the Judgment of God', 446–51; Kirchhoff, *Construction of a Male Self*, 26–57.
8 Thompson, *Romantic to Revolutionary*, 7; MacCarthy, *A Life*, 87–8 and 98–102.
9 Hodgson, *Romances*, 39.
10 Silver, *Romance*, 9.
11 Sasso, '"The Road of War" and "The Path of Peace"', 483–96.
12 Mackail, *Life*, I: 100.
13 Burne-Jones was turned down on grounds of health. Burne-Jones, *Memorials*, I: 109–10.

14 Henry J. MacDonald, 'Recent Poems and Plays', 717–24.
15 Malory, *Morte Darthur*, Jill Mann, 'Knightly Combat', 334.
16 Rylance, *Victorian Psychology*, 194.
17 Burne-Jones, 'Essay on *The Newcomes*', 53.
18 Carlyle, *Works*, X: *Past and Present*, 2–6; Morris, *Letters*, II: 472.
19 La Motte Fouqué, *Sintram*, first translated into English in 1820; Tennyson, *Maud*, in *Poems*, II: 513–84; Fulford, 'Alfred Tennyson', 136–145.
20 Burne-Jones, *Memorials*, II: 56.
21 'The real, final reason for all the poverty, misery, and rage of battle, throughout Europe, is simply that you women, however good, however religious, however self-sacrificing for those whom you love, are too selfish and too thoughtless to take pains for any creature out of your own immediate circles.' Ruskin, 'War', in *Works*, XXVIII: *The Crown of Wild Olive*, 459–493 (491).
22 Aytoun, 'The New Reform Bill', 369.
23 William Howard Russell's first-hand accounts of the Crimean War were published in the *Times* between 1854 and 1856. For his own edited collection of despatches, see Russell, *The British Expedition*.
24 Carter Wood discusses the public discourse of violence, class and civilization in *Violence and Crime*, 14–26; see also J. S. Mill's influential 1836 essay, 'Civilization', in *Essays on Politics and Culture*, 45–76.
25 Peck, Preface to *War*, ix–x.
26 Peck, *War*, 21.
27 Markovits, *Crimean War*, 135. Tennyson, 'The Charge of the Light Brigade', in *Poems*, II: 510–13; Tate discusses the poem's 'ambivalent sense of mourning', in 'On Not Knowing Why', 179; Bevis notes 'a ghost of the words "err" and "erred"' in 'the sounds that drum through the poem'. 'Fighting Talk', 16.
28 Peck, *War*, 23.
29 For a discussion of the shifting understanding of violence from the mid-nineteenth century, see Carter Wood, *Violence and Crime*, 36–9.
30 Tennyson, *Idylls of the King* in *Poems*, III: 263–563 (417).
31 Merleau-Ponty, *Phenomenology*, 93.
32 Aristotle, *Works*, III: *De Anima*, 2.2.413b; 2.11.424a.
33 As Bain notes, the difference between pleasure and pain, in stimulation (as between a caress and a blow, perhaps) arises from excess, that is violence. Bain, *Mind and Body*, 70–71.
34 Carlyle's essay includes translated excerpts, like the one that Morris uses as an epigraph. See Carlyle, 'The Nibelungen Lied', in *Works*, XXVII: *Critical and Miscellaneous Essays*, II, 216–73 (238).
35 Michel Serres suggests that 'the skin is a variety of contingency: in it, through it, with it, the world and my body touch each other. [...] In it the world and the body intersect and caress each other.' Serres, *The Five Senses*, 80. See also Connor, *The Book of Skin*, 27–9.
36 For accounts of the disjunction between public declarations about women's needs for safety and protection in nineteenth-century Britain, and legal and judicial practice to uphold their rights to that protection, see Carter Wood, *Violence and Crime*, 44; Stevenson, 'Ingenuities of the Female Mind', 89–103.
37 Hodgson, *Romances*, 41–4.
38 In the *Merlin Continuation*, the devastated land is described as 'the kingdom of Waste Land and the Kingdom of Strange Land'. Quoted in Kaeuper, *Chivalry*, 27. Morris,

'The Wasted Land' fragment, Morris Literary Manuscripts, fols 194–5. May Morris publishes part of this tale in the Introduction to *Collected Works*, XVII: xviii–xix.
39 Markovits, *Crimean War*, 157.
40 Sartre, *Being and Nothingness*, 613.
41 Merleau-Ponty, *The Visible and the Invisible*, 227; 196.
42 Beer, *The Romance*, 68.
43 See Paul Rodaway's discussion of 'haptic geographies', in which he explores the idea that touch 'is a kind of communication between person and world, a corporeal situation rather than a cognitive positioning'. *Sensuous Geographies*, 41; 44.
44 Dickens, *Bleak House*, 13–14. Markovits notes the significance of fog, 'meteorological as well as figurative' in both the conduct and the reporting of the Crimean War, and makes a connection between a soldier's wittily expressed frustration at the mismanagement of war resources and the fog in *Bleak House*. *Crimean War*, 42–3.
45 Russell, 'The Battle of Inkermann', 6; 'The British Expedition', 7. See Peck, *War*, 29–32, for comparisons between Russell's reporting of the Crimean War and Dickens's novels.
46 Jones, *In Parenthesis*, 179.
47 Das, *Touch and Intimacy*, 35–72.
48 Sartre, *Being and Nothingness*, 610.
49 Carlyle, 'The Hero as Priest', in *Works*, V: *On Heroes, Hero-Worship and the Heroic in History*, 115–53 (135).
50 Gibson, *The Senses*, 123.
51 Kaeuper, *Chivalry*, 143.
52 For a detailed consideration of Christian manliness in the works of Kingsley and Hughes, see Vance, *The Sinews of the Spirit*.
53 See Mackail, *Life*, I: 37–8, and Morris's September 1883 letter to Andreas Scheu, in *Letters*, II: 228.
54 Smith, 'The Physiology of the Will', 81.
55 Bourke, *Intimate History*, 31. See below, Chapter Four, for further discussion of battle joy.
56 Douglas, *Purity and Danger*, 118.
57 Genesis 32.24–31.
58 Hodges, 'Wounded Masculinity', 21.
59 Burne-Jones's inspiration for the painting is a story in Digby's *Broad Stone of Honour*, as Allen J. Frantzen records in *Bloody Good*, 17–18.
60 Douglas, *Purity and Danger*, 142.
61 Clausewitz, *On War*, 101; 117.
62 Bourke, *Intimate History*, 1.
63 Bataille, Preface to *The Accursed Share*, I: 'Consumption', 12; 'La Notion du Dépense', in Bataille, *Essential Writings*, 70.
64 Bataille, 'Consumption', 71.
65 Carlyle, *Past and Present*, 136.
66 I discuss the idea of manliness and a range of models of masculinity current in Victorian Britain in Chapter Three; 'manly' is a recurring word in Morris's letters and lectures, and here I use it to signify an expression of masculinity, with its concomitant ideas of courage, honesty and strength, which in these early stories is closely tied to biological maleness.
67 Heeley, 'Sir Philip Sidney, Part 1', 2.

68 For an extended description of the Eglinton tournament and its aftermath, see Girouard, *Return to Camelot*, 92–105.
69 Carlyle, *Past and Present*, 146.
70 'Because England is a money-making country, and money-making is an effeminate pursuit, therefore all sedentary and spoony sins, like covetousness, slander, bigotry, and self-conceit, are to be cockered and plastered over, while the more masculine vices, and no-vices also, are mercilessly hunted down.' Kingsley, *Yeast*, 28.
71 Carlyle, *Past and Present*, 190.
72 Digby, *Broad Stone of Honour*, 556.
73 Ruskin, 'War', 464.
74 Ruskin, 'War', 464–5. There is an echo here of Kant's argument that, in contrast to the sublimity of war, 'a prolonged peace tends to make prevalent a mere[ly] commercial spirit, and along with it base selfishness, cowardice, and softness, and to debase the way of thinking of that people'. Immanuel Kant, 'Critique of Aesthetic Judgment', 263, in *Critique of Judgment*, 122.
75 Stewart, *Poetry and the Fate of the Senses*, 8.
76 Aristotle, *De Anima*, 2.10.422b.
77 Dixon, 'Prospects of Peace', 189.
78 Kaeuper, *Chivalry*, 22.
79 Scarry, *Dreaming by the Book*, 10–30.
80 Dixon, 'Prospects of Peace', 189.
81 Dixon, 'Prospects of Peace', 189.
82 Armstrong makes this connection in her discussion of Morris's *The Defence of Guenevere*, in *Poetry, Poetics and Politics*, 241. The evocation of the absent factory hand seems less apparent to me, however, in the poems, where so many disparate body parts appear alongside the hands: lips, hair, eyes – mostly women's – are equally isolated and distorted.
83 Ruskin, 'The Nature of Gothic', in *Works*, X: *The Stones of Venice*, II: 192.
84 By the nineteenth century, even the one-to-one pistol duels that had largely superseded the intimacy of swordfights since the later eighteenth century were increasingly rare. The last recorded duel in England was fought in 1852. Baldick, *The Duel*, 114.
85 Carlyle, *Past and Present*, 191.
86 Carlyle, *Past and Present*, 201–2.
87 Morris, 'Gothic Architecture', in *Artist Writer Socialist*, I: 276.
88 Carlyle, 'Signs of the Times', in *Works*, XXVII: *Critical and Miscellaneous Essays*, II, 63.
89 On 3 April 1855, Morris wrote to Cormell Price: 'The other day I went a-brassing near the Thames'; and, later the same month: 'I am going a-brassing again sometime soon'. *Letters*, I: 10–11.
90 Letter to Frederick Startridge Ellis, 4 March(?) 1891. *Letters*, III: 280.
91 Clausewitz, *On War*, 202; 165.
92 Rowe, '"God's Handy Worke": Divine Complicity and the Anatomist's Touch', 287.
93 Catherine Batt argues that hands in the *Morte Darthur* provide an indicator of status and power, as well as stability, in Batt, '"Hand for Hand" and "Body for Body"', 269–87; See also Kaeuper, *Chivalry*, 146–7.
94 Malory, *Morte Darthur*, II.10.7; II.10.52.
95 Malory, *Morte Darthur*, I.1.10; I.7.1; I.7.28. Kaeuper discusses the significance of hands in the *Morte Darthur* and other fictional and historical tales of medieval chivalry in *Chivalry*, 146–7.

96 Kingsley, *Yeast*, 27–8. For a more developed discussion of Morris's ideas of manliness, see Chapter Three, below.
 97 For a useful overview of critical work on the material imagination in the nineteenth century, see Victoria Mills, 'Introduction: Victorian Fiction and the Material Imagination'.
 98 Bachelard, 'Introduction: Imagination and Matter', *Water and Dreams*, 1.
 99 In one of her few comments on the early romances, MacCarthy astutely observes that 'the interesting thing about this story of obsession, a highly wrought dream narrative, a dream within a dream, is the way it focuses on the activity of *making*.' MacCarthy, *A Life*, 88.
100 Das, *Touch and Intimacy*, 146. Das discusses Owen's frequent use of the image of the hand in both war poetry and erotic poetry, commenting that 'hands become a fraught image in Owen's poetry'.
101 Wilde, 'The English Renaissance', 256.
102 Jeffrey Richards makes a detailed case to show that a clear and widely understood distinction was made in early Victorian literature and society between legitimate, deeply intimate male friendship and the 'bestiality' of active homosexuality, in Richards, '"Passing the Love of Women"', 92–122. However, his account is occasionally unsatisfying in its acceptance without qualification of a sharp division between intimate loving friendship and 'bestial' sexual desire, allowing for no possibility of reading against the explicit purpose of the Victorian texts he cites.
103 Kaeuper, *Chivalry*, 216.
104 Carlyle, *Past and Present*, 183; 189; 192.
105 Lemire, Introduction to William Morris, *The Hollow Land*, xxviii.
106 Merleau-Ponty, *Phenomenology*, 144.
107 On the powerful, symbolic right hand see Onians, *The Origins of European Thought*, 97; Hebrews 10.12 and Isaiah 41.10; Ruskin, 'The Nature of Gothic', in *Works*, X: *The Stones of Venice*, II, 180–269 (196–202).
108 Malory, *Morte Darthur*, II.10.2.
109 'Ye are the knyght with the two swerdys, and the man of moost prowesse of your handes lyvyng'. Malory, *Morte Darthur*, I.2.16.
110 Kingsley, *Hereward the Wake*, 76.
111 Serres, *Genesis*, 34–5.
112 Tennyson, 'The Charge of the Light Brigade', in *Poems*, II: 510–13, and 'The Charge of the Heavy Brigade at Balaclava', in *Poems*, III: 91–7.
113 Arnold, 'On the Modern Element in Literature', in *Complete Prose Works*, I: 23.
114 Bevis, 'Fighting Talk', 11.

Chapter Two   Knightly Women and the Imagination of Battle in *The Defence of Guenevere, and Other Poems*

 1 'King Arthur's Tomb' in *The Defence of Guenevere, and Other Poems*, 21–42 (41). Further references to poems in the volume are taken from *Collected Works*, I: 1–145. Page numbers are given in abbreviated form in the text.
 2 Bullen, *The Pre-Raphaelite Body*, 79.
 3 Armstrong, 'Victorian Poetry', 287; Peck, *War*, 21.
 4 For instance: 'He combines the mawkish simplicity of the Cockney school with the prosaic baldness of the worst passages of Tennyson, and the occasional obscurity

and affectation of plainness that characterize Browning and his followers.' Unsigned notice in the *Spectator*, 27 February 1858, 238. For further contemporary criticism, see Faulkner, *The Critical Heritage*, 31–49.

5 Herbert, 'Dissident Language', 313–27; Hassett, 'The Style of Evasion', 113.
6 Boos, '*The Defence of Guenevere*: A Morrisian Critique', 18.
7 Morris and Bax, *Socialism*, 66–7.
8 See Armstrong, *Poetry, Poetics and Politics*, 241; 243; 245.
9 Armstrong, Introduction to *Poetry, Poetics and Politics*, 14.
10 Coventry Patmore, *The Angel in the House: The Betrothal* (1854); Barrett Browning, *Aurora Leigh*, in *Poetical Works*, 352–504.
11 Woolford and Karlin, *Robert Browning*, 178.
12 Scarry, *The Body in Pain*, 33.
13 Chandler, *A Dream of Order*, 1.
14 Morris, '"Men and Women"', in *Collected Works*, I: 326–48 (330–31).
15 Morris, '"Men and Women"', 334.
16 See Arnold H. Modell, who borrows the term, 'corporeal imagination' from Greek philosopher Cornelius Castoriadis to argue that 'the body is both the initial source and the sustaining source of an autonomous imagination'. Modell, *Imagination*, 69.
17 Twenty-one out of the volume's thirty poems include images or acts of kissing or attempted kissing.
18 Like Malory's this is a world rooted in the earthly rather than the spiritual. Terence McCarthy discusses how Malory reorganizes source material according to his own, more material than spiritual values of 'prowess, loyalty and martial achievement'. McCarthy 'Malory and His Sources', 82.
19 See Mackail, *Life*, I: 60 and 136 for Morris's comments on Barrett Browning's and Robert Browning's influence. Barrett Browning, *Poems*, 2 vols. Further references are taken from Barrett Browning, *Poetical Works*.
20 For a celebration of the 'martial maiden', see Robert Southey, 'Joan of Arc', *Poetical Works*, I: 163.
21 Inga Bryden details the various nineteenth-century versions of the Launcelot and Guenevere tale in *Reinventing King Arthur*, 95–111.
22 May Morris recalls happy family evenings around the fireplace, 'Father reading aloud one of the family classics', including 'the most of Lane's Thousand and One Nights'. Introduction to *Collected Works*, XXII: xvii.
23 Freedman, 'Ideological Battleground', 242–3. The identification of Guenevere as a manly warrior is also briefly noted by Robert L. Stallman, in 'The Lovers' Progress', 657–70.
24 Scott, *Ivanhoe*, 509–14.
25 Freedman, 'Ideological Battleground', 243.
26 Morris, 'The Influence of the North', in *Artist Writer Socialist*, I: 452.
27 Armstrong, *Poetry, Poetics and Politics*, 243.
28 Tennyson, *Idylls of the King* in *Poems*, III: 263–563 (540). Gustav Doré's illustration of Guinevere at Arthur's feet cemented this image of Arthur's queen in the popular imagination. For a discussion of this and other visual representations of Morris's Guenevere and Tennyson's Guinevere, see Broome Saunders, *Women Writers*, 153–83.
29 Bain, *The Senses*, 52. A review in January 1856 in the popular *Chambers's Journal* summarized the ideas contained in *The Senses*, making specific mention of the effects of sound. Anon., 'Psychological Novelties', 20–22. It was also reviewed in the *Saturday*

Review, 1 December 1855, 84–5. This is the same journal that reviewed both Morris's early literary work in the *Oxford and Cambridge Magazine* in February 1857, and *The Defence of Guenevere*, in November 1858.
30 Bain, *The Senses*, 198–9.
31 Bain, *The Senses*, 199.
32 Rudy constructs a 'physiological poetics' that explores the politics and physicality of Victorian poetry through an understanding of developments in the science of electricity. *Electric Meters*, 3.
33 Shaw, 'Arthurian Ghosts', 305.
34 Browning, 'Count Gismond' in *Poems*, 161–6.
35 Austin, *How to Do Things with Words*, 1–24.
36 Pearsall, Introduction to *Tennyson's Rapture*, 10–11.
37 Walter Pater, 'Poems by William Morris', 301.
38 In an observation that strengthens the sense of Morris's emphasis on the instability of material meanings, Shaw suggests that 'Morris may expect us to know that blue, originally a symbol of fidelity in love, came in the Middle Ages to represent its own opposite.' 'Arthurian Ghosts', 310.
39 Similar observations have been made on Malory's approach to the spiritual. On Launcelot's decision to go into a religious house as Guenevere has done, 'for the pleasure of Jesu', C. David Benson writes, 'Jesus is mentioned, but he seems decidedly secondary'. Benson, 'The Ending of the *Morte Darthur*', 236.
40 It is bodies, specifically, that go into combat in the *Morte Darthur*. Travelling with La Cote Male Tayle, Launcelot offers to be first in fighting some knights who are in their way. La Cote Male Tayle begs to go first himself, saying, 'I praye you lete me putte my body in this adventure'. Malory, *Morte Darthur*, I.9.7.
41 Blair, *The Culture of the Heart*, 65.
42 Harrison, *Victorian Poets*, 25.
43 See D. S. Brewer, 'The Ideal of Feminine Beauty', 262. He suggests that 'by the late sixteenth century there must be few examples of typically beautiful heroines whose physical beauty does not reflect moral beauty.' Significantly, he offers 'Arthur's Guinivere' as a possible exception to this rule.
44 Hassett, 'The Style of Evasion', 105.
45 John Keats, Letter to Benjamin Bailey, 22 November, 1817, in Keats, *Selected Letters*, 36.
46 Arthur's main concern is the dissolution of the fellowship. When Launcelot, in rescuing Guenevere from the fire, inadvertently kills Sir Gareth and Sir Gaherys, Arthur laments, 'Allas that ever I bare croun upon my hede. For now have I loste the fayrest felaushyp of noble knyghtes that ever helde crysten kynge to gyders.' Malory, *Morte Darthur*, II.20.8.
47 Malory, *Morte Darthur*, I.3.8.
48 Malory, *Morte Darthur*, I.4.23. However, Bonnie Wheeler analyses the interaction between language, act and truth in this incident to suggest that 'Gawain's statement to Pelleas, his "truth", corresponds exactly with the achieved effect'. 'Romance and Parataxis and Malory', 109–32.
49 Malory, *Morte Darthur*, II.20.16.
50 Malory, II.20.8. By rescuing the queen, Launcelot saves her – but also and more importantly for Malory, himself – from shame. Malory, *Morte Darthur*, II.20.6.
51 Bullen, *The Pre-Raphaelite Body*, 80; Foucault, *History of Sexuality*, 18–19, quoted by Bullen, 80.

52 Anon., 'The Defence of Guenevere, and Other Poems', 238.
53 Hassett notes that 'within the compass of thirty poems, there is an odd reduplication of Roberts and Gileses, Alices and Isabeaux', but suggests that this is a 'manifestation of linguistic arbitrariness.' 'Style of Evasion', 105.
54 Anon., 'Morris's Defence of Guenevere', 507.
55 Morris and Bax, *Socialism*, 67.
56 Praz, Preface to *The Romantic Agony*, xxi.
57 Merleau-Ponty, 'Working Notes', *The Visible and the Invisible*, 165–275 (197).
58 Anon., 'Morris's Defence of Guenevere', 507.
59 Statham, unsigned article, 'William Morris, Poet and Craftsman', 66.
60 Froissart, *Antient Chronicles*, II: 419.
61 Henderson, *Romanticism*, 5.
62 Morris, 'Prologue', in *Collected Works*, III: *The Earthly Paradise*, I, 80.
63 Bain, *The Senses*, 341.
64 For an account of the role of memory in Victorian discussions of shock, see Jill Matus, *Shock*, 183–4. Although the concept of trauma is not articulated until later in the century, elements of the ideas of mind, memory and the senses that it draws on are present in much mid-Victorian psychological and physiological thinking, as Matus shows in the Introduction to *Shock*, 1–60.
65 See my Introduction for a brief account of Morris's fondness for singlestick, and Chapter One for his letter about going 'a-brassing'. *Letters*, I: 10–11.
66 See Ignatius, 'The First Contemplation: the Incarnation', 45–6.
67 'Let us go then, you and I, /When the evening is spread out against the sky / Like a patient etherised upon a table.' 'The Love Song of J. Alfred Prufrock', in Eliot, *Collected Poems*, 13.
68 See Algernon Swinburne's use of the same phrase, in the context of pain and passion: 'her neck, kissed over close'. *Laus Veneris* (1866) in Swinburne, *Poems*, 11.
69 Lucy Bending notes that between the 1840s and the 1880s the idea of earthly pain as instructive in turning people to God and of the pain of hell as due punishment for sin gave way to a more medicalized understanding of pain, amid much doctrinal controversy. The romanticization of pain, evident in these works of Morris's, suggests a different use for it, which draws on both these conceptions. Bending, *The Representation of Bodily Pain*, 5–42.
70 Silver, *Romance*, 37–8.
71 Feuerbach, *Essence of Christianity*, 148.
72 Kirchhoff, *Construction of a Male Self*, 77.
73 Morris, *Novel on Blue Paper*, 7.
74 Merleau-Ponty, *The Visible and the Invisible*, 153.
75 A literal – rather than an etymologically accurate – reading of Godmar's name reinforces the sense of his malign purpose, and the suggestion of God as an idea incarnate in Jehane's body rather than an external, purposeful will or benign ordering presence.
76 Hodges, 'Wounded Masculinity', 29.
77 Scarry, *The Body in Pain*, 164–5.
78 Froissart notes the burning of women as a frequent event in the Jacquery, but the addition of the church is Morris's own. *Antient Chronicles*, I: 392–3. See 'Svend and his Brethren', in *Collected Works*, I: 226–44 (231), in which the people are punished year after year for the atrocity of setting fire to women in a church.

79 Brantlinger, 'A Reading of Morris' *The Defence*', 20.
80 Armstrong, *Poetry, Poetics and Politics*, 245.
81 Morris, 'Art Under Plutocracy', in *Collected Works*, XXIII: 164–91 (190).
82 For an alternative account of entrapment and gender in the volume, see Boos, 'Sexual Polarities', 181–200.
83 Brombert, Introduction to *The Romantic Prison*, 6.
84 Morris, 'The Boy Farms at Fault', 241; 'On Some Practical Socialists', 52.
85 Pater, 'Poems by William Morris', 311.
86 Morris, 'Art: A Serious Thing' (1882), in *Unpublished Lectures*, 38–9.
87 Pater, 'Poems by William Morris', 312.
88 See also Morris, *Letters*, II: 735: 'The whole prison system in its folly, stupidity, and cruelty, is a disgrace to mankind.'
89 Morris, *News from Nowhere*, in *Collected Works*, XVI: 3–211 (43); see also the 'sense of isolation and imprisonment', of *Novel on Blue Paper*, 4.
90 Tennyson, 'Mariana', in *Poems*, I: 82. 'The Raven', in Poe, *Complete Tales and Poems*, 943–6; Barrett Browning, *Poetical Works*, 202.
91 Browning, 'My Last Duchess', in *Poems*, II: 157–60.
92 Bain, *The Senses*, 602.
93 'Gertha's Lovers', in *Collected Works*, I: 176–225.
94 Riede, 'Morris, Modernism and Romance', 97.
95 Bain uses Mariana's cry of weariness to illustrate the effects of 'nervous fatigue and exhaustion', the 'most virulent forms' of which may lead to suicide. 'Hence the final triumph of ennui:– "I am aweary, aweary, O God that I were dead!"' He goes on to suggest that 'this state is the termination or final issue of a great many other forms of pain, [...] whether bodily or mental'. *The Senses*, 113–14. For an extended comparison of 'Mariana' and 'Golden Wings', see Saltzman, 'William Morris' "Golden Wings"', 285–99.
96 *Pilgrims* (1885–86) tells a tale of hopeful battle for change, as I discuss in Chapter Five. The idea of hope comes up again and again in Morris's work, in the contexts of politics, personal life and work. See, for instance, 'Useful Work *versus* Useless Toil' (1884): 'what is the nature of the hope which, when it is present in work, makes it worth doing? It is threefold, I think – hope of rest, hope of product, hope of pleasure in the work itself; and hope of these also in some abundance and of good quality'. *Collected Works*, XXIII: 98–120 (99).
97 Rossetti, *Poems*, 3–7.
98 Gallagher, 'George Eliot: Immanent Victorian', 72–3.
99 Rossetti, William Holman Hunt and John Millais conceived the Pre-Raphaelite Brotherhood in explicit opposition to the establishment values of the Royal Academy: 'The British School of painting was in 1848 wishy-washy to the last degree; nothing imagined finely, nor descried keenly, nor executed puissantly. The three young men hated all this [...] They determined to make a new start on a firm basis.' Rossetti, *Dante Gabriel Rossetti: His Family-Letters*, I: 126–7.
100 See, for instance, *Laus Veneris* (1873–78). For a useful analysis of the androgyny of Burne-Jones' paintings, and their reception, see Bullen, *The Pre-Raphaelite Body*, 182–216.
101 Helsinger, *Pre-Raphaelite Arts*, 57.
102 Morris, 'The Churches of North France', in *Collected Works*, I: 349–66 (349).
103 Keats, Letter to Benjamin Bailey, in *Selected Letters*, 36.

Chapter Three *Sigurd the Volsung* and the Parameters of Manliness

1. Thomas Carlyle, 'The Hero as Divinity', in *Works*, V: *On Heroes, Hero-Worship and the Heroic in History*, 1–41 (32).
2. 1 Corinthians 16.13.
3. Tosh, *Manliness and Masculinities*, 201.
4. For discussions of the varieties of Victorian ideas of manliness, see Sussman, *Victorian Masculinities*; Adams, *Dandies and Desert Saints*; Tosh, *Manliness and Masculinities*; Nelson, 'Sex and the Single Boy'.
5. Wawn, *The Vikings*, 3.
6. *Sigurd the Volsung*, vol. XII of Morris, *Collected Works*.
7. Tucker, *Epic: Britain's Heroic Muse*, 515; Dentith, *Epic and Empire*, 78–83.
8. Dentith, 'Morris, "The Great Story of the North" and the Barbaric Past', 251.
9. Sussman, Introduction to *Victorian Masculinities*, 1–15 (13).
10. Tennyson, *The Princess*, in *Poems*, II: 185–296.
11. For Victorian constructions of the Norse, see Arnold, *Balder Dead*, in *Poems*, 376–421; Haggard, *Eric Brighteyes*; Dasent, 'The Norsemen in Iceland', 165–214; Dasent, *The Story of Burnt Njal*; Kingsley, *Hereward the Wake*. See also Wawn, *The Vikings and the Victorians*.
12. On the interconnection of the discourse of manliness and counter-revolutionary activity, see Alderson, *Mansex Fine*, 15–45.
13. Anon., 'Recent Literature', 501: '*Sigurd, the Volsung*, is the second great English epic of our generation'.
14. Dentith, *Epic and Empire*, 83; 79. Morris's poetic strategy is similar to one identified by Chris Jones in the works of later poets who draw on Old English writings (and are influenced by Morris). Jones borrows a term from Geoffrey Hill to suggest that 'the "strange likeness" of Old English accords neatly with modernist strategies of defamiliarization, a mode of refreshing the intensity of sensory perception by first making strange the act of perception and then allowing refamiliarization [...] to occur.' Introduction to Jones, *Strange Likeness*, 6–7.
15. Dentith, *Epic and Empire*, 69–74.
16. Although, as Morris predicted, the public were less convinced by it, and the poem did not sell well at first. See letter to Theodore Watts-Dunton, 16 December 1886: 'I am bringing out a cheap Edition of Sigurd 6s/0: since the old one did not sell.' *Letters*, II: 602.
17. Watts, unsigned review, 'Literature: *The Story of Sigurd the Volsung*', 755. Gosse, 'Literature', 557; Anon., 'Contemporary Literature', 325.
18. Colvin, 'General Literature and Art: *The Earthly Paradise*', 58; Simcox, '*The Earthly Paradise*: Poem', 121; Anon., '*The Earthly Paradise* – Part III', 333.
19. Austin, 'The Poetry of the Period: Morris', 51.
20. For comparisons of the North with the South, see Ruskin, 'The Nature of Gothic', in *Works*, X: *The Stones of Venice*, II, 180–269. For comparisons of the 'effeminate' East with the 'masculine' North, see FitzGerald, *Letters*, II: 190 and II: 184.
21. For an overview of critical responses to *Sigurd*, see Faulkner, *The Critical Heritage*, 230–87.
22. Buchanan [Thomas Matiland], 'The Fleshly School', 335.
23. Buchanan, 'The Fleshly School', 341; 344; 336; 337.
24. Wilmer, 'Maundering Medievalism', 69–73 (70).
25. Morris, 'The Aims of Art', in *Collected Works*, XXIII: 81–97 (97).

26 Morris, 'How We Live and How We Might Live', in *Collected Works*, XXIII: 3–26 (23).
27 A. P. Stanley, *The Life of Thomas Arnold*, 103.
28 See my Introduction for the use of holism in relation to Smuts's original use of the term. The importance of parts working together to express a whole at the same time as the whole shapes the parts is particularly relevant here, as is Smuts's view of the 'natural shading-off continuities which are or should be well-known to science and philosophy alike'. Smuts, *Holism and Evolution*, 18.
29 Carlyle, 'Early Kings of Norway' in *Works*, XXX: *Critical and Miscellaneous Essays*, V, 201–310 (309).
30 Morris, letter to Andreas Scheu, 1883 in *Letters*, II: 229.
31 Buchanan, 'The Voice of the Hooligan', 776–89.
32 Arata, *Fictions of Loss*, 13. Arthur de Gobineau's 1853–55 *Essay on the Inequality of the Human Races* further contributed to the development of a discourse of racial degeneracy; although it received little attention on first publication, it was partially translated into English in 1856 and began to be widely known in the 1870s due to Wagner's enthusiastic support. See Biddiss, Introduction to *Gobineau: Selected Political Writings*, 29–30.
33 Nordau notes airily of Morris, that he is 'intellectually far more healthy than Rossetti and Swinburne'. *Degeneration*, 98–9.
34 Tucker, 'All for the Tale', 373–95.
35 Goode, *Collected Essays*, 287.
36 'Gender proves to be performative – that is, constituting the identity it is purported to be. In this sense, gender is always a doing, though not a doing by a subject who might be said to preexist the deed.' Butler, *Gender Trouble*, 34.
37 See Tosh for an account of the ways in which 'empire was seen as a projection of masculinity' and 'a test of the nation's virility'. *Manliness and Masculinities*, 193.
38 Morris and Magnússon, *Völsunga Saga*, 291–2.
39 Morris affirms the importance of 'a free and unfettered animal life for man first of all' in his lecture given in Ancoats, Manchester, in 1888, later published as 'The Society of the Future', in *Artist Writer Socialist*, II: 453–68 (457).
40 Morris and Magnússon, *Völsunga Saga*, 299.
41 Theweleit, *Male Fantasies*, II: *Male Bodies*, 178–84.
42 Well before the publication of fin-de-siècle texts of monstrous Otherness, threats to the integrity of institutions or nations are figured as bestial. See, for instance, the *Punch* and George Cruikshank cartoons of simian Fenians that Curtis discusses in *Apes and Angels*, 32–41. For the opposition of bestiality and manhood, see Ruskin's 1873 lecture on art, in 'Lectures on Art: Lecture I, Inaugural', in *Works*, XX: *Lectures on Art and Aratra Pentelici*, 17–44 (42–3).
43 Machann, 'Tennyson's King Arthur', 202–3.
44 Tennyson, *Idylls of the King*, in *Poems*, III: 263–563 (389).
45 Tennyson, *Idylls of the King*, in *Poems*, III: 263–563 (512).
46 Letter to Franklin Sieveright Peterson, 12 September 1894, in *Letters*, IV: 206.
47 However, it is worth noting that Sigurd too is prepared for his life of mighty deeds by a level of identification with the bestial. The act of eating the heart of Fafnir awakens him to the complexities of evil: 'There came a change upon him [...] he felt beset of evil in a world of many foes'. *Sigurd*, 115.
48 Dasent, Introduction to *The Story of Burnt Njal*, xx–xxi.
49 Kingsley, 'The Explosive Forces', 88.
50 Kingsley, *Letters and Memories*, II: 26. In a further letter Kingsley suggests that the effeminacy of the middle classes arises from the attempt to suppress 'manly *thumos*,

which Plato saith is the root of all virtue'. *Letters and Memories*, II: 27. Angela Hobbs suggests that in Plato, *thumos* is associated with *andreia*, 'manliness', or 'courage', and that women as well as men may show or possess *andreia*. Hobbs, *Plato and the Hero*, 8–11 and 68–73.

51 Rosen, 'The Volcano and the Cathedral', 30.
52 Morris, 'How We Live and How We Might Live', 23.
53 For a discussion of the perceived threat of the rage of the working class, see Stedman Jones, *Outcast London*, 285–94; women's disruptive power is suggested by their association with hysteria, as Poovey demonstrates in *Uneven Developments*, 36–7; Sussman argues for the importance of boundaries in the idea of manliness delineated by Carlyle, as opposed to the formlessness of both the female and the revolutionary. *Victorian Masculinities*, 16–72.
54 The physiologist William Carpenter writes in 1874: 'it is a doctrine now generally received among practical men, that paroxysms of violent Emotional excitement are much more likely to subside, when they are allowed to "work themselves off" freely'. Carpenter, *Principles of Mental Physiology*, 325.
55 For an overview of contemporary criticism of *Maud*, see Shannon, Jr, 'The Critical Reception of Tennyson's *Maud*', 397–417; MacCarthy draws attention to the emphasis in Morris's works on fits, swoons and temporary losses of self-possession, and convincingly relates it to his own well-documented fits of rage or passion. 'Perhaps those who have experienced this sort of otherworldliness have the equipment to get closer to the truth', she writes, in *A Life*, 79.
56 Carlyle, *On Heroes*, 32.
57 Silver, *Romance*, 112.
58 Dentith, *Epic and Empire*, 81. Morris himself disliked Wagner's treatment of the material of the *Nibelungenlied*, writing to Buxton Forman that he felt it was 'nothing short of desecration to bring such a tremendous and world-wide subject under the gaslights of an opera: the most rococo and degraded of all forms of art.' *Letters*, I: 205. Brian Magee notes that Wagner's rendition of the tale 'shows things acting on people, but not people acting on things', quite the reverse of Morris's approach. Magee, *Aspects of Wagner*, 14.
59 Letter to Charles Eliot Norton, May 1869, in *Letters*, I: 76. Compare Morris's emphasis on Sigurd as 'gold' or 'golden' with Dasent's comment that, 'only the fair in face, and hair and eye, could pass for beautiful and well-born. This feeling runs through the whole history of the race like a golden thread'. 'The Norsemen in Iceland', 170.
60 Klaus Theweleit's extensive psychoanalytic reading of novels, letters, autobiographies and other documents relating to the German Freikorps argues for the importance of rigid boundaries and the rejection of any kind of hybridity as unmanly, in the psyche and practice of the soldier male in pre-First World War Germany. See Theweleit, *Male Fantasies*, I: *Women, Floods, Bodies, History*, 408–12 for a summary of the contrast between boundaried bodies, fluidity and hybridity.
61 Morris, *Letters*, I: 241.
62 Morris suggests that work in the nineteenth century, 'seldom, very seldom, comes to the pitch of compelling the workman, out of the fullness of his heart, to impress on the work itself the tokens of his manly pleasure. [...] This is the kind of work which the world has lost, supplying its place with the work which is the result of the division of labour.' 'Art and the Beauty of the Earth', in *Collected Works*, XXII: 155–74 (164).
63 Browning, 'My Last Duchess', *Poems*, II: 158–60.
64 Morris, Letter to the *Daily News*, 24 October 1876, *Letters*, I: 323; 324.

65 Morris, *Letters*, I: 325.
66 Kingsley, Preface, *Hypatia*, xiv.
67 Dasent, 'The Norsemen in Iceland', 166.
68 Ruskin, 'Lectures on Art: I, Inaugural', 41. Also see Gobineau: 'the word degenerate [...] means [...] that the people had no longer the same blood in its veins, continual alterations having gradually affected the quality of that blood.' Gobineau, *Political Writings*, 59.
69 Sørensen, *The Unmanly Man*, 11.
70 Morris and Magnússon, *Völsunga Saga*, 309.
71 Hatto, trans., *The Nibelungenlied*, 87–9; Morris and Magnússon, *Völsunga Saga*, 354.
72 Spatt, 'Morrissaga', 371.
73 Smiles, *Self-Help*, 192.
74 Mill, *A System of Logic*, 584. For a useful discussion of the interaction of habit, will and character in the thought of Mill and his contemporaries, see Collini, *Public Moralists*, 91–118.
75 Morris, *Letters*, I: 89.
76 'I don't think people really want to die because of mental pain'. *Letters*, I: 128. Morris also discusses cowardice in terms of mental pain in relation to himself. In a letter of 1872, just prior to his second trip to Iceland, Morris writes: 'When I said there was no cause for my feeling low, I meant that my friends had not changed at all towards me in any way and that there had been no quarrelling: and indeed I am afraid it comes from some cowardice or unmanliness in me'. *Letters*, I: 171–3 (172).
77 Letter to Thomas Hughes in 1857: 'I have good hopes of our class, and better than those of the class below. They are effeminate, and that makes them sensual.' Charles Kingsley, *Letters and Memories*, II: 27. See also Rosen, 'The Volcano and the Cathedral', 33.
78 Morris and Magnússon, *Völsunga Saga*, 290.
79 Quoted in Mackail, *Life*, I: 359.
80 See, for example: 'they told you there should be mockers in the last time, who should walk after their own ungodly lusts'. Jude 1.18.
81 Morris, 'The Early Literature of the North – Iceland', in *Unpublished Lectures*, 186.
82 Silver, *Romance*, 112.
83 Morris, 'The Early Literature of the North – Iceland', in *Unpublished Lectures*, 185.
84 Valente, 'The Manliness of Parnell', 67.
85 See, for instance, August Bebel's argument in *Woman in the Past, Present and Future*, 7: 'From the beginning of time oppression has been the common lot of woman and the labouring man.' Morris ordered a copy of the book for himself in July 1885. See *Letters*, II: 442. For Morris's own comment on the woman question, see 'Notes on News', *Commonweal*, 28 May 1887, 172. He argues that women's groups 'are far too apt to put forward women as *competitors* with men, and thereby injure the cause of the emancipation of women which every Socialist is bound to further'.
86 George P. Marsh, Preface to *A Compendious Grammar*, x.
87 Clover, 'Regardless of Sex', 75.
88 Clover, 'Regardless of Sex', 76. Also see Laqueur, *Making Sex*, 1–24.
89 Morris, 'Concerning Geffray Teste Noire', in *Collected Works*, I: 75–81.
90 Torfrida in Kingsley's *Hereward the Wake* exemplifies this strong, pure, beautiful, morally guiding spirit, gifted with spiritual insight if not foresight.
91 Dasent, 'The Norsemen in Iceland', 212.

92 Ruskin, 'Of Queens' Gardens', in *Works*, XVIII: 109–44 (114). While this essay has often been characterized as an anti-feminist diatribe, Dinah Birch draws attention to Ruskin's own 'womanliness' and to the 'strange cross-gender movements of thought' in his argument in 'Of Queen's Gardens'. She argues that, 'defining the perfect woman, Ruskin is again talking about himself'. Birch, 'Ruskin's "Womanly Mind"', 113. See also Peterson, 'Feminist Origins of "Of Queens' Gardens"'.
93 Mill, *The Subjection of Women*, 484; 486.
94 Quoted in Aileen Smiles, *Samuel Smiles*, 67; as Tosh points out, 'he meant that she had surpassed the capacities of women, not that she equalled those of men'. *Manliness and Masculinities*, 92.
95 Hughes, *The Manliness of Christ*, 36. For a discussion of Hughes and the feminine characteristics of Christian masculinity, see Nelson, 'Sex and the Single Boy', 530–49.
96 Marsh, 'William Morris and Victorian Manliness', 191.
97 Laycock, *A Treatise on the Nervous Diseases of Women*, 71–2.
98 Lévi-Strauss, *The Elementary Structures of Kinship*, 435.
99 De Beauvoir, *The Second Sex*, 295–6.
100 Carpenter, *The Intermediate Sex*, 17.
101 Irigaray, *This Sex Which is Not One*, 80; 78.
102 Sedgwick, Preface to *Between Men*, vii–x (viii).
103 See Hughes: 'the last requisite for a good fight, the last proof and test of our courage and manfulness, must be loyalty to truth — the most rare and difficult of all human qualities. For such loyalty, as it grows in perfection, asks ever more and more of us, and sets before us a standard of manliness always rising higher and higher.' *Manliness*, 34–5. See also Smiles, *Self-Help*, 316–18.
104 Morris, 'The Aims of Art', in *Collected Works*, XXIII: 81–97 (96–7). Set against this, it should be noted that Morris very much enjoys the use of deception in stories: May Morris notes how he read the Uncle Remus stories to the family. Introduction to *Collected Works*, XXII; as discussed in Chapter Two, he notes and partially justifies the role of lying in Norse and Greek tales in Morris, 'The Influence of the North', in *Artist Writer Socialist*, I: 452.
105 Morris, 'The Aims of Art', 97.
106 Mallet, *Northern Antiquities*, 149.
107 Morris allows his heroes wild courage or solemn determination, without forcing on them the joy of death. Later worshippers of courage, the Nazis, enjoined their young men to 'Live Faithfully, Fight Bravely, and Die Laughing!'. Koonz, *Mothers in the Fatherland*, 196.
108 Arnold, 'Courage', in *Poems*, 147–8.
109 Tucker, 'All for the Tale', 374.
110 As Tucker suggests in relation to Brynhild and Sigurd, insisting on the completeness and self-referentiality of the narrative itself: 'When "all those shall be as the dead" – and only then – will our lovers, bedded in the tale, live again on earth, as they do in the breath of Morris's hexameter.' *Epic*, 522.
111 Spatt, 'Morrissaga', 357; 371.
112 Gates, *Victorian Suicide*, 82–5.
113 The influence of Thomas Bartholin's *Antiquitatum Danicarum*, with its account of the Nordic laughter in the face of death and desire for the glories of Valhalla and the battle to come, was evident in Mallet's work, and continued to be felt in the work of Victorian writers, as Wawn notes in *The Vikings*, 18–19 and 316.

114 Stephen, 'Gentlemen', 336.
115 Morris and Magnússon, *Völsunga Saga*, 286.
116 Quoted in May Morris, Introduction to *Collected Works*, VII: xv–xxxiii (xvii–xviii).
117 For Carlyle's pro-German thought, see Carlyle, *Works*, XII–IXX: *History of Friedrich II of Prussia, called Frederick the Great*, 8 vols; also Carlyle, Letter to Goethe, 18 April, 1828, in Norton, *Correspondence Between Goethe and Carlyle*, 85; Harrold, *Carlyle and German Thought*; Wawn gives this description of Stephens's approach to his work in *The Vikings*, 218; William Howitt and Mary Howitt, *The Literature and Romance of Northern Europe*, I: 5–13.
118 Smith, '*Past and Present*, by Carlyle', 137–8. For attribution, see Seigel, *Thomas Carlyle*, 208.
119 Austin, 'The Poetry of the Period: Mr Swinburne', 460.
120 Writing is itself a kind of alternative use of male energy. Morris's lecture on 'The Aims of Art' suggests that the labour of art 'is undertaken with the aim of satisfying the mood of energy by employing it to produce something worth doing'. *Collected Works*, XXIII: 83–4.

Chapter Four Crossing the River of Violence: The Germanic Antiwars and the Uncivilized Uses of Work and Play

1 *The House of the Wolfings*, in *Collected Works*, XIV: 2–208; *The Roots of the Mountains*, vol. XV of *Collected Works*. Hereafter referred to as *Wolfings* and *Roots*, with references given in the text.
2 Morris, 'Misery and the Way Out', in *Artist Writer Socialist*, II: 162.
3 Boos, 'Dystopian Violence', 33; 39; 36. Boos discusses the Germanic romances in greater detail in 'Morris's German Romances', 321–42.
4 Brantlinger, 'Morris's Socialist Anti-Novel', 35. It should be noted, however, that Morris's letters show that he was widely read in contemporary literature, including popular novels as well as imperial romances.
5 Morris, 'How We Live and How We Might Live', in *Collected Works*, XXIII: 3–26. He refers to Victorian society as a state of 'commercial war' in 'Notes on News', *Commonweal*, 12 January 1889, 12, and in 'Art and Socialism', in *Collected Works*, XXIII: 192–214 (206).
6 See, for instance, Salmon, 'A Study in Victorian Historiography', 62–4; Waithe, '*William Morris's Utopia of Strangers*', 118–19.
7 Letter to Thomas Coglan Horsfall, 17 February 1883, in *Letters*, II: 157.
8 Morris and Bax, *Socialism*, 215. First published in 1886–88 as a series of articles in the Socialist League journal, *Commonweal*, entitled 'Socialism From the Root Up', later edited into a book.
9 Letter to Robert Thompson, 24 July 1884, in *Letters*, II: 307. As Kelvin shows, before writing 'purpose', Morris writes 'our aim', or 'our object', then deletes them both and substitutes 'our purpose'. It is evidently a slightly anxious issue for him.
10 See 'The Hopes of Civilization' in *Collected Works*, XXIII: 59–80 (74–5).
11 'Notes on News', *Commonweal*, 6 October 1888, 313–14 (313).
12 Brantlinger, 'Morris's Socialist Anti-Novel', 35.
13 Daly, Introduction to *Modernism, Romance, and the Fin de Siècle*, 17–19.
14 Vaninskaya, *The Idea of Community*, 41.

15 Morris's complicated relationship with imperialism is not often acknowledged. Edward Said described Morris as one of the few Victorians to be thoroughly anti-imperialist, in *Culture and Imperialism*, 291. But Brantlinger rightly points out that it is not entirely the case that Morris was 'totally opposed to imperialism', in 'A Postindustrial Prelude to Postcolonialism', 472. See also Vaninskaya, *The Idea of Community*, 38.
16 Morris, 'Notes on News', *Commonweal*, 6 October 1888, 313–14 (313).
17 Morris, 'Address at the Twelfth Annual Meeting of the Society for the Protection of Ancient Buildings, 3 July 1889', in *Artist Writer Socialist*, I: 146–57 (148).
18 Morris's impatience with a purely literal understanding of truth is evident in the story of his response to a German professor who wrote asking for clearer details of the people of the German Mark in *Wolfings*: 'Doesn't the fool realise […] that it's a romance, a work of fiction – that it's all LIES!' Quoted in Sparling, *The Kelmscott Press*, 50.
19 Morris, 'How I Became a Socialist', in *Collected Works*, XXIII: 277–81 (279); 'The Society of the Future', in *Artist Writer Socialist*, II: 453–68 (456–7).
20 Buchanan, 'The Voice of the Hooligan', 776–89.
21 Deane, 'Imperial Barbarians', 205.
22 Deane, 'Imperial Barbarians', 205.
23 Deane discusses, as key examples of the genre he proposes, Haggard's *King Solomon's Mines*, Conan Doyle's *The Lost World* and Kipling's 'The Man Who Would Be King'.
24 Bakhtin, *The Dialogic Imagination*, 16.
25 *The Dialogic Imagination*, 17–18.
26 Morris, *Letters*, II: 426. Vaninskaya, *The Idea of Community*, 58.
27 13 May 1885. Morris, *Letters*, II: 436. See Engels, *Origin of the Family*, 194: 'only barbarians are able to rejuvenate a world in the throes of collapsing civilization'.
28 Macaulay, *Miscellaneous Writings*, I: 314.
29 Engels, *Origin of the Family*, 195–6; Morgan, *Ancient Society*, 122. For a detailed account of the intersection of Morris and Bax's ideas of the barbarism of Teutonic society with those of Engels, Morgan and contemporary historians, see Vaninskaya, *The Idea of Community*, 75–113.
30 Morris and Bax, *Socialism*, 27.
31 Morris, 'How We Live and How We Might Live', 5.
32 See Mill, 'Civilization', 45–76. Michael Levin gives a detailed account of Mill's attitudes in the context of the wider debate in *J. S. Mill on Civilization and Barbarism*.
33 Tylor, *Primitive Culture*, I: 29.
34 Millin, *Rhodes*, 144, 'The Native Question', in Vindex, *Cecil Rhodes*, 361–96 (383); see Deane, *Imperial Barbarians*, 205, for a discussion of Rhodes' claims to barbarianism and the similar claims made against him by critics; for an assertion of the supremacy of the Anglo-Saxon race, see 'Rhodes' "Confession of Faith" of 1877', in Flint, *Cecil Rhodes*, 248–52.
35 See Stead, 'Chinese Gordon for the Soudan': 'We cannot send a regiment to Khartoum, but we can send a man who on more than one occasion has proved himself more valuable in similar circumstances than an entire army.'
36 For a survey of depictions of Gordon after his death, see Behrman, 'After-life', 47–61.
37 Tennyson, epitaph for Charles Gordon, in 'Gordon, Tennyson, and Whittier'.
38 Oliphant, 'General Gordon', 247; 250; 259; 247. For an account of the ways in which Gordon fits in with broader myths of imperial heroism, see MacKenzie, 'Heroic Myths of Empire' in MacKenzie, *Popular Imperialism*, 109–38.
39 Bax, 'Gordon and the Soudan', 10.
40 Morris, Letter to Wilfred Scawen Blunt, 3 March 1885, in *Letters*, II: 397.

41 Morris, 'Notes on News', *Commonweal*, 2 February 1889, 33.
42 Morris, 'Notes on News', *Commonweal*, 27 October 1888, 337.
43 Morris, *Letters*, II: 496. Later, in 1888, Morris mentioned to Magnússon that Haggard had approached him for introductions in Iceland in preparation for writing his Nordic tale, *Eric Brighteyes*. *Letters*, II: 785.
44 Haggard, 'A Zulu War-Dance', 97.
45 Haggard, 'A Zulu War-Dance', 107; 96. Morris turns the tables on Christian missionaries who complained of the traders' activities, and whom Haggard lets off more lightly, when he writes, of their approach: 'one day it is rum-and-bible, another sword-and-bible'. *Commonweal*, 12 January 1889, 12. See below, Chapter Five, for more extensive discussion of this.
46 Tosh, 'Masculinities in an Industrializing Society', 339.
47 Bhabha, *The Location of Culture*, 160.
48 Genette, *Paratexts*, 1–12.
49 'The Development of Modern Society', *Commonweal*, 16 August 1890, 260–61 (261).
50 Rudyard Kipling's famous formulation perfectly encapsulates this idea: 'Take up the White Man's Burden – / The savage wars of peace'. 'The White Man's Burden', in *Kipling's Verse*, 323–4 (324).
51 Morris, 'The Hopes of Civilization', 74.
52 'Gertha's Lovers', in Morris, *Collected Works*, I: 176–225.
53 Newman, *The Idea of a University*, 179.
54 Morris writes of reading Mill's critique of socialism: 'Those papers put the finishing touch to my conversion to Socialism', in 'How I Became a Socialist', 278.
55 Mill, 'Civilization', 57.
56 Mill, 'Civilization', 58; 46.
57 Reid, '"King Romance" in *Longman's Magazine*', 360.
58 Lang, 'Realism and Romance', 690.
59 Lang, 'Realism and Romance', 689; 690.
60 Cf. *The Tale of Beowulf Sometime King of the Folk of the Weder Geats*, trans. William Morris and A. J. Wyatt, in *Collected Works* X: 174–284: 'mere-farer' (194); 'mead-bench' (202); 'bone-house' (273).
61 Cf. Morris, *Beowulf*: 'war-weed' (190); 'slaughter-shafts' (190); 'war-race' (195); 'wartide' (211); 'war-grip' (222); 'battle-steep war-helm' (243); 'war-hosts' (244); 'war-swing' (256); 'battle-gleams' (256). While these are, of course, Morris's own renditions of *Beowulf*'s language, they reflect its preoccupations: Andy Orchard lists 103 compound words based on war or battle used in *Beowulf*, in *A Critical Companion*, 70–72.
62 Malory, *Morte Darthur*, I.2.1.
63 Malory, *Morte Darthur*, II.21.4
64 Morris, 'Art under Plutocracy', in *Collected Works*, XXIII: 164–91 (186).
65 Haggard, *King Solomon's Mines*, 183; 190.
66 Andrew Lang, quoted in Appendix A to Haggard, *King Solomon's Mines*, 245.
67 Anon., 'The Roots of the Mountains', 688.
68 Morris, 'Unattractive Labour', Supplement to *Commonweal*, May 1885, 37.
69 Morris, 'Unattractive Labour', 37.
70 Bloch, *Principle of Hope*, II: 614.
71 Morris, 'Unattractive Labour', 37.
72 See, for instance, Morris, *The Odyssey of Homer Done into English Verse*, vol. XIII of *Collected Works*, 44–63; 102–3; 304.

73 Morris, 'The Society of the Future', 457.
74 Marx, *Economic and Philosophic Manuscripts of 1844*, in Marx and Engels, *Collected Works*, III: 232–46 (310).
75 Morris, 'Modern Society', *Commonweal*, 26 July 1890, 237; 'Modern Society', *Commonweal*, 19 July 1890, 225–6 (226).
76 Waithe, *Utopia of Strangers*, 130.
77 Morris, 'Looking Backward', *Commonweal*, 22 June 1889, 194–5.
78 Boos, 'Morris's German Romances', 329–30.
79 'The Early Literature of the North – Iceland', 181. See Dasent on the qualities of ugliness and evil associated with dark skin in 'The Norsemen in Iceland', 171.
80 In a rather different, but related usage, see Stevenson, *Dr Jekyll and Mr Hyde*, 61, in which Hyde's hands are oddly described as 'of a dusky pallor and thickly shaded with a smart growth of hair' – drawing in images of degeneracy as well as racial otherness.
81 Pfeiffer, 'The Fight at Rorke's Drift', in *Under the Aspens*, 98–104 (99–100).
82 Anon., 'The Zulu War', *Times*, 5 May 1879, 13; Anon., 'The Zulu War', *Times*, 6 March 1879, 6; Anon., 'Latest Telegrams: The Disaster at the Cape', *Daily News*, 14 February 1879, 5.
83 Lawrence, 'I'sandula!'. For a further account of responses to the Anglo–Zulu War, see Lieven, 'Heroics and the Making of Heroes', 419–38.
84 Lawrence, 'I'sandula!', 256.
85 Morris's own awareness of the Zulu War had a personal as well as a political element. His soldier brother Arthur was on active service in South Africa in 1879. Although the brothers were not close, Morris would have been aware of the events of the war from this angle.
86 Salmon, 'Victorian Historiography', 83–4.
87 Regarding the Eloi's feebleness and lack of vigour, Wells's narrator asks, 'What, unless biological science is a mass of errors, is the cause of human intelligence and vigour? Hardship and freedom.' Wells, *The Time Machine*, 32; James, *Maps of Utopia*, 60.
88 Herbert Spencer, Letter 9, 'The Proper Sphere of Government', in *Political Writings*, 1–57 (49). Morris primarily objected to Spencer's use of evolutionary theory to bolster his own view of capitalism as the natural state of society, as against socialism.
89 Spencer, 'Bain on the Emotions and the Will', in *Essays*, 252; Darwin, *Descent of Man*, 142; 143.
90 See Morris, *Beowulf*, 250: 'he, the man victory-happy had cleansed the hall' of Grendel. Again, when Beowulf kills Grendel's mother, it is described in terms of cleansing: 'And now were the wave-welters cleansed full well.' Morris, *Beowulf*, 227.
91 Morris, *Beowulf*, 201.
92 Salmon, 'Victorian Historiography', 83.
93 'Pacific-ism rules out all aggressive wars and even some defensive ones […] but accepts the need for military force to defend its political achievements against aggression.' Ceadel, *Thinking about Peace and War*, 5. Paul Laity, borrowing from Ceadel's definitions, points out that nineteenth-century 'pacif-ists and pacifists united in arguing against every "small" war in which Britain was involved'. Laity, *The British Peace Movement*, 8.
94 'From the moment the first shot is fired, or the first blow is struck in a dispute, then farewell to all reason and argument; you might as well attempt to reason with mad dogs as with men when they have begun to spill each other's blood in mortal combat'. Cobden, *Speeches*, II: 314.

95 Letter to Wilfred Scawen Blunt, 3 March 1885, about Sudan: 'it would really be worth while to try to make a big thing of the antiwar agitation, and that not on the mere Peace-Society platform, but on wider grounds', *Letters*, II: 397–9; in *Commonweal*, 26 July 1890, 235, he refers to the Peace Society in one breath with 'your innocent bourgeois' and accuses them of ignoring fundamental questions of justice.
96 Morris, 'Art and Socialism', 200.
97 Quoted in Bourke, *Intimate History*, 31; 52.
98 Morris, 'Useful Work *versus* Useless Toil', in *Collected Works*, XXIII: 98–120 (100).
99 Livesey, *Culture of Aestheticism*, 13.
100 Morris, 'How We Live and How We Might Live', 23.
101 Goode, *Collected Essays*, 313.
102 Morris does use the term leisure, both in the common sense of rest from labour, and in the sense of labour itself. See Kinna, 'Art, Work and Leisure', 493–512.
103 Marx and Engels, *Collected Works*, V: *The German Ideology*, 36.
104 Gibbon, *Decline and Fall*, I: 227; Boos notes Morris's familiarity with Gibbon and discusses other particulars of his debt to Gibbon's account of Germanic tribal society, in 'Morris's German Romances', 324–30.
105 Morris, 'Art under Plutocracy', 176.
106 Brittain, *Testament of Youth*, 263–4.
107 Quoted in Bourke, *Intimate History*, 31.
108 Brittain, *Testament of Youth*, 264.
109 Morris, *The Aeneids of Virgil*, vol. XI of *Collected Works*, 317. See also XI: 63: 'For I am Polydore: pierced through, by harvest of the spear / O'ergrown, that such a crop of shafts above my head doth bear.' The image of war as a harvest occurs again in *The Odyssey*, which Morris translated in 1887. *Collected Works*, XIII: 203.
110 Sassoon, 'Autumn', in *War Poems*, 109; 'The Harvest of the Sea', in McCrae, *In Flanders Fields*, 55. See also Meynell 'Summer in England, 1914', for a more complex reflection on the relation between harvest and war.
111 The use of nature imagery is common among socialist poets of the 1880s and 1890s, but usually as a metaphor for change that stands in place of ideas of war, rather than being, as it is here, intrinsic to them.
112 By contrast, the speaker in Tennyson's *Maud* presents war as a welcome interruption to the harvest of a corrupt peace, allied with commerce, who will no more 'Pipe on her pastoral hillock a languid note, / And watch her harvest ripen'. *Maud*, in Tennyson, *Poems*, II: 513–84 (583).
113 Morris, 'The Hopes of Civilization', 72.
114 For an account of similarities between the Holocaust and the Rwandan genocide, including the ideas of work and the methodical organization of killing, see Stone 'Holocaust and "The Human"', 240.
115 The celebration of General Gordon's exploits, discussed earlier in this chapter, offers a version of this idea in relation to imperialism.
116 'Their's not to reason why / Their's but to do and die', 'The Charge of the Light Brigade', 512.
117 Appendix B, Shannon and Ricks, 'The Charge of the Light Brigade' in Ricks, *Tennyson*, 324–63 (359).
118 Clausewitz refers approvingly to 'the military machine, the Army', in *On War*, 164. Cobden complains that 'this principle of subordination, which is the very essence of military discipline […] deprives us of the man and gives us instead a machine.' *Political Writings*, I: 370.

119 Newbolt, 'Vitaï Lampada', 95.
120 MacDonald, *The Language of Empire*, 23.
121 MacDonald, *The Language of Empire*, 23.
122 Morris, *Beowulf*, 196; 210; 214; 226. Sam Newton discusses the connections of Hrothgar's queen to the Wolfings in *The Origins of Beowulf*, 123–4.
123 Campbell, ed., *Battle of Brunanburh*, 86. Tennyson: 'hard was his hand-play', 'The Battle of Brunanburh', in *Poems*, III: 18–23 (20). On the relatively rare occurrence and uses of 'handplay' (hand-plegan) in Old English literature, see Hill, *The Anglo-Saxon Warrior Ethic*, 104. Morris also links with a contemporary tradition of writing about the past: that 'handplay' was a word associated both with Nordic tales and with Victorian northernism and archaicizing is suggested by its use in Grant Allen's 1881 comic satire on heroic Nordic tales, 'The Story of Wulfgeat', 553.
124 See, for example, 'Tommy' in *Barrack Room Ballads*, 31–2.
125 Woolf, *Three Guineas*, 13; for a subtle and detailed account of the varied roles of women in Nazi Germany, see Koonz, *Mothers in the Fatherland*, especially 387–420; Bourke draws on first-hand accounts for an examination of the roles of British, American and Australian women in twentieth-century war in *Intimate History*, 306–44.
126 Morris writes to Charles Eliot Norton about *Roots* in 1889, 'I will rather carry out Oscar Wilde's theory of the beauty of lying, as it will have neither time, place, history nor theory in it.' *Letters*, III: 77.
127 O'Brien, 'How to Tell a True War Story', in *The Things They Carried*, 68.

Chapter Five 'All for the Cause': Fellowship, Sacrifice and Fruitful War

1 William Morris, Untitled note, Supplement to *Commonweal*, June 1885, 52.
2 Bourdieu and Wacquant, *An Invitation to Reflexive Sociology*, 112. Bourdieu defines the state as 'the ensemble of fields' that are the site of struggle to establish 'the monopoly of legitimate symbolic violence, i.e., the power to constitute and to impose as universal and universally applicable within a given "nation" [...] a common set of coercive norms'. See also Bourdieu, *Language and Symbolic Power*, trans. Gino Raymond and Matthew Adamson, 167. Although Bourdieu's term is more nebulous than Morris's and deals primarily with the sociological effects of violent power rather than its physical ones, it helpfully highlights the hiddenness of structures of domination, which is important for Morris's argument.
3 Boos, 'Dystopian Violence', 9; 23; 39.
4 Latham, 'To Frame a Desire', 162.
5 For an outline of Marxist ideas about active, passive and reactive violence, see John Harris, 'The Marxist Conception of Violence', 192–220. Harris makes a useful distinction between violent acts which necessarily require force, and violence which may not be active, but results nonetheless in destruction and loss of life.
6 'The Arts and Crafts of To-day', in *Collected Works*, XXII: 356–74 (372).
7 'Useful Work *versus* Useless Toil', in *Collected Works*, XXIII: 98–120 (119).
8 Cobden, 'Russia', in *Political Writings of Richard Cobden*, I: 323.
9 Morris, 'Notes on News', *Commonweal*, 12 January 1889, 12.
10 Fanon, *The Wretched*, 63–4.
11 Fanon talks of the pre-independence acts by the colonial powers as 'mass slaughter in the colonies'. *The Wretched*, 56; see also *News from Nowhere*, in *Collected Works*, XVI: 3–211 (123): 'the soldiery [...] were so daunted by the slaughter which they had made'.

12 'Useful Work *versus* Useless Toil', 119.
13 The idea of pain and suffering as preferable to dullness is a recurring one for Morris; in 1888, writing about the future, he asks disparagingly, 'shall we all [...] as the "refined" middle classes now do, wear ourselves away in the anxiety to stave off all trouble, emotion, and responsibility?'. 'On Some "Practical" Socialists', 52. He sees the same kind of deadening, in political terms, in the move towards what he describes to John Bruce Glasier as 'unideal and humdrum "gradual improvement"; i.e. towards general deadlock and break up'. *Letters*, III: 218.
14 Describing the destruction of capitalism through civil war, Old Hammond observes, 'Surely the sharper, shorter remedy was the happiest'. *News from Nowhere*, 132.
15 'In terms of historical function, there is a difference between revolutionary and reactionary violence, between violence practiced by the oppressed and by the oppressors.' Marcuse, 'Repressive Tolerance', 117. Marcuse goes on to argue that a measure of freedom, progress and justice was brought about historically by violence from 'the oppressed classes' in a way that it has not been by violence from the ruling class (121–2).
16 11 February 1886, in *Letters*, II: 523.
17 Letter to John Glasse, 10 February 1886, in *Letters*, II: 520.
18 'Hopes of Civilization', in *Collected Works*, XXIII: 59–80 (76).
19 Anon., 'Books of To-day', November 1888, 153; 'The Earthly Inferno', 608.
20 Bevington, *Anarchism and Violence*, 3. See also Kropotkin, 'Anarchism', 116–17: 'violence is resorted to by all parties in proportion as their open action is obstructed by repression, and exceptional laws render them outlaws.'
21 Morris writes in the *Pall Mall Gazette* on 7 November 1887, that the anarchists 'had a right to defend themselves as best they could; and [...] the police who were slain brought their death upon themselves by their own violence'. *Letters*, II: 708. This instrumental objection is noted by May Morris in her avowal that 'one cannot too much emphasize Morris's dislike of violence which leads nowhere save to suffering and loss of life and his constant plea for caution in this respect.' *Artist Writer Socialist*, II: 222.
22 He writes to James Tochatti in December 1893 that he cannot imagine how anarchism can 'admit of promiscuous slaughter as a means of converting people'. *Letters*, IV: 113.
23 That he was willing to countenance war abroad as a means of changing Britain is evident in a letter to Edward Carpenter in 1885. He writes that he regrets that the mooted war between Britain and Russia in Afghanistan is averted: 'I confess, brutal as it may seem, I am sorry for it; I hoped that *civilization* was going to give herself an ugly wound'. *Letters*, II: 430.
24 Morris, *Our Country Right or Wrong*, 53.
25 Morris, *Our Country Right or Wrong*, 57; 68.
26 Bevington, 'Why I am a Communist', 6.
27 Brantlinger, '*News from Nowhere*: Morris's Socialist Anti-Novel', 40.
28 First published in *Commonweal*, March 1885–July 1886. All my references are taken from *The Pilgrims of Hope*, in *Collected Works*, XXIV: 369–408; *Pilgrims*, 383.
29 My references are taken from the 1885 pamphlet with seven poems (an earlier 1885 edition had only six), *Chants for Socialists* (London: Socialist League, 1885).
30 Anne Janowitz, *Lyric and Labour*, 217.
31 *Commonweal*, February 1885, 1. The *Chants* published in *Commonweal* were: 'The March of the Workers' (February 1885, 4); 'The Message of the March Wind' (March 1885, 12); and 'All for the Cause' (16 March 1889, 85). For a fuller – though not complete –

record of the publication of Morris's poetry in socialist journals, see Deborah Mutch, *English Socialist Periodicals*, 182–3.

32 Livesey discusses how Carpenter's and Shaw's 'fads' 'opened out spaces for the exploration and discussion of the masculine body', in *Culture of Aestheticism*, 103.

33 The protoanarchist Godwin wrote in 1794, 'it is the nature of the human mind to be great in proportion as it is acted upon by great incitements'. Appendix 3, 'Godwin's Letter to Joseph Gerrald, 23 January 1794', *Caleb Williams*, 355–8 (356). Evocations of injustice and unequal battle function as just this kind of 'incitement' for Morris, transforming the individual moral mind rather than rousing immediate communal action.

34 See the following poems by Freiligrath, trans. J. L. Joynes, in *Commonweal*: 'Freiligrath's Revolution Song: "The Way It's Done"', September 1885, 87; 'Revolution', 21 August 1886, 163; 'A Song of Death', 27 August 1887, 275. Reports on Socialist League events in *Commonweal* frequently note the singing of the 'Marseillaise'. See, for example, *Commonweal*, July 1885, 60; 7 August 1886, 150; 1 January 1887, 7; 19 May 1888, 160; 22 March 1890, 95.

35 Processional: 'Onward Christian Soldiers', in *Hymns Ancient and Modern*, 553; 'Stand Up! – Stand Up for Jesus!', in *Hymns Ancient and Modern*, 775; 'We Are Soldiers of Christ', in *Hymns Ancient and Modern*, 773. These hymns draw on New Testament imagery of Christians as soldiers in, for instance, Ephesians 6.11–17, 1 Timothy 6.12, or 2 Timothy 2.3. For John Glasse's socialist version of 'Onward Christian Soldier' [*sic*], entitled 'A Processional Hymn', see *Commonweal*, 27 October 1887, 33.

36 'All for the Cause', *Chants for Socialists*, 8–9 (9). Cf. 'Stand Up! – Stand Up for Jesus!': 'To him that overcometh / A crown of life shall be; / He with the King of Glory / Shall reign eternally.' *Ancient and Modern*, 775.

37 Janowitz, *Lyric and Labour*, 225–6. May Morris, Introduction to *Collected Works*, XXIV: xxxii–xxxiii (xxxii); she goes on to say that they 'were in steady demand at meetings and open-air demonstrations'.

38 Although see May Morris on the rhythm: 'The measure of The March of the Workers is very heavy for the air – "John Brown's Body lies Mouldering in the Grave," but someone unluckily furnished my father not with the original words as a guide, but with another set of verses, the long racing metre of which he followed. When he found out how much simpler the original John Brown song was, he was vexed.' Introduction to *Collected Works*, XXIV: xxxii–xxxiii.

39 'No Master', in *Chants for Socialists*, 10; 'Wake London Lads', reprinted in *Letters*, I: 436–7. In 1897 Dean Hole (Samuel Reynolds Hole) is reported as writing that 'no song went home to our English hearts, roused us from our lethargic and drear gentility, and made us clap our English hands, save "The Song of the Hardy Norsemen" [*sic*]'. Quoted in 'From my Study', (signed X), 518. The 'Hardy Norseman's House of Yore' is included in a list of patriotic 'Boys' Songs' in the *Musical Herald*, 1 December 1910, 67.

40 Quoted in Bradley, *Abide with Me: The World of Victorian Hymns*, 81.

41 On the complex history of the tune of 'John Brown's Body' and its revolutionary, conservative and religious uses, see Annie J. Randall, 'A Censorship of Forgetting', 5–24.

42 Chris Waters, *British Socialists*, 111.

43 Carpenter, 'England Arise', in *Chants of Labour*, 18–19; Waters, *British Socialists*, 111.

44 'First General Meeting of the Socialist League', Supplement to *Commonweal*, August 1885, 75.

45 Sanders, *The Poetry of Chartism*, 69–86. Morris does not encourage poetic contributions to *Commonweal*, emphasizing instead the importance of political action. See *Letters*, II: 484.
46 'First General Meeting', 75.
47 Tennyson, *Maud*, in *Poems*, II: 513–584 (584).
48 The 'Marseillaise', quoted in Laura Mason, *Singing the French Revolution*, 99. For the modified English version used by Morris and his fellow socialists, which omits the 'pitiless tigers', see *Commonweal*, 16 March 1889, 85. For an article on the composition and history of 'this fine song', see *Commonweal*, 31 December 1887, 420.
49 For an analysis of the idea of natural power in Chartist poetry, see Sanders, 'Poetic Agency: Metonymy and Metaphor in Chartist Poetry', 114–19.
50 Plotz, *Portable Property*, 156.
51 For a detailed account of the varieties and uses of nineteenth-century socialist songs, see Waters, *British Socialists*, 97–130.
52 Glasier, *Early Days*, 40–41.
53 Sanders, *The Poetry of Chartism*, 21.
54 The term 'deedless' crops up frequently in Morris's work, in the context of missing acts that ought to be carried out. See, for instance, Gudrun's 'deedless hands' in the face of her brothers' imminent deaths in *Sigurd*, 280, discussed in Chapter Three; or the description of Hogni's wife in *Sigurd*, who foresees Gunnar and Hogni's deaths, but strives with 'speechless sleep' and cannot utter the curses she forms, waking finally to 'the light of a deedless dawning' (266).
55 Anne Janowitz draws on Derek Attridge's account of rhythm to suggest that 'the underlying pattern of six-beat metres is three beats, one unrealised beat, repeated' and therefore the hexameter poems of *Pilgrims* carry the echo of the popular four-beat song rhythm in which the first two poems are written. Janowitz, *Lyric and Labour*, 225.
56 Glasier, 'The Ballade of "Law and Order"', *Commonweal*, April 1886, 27.
57 Morris, 'The Hollow Land', in *Collected Works*, I: 254–90 (285).
58 Tennyson, 'In Memoriam A. H. H.', in *Poems*, II: 304–458 (322).
59 Beaumont, 'Cacotopianism', 474.
60 Campbell, *Rhythm and Will*, 187–209.
61 Wright Mills, *The Marxists*, 35; Thompson, *Romantic to Revolutionary*, 641.
62 Boos, 'Narrative Design', 152.
63 Tennyson, *Maud*, 523.
64 Boos, 'Narrative Design', 152; Tennyson, *Maud*, 584. See Jeremiah 6.14; Ezekiel 13.10.
65 Ed Vaillant, 'Vive La Commune', *Commonweal*, April 1885, 17.
66 Sorel, *Reflections on Violence*, 148.
67 Anon., 'Books of To-day', June 1888, 185.
68 Following its serialization in *Commonweal*, it was quickly brought out as a book in 1888 – with minor alterations, as Salmon details in 'The Revision', 15–17. My references are taken from Morris, *Collected Works*, XVI: 215–88.
69 Waithe, *Utopia of Strangers*, 139–41; Goode, *Collected Essays*, 296–304.
70 Vaninskaya, *William Morris and the Idea of Community*, 123.
71 Sartre, Preface, 25.
72 Sartre, Preface, 11.
73 Vaninskaya offers an overview of the various nineteenth-century uses of the history of the Peasants' Revolt, while Stephen F. Eisenman analyses the sources and reception

of Morris's version of the tale. Vaninskaya, 'Dreams of John Ball', 45–57; Eisenman, 'Communism in Furs', 92–110.

74 Its continuing hold on the public imagination can be seen by the fact that in 1888, *John Ball* takes its place in the review section of *Academy* alongside two newly-written novels based on the events of 1381. See a review of all three works in Anon., 'Gift Books', 400.
75 Stubbs, *Constitutional History*, II: 473; Thorold Rogers, *Work and Wages*, 255; Hyndman, *Historical Basis of Socialism*, 20. See also 3–4 for John Ball's speech.
76 Froissart, *Antient Chronicles*, II: 405–28; Green, *A Short History*, 244–55; Maurice, *Lives of English Popular Leaders*, 143.
77 Morris and Bax refer to Green and Stubbs, as well as Edward Freeman, as 'enlightened historians' in *Socialism, Its Growth and Outcome*, 63. Rogers's *Work and Wages* is repeatedly advertised in *Commonweal* in 1886 and 1887.
78 Morris, 'The Lord Mayor's Show', 2.
79 Morris, *Letters*, II: 326.
80 Glasier, *Early Days*, 40.
81 For an outline of rites of intensification, see Rosman and Rubel, *The Tapestry of Culture*, 231–2.
82 For other accounts of Morris reading aloud, see Mackail, *Life* I: 49; May Morris, Introduction to *Collected Works*, XXII: xvii–xviii; Carpenter, *My Days and Dreams*, 217, in which he describes Morris reading aloud 'page after page' of Jefferies's *After London* 'with glee'. W. B. Yeats notes Morris's commitment to the rhythmic reading of poetry in his Introduction to a reading of 'The Lake Isle of Innisfree', broadcast on the BBC on 10 April 1932. 'The Spoken Word: Poets' CD.
83 Goode, *Collected Essays*, 273; 282; 293 Sorel, *Reflections*, 41–2; 126.
84 Holzman, 'The Encouragement and Warning of History', 104.
85 Girard, *Violence and the Sacred*, 1.
86 Girard, *Violence and the Sacred*, 8.
87 In this Morris's heroes resemble the terrorist described by the anarchist Stepniak, in *Underground Russia*, a book Morris read and admired: 'he is noble, terrible, irresistibly fascinating, for he combines in himself the two sublimities of human grandeur: the martyr and the hero'. *Underground Russia*, 42. The individualism of Stepniak's terrorist, however, sets him apart from Morris's characters.
88 Girard, *Violence and the Sacred*, 156–8. Girard identifies mimetic desire as necessarily productive of violence (158).
89 Waithe, *Utopia of Strangers*, 141.
90 Morris, *Pilgrims of Hope*, 377.
91 Allen J. Frantzen, *Bloody Good*, 94. See 39–48 for his account of Girard's model in relation to medieval chivalry.
92 For Morris's own accounts of campaigning in late 1886 and 1887, see *Letters*, II: 582; 597–600; and his *Socialist Diary*.
93 May Morris, Introduction to *Collected Works*, XVII: xiii.
94 Matthew 16.18.
95 'They are clothed in velvet, and warm in their furs and their ermines, while we are covered with rags. [...] They have leisure and fine houses; we have pain and labour, the rain and the wind in the fields'. *A Short History*, 250. Green draws closely on Froissart here. See Froissart, *Antient Chronicles*, II: 406.
96 Rogers, *Work and Wages*, 254.

97 'By Wiklif's labours, the Bible men had been introduced to the new world of the Old Testament.' Rogers, *Work and Wages*, 254. See Micah 4.4–5; Isaiah 65.20–22; Isaiah 55.1.
98 Morris, *Letters*, II: 777; 219; 777. This concept of socialism as a religion is not unique to Morris; the scientifically-minded Bax was particularly committed to the idea, evident in *The Religion of Socialism*. Although Bax's account of socialism as a religion usually draws on practical rather than numinous values, see his comment on the deaths of the Paris Communards (quoting Tertullian): 'the blood of the martyrs is the seed of the church'. The "Bloody Week", 73.
99 Arendt, *On Violence*, 68.
100 'Art and Socialism', in *Collected Works*, XXIII: 192–214 (212).
101 Waithe, *Utopia of Strangers*, 141.
102 Stubbs and Green put the number of deaths at seven thousand, Froissart (notoriously unreliable on figures) and Rogers at one thousand five hundred. *Constitutional History*, II: 482; *Short History*, 254; *Antient Chronicles*, II: 428; and *Work and Wages*, 261.
103 Marx Aveling, 'Record of the International Movement: Germany', 83.
104 'Revolutionary Rumblings: France', 20 November 1886, 270; 'The Socialists in Holland', 15 January 1887, 19; 'The Labour Struggle', 27 November 1886, 279; the factory workers, *Commonweal* notes, could return to work if they would accept a pay reduction. However: 'the workers, feeling that they are fighting the battle of so many others besides themselves, are determined to resist to the uttermost'.
105 Alex Houen, 'Sacrificial Militancy', 131.
106 Houen, 'Sacrificial Militancy', 134.
107 Houen, 'Sacrificial Militancy', 131. For a discussion of the dream-form of *John Ball*, see Cowan, '"Paradyse Erthly"', 137–53. However, Cowan makes only passing reference to Langland's *Piers Plowman* and none to John Gower's aristocratic Latin poem, *Vox Clamantis*, the tale's dream narrative predecessors most frequently alluded to by nineteenth-century historians. See Green, *Short History*, 255–7; Maurice, *Lives*, vii and 159; and Stubbs, *Constitutional History*, II: 475–6, note 1; 480, note 5.
108 Stubbs, *Constitutional History*, II: 478–81; Froissart, *Antient Chronicles*, II: 414.
109 See Frantzen, *Bloody Good*, 13–118, for a useful discussion of the combination of Christianity, violence, and self-perpetuating self-sacrifice in the rhetoric and practice of the Crusades.
110 Douglas, *Purity and Danger*, 79.
111 Fredric Jameson suggests that in order for a utopia to be effective in representing change, 'the modification of reality must be absolute and totalizing'. Jameson, *Archaeologies of the Future*, 39. *News from Nowhere* was published serially in *Commonweal* in 1890; my references are from *Collected Works*, XVI: 3–211.
112 Godwin, *Enquiry Concerning Political Justice*, xxiv.
113 *The Communist Manifesto* posits the 'history of all hitherto existing society' as 'the history of class struggles' and states that the aim of Communism is 'the forcible overthrow of all existing social conditions' – the end of history. Marx and Engels, *The Communist Manifesto*, 219; 258. See also Francis Fukuyama's adaptation of Hegelian and Marxist thought to offer a politically very different, liberal idea of the 'end of history', revised in the light of 9/11 and other world events. Fukuyama, *The End of History*, 341–54.
114 Beaumont, '*News from Nowhere* and the Here and Now', 43.
115 Pinkney, '*News from Nowhere*, Modernism, Postmodernism', para. 1 of 29.
116 Pinkney, '*News from Nowhere*, Modernism, Postmodernism', para. 17 of 29; para. 7 of 29. Waithe is among the few to note the possibilities of coercion implicit in

News from Nowhere's narratives of change, in *Utopia of Strangers*, 142–69. See also Paul Meier, *Marxist Dreamer*, II: 288–305, for a brief account of Morris's 'first stage' of revolution.

117 Letter to Tochatti, 2 December 1893: 'I don't for a moment suppose that you agree with such "propaganda by deed"', *Letters*, IV: 113; 'I shall vote against a parliamentary and palliative programme. [...] A parliamentary programme *must* carry with it support of palliative measures'. Letter to Joseph Lane, 30 March 1887, *Letters*, II: 632.

118 Meier, *Marxist Dreamer*, II: 307.

119 Arendt, *On Violence*, 56.

120 Fanon, *The Wretched*, 73.

121 See Evans and Phillips, *Algeria*, 73: 'Although the liberation struggle was now at an end, the experience of the war would continue to define the fundamental aspects of post-independence Algeria'.

122 Johnson, '*News from Nowhere*. By William Morris', 483.

123 Indeed, Boos suggests that 'Morris's pastoral utopia, in short, enacts non-violent transformation'. Boos, 'Personal and Political *Lieux d'Anticipation*', 106.

124 In his 1885 lecture, 'How we Live and How We Might Live', Morris explains that revolution in itself 'does not necessarily mean a change accompanied by riot and all kinds of violence'. *Collected Works*, XXIII: 3–26 (3). Organization, rather than the randomness of 'riot' is central to success, but does not preclude violence.

125 For Lamarck's ideas on need, habit and adaptation, see McKinney, ed., *Lamarck to Darwin*, 9–17. Livesey notes that Morris's fellow socialist Edward Carpenter drew on Lamarck's ideas for his own understanding of social development and the importance of desire (*Culture of Aestheticism*, 111–17).

126 May Morris records her father saying of Bellamy's utopia that 'if they brigaded *him* into a regiment of workers, he would just lie on his back and kick'. Introduction to *Collected Works*, XVI: xxviii. On ethics and eugenics in *News from Nowhere*, see Parrinder, 'Eugenics and Utopia', 1–12.

127 Hudson, *A Crystal Age*, 79–81; Jefferies, *After London*, 14–17.

128 Kenworthy, 'William Morris: A Memory', 130. Kenworthy goes on to suggest that Morris would have espoused 'the principle of "non-resistance"', but offers no convincing evidence of this. MacCarthy, in *A Life*, 570, more convincingly observes that 'Morris, with his literary imaginings of the clashes of the swordsmen, the armed conflicts of the sagas, had no concept of the power of non-violent resistance'.

129 Letter to The Chairman of the Meeting, Commune Celebration, 16 March 1889, in *Letters*, III: 45.

130 For the Russian Stepniak's discussion of bombs and anarchism fears, see 'The Dynamite Scare and Anarchy', 529–41. For socialists as agitators, see Anon., 'The New Suffering of the Poor', 317–19. See also Cole, 'Dynamite Violence and Literary Culture', 301–28.

131 Baudrillard, 'The Violence of the Global', 87; 93.

132 Morris, 'London in a State of Siege', *Commonweal*, 19 November 1887, 369–70.

133 May Morris, Introduction to *Collected Works*, XX: xvii–lvii (xxxii).

134 Bloch, *Principle of Hope*, II: 614.

135 Marx and Engels, *Communist Manifesto*, 258.

136 Morris's narrative avoids any details about the process of the destruction of goods, so that the violence that it necessarily implies is not made specific. Nonetheless this faith

in the renewing capacity of destruction reflects the thinking of the anarchist Bakunin and echoes his phrasing: 'Revolution requires extensive and widespread destruction, a fecund and renovating destruction, since in this way and only in this way are new worlds born.' Bakunin, *Bakunin on Anarchy*, 334.
137 Spencer, *Principles of Sociology*, II: 736.
138 Ezekiel 37.1–14.
139 Hegel, *Elements of the Philosophy of Right*, 361, para. 324; Hegel argues for the necessity of recurring war rather than its contingency.
140 Waithe, *Utopia of Strangers*, 164.
141 Jameson, *Archaeologies*, 157.
142 See Plotz, 'Nowhere and Everywhere', 939: 'Morris is committed not to obliterating but to universalizing the bonds of romantic love'.
143 See Derrida, *Of Grammatology*, 62: 'without a trace retaining the other as other in the same, no difference would do its work and no meaning would appear'.
144 Holzman, 'Anarchism and Utopia', 594–5.
145 Popper, 'Utopia and Violence', 359.
146 See Chapter Three for a discussion of Irigaray's use of 'phallocratism' and 'phallocentrism'.
147 Pinkney highlights Ellen's role as agent of change and disturbance, in '*News from Nowhere*, Modernism, Postmodernism', para. 28 of 29.
148 Despite the arguments made by critics for Morris's affirmation of women's value in *Nowhere*, the text requires them not only to enjoy being generally desired, but to enjoy domesticity. See Levitas's 'partial vindication' in '"Who Holds the Hose?"', 65–84, or Kinna's 'qualified defence' in 'Socialist Fellowship and the Woman Question', 183–96.
149 See Morris, *Letters*, II: 430: 'The passions have to be reckoned with by almost everyone; and thence come all kinds of entanglements, which we could not wholly get rid of in any state of society'.
150 Jones, Preface to *In Parenthesis*, ix–xv (xv).
151 Jameson, 'The Politics of Utopia', 43.
152 Popper, 361.
153 Morris, *Letters*, II: 435–6; 472.

Afterword   'Hopeful Strife and Blameless Peace'

1 Henty, Preface to *St George for England*, vii.
2 See MacCarthy, *A Life*, 548.
3 Livesey, in *Culture of Aestheticism*, 200–27, discusses the effects of the corporeal aesthetic ideals associated with the fin-de-siècle socialist movement on the men and women who succeeded Morris and lived on through the Boer War and the First World War, including George Bernard Shaw, Olive Schreiner, Virginia Woolf and Rupert Brooke. She notes emerging 'racist and anti-Semitic tendencies', and records former guild socialist Arthur Penty's turn to fascism in the 1920s, in what he saw as 'the natural reaction to the poison and ugliness of modernism and Bolshevism' (203; 227).
4 See Hedges, *War is a Force*, 1–3.
5 Fussell, *The Great War*, 168–9. For a counterargument, see Vaninskaya, *The Idea of Community*, 43.

6 T. E. Lawrence, *Minorities*, 240.
7 Calder, Introduction to T. E. Lawrence, *Seven Pillars*, v–xxv (x).
8 Thomas, *Collected Poems*, 384. Peter Howarth notes this connection in *British Poetry*, 211, note 69 – although the redemptive nature of Morris's Hollow Land complicates the intertextual meanings.
9 Blunden, *Votive Tablets*, 218.
10 The first version of Froissart for boys was published in 1880: *The Boys' Froissart*, ed. Sidney Lanier.
11 Jones, *Strange Likeness*, 21; 69; and the notes on 32–3. Hilda Doolittle describes Pound's reading of Morris's 'The Gilliflower of Gold' and other poems from *The Defence*, in H. D., *End to Torment*, 22–3.
12 From a letter to Professor L. W. Forster, 31 December 1960, in Tolkien, *Letters*, 303.
13 McLoughlin, *Representing War*, 20.
14 Brittain, *Testament of Youth*, 263–4.
15 Hedges, *War is a Force*, 3.
16 In 'Why I Am a Communist' (1894), 10, Morris refers to 'a wide spread and definite Socialist party, which will, by using the vote, wrest from the present possessing classes the instruments which are now used to govern the people in the interests of the possessing classes, and will use them for effecting the change in the basis of society'.
17 Lennox, Jr, 'Romance and Reality', 58.
18 Morris, 'Useful Work *versus* Useless Toil', in *Collected Works*, XXIII: 98–120 (119).
19 Morris, 'The Hollow Land', in *Collected Works*, I: 254–90 (254).

BIBLIOGRAPHY

Books and Articles

Adams, James Eli. *Dandies and Desert Saints: Styles of Victorian Manhood*. Ithaca: Cornell University Press, 1995
Alderson, David. *Mansex Fine: Religion, Manliness and Imperialism in Nineteenth-Century British Culture*. Manchester: Manchester University Press, 1998
Allen, Grant. 'The Story of Wulfgeat'. *Gentleman's Magazine* (November 1881): 551–62
Anon. 'Books of To-day'. *To-day: The Monthly Magazine of Scientific Socialism* (June 1888): 182–8
_____. 'Books of To-day'. *To-day: The Monthly Magazine of Scientific Socialism* (November 1888): 153–6
_____. 'Boys' Songs'. *Musical Herald* (1 December 1910): 67. British Periodicals. Online: http://britishperiodicals.chadwyck.co.uk (accessed 11 April 2010)
_____. 'Contemporary Literature'. *North American Review* (March 1877): 323–5. Making of America. Online: http://digital.library.cornell.edu/n/nora/index.html (accessed 13 February 2010)
_____. 'The Defence of Guenevere and Other Poems'. *Spectator* (27 February 1858): 238
_____. 'The Earthly Inferno'. *Saturday Review*, 19 May 1888, 607–8
_____. '*The Earthly Paradise* – Part III'. *Spectator* (12 March 1870): 332–4
_____. 'First General Meeting of the Socialist League'. Supplement to *Commonweal*, August 1885, 73–5
_____. 'Gift Books'. *Academy* (22 December 1888): 400
_____. 'The Labour Struggle'. *Commonweal*, 27 November 1886, 279
_____. 'Latest Telegrams: The Disaster at the Cape'. *Daily News*, 14 February 1879, 5
_____. 'Morris's Defence of Guenevere'. *Saturday Review*, 20 November 1858, 506–7
_____. 'The New Suffering of the Poor'. *Spectator* (10 March 1883): 317–19
_____. 'Psychological Novelties'. *Chambers's Journal* (12 January 1856): 20–22
_____. 'Recent Literature'. *Atlantic Monthly* (April 1877): 501–4. Making of America. Online: http://digital.library.cornell.edu/n/nora/index.html (accessed 13 February 2010)
_____. 'Revolutionary Rumblings: France'. *Commonweal*, 20 November 1886, 270
_____. 'The Roots of the Mountains'. *Saturday Review*, 14 December 1889, 688
_____. 'The Senses and the Intellect'. *Saturday Review*, 1 December 1855, 84–5
_____. 'The Socialists in Holland'. *Commonweal*, 15 January 1887, 19
_____. 'Undergraduate Literature'. *Saturday Review*, 28 February 1857, 196–7
_____. 'The Zulu War'. *Times*, 6 March 1879, 6
_____. 'The Zulu War'. *Times*, 5 May 1879, 13
Aquinas, Thomas. *Summa Theologiae*. Edited and translated by Anthony Kenny. London: Blackfriars, 1964

Arata, Stephen. *Fictions of Loss in the Victorian Fin de Siècle: Identity and Empire*. Cambridge: Cambridge University Press, 1996

Arendt, Hannah. *On Violence*. Orlando: Harcourt Books, 1969

Aristotle. *The Works of Aristotle*. Edited by W. D. Ross. 12 vols. Oxford: Clarendon Press, 1908–1952

Armstrong, Isobel. 'Victorian Poetry'. In *Encyclopedia of Literature and Criticism*, edited by Martin Coyle et al., 278–94. London: Routledge, 1990

———. *Victorian Poetry: Poetry, Poetics and Politics*. London: Routledge, 1993

Arnold, Matthew. *The Complete Prose Works of Matthew Arnold*. 11 vols. Ann Arbor: University of Michigan Press, 1960–1977

———. *The Poems of Matthew Arnold*. Edited by Kenneth Allott and Miriam Allott. 2nd ed. London: Longman, 1979

Austin, Alfred. 'The Poetry of the Period: Morris'. *Temple Bar* 27 (1869): 35–51

———. 'The Poetry of the Period: Mr Swinburne'. *Temple Bar* 26 (1869): 457–74

Austin, J. L. *How to Do Things with Words*. 2nd ed. Cambridge, MA: Harvard University Press, 1975

Aveling, Eleanor Marx. 'Record of the International Movement: Germany'. *Commonweal*, September 1885, 83

Aytoun, William Edmonstoune. 'The New Reform Bill'. *Blackwood's Edinburgh Magazine* 75 (March 1854): 369–80

Bachelard, Gaston. *Water and Dreams: An Essay on the Imagination of Matter*. Translated by Edith R. Farrell. Dallas: The Pegasus Foundation, 1983

Bain, Alexander. *Mind and Body: The Theories of Their Relation*. 2nd ed. London: King, 1873

———. *The Senses and the Intellect*. 3rd ed. London: Longmans, Green, and Co., 1868

Bakhtin, M. M. *The Dialogic Imagination: Four Essays*. Austin: University of Texas Press, 1990

Bakunin, Mikhail. *Bakunin on Anarchism*. Edited and translated by Sam Dolgoff. Montreal: Black Rose, 1980

Baldick, Robert. *The Duel: A History of Duelling*. London: Chapman and Hall, 1965

Ballantyne, Tony. *Orientalism and Race: Aryanism in the British Empire*. Basingstoke: Palgrave Macmillan, 2006

Barrett Browning, Elizabeth. *Poems*. 2 vols. London: Moxon, 1844

———. *The Poetical Works of Elizabeth Barrett Browning*. London: Smith Elder, 1897

Bartholin, Thomas. *Antiquitatum Danicarum de Causis Contemptae a Danis adhuc Gentilibus Mortis*. Bockenhoffer: Hafniae, 1689

Bataille, Georges. *The Accursed Share: An Essay on General Economy*, I: *Consumption*. Translated by Robert Hurley. New York: Zone Books, 1988

———. *Essential Writings*. Edited by Michael Richardson. London: Sage Publications, 1998

Batt, Catherine. '"Hand for Hand" and "Body for Body": Aspects of Malory's Vocabulary of Identity and Integrity with Regard to Gareth and Lancelot'. *Modern Philology* 91 (1994): 269–87

Baudrillard, Jean. 'The Violence of the Global'. In *The Spirit of Terrorism and Other Essays*, 87–105. Translated by Chris Turner. London: Verso, 2003

Bax, Ernest Belfort. 'Gordon and the Soudan'. *Commonweal*, 1 March 1885, 9–10

———. *The Religion of Socialism: Being Essays in Modern Socialist Criticism*. London: Swann Sonnenschein, 1887

Beaumont, Matthew. 'Cacotopianism, The Paris Commune, and England's Anti-Communist Imaginary, 1870–1900'. *ELH* 73 (2006): 465–87

———. 'News from Nowhere and the Here and Now: Reification and the Representation of the Present in Utopian Fiction'. *Victorian Studies* 47 (2004): 33–54

Bebel, August. *Woman in the Past, Present and Future*. Translated by H. B. Adams Walther. London: William Reeves [n.d.]

Beer, Gillian. *The Romance*. London: Methuen, 1970

Behrman, Cynthia F. 'The After-life of General Gordon'. *Albion* 3 (1971): 47–61

Bellamy, Edward. *Looking Backward, 2000–1887*. Oxford: Oxford University Press, 2007

Bending, Lucy. *The Representation of Bodily Pain in Late Nineteenth-Century English Culture*. Oxford: Oxford University Press, 2000.

Benthien, Claudia. *Skin: On the Cultural Border Between Self and the World*. New York: Columbia University Press, 2002

Bevington, Louisa Sarah. *Anarchism and Violence*. London: Tochatti, Liberty Press, 1896

Bevis, Matthew. 'Fighting Talk: Victorian War Poetry'. In *The Oxford Handbook of British and Irish War Poetry*, edited by Tim Kendall, 7–33. Oxford: Oxford University Press, 2007

Bhabha, Homi. 'Signs Taken for Wonders'. In *The Location of Culture*, 145–74. London: Routledge, 1994

Biddiss, Michael D. Introduction to *Gobineau: Selected Political Writings*, 13–35. Edited by Michael D. Biddiss. London: Cape, 1970

Binning, Thomas. 'The Blessings of Civilisation'. Supplement to *Commonweal*, September 1885, 85–6

Birch, Dinah. 'Ruskin's "Womanly Mind"'. In *Ruskin and Gender*, edited by Dinah Birch and Francis O'Gorman, 107–20. Basingstoke: Palgrave Macmillan, 2002.

Blair, Kirstie. *Victorian Poetry and the Culture of the Heart*. Oxford: Clarendon Press, 2006

Bloch, Ernst. *The Principle of Hope*. Translated by Neville Plaice, Stephen Plaice and Paul Knight. 2 vols. Oxford: Blackwell, 1986

Blunden, Edmund. *Votive Tablets: Studies Chiefly Appreciative of English Authors and Books*. 1931. Reprint, New York: Books for Libraries Press, 1932

Boos, Florence S. 'Alternative Victorian Futures: "Historicism", *Past and Present* and *A Dream of John Ball*'. In *History and Community: Essays in Victorian Medievalism*, edited by Boos, 3–37. New York: Garland, 1992

———. '*The Defence of Guenevere*: A Morrisian Critique of Medieval Violence'. *Journal of William Morris Studies* 18, no. 4 (2010): 8–21

———. 'Dystopian Violence: William Morris and The Nineteenth-Century Peace Movement'. In *William Morris, Our Country Right or Wrong: A Critical Edition*, 9–48. Edited by Florence S. Boos. London: William Morris Society, 2008

———. 'Justice and Vindication in William Morris's "The Defence of Guenevere"'. In *King Arthur through the Ages*, edited by Valerie M. Lagorio and Mildred Leake Day, 83–104. New York: Garland, 1990

———. 'Morris's German Romances as Socialist History'. *Victorian Studies* 27 (1984): 321–42

———. 'Narrative Design in the Pilgrims of Hope'. In *Socialism and the Literary Artistry of William Morris*, edited by Florence S. Boos and Carole G. Silver, 147–66. Columbia: University of Missouri Press, 1990

———. 'Personal and Political *Lieux d'Anticipation* in *News from Nowhere*', in *William Morris's News from Nowhere*, edited by Béatrice Laurent, 93–107. Nantes: Edition du Temps.

———. 'Sexual Polarities in The Defence of Guenevere'. *Browning Institute Studies* 13 (1985): 181–200
Bourdieu, Pierre. *An Invitation to Reflexive Sociology*. Translated by Loïc J. D. Wacquant. Cambridge: Polity Press, 1992
———. *Language and Symbolic Power*. Translated by Gino Raymond and Matthew Adamson. 1992. Reprint, Cambridge: Polity Press, 2005
Bourke, Joanna. *An Intimate History of Killing*. London: Granta Books, 1999
Bradley, Ian C. *Abide with Me: The World of Victorian Hymns*. London: SCM Press, 1997
Brantlinger, Patrick. '*News from Nowhere*: Morris's Socialist Anti-Novel'. *Victorian Studies* 19 (1975): 35–49
———. 'A Postindustrial Prelude to Postcolonialism: John Ruskin, William Morris, and Ghandism'. *Critical Inquiry* 22 (1996): 466–85
———. 'A Reading of Morris' *The Defence of Guenevere and Other Poems*'. *Victorian Newsletter* 44 (1973): 18–24
Brewer, D. S. 'The Ideal of Feminine Beauty in Medieval Literature, especially "Harley Lyrics", Chaucer, and some Elizabethans'. *Modern Language Review* 50 (1955): 257–69
Brittain, Vera, *Testament of Youth: An Autobiographical Study of the Years 1900–1925*. 1933. Reprint, London: Virago, 2004
Brombert, Victor. *The Romantic Prison: The French Tradition*. Princeton: Princeton University Press, 1978
Brontë, Charlotte. *Jane Eyre*. Edited by Q. D. Leavis. 1966. Reprint, Harmondsworth: Penguin, 1985
Broome Saunders, Clare. *Women Writers and Nineteenth-Century Medievalism*. Basingstoke: Palgrave Macmillan, 2009
Browning, Robert. *The Poems of Browning*. Edited by John Woolford et al. 3 vols. London: Longman, 1991–2007
Bryden, Inga. *Reinventing King Arthur: The Arthurian Legends in Victorian Culture*. Aldershot: Ashgate, 2005
Buchanan, Robert [Thomas Matiland]. 'The Fleshly School of Poetry: Mr D. G. Rossetti'. *Contemporary Review* (October 1871): 334–50
———. 'The Voice of the Hooligan'. *Contemporary Review* (December 1899): 776–89
Bullen, J. B. *The Pre-Raphaelite Body: Fear and Desire in Painting, Poetry and Criticism*. Oxford: Clarendon Press, 1998
Burne-Jones, Edward. 'Essay on *The Newcomes*'. *Oxford and Cambridge Magazine* (January 1856): 50–61
Burne-Jones, Georgiana. *Memorials of Edward Burne-Jones*. 2 vols. London: Lund Humphries, 1993
Butler, Judith. *Gender Trouble: Feminism and the Subversion of Identity*. Rev. ed. New York: Routledge, 2006
Buxton Forman, H. *The Works of William Morris Described: With Some Account of his Doings in Literature and the Allied Crafts*. London: Frank Hollings, 1897
Campbell, Alistair, ed. *The Battle of Brunanburh*. London: Heineman, 1938
Campbell, Matthew. *Rhythm and Will in Victorian Poetry*. Cambridge: Cambridge University Press, 1999
Carlyle, Thomas. *The Works of Thomas Carlyle*. Centenary edition. Edited by H. D. Traill. 30 vols. London: Chapman and Hall, 1896–1901
Carpenter, Edward, ed. *Chants of Labour: A Songbook of the People*. London: Swann Sonnenschein, 1888

———. *The Intermediate Sex*. 2nd ed. London: Swan Sonnenschein, 1909
———. *My Days and Dreams*. London: George Allen & Unwin, 1916
———. 'William Morris'. *Freedom* 10 (December 1896): 188
Carpenter, William B. *Principles of Mental Physiology, with their Applications to the Training and Discipline of the Mind, and the Study of its Morbid Conditions*. London: King, 1874
Carter Wood, J. *Violence and Crime in Nineteenth-Century England: The Shadow of Our Refinement*. London: Routledge, 2004
Ceadel, Martin. *Semi-Detached Idealists: The British Peace Movement and International Relations, 1854–1945*. Oxford: Oxford University Press, 2000
———. *Thinking about Peace and War*. Oxford: Oxford University Press, 1989
Chandler, Alice. A *Dream of Order: The Medieval Ideal in Nineteenth-Century English Literature*. London: Routledge and Kegan Paul, 1971
Clausewitz, Carl von. *On War*. Edited by Anatol Rapoport. Harmondsworth: Penguin, 1976
Clover, Carol. 'Regardless of Sex: Men, Women and Power in Early Northern Europe'. In *Studying Medieval Women: Sex, Gender, Feminism*, edited by Nancy F. Partner, 61–85. Cambridge, MA: Medieval Academy of America, 1993
Cobden, Richard. *Political Writings of Richard Cobden*. 2nd ed. London: Ridgeway, 1868
———. *Speeches on Questions of Public Policy*. Edited by John Bright and James E. Thorold Rogers. 2 vols. London: Macmillan, 1870
Cole, Sarah. 'Dynamite Violence and Literary Culture'. *Modernism/Modernity* 16 (2009): 301–28
Collini, Stefan. *Public Moralists: Political Thought and Intellectual Life in Britain*. Oxford: Clarendon, 1991
Colvin, Sidney. 'General Literature and Art: *The Earthly Paradise*'. *Academy* 15 (December 1870): 57–8
Connor, Steven. *The Book of Skin*. London: Reaktion, 2004
Cowan, Yuri. '"Paradyse Erthly": *John Ball* and the Medieval Dream-Vision'. In *Writing on the Image: Reading William Morris*, edited by David Latham, 137–53. Toronto: University of Toronto Press, 2007
Coyle, Martin et al., eds. *Encyclopedia of Literature and Criticism*. London: Routledge, 1990
Crane, Walter. *An Artist's Reminiscences*. 2nd ed. London: Methuen, 1907
Creasey, Edward. *The Fifteen Decisive Battles of the World: From Marathon to Waterloo*. London: Macmillan, 1907
Crump, John. 'How the Change Came: News from Nowhere and Revolution'. In *William Morris and News from Nowhere: A Vision for our Time*, edited by Stephen Coleman and Paddy O'Sullivan, 57–73. Totnes, Devon: Green Books, 1990
Curtis, L. Perry. *Apes and Angels: The Irishman in Victorian Caricature*. Newton Abbot: David and Charles, 1971
Daly, Nicholas. *Modernism, Romance, and the Fin de Siècle: Popular Fiction and British Culture, 1880–1914*. Cambridge: Cambridge University Press, 1999
Darwin, Charles. *The Descent of Man*. London: Penguin, 2004
Das, Santanu. *Touch and Intimacy in First World War Literature*. Cambridge: Cambridge University Press, 2005
Dasent, George Webbe, trans. *Icelandic Sagas and Other Historical Documents Relating to the Settlements and Descents of the Northmen on the British Isles*. 4 vols. London: Eyre & Spottiswoode, 1887–1894
———. 'The Norsemen in Iceland'. In *Oxford Essays, Contributed by Members of the University*, 165–214. London: John Parker, 1858

———, trans. *Popular Tales from the Norse: With an Introductory Essay on the Origin and Diffusion of Popular Tales*. Edinburgh: Edmonston and Douglas, 1859

———. *The Story of Burnt Njal, or Iceland at the End of the Tenth Century*. Edinburgh: Edmonston and Douglas, 1861

Dawson, Graham. *Soldier Heroes: British Adventure, Empire and the Imagining of Masculinities*. London: Routledge, 1994

D'Cruze, Shani. *Crimes of Outrage: Sex, Violence and Victorian Working Women*. London: UCL Press, 1998

———, ed. *Everyday Violence in Britain 1850–1950: Gender and Class*. Harlow: Longman, 2000

Deane, Bradley. 'Imperial Barbarians: Primitive Masculinity in Lost World Fiction'. *Victorian Literature and Culture* 36 (2008): 205–25

De Beauvoir, Simone. *The Second Sex*. London: Picador, 1988

De Gobineau, Arthur. *Gobineau: Selected Political Writings*. Edited by Michael D. Biddiss. London: Cape, 1970

Dentith, Simon. *Epic and Empire in Nineteenth-Century Britain*. Cambridge: Cambridge University Press, 2006

———. 'Morris, "The Great Story of the North", and the Barbaric Past'. *Journal of Victorian Culture* 14 (2009): 238–54

Derrida, Jacques. *Of Grammatology*. Translated by Gayatri Chakravorty Spivak. Baltimore: Johns Hopkins University Press, 1974

Dickens, Charles. *Bleak House*. London: Penguin, 1996

Digby, Kenelm. *The Broad Stone of Honour: Or, Rules for the Gentlemen of England*. London: Rivington, 1823

Dixon, R. W. 'The Barrier Kingdoms'. *Oxford and Cambridge Magazine* (February 1856): 65–73

———. 'The Prospects of Peace'. *Oxford and Cambridge Magazine* (March 1856): 185–9

Doolittle, Hilda (H. D.). *End to Torment: A Memoir of Ezra Pound*. Edited by Norman Holmes Pearson and Michael King. Manchester: Carcanet, 1980

Douglas, Mary. *Purity and Danger: An Analysis of Concept of Pollution and Taboo*. London: Routledge and Kegan Paul, 2002

Eisenman, Stephen F. 'Communism in Furs: A Dream of Prehistory in William Morris's *John Ball*'. *Art Bulletin* 87 (2005): 92–110

Eliot, T. S. *Collected Poems 1909–1962*. London: Faber and Faber, 1974

Engels, Friedrich. *The Origin of the Family, Private Property and the State*. London: Lawrence and Wishart, 1972. Reprint, London: Penguin, 2010

Evans, Martin and John Phillips. *Algeria: Anger of the Dispossessed*. London: Yale University Press, 2007

Fanon, Frantz. *The Wretched of the Earth*. Translated by Constance Farrington. 1967. Reprint, London: Penguin, 1990

Faulkner, Peter, ed. *William Morris: The Critical Heritage*. London: Routledge and Kegan Paul, 1973

Feuerbach, Ludwig. *The Essence of Christianity*. Translated by George Eliot. New York: Harper and Row, 1957

FitzGerald, Edward. *Rubáiyát of Omar Khayyám*. Edited by Daniel Karlin. Oxford: Oxford University Press, 2009

Flint, John. *Cecil Rhodes*. London: Hutchinson, 1976

Forman, H. Buxton. *The Works of William Morris Described: With Some Account of his Doings in Literature and the Allied Crafts*. London: Frank Hollings, 1897

Foucault, Michel. *The History of Sexuality*, I: *An Introduction*. Translated by Robert Hurley. London: Allen Lane, 1979

Fouqué, Friedrich Heinrich Carl de la Motte. *Sintram and His Companions*. London: James Burns, 1842

Franey, Laura E. *Victorian Travel Writing and Imperial Violence*. Basingstoke: Palgrave Macmillan, 2003

Frantzen, Allen J. *Bloody Good: Chivalry, Sacrifice and the Great War*. Chicago: University of Chicago Press, 2004

Freedman, Jonathan. 'Ideological Battleground: Tennyson, Morris and the Pastness of the Past'. In *The Passing of Arthur: New Essays in Arthurian Tradition*, edited by Christopher Baswell and William Sharpe, 235–48. New York: Garland, 1988

Freiligrath, Ferdinand. 'Freiligrath's Revolution Song: "The Way It's Done"'. Translated by J. L. Joynes. *Commonweal*, September 1885, 87

———. 'Revolution'. Translated by J. L. Joynes. *Commonweal*, 21 August 1886, 163

———. 'A Song of Death'. Translated by J. L. Joynes. *Commonweal*, 27 August 1887, 275

Froissart, Jean. *The Antient Chronicles of Sir John Froissart: of England, France, Spain, Portugal, Scotland, Brittany, and Flanders, and the Adjoining Countries*. Translated by John Bourchier, Lord Berners. 4 vols. London: Davis, 1814–1816

———. *The Boys' Froissart*. Selected by M. Edgar. London: Harrap, 1913

———. *The Boys' Froissart: Being Selections From Sir J. Froissart's Chronicles*. Edited by Sidney Lanier. London: Sampson & Low, 1880

———. *Chronicles of England, France and the Adjoining Countries from the latter part of the reign of Edward II to the Coronation of Henry IV*. Translated by Thomas Johnes. 4 vols. London: Henderson, 1805

Fulford, William, 'Alfred Tennyson: An Essay. In Three Parts. III. *Maud, and Other Poems*'. *Oxford and Cambridge Magazine* (March 1856): 136–45

Fukuyama, Francis. *The End of History and the Last Man*. With a new afterword. New York: Free Press, 2006

Fussell, Paul. *The Great War and Modern Memory*. Illustrated ed. Oxford: Oxford University Press, 1974. Reprint, New York: Sterling, 2009

Gallagher, Catherine. 'George Eliot: Immanent Victorian'. *Representations* 90 (2005): 61–74

Galton, Francis. *Inquiries into Human Faculty and its Development*. Basingstoke: Palgrave Macmillan, 1883

Gaskell, Elizabeth. *North and South*. London: Penguin, 1994

Genette, Gérard. *Paratexts: Thresholds of Interpretation*. Translated by Jane E. Lewin. Cambridge: Cambridge University Press, 1997

Gibbon, Edward. *The Decline and Fall of the Roman Empire*. Introduced by Christopher Dawson. 6 vols. London: Dent, 1910

Gibson, James J. *The Senses Considered as Perceptual Systems*. London: George Allen & Unwin, 1968

Girard, René. *Things Hidden Since the Foundation of the World*. Translated by Stephen Bann and Michael Metteer. Stanford: Stanford University Press, 1987

———. *Violence and the Sacred*. Translated by Patrick Gregory. Baltimore: Johns Hopkins University Press, 1972

Girouard, Mark. *The Return to Camelot: Chivalry and the English Gentleman*. New Haven: Yale University Press, 1981

Glasier, J. Bruce, 'Ballade of Law and Order'. *Commonweal*, March 1886, 27

———. *The Meaning of Socialism*. Introduction by J. A. Hobson. Manchester: National Labour Press, 1919
———. *William Morris and the Early Days of the Socialist Movement*. London: Longmans, Green, and Co., 1921
Glasse, John, 'A Processional Hymn'. *Commonweal*, 22 October 1887, 339
Godwin, William. *Caleb Williams*. Edited by Maurice Hindle. London: Penguin, 2005
———. *Enquiry Concerning Political Justice*. 3 vols. Toronto: University of Toronto, 1946
Goode, John. *Collected Essays of John Goode*. Edited by Charles Swann, introduction by Terry Eagleton. Keele: Keele University Press, 1995
Gosse, Edmund W. 'Literature'. *Academy* 9 (December 1876): 557–8
Graham, Desmond. *The Truth of War: Owen, Blunden, Rosenberg*. Manchester: Carcanet Press, 1984
Green, John R. *A Short History of the English People*. 1874. Rev. ed. London: Macmillan, 1916
Gregory, Barry. *A History of the Artists Rifles 1859–1947*. Barnsley: Pen and Sword Military, 2006
Haggard, H. Rider. *Eric Brighteyes*. Illustrated by Lancelot Speed. 2nd ed. London: Longmans, Green, 1891
———. *King Solomon's Mines*. Edited by Gerald Monsman. Peterborough, ON: Broadview, 2002
———. *She*. Oxford: Oxford University Press, 1991
———. 'A Zulu War-Dance'. *Gentleman's Magazine* 241 (July 1877): 94–107
Hake, A. Egmont. *The Story of Chinese Gordon*. 4th ed. London: Remington, 1884
Hale, Virginia S. and Catherine Barnes Stevenson. 'Morris' Medieval Queen: A Paradox Resolved'. *Victorian Poetry* 30 (1992): 171–8
Hall, Donald E., ed. *Muscular Christianity: Embodying the Victorian Age*. Cambridge: Cambridge University Press, 1994
Harris, John. 'The Marxist Conception of Violence'. *Philosophy and Public Affairs* 3 (1974): 192–220
Harrison, Antony H. *Victorian Poets and the Politics of Culture: Discourse and Ideology*. Charlottesville: University Press of Virginia, 1998
Harrold, Charles Frederick. *Carlyle and German Thought, 1819–1834*. London: Archon, 1963
Hassett, Constance W. 'The Style of Evasion: William Morris' *The Defence of Guenevere, and Other Poems*'. *Victorian Poetry* 29 (1991): 99–114
Hatto, Arthur Thomas, trans. *The Nibelungenlied*. Rev. ed. Harmondsworth: Penguin, 1969
Hedges, Chris. *War is a Force that Gives Us Meaning*. New York: Anchor, 2003
Heeley, Wilfred. 'Sir Philip Sidney, Part I: The Prelude'. *Oxford and Cambridge Magazine* (January 1856): 1–7
Hegel, G. W. F. *Elements of the Philosophy of Right*. Edited by Allen W. Wood, translated by H. B. Nisbet. Cambridge: Cambridge University Press, 1995
Helsinger, Elizabeth K. *Poetry and the Pre-Raphaelite Arts*. New Haven: Yale, 2008
Henderson, Andrea K. *Romanticism and the Painful Pleasures of Modern Life*. Cambridge: Cambridge University Press, 2008
Henty, G. A. *St George for England*. London: Dean [n.d.]
Herbert, Karen. 'Dissident Language in *The Defence of Guenevere*'. *Victorian Poetry* 34 (1996): 313–27
Hill, John M. *The Anglo-Saxon Warrior Ethic: Reconstructing Lordship in Early English Literature*. Gainesville: University of Florida Press, 2000

Hoare, Dorothy M. *The Works of Morris and of Yeats in Relation to Early Saga Literature*. Cambridge: Cambridge University Press, 1937

Hobbs, Angela. *Plato and the Hero: Courage, Manliness and the Impersonal Good*. Cambridge: Cambridge University Press, 2000

Hodges, Kenneth. 'Wounded Masculinity: Injury and Gender in Sir Thomas Malory's *Le Morte Darthur*'. *Studies in Philology* 106 (2009): 14–31

Hodgson, Amanda. *The Romances of William Morris*. Cambridge: Cambridge University Press, 1987

Hollow, John. 'William Morris and the Judgement of God'. *PMLA* 86 (1971): 446–51

Holy Bible. King James Version. Oxford: Oxford University Press, 2010

Holzman, M. 'Anarchism and Utopia: William Morris's *News from Nowhere*'. *ELH* 51 (1984): 589–603

———. 'The Encouragement and Warning of History: William Morris's *A Dream of John Ball*'. In *Socialism and the Literary Artistry of William Morris*, edited by Florence S. Boos and Carole G. Silver, 98–116. Columbia: University of Missouri Press, 1990

Hosman, Robert Stahr. 'The Oxford and Cambridge Magazine'. In *British Literary Magazines: The Victorian and Edwardian Age, 1837–1913*, edited by Alvin Sullivan, 294–302. Westport: Greenwood Press, 1984

Houen, Alex. 'Sacrificial Militancy and the Wars Around Terror'. In *Terror and the Postcolonial*, edited by Elleke Boehmer and Stephen Morton, 113–40. Oxford: Blackwell, 2010

———. *Terrorism and Modern Literature: From Joseph Conrad to Ciaran Carson*. Oxford: Oxford University Press, 2002

Howarth, Peter. *British Poetry in the Age of Modernism*. Cambridge: Cambridge University Press, 2005

Howitt, William and Mary Botham Howitt. *The Literature and Romance of Northern Europe: Constituting a Complete History of the Literature of Sweden, Denmark, Norway and Iceland*. 2 vols. London: Colburn, 1852

Hudson, W. H. *A Crystal Age*. London: Duckworth [n.d.]

Hughes, Thomas. *The Manliness of Christ*. London: Macmillan, 1879

Hymns Ancient and Modern. London: William Clowes, 1889

Hyndman, H. M. *The Historical Basis of Socialism in England*. London: Kegan Paul, 1883

Ignatius. *The Spiritual Exercises of Saint Ignatius*. Translated by Thomas Corbishly. London: Burns and Oats, 1963

Irigaray, Luce. *This Sex Which is Not One*. Translated by Catherine Porter with Carolyn Burke. Ithaca: Cornell University Press, 1985

James, Simon. *Maps of Utopia: H.G. Wells, Modernity and the End of Culture*. Oxford: Oxford University Press, 2012

James, William. 'The Moral Equivalent of War'. In *The Writings of William James: A Comprehensive Edition*, 660–71. New York: Random House, 1968

Jameson, Fredric. *Archaeologies of the Future: The Desire Called Utopia and Other Science Fictions*. London: Verso, 2005

———. 'The Politics of Utopia'. *New Left Review* 25 (2004): 35–54

Janowitz, Anne. *Lyric and Labour in the Romantic Tradition*. Cambridge: Cambridge University Press, 1998

Jefferies, Richard. *After London and Amaryllis at the Fair*. London: Dent; New York: Dutton, 1939

Johnson, Lionel. '*News from Nowhere*, by William Morris'. *Academy* 23 (May 1891): 483–4

Jones, Chris. 'The Reception of Morris's *Beowulf*'. In *Writing on the Image: Reading William Morris*, edited by David Latham, 197–208. Toronto: University of Toronto Press, 2007

———. *Strange Likeness: The Uses of Old English in Twentieth-Century Poetry*. Oxford: Oxford University Press, 2006

Jones, David. *In Parenthesis*. London: Faber and Faber, 1937

Kaeuper, Richard W. *Chivalry and Violence in Medieval Europe*. Oxford: Oxford University Press, 1999

Kant, Immanuel. *Critique of Judgment*. Translated by Werner S. Pluhar. Indianapolis: Hackett, 1987

Karlin, Daniel. 'From Dark Defile to Gethsemane: Rudyard Kipling's War Poetry'. In *The Oxford Handbook of British and Irish War Poetry*, edited by Tim Kendall, 51–72. Oxford: Oxford University Press 2007

Keats, John. *Selected Letters*. Edited by Robert Gittings, revised and introduced by Jon Mee. Oxford: Oxford University Press, 2002

Kennedy, Edward D. 'Malory and his English Sources'. In *Aspects of Malory*, edited by Toshiyuki Takamiya and Derek Brewer, 27–55. Cambridge: Brewer, 1981

Kenworthy, John C. 'William Morris: A Memory, Personal and Otherwise: Part II'. *New Century Review* (February 1897): 124–32

King, Richard H. and Dan Stone, eds. *Hannah Arendt and the Uses of History*. New York: Berghahn Books, 2008

Kingsley, Charles. *Alton Locke*. 1910. Reprint, London: J. M. Dent, 1928

———. *Charles Kingsley, His Letters and Memories of his Life*. Edited by Frances Kingsley. 2 vols. 8th ed. London: King, 1877

———. 'The Explosive Forces'. In *Three Lectures: Delivered at the Royal Institution, on The Ancien Regime*, 86–136. London: Macmillan, 1867

———. *Hereward the Wake*. London: T. Nelson and Sons: [n.d.]

———. *Hypatia, or New Foes With an Old Face*. 10th ed. London: Macmillan, 1878

———. *Two Years Ago*. London: Cassell, 1909

———. *Yeast: A Problem*. London: Macmillan, 1908

Kinna, Ruth. 'Socialist Fellowship and the Woman Question'. In *Writing on the Image: Reading William Morris*, edited by David Latham, 183–5. Toronto: University of Toronto Press, 2007

———. 'William Morris: Art, Work and Leisure'. *Journal of the History of Ideas* 61 (2000): 493–512

Kipling, Rudyard. *Barrack Room Ballads*. 1899. 16th ed. Reprint, London: Methuen, 1974

———. *Rudyard Kipling's Verse*. Definitive ed. London: Hodder and Stoughton, 1940

Kirchhoff, Frederick. *William Morris: The Construction of a Male Self, 1856–1872*. Athens: Ohio University Press, 1990

Koonz, Claudia. *Mothers in the Fatherland: Women, the Family and Nazi Politics*. London: Jonathan Cape, 1987

Kropotkin, Peter. *The Conquest of Bread*. London: Chapman and Hall, 1913

———. *The Essential Kropotkin*. Edited by Emile Capouya and Keitha Tomkins. New York: Liveright, 1975

———. 'In Memory of William Morris'. *Freedom*, December 1896, 109–10

———. *Kropotkin's Revolutionary Pamphlets*. Edited by Roger N. Baldwin. 1927. Reprint, New York: Benjamin Bloom, 1968

Laity, Paul. *The British Peace Movement 1870–1914*. Oxford: Clarendon Press, 2001
Lane, Edward William, trans. *The Thousand and One Nights: Commonly Called, in England, The Arabian Nights' Entertainment*. 3 vols. London: Knight and Co. 1840
Lang, Andrew. 'Realism and Romance'. *Contemporary Review* (November 1887): 683–93
Laqueur, Thomas. *Making Sex: Body and Gender from the Greeks to Freud*. Cambridge, MA: Harvard University Press, 1990
Latham, David. 'To Frame a Desire: Morris's Ideology of Work and Play'. In *Writing on the Image: Reading William Morris*, edited by David Latham, 155–72. Toronto: University of Toronto Press, 2007
Lawrence, Harding. 'I'sandula!'. *Chambers's Journal of Popular Literature, Science and Arts* (April 1879): 256
Lawrence, T. E. *Minorities*. Edited by J. M. Wilson, preface by C. Day Lewis. London: Jonathan Cape, 1971
———. *Seven Pillars of Wisdom*. Introduction by Angus Calder. Ware: Wordsworth, 1997
Laycock, Thomas. *A Treatise on the Nervous Diseases of Women: Comprising an Inquiry into the Nature, Causes and Treatment of Spinal and Hysterical Disorders*. London: Longman, Orme, Brown, Green and Longmans, 1840
Lecercle, Jean-Jacques. *The Violence of Language*. London: Routledge, 1990
Lemire, Eugene D. *A Bibliography of William Morris*. New Castle: Oak Knoll Press; London: British Library, 2006
Levin, Michael. *J. S. Mill on Civilization and Barbarism*. London: Routledge, 2004
Lévi-Strauss, Claude. *The Elementary Structures of Kinship*. Translated by James Harle Bell, John Richard von Sturmer and Rodney Needham. Rev. ed. London: Eyre and Spottiswood, 1969
Levitas, Ruth. *The Concept of Utopia*. Hemel Hempstead: Philip Allan, 1990
———. '"Who Holds the Hose?" Domestic Labour in the Work of Bellamy, Gilman and Morris'. *Utopian Studies* 6, no. 1 (1995): 65–84
Lewis, C. S. *Rehabilitations and Other Essays*. London: Oxford University Press, 1939
Lieven, Michael. 'Heroics and the Making of Heroes: The Anglo–Zulu War of 1879'. *Albion* 30 (1998): 419–38
Livesey, Ruth. 'Morris, Carpenter, Wilde and the Political Aesthetics of Labor'. *Victorian Literature and Culture* 32 (2004): 601–16
———. *Socialism, Sex and the Culture of Aestheticism in Britain, 1880–1914*. Oxford: Oxford University Press/British Academy, 2007
Macaulay, Thomas Babington. *The Miscellaneous Writings of Lord Macaulay*. 2 vols. London: Longman, Green, Longman, and Roberts, 1860
MacCarthy, Fiona. *William Morris: A Life for Our Time*. London: Faber and Faber, 1994
MacDonald, Henry J. 'Recent Poems and Plays'. *Oxford and Cambridge Magazine* (December 1856): 717–32
MacDonald, Robert H. *The Language of Empire: Myths and Metaphors of Popular Imperialism, 1880–1918*. Manchester: Manchester University Press, 1994
Machann, Clinton. 'Tennyson's King Arthur and the Violence of Manliness'. *Victorian Poetry* 38 (2000): 199–226
Mackail, J. W. *The Life of William Morris*. 2 vols. London: Longmans, Green, and Co., 1912
MacKenzie, John M., ed. *Popular Imperialism and the Military, 1850–1950*. Manchester, Manchester University Press, 1992
Magee, Brian. *Aspects of Wagner*. Oxford: Oxford University Press, 1988

Mahon, J. L. 'Discovery of Fresh Nihilist Plots in Russia'. *Commonweal*, 1 January 1887, 7

Mallet, Paul Henri. *Northern Antiquities: Or, an Historical Account of the Manners, Customs, Religion and Laws, Maritime Expeditions and Discoveries, Language and Literature of the Ancient Scandinavians*. Translated by Bishop Percy, introduction by I. A. Blackwell. London: Henry Bohn, 1847

Malory, Thomas. *The Byrth, Lyf and Actes of King Arthur; of his Noble Knyghtes of the Rounde Table, Theyr Merveyllous Enquestes and Adventures, Thachyevyng of the Sanc Greal; and in the End Le Morte Darthur, with the Dolorous Deth and Departyng out of this Worlde of Them Al*. 2 vols. London: Longman, Rees, Orme and Brown, 1817

Mann, Jill. 'Malory: Knightly Combat in *Le Morte D'Arthur*.' In vol. I, part 1 of *The New Pelican Guide to English Literature*, edited by Boris Ford, 331–9. 11 vols. Pelican, 1982. Reprint, Harmondsworth: Penguin, 1990

Marcuse, Herbert. 'Repressive Tolerance.' In *A Critique of Pure Tolerance*, by Robert Paul Wolff, Barrington Moore, Jr, and Herbert Marcuse, 95–137. London: Jonathan Cape, 1969

Markovits, Stefanie. *The Crimean War in the British Imagination*. Cambridge: Cambridge University Press, 2009

Marsh, George P. *A Compendious Grammar of the Old Northern or Icelandic Language: Compiled and Translated from the Grammars of Rask*. Burlington: Hiram Johnston, 1848

Marsh, Jan. 'William Morris and Victorian Manliness.' In *William Morris: Centenary Essays*, edited by Peter Faulkner and Peter Preston, 185–99. Exeter: University of Exeter Press, 1999

Marx, Karl and Friedrich Engels. *Collected Works*. Translated by Jack Cohen et al. 50 vols. London: Lawrence and Wishart, 1975–2004

———. *The Communist Manifesto*. Edited and with an introduction by Gareth Stedman Jones. London: Penguin, 2002

Mason, Laura. *Singing the French Revolution: Popular Culture and Politics, 1789–1799*. Ithaca: Cornell University Press, 1996

Matus, Jill. *Shock, Memory and the Unconscious in Victorian Fiction*. Cambridge: Cambridge University Press, 2009

Maurice, C. E. *Lives of English Popular Leaders in the Middle Ages: Tyler, Ball and Oldcastle*. London: King, 1875

McCarthy, Terence. 'Malory and his Sources'. In *A Companion to Malory*, edited by Elizabeth Archibald and A. S. G. Edwards, 75–95. Cambridge: Brewer, 1996

McCrae, John. *In Flanders Fields and Other Poems*. Hodder and Stoughton, 1919

McKinney, H. Lewis, ed. *Lamarck to Darwin*. Lawrence: Coronado Press, 1971

McLoughlin, Kate. *Authoring War: The Literary Representation of War from the Iliad to Iraq*. Cambridge: Cambridge University Press, 2011

Meier, Paul. *William Morris, Marxist Dreamer*. Translated by Frank Gubb. 2 vols. Sussex: Harvester Press, 1978

Merleau-Ponty, Maurice. *Phenomenology of Perception*. Translated by Colin Smith. London: Routledge and Kegan Paul, 1962

———. *The Visible and the Invisible: Followed by Working Notes*. Edited by Claude Lefort, translated by Alphonso Lingis. Evanston: Northwestern University Press, 1968

Meynell, Alice. 'Summer in England, 1914'. In *The Penguin Book of First World War Poetry*, edited by Jon Silkin, 149–50. London: Penguin, 1996

Mill, John Stuart. 'Civilization'. In *Essays on Politics and Culture*, 45–76. Garden City: Anchor/Doubleday, 1963

———. *The Subjection of Women*. 1869. In *On Liberty and Other Essays*, edited and with an introduction by John Gray, 471–582. Oxford: Oxford University Press, 1991

———. *A System of Logic, Ratiocinative and Inductive: Being a Connected View of the Principles of Evidence, and the Methods of Scientific Investigation*. 8th ed. New York: Harper, 1882

Miller, Elizabeth Carolyn, 'William Morris, Print Culture, and the Politics of Aestheticism'. *Modernism/Modernity* 15 (2008): 477–502

Mills, C. Wright. *The Marxists*. Harmondsworth: Penguin Books, 1962

Mills, Victoria. 'Introduction: Victorian Fiction and the Material Imagination'. *19: Interdisciplinary Studies in the Long Nineteenth Century*, 6 (April 2008). Online: http://19.bbk.ac.uk/index.php/19/article/view/468 (accessed 12 March 2012)

Modell, Arnold H. *Imagination and the Meaningful Brain*. Cambridge, MA: MIT Press, 2003

Morgan, Lewis H. *Ancient Society, or Researches in the Lines of Human Progress from Savagery through Barbarism to Civilization*. New York: Holt, 1907

Morris, William. 'The Boy Farms at Fault'. *Commonweal*, 30 July 1887, 241

———. *Chants for Socialists*. London: Socialist League, 1885

———. *The Collected Letters of William Morris*. Edited by Norman Kelvin. 4 vols. Princeton: Princeton University Press, 1984–96

———. *The Collected Works of William Morris*. Edited by May Morris. 24 vols. London: Longmans, Green, and Co., 1910–1915

———. *The Defence of Guenevere, and Other Poems*. London: Bell and Daldy, 1858

———. *The Defence of Guenevere, and Other Poems*. Edited by Margaret A. Lourie. New York: Garland Publishing, 1981

———. 'The Development of Modern Society.' *Commonweal*, 19 July 1890, 225–6

———. 'The Development of Modern Society'. *Commonweal*, 26 July 1890, 237

———. 'The Development of Modern Society'. *Commonweal*, 16 August 1890, 260–61

———. *The Hollow Land and Other Contributions to the Oxford and Cambridge Magazine*. Edited and with an introduction by Eugene D. Lemire. Bristol: Thoemmes Press, 1996

———. 'Introductory'. *Commonweal*, February 1885, 1

———. *Journalism: Contributions to Commonweal, 1885–1890*. Edited by Nicholas Salmon. Bristol: Thoemmes Press, 1996

———. 'London in a State of Siege'. *Commonweal*, 19 November 1887, 369–70

———. 'Looking Backward'. *Commonweal*, 22 June 1889, 194–5

———. 'The Lord Mayor's Show'. *Justice*, 15 November 1884, 2

———. 'Notes on News'. *Commonweal*, 28 May 1887, 172

———. 'Notes on News'. *Commonweal*, 6 October 1888, 313–14

———. 'Notes on News'. *Commonweal*, 27 October 1888, 337–8

———. 'Notes on News'. *Commonweal*, 12 January 1889, 12

———. 'Notes on News'. *Commonweal*, 2 February 1889, 33

———. 'Notes on News'. *Commonweal*, 26 July 1890, 235

———. *The Novel on Blue Paper*. Edited by Penelope Fitzgerald. London: Journeyman, 1982

———. 'On Some Practical Socialists'. *Commonweal*, 18 February 1888, 52–3

———. *Our Country Right or Wrong*. Edited by Florence Boos. London: William Morris Society, 2008

———. *Political Writings: Contributions to Justice and Commonweal, 1883–1890*. Edited by Nicholas Salmon. Bristol: Thoemmes Press, 1994

———. *The Tables Turned Or, Nupkins Awakened: A Socialist Interlude*. London: Office of the *Commonweal*, 1887

———. *Three Northern Love Stories*. Introduction by Gary Aho. Bristol: Thoemmes Press, 1996

———. 'Unattractive Labour'. Supplement to *Commonweal*, May 1885, 37
———. *The Unpublished Lectures of William Morris*. Edited by Eugene Lemire. Detroit: Wayne State University, 1969
———. Untitled note. Supplement to *Commonweal*, June 1885
———. 'Why I am a Communist.' 2nd series. London: Tochatti, Liberty Press, 1894
———. *William Morris: Artist Writer Socialist*. Edited by May Morris. 2 vols. Oxford: Basil Blackwell, 1936
———. *William Morris's Socialist Diary*. Edited by Florence Boos. London: Journeyman, 1985
——— and E. Belfort Bax. *Socialism, Its Growth and Outcome*. Chicago: Kerr, 1913
Mutch, Deborah. *English Socialist Periodicals, 1880–1900: A Reference Source*. Aldershot: Ashgate, 2005
Nakayama, Shuichi. 'The Impact of William Morris in Japan, 1904 to the Present'. *Journal of Design History* 9 (1996): 273–83
Nelson, Claudia. 'Sex and the Single Boy: Ideals of Manliness and Sexuality in Victorian Literature for Boys'. *Victorian Studies* 32 (1989): 525–50
Newbolt, Henry. *Poems New and Old*. 2nd ed. London: Murray, 1919
Newman, J. H. *The Dream of Gerontius and Other Poems*. Oxford: Oxford University Press, 1914
———. *The Idea of a University: Defined and Illustrated*. Edited by I. T. Ker. Oxford: Clarendon Press, 1976
Newton, Sam. *The Origins of Beowulf and the Pre-Viking Kingdom of East Anglia*. Cambridge: Brewer, 1993
Nordau, Max. *Degeneration*. 2nd ed. London: Heinemann, 1896
Norton, Charles Eliot, ed. *Correspondence Between Goethe and Carlyle*. London: Macmillan, 1887
Oberg, Charlotte H. *A Pagan Prophet: William Morris*. Charlottesville: University Press of Virginia, 1978
Oliphant, Margaret. 'General Gordon'. *Blackwood's Edinburgh Magazine* (August 1885): 247–72
Onians, Richard Broxton. *The Origins of European Thought about the Body, the Mind, the Soul, the World, Time and Fate*. Cambridge: Cambridge University Press, 1951
Orchard, Andy, ed. *A Critical Companion to Beowulf*. Cambridge: Brewer, 2003
O'Sullivan, Paddy. 'The Ending of the Journey: William Morris, *News from Nowhere* and Ecology'. In *William Morris and News from Nowhere: A Vision for Our Time*, edited by Stephen Coleman and Paddy O'Sullivan, 169–81. Totnes, Devon: Green Books, 1990
Parrinder, Patrick. 'Eugenics and Utopia: Sexual Selection from Galton to Morris.' *Utopian Studies* 8, no. 2 (1997): 1–12
Pater, Walter. 'Poems by William Morris.' *Westminster Review* (October 1868): 300–12
Patmore, Coventry. *The Angel in the House*. London: Parker, 1854
Pearsall, Cornelia D. J. *Tennyson's Rapture: Transformation in the Victorian Dramatic Monologue*. Oxford: Oxford University Press, 2008
Peck, John. *War, the Army and Victorian Literature*. Basingstoke: Palgrave Macmillan, 1998
Peterson, Linda H. 'The Feminist Origins of "Of Queens' Gardens"'. In *Ruskin and Gender*, edited by Dinah Birch and Francis O'Gorman, 86–106. Basingstoke: Palgrave Macmillan, 2002
Pfeiffer, Emily. *Under the Aspens: Lyrical and Dramatic*. London: Kegan Paul, 1882

Pick, Daniel. *War Machine: The Rationalisation of Slaughter in the Modern Age*. New Haven: Yale University Press, 1993
Pinkney, Tony. '*News from Nowhere*, Modernism, Postmodernism'. *AE: Canadian Aesthetics Journal* 15 (2008). Online: http://www.uqtr.uquebec.ca/AE/Vol_15 (accessed 25 June, 2010)
_____, ed. *We Met Morris: Interviews with William Morris, 1885–1896*. Reading: Spire Books/William Morris Society, 2005
Plotz, John. 'Nowhere and Everywhere: The End of Portability in William Morris's Romances'. *ELH* 74 (2007): 931–56
_____. *Portable Property: Victorian Culture on the Move*. Princeton: Princeton University Press, 2008
Poe, Edgar Allan. *The Complete Tales and Poems of Edgar Allan Poe*. London: Penguin, 1982
Poovey, Mary. *Uneven Developments: The Ideological Work of Gender in Mid-Victorian England*. Chicago: University of Chicago Press, 1988
Popper, Karl R. *Conjectures and Refutations: The Growth of Scientific Knowledge*. 3rd rev. ed. London: Routledge and Kegan Paul, 1974
Praz, Mario. *The Romantic Agony*. Translated by Angus Davidson. 2nd ed. Oxford: Oxford University Press, 1970
Randall, Annie, J. 'A Censorship of Forgetting: Origins and Origin Myths of "Battle Hymn of the Republic"'. In *Music, Power and Politics*, edited by Annie J. Randall, 5–24. New York: Routledge, 2005
Reed, John R. *Victorian Will*. Athens: Ohio University Press, 1989
Reid, Julia, '"King Romance" in *Longman's Magazine*: Andrew Lang and Literary Populism', *Victorian Periodicals Review* 44 (2011): 354–76
Richards, Jeffrey. '"Passing the Love of Women": Manly Love and Victorian Society'. In *Manliness and Morality: Middle Class Masculinities in Britain and America 1800–1940*, edited by J. A. Mangan and James Walvin, 92–122. Manchester: Manchester University Press, 1987
Ricks, Christopher. *Tennyson*. 2nd ed. Basingstoke: Macmillan, 1989
Riede, David G. 'Morris, Modernism and Romance'. *ELH* 51 (1984): 85–106
Rodaway, Paul. *Sensuous Geographies: Body, Sense and Place*. London: Routledge, 1994
Rogers, James E. Thorold. *A History of Agriculture and Prices in England*. 7 vols. Oxford: Clarendon Press 1866–1902
_____. *Six Centuries of Work and Wages: The History of English Labour*. London: Swan Sonnenschein, 1894
Roper, Michael, and John Tosh, eds. *Manful Assertions: Masculinities in Britain since 1800*. London: Routledge, 1991
Rosen, David. 'The Volcano and the Cathedral: Muscular Christianity and the Origins of Primal Manliness.' In *Muscular Christianity: Embodying the Victorian Age*, edited by Donald E. Hall, 17–44. Cambridge: Cambridge University Press, 1994
Rosman, Abraham, P. G. Rubel and M. Weisgrau. *The Tapestry of Culture: An Introduction to Cultural Anthropology*. 9th ed. Plymouth: AltaMira, 2009
Rossetti, Dante Gabriel. *His Family-Letters, With a Memoir by William Michael Rossetti*. 2 vols. London: Ellis & Elvey, 1895
_____. *Poems*. Edited and with an introduction by Oswald Doughty. London: Dent; New York: Dutton, 1974
Rowe, Katharine. '"God's Handy Worke": Divine Complicity and the Anatomist's Touch.' In *The Body in Parts: Fantasies of Corporeality in Early Modern Europe*, edited by David Hillman and Carla Mazzio, 284–309. New York: Routledge, 1997

Rudy, Jason R. *Electric Meters: Victorian Physiological Poetics*. Ohio: Ohio University Press, 2009

Ruskin, John. *The Works of John Ruskin*. Edited by E. T. Cook and Alexander Wedderburn. 39 vols. London: George Allen, 1903–1912

Russell, William Howard. 'The Battle of Inkermann.' *Times*, 23 November 1854, 6

——. 'The British Expedition.' *Times*, 25 December 1854, 7

——. *The British Expedition to the Crimea*. London: Routledge, 1858

Rylance, Rick. *Victorian Psychology and British Culture, 1850–1880*. Oxford: Oxford University Press, 2000

Said, Edward. *Culture and Imperialism*. London: Vintage, 1994

Salmon, Nicholas. 'The Revision of *A Dream of John Ball*'. *Journal of the William Morris Society* 10, no. 2 (1993): 15–17

——. 'A Study in Victorian Historiography: William Morris's Germanic Romances', *Journal of the William Morris Society* 14, no. 2 (2001): 59–89

Saltzman, Benjamin A. 'William Morris' "Golden Wings" as a Poetic Response to the "Delicate Sentiment" of Tennyson's "Mariana"'. *Victorian Poetry* 49 (2011): 285–99

Sanders, Mike. *The Poetry of Chartism: Aesthetics, Politics, History*. Cambridge: Cambridge University Press, 2009

Sargent, Lyman Tower. 'William Morris and the Anarchist Tradition'. In *Socialism and the Literary Artistry of William Morris*, edited by Florence S. Boos and Carole G. Silver, 61–73. Columbia: University of Missouri Press, 1990

Sartre, Jean Paul. *Being and Nothingness*. Translated by Hazel E. Barnes, introduction by Mary Warnock. London: Methuen, 1958. Reprint, London: Routledge, 1996

——. Preface to *The Wretched of the Earth*, by Frantz Fanon, 7–26. Translated by Constance Farrington. 1967. Reprint, London: Penguin, 2001

Sasso, Eleonora. '"The Road of War" and "The Path of Peace": William Morris's Representation of Violence'. *Cahiers Victoriens et Edouardiens* 66 (2007): 483–96

Sassoon, Siegfried. *The War Poems of Siegfried Sassoon*. London: Faber, 1983

Scarry, Elaine. *The Body in Pain: The Making and Unmaking of the World*. New York: Oxford University Press, 1985

——. *Dreaming by the Book*. Princeton: Princeton University Press, 1999

Scott, Walter. *Ivanhoe*. Vol. 9 of *The Waverley Novels*. Bouverie ed. 25 vols. London: Daily News, 1901

——. 'Johnes's Translation of Froissart'. *Edinburgh Review* (January 1805): 347–62

Sedgwick, Eve Kosofsky. *Between Men: English Literature and Male Homosocial Desire*. With a new preface by the author. New York: Columbia University Press, 1985

Seigel, Jules Paul. *Thomas Carlyle: The Critical Heritage*. London: Routledge and Kegan Paul, 1996

Serres, Michel. *The Five Senses: A Philosophy of Mingled Bodies*. Translated by Margaret Sankey and Peter Cowley. London: Continuum, 2008

——. *Genesis*. Translated by Geneviève James and James Nielson. Ann Arbor: University of Michigan Press, 1995

Shannon, Edgar F. Jr, 'The Critical Reception of Tennyson's Maud'. *PMLA* 68 (1953): 397–417

—— and Christopher Ricks. 'The Charge of the Light Brigade', Appendix B in Ricks, *Tennyson*, 324–63. 2nd ed. Basingstoke: Macmillan, 1989

Shaw, W. David. 'Arthurian Ghosts: The Phantom Art of "The Defence of Guenevere"'. *Victorian Poetry* 34 (1996): 299–312

Silkin, Jon, ed. *The Penguin Book of First World War Poetry*. London: Penguin, 1996
Silver, Carole. *The Romance of William Morris*. Athens: Ohio University Press, 1982
Simcox, G. A. '*The Earthly Paradise*: Poem, by William Morris, Author of *The Life and Death of Jason*. Part III'. *Academy* (12 February 1870): 121–2
Smiles, Aileen. *Samuel Smiles and His Surroundings*. London: Robert Hale, 1956
Smiles, Samuel. *Self-Help*. 1859. Oxford: Oxford University Press, 2002
Smith, Roger. 'The Physiology of the Will: Mind, Body, and Psychology in the Periodical Literature, 1855–1875.' In *Science Serialized: Representations of the Sciences in Nineteenth-Century Periodicals*, edited by Geoffrey Cantor and Sally Shuttleworth, 81–110. Cambridge, MA: MIT Press, 2004
Smith, William Henry. '*Past and Present*, by Carlyle'. *Blackwood's Edinburgh Magazine* (July 1843): 121–38
Smuts, Jan Christiaan. *Holism and Evolution*. London: Macmillan, 1926
Sorel, Georges. *Reflections on Violence*. Translated by T.E. Hulme and J. Roth. New York: Collier Books, 1972
Sørensen, Preben Meulengracht. *The Unmanly Man: Concepts of Sexual Defamation in Early Northern Society*. Translated by Joan Turville-Petre. Odense: Odense University Press, 1983
Southey, Robert. *The Poetical Works of Robert Southey: Collected by Himself*. 10 vols. London: Longman, Orme, Brown, Green and Longmans, 1837
Sparling, Halliday H. *The Kelmscott Press and William Morris, Master-Craftsman*. Folkstone, Kent: Dawsons, 1975
Spatt, Hartley S. 'Morrissaga: *Sigurd the Volsung*'. *ELH* 44 (1977): 355–75
Spencer, Herbert. 'Bain on the Emotions and the Will'. In vol. I of *Essays: Scientific, Political, and Speculative*, 241–64. 3 vols. Library edition. London: Williams and Norgate, 1901
_____. *Principles of Sociology*. 3 vols. London: Williams and Norgate, 1879
_____. 'The Proper Sphere of Government.' In *Political Writings*, 1–57. Edited by John Offer. Cambridge: Cambridge University Press, 1994
Staines, David. 'Morris' Treatment of His Medieval Sources in *The Defence of Guenevere and Other Poems*'. *Studies in Philology* 70 (1973): 439–64
Stallman, Robert L. 'The Lovers' Progress: An Investigation of William Morris' "The Defence of Guenevere" and "King Arthur's Tomb"'. *Studies in English Literature 1500–1900* 15 (1975): 657–70
Stanley, A. P. *The Life of Thomas Arnold, D. D, Head-Master of Rugby*. London: John Murray, 1904
Statham, H. H. 'William Morris: Poet and Craftsman.' *Edinburgh Review* (January 1897): 63–83
Stead, W. T. 'Chinese Gordon for the Soudan.' *Pall Mall Gazette*, 9 January 1884, 1
_____. 'The Seamy Side of Empire.' *Pall Mall Gazette*, 27 January 1887, 1
Stedman Jones, Gareth. *Outcast London: A Study in the Relationship Between Classes in Victorian Society*. Harmondsworth: Penguin, 1976
Stephen, James Fitzjames. 'Gentlemen.' *Cornhill Magazine* 5 (1862): 327–42
Stepniak. 'The Dynamite Scare and Anarchy.' *The New Review*, 6 May 1892, 529–41
_____. *Underground Russia: Revolutionary Profiles and Sketches from Life*. London: Smith Elder, 1883
Stevenson, Kim. 'Ingenuities of the Female Mind: Legal and Public Perceptions of Sexual Violence in Victorian England 1850–1890'. In *Everyday Violence in Britain 1850–1950: Gender and Class*, edited by Shani D'Cruze, 89–103. Harlow: Longmans, 2000
Stevenson, Robert Louis. *The Strange Case of Dr Jekyll and Mr Hyde*. In *The Strange Case of Dr Jekyll and Mr Hyde and Other Tales of Terror*, 5–70. London: Penguin, 2003

Stewart, Garrett. *Novel Violence: A Narratography of Victorian Fiction*. Chicago: University of Chicago Press, 2009

Stewart, Susan. *Poetry and the Fate of the Senses*. Chicago: University of Chicago Press, 2002

Stirling, A. M. W., ed. *The Richmond Papers: From the Correspondence and Manuscripts of George Richmond RA and His Son Sir William Richmond RA, KCB*. London: Heinemann, 1926

Stone, Dan. 'Holocaust and "The Human"'. In *Hannah Arendt and the Uses of History*, edited by Richard H. King and Dan Stone, 232–49. New York: Berghahn Books 2008

Stubbs, William. *The Constitutional History of England in its Origin and Development*. 3 vols. 4th ed. Oxford: Clarendon Press, 1896

Sussman, Herbert. *Victorian Masculinities: Manhood and Masculine Poetics in Early Victorian Literature and Art*. 1995. Reprint, Cambridge: Cambridge University Press, 2008

Swinburne, Algernon. *The Poems of Algernon Charles Swinburne*. 6 vols. London: Chatto and Windus, 1904

Tate, Trudi. 'On Not Knowing Why: Memorializing the Light Brigade'. In *Literature, Science, Psychoanalysis, 1830–1970: Essays in Honour of Gillian Beer*, edited by Helen Small and Trudi Tate, 160–80. Oxford: Oxford University Press, 2003.

Tennyson, Lord Alfred. Epitaph for Charles Gordon. 'Gordon, Tennyson, and Whittier', *Times*, 7 May 1885, 6

———. *The Poems of Tennyson*. Edited by Christopher Ricks. 2nd ed. 3 vols. Harlow: Longman, 1987

Thackeray, William Makepeace. *The Memoirs of Barry Lyndon, Esq*. In vol. IV of *The Works of William Makepeace Thackeray*, 3–270. Biographical edition. 13 vols. London: Smith, Elder, 1898

Theweleit, Klaus. *Male Fantasies*, I: *Women, Floods, Bodies, History*. Translated by Stephen Conway in collaboration with Erica Carter and Chris Turner. Cambridge: Polity Press, 1987

———. *Male Fantasies*, II: *Male Bodies: Psychoanalyzing the White Terror*. Translated by Chris Turner and Erica Carter in collaboration with Stephen Conway. Cambridge: Polity Press, 1989

Thomas, Edward. *The Collected Poems of Edward Thomas*. Edited and with an introduction by R. George Thomas. Oxford: Clarendon Press, 1978

Thompson, E. P. *William Morris, Romantic to Revolutionary*. 2nd ed. London: Merlin Press, 1977

Thorpe, Benjamin. *Northern Mythology: Comprising the Principal Popular Traditions and Superstitions of Scandinavia, North Germany and the Netherlands*. 3 vols. London: Edward Lumley, 1851–1852

Tolkien, J. R. R. *Letters of J R. R. Tolkien*. Edited by Humphrey Carpenter, with the assistance of Christopher Tolkien. London: Allen and Unwin, 1981

Tosh, John. *Manliness and Masculinities in Nineteenth-Century Britain: Essays on Gender, Family and Empire*. Harlow: Pearson Education, 2005

———. 'Masculinities in an Industrializing Society: Britain 1800–1914'. *Journal of British Studies* 44 (April 2005): 330–42

Tucker, Herbert F. 'All for the Tale: The Epic Macropoetics of Sigurd the Volsung'. *Victorian Poetry* 34 (1996): 373–95

———. *Epic: Britain's Heroic Muse 1790–1910*. Oxford: Oxford University Press, 2008

Tylor, Edward B. *Primitive Culture: Researches into the Development of Mythology, Philosophy, Religion, Language, Art, and Custom*. 2 vols. 4th rev. ed. London: Murray, 1903
Vaillant, Ed. 'Vive La Commune'. *Commonweal*, April 1885, 17
Valente, Joseph. 'The Manliness of Parnell.' *Éire-Ireland* 41 (2006): 64–113
Vance, Norman. *The Sinews of the Spirit: The Ideal of Christian Manliness in Victorian Literature and Religious Thought*. Cambridge: Cambridge University Press, 1985
Vaninskaya, Anna. 'Dreams of John Ball: Reading the Peasants' Revolt in the Nineteenth Century'. *Nineteenth-Century Contexts* 31 (2009): 45–57
_____. *William Morris and the Idea of Community: Romance, History and Propaganda, 1880–1914*. Edinburgh: Edinburgh University Press, 2010
Vindex. *Cecil Rhodes: His Political Life and Speeches 1881–1900*. London: Chapman and Hall, 1900
Vrettos, Athena. 'Defining Habits: Dickens and the Psychology of Repetition'. *Victorian Studies* 42 (2000): 399–436
Waithe, Marcus. '*News from Nowhere*, Utopia, and Bakhtin's Idyllic Chronotope'. *Textual Practice* 16 (2002): 459–72
_____. *William Morris's Utopia of Strangers: Victorian Medievalism and the Ideal of Hospitality*. Cambridge: Brewer, 2006
Walton, Susan. *Imagining Soldiers and Fathers in the Mid-Victorian Era: Charlotte Yonge's Models of Manliness*. Farnham, Surrey: Ashgate, 2010
Waters, Chris. *British Socialists and the Politics of Popular Culture, 1884–1914*. Manchester: Manchester University Press, 1990
_____. 'Morris's "Chants" and the Problems of Socialist Culture'. In *Socialism and the Literary Artistry of William Morris*, edited by Florence S. Boos and Carole G. Silver, 127–46. Columbia: University of Missouri Press, 1990
Watts, Theodore. 'Literature: *The Story of Sigurd the Volsung*'. *Athenaeum* (9 December 1876): 753–5
Wawn, Andrew. *The Vikings and the Victorians: Inventing the Old North in Nineteenth-Century Britain*. Cambridge: Brewer, 2002
Wells, H. G. *The Time Machine*. Edited by Patrick Parrinder, introduction by Marina Warner. London: Penguin, 2005
Wheeler, Bonnie. 'Romance and Parataxis and Malory: The Case of Sir Gawain's Reputation'. *Arthurian Literature* 12 (1993): 109–32
Wiener, Martin J. *Men of Blood: Violence, Manliness and Criminal Justice in Victorian England*. Cambridge: Cambridge University Press, 2004
Wiens, Pamela Bracken. 'The Reviews Are In: Reclaiming the Success of Morris's Socialist Interlude'. *Journal of the William Morris Society* 9, no. 2 (1991): 16–21
Wilde, Oscar. "The English Renaissance." In *Miscellanies*. Vol. 6 of *Complete Writings of Oscar Wilde*. 10 vols. New York: The Nottingham Society, 1909
Williams, Raymond. *Keywords: A Vocabulary of Culture and Society*. London: Fontana, 1983
Wilmer, Clive. 'Maundering Medievalism: Dante Gabriel Rossetti and William Morris's Poetry.' *PN Review* 29, no. 3 (2003): 69–73
Woolf, Virginia. *Three Guineas*. London: Hogarth Press, 1938
Woolford, John and Daniel Karlin. *Robert Browning*. London: Longman, 1996
Wordsworth, William and Samuel Taylor Coleridge. *Lyrical Ballads*. Edited by Michael Mason. 2nd ed. Harlow: Pearson Education, 2007
X. 'From My Study'. *Musical Times* (1 August 1897): 518–21
Yonge, Charlotte M. *The Heir of Redclyffe*. London: Macmillan, 1888

Manuscripts

Morris, William. 'The Wasted Land'. London, British Library, Add. MS. 45328, William Morris Literary Manuscripts, fols 194–5

Sound Recordings

Yeats, W. B. Introduction to a reading of 'The Lake Isle of Innisfree', broadcast on the BBC on 10 April 1932. 'The Spoken Word: Poets' CD: Historic Recordings from the British Library Sound Archive

INDEX

aestheticism 101
After London (Jefferies) 102–3, 158
anarchists xiv, xx, 134, 154, 156, 159–60; Chicago 135
Angel in the House, The (Patmore) 33
Arata, Stephen 71
Arendt, Hannah 151, 157
Armstrong, Isobel 31–2, 37, 45, 54
Arnold, Matthew xviii, 30, 92–3
Arnold, Thomas 70
Auden, W. H. 169
Austin, Alfred 68, 95
Austin, J. L. 39
Aytoun, W. E. 5

Bachelard, Gaston 25
Bain, Alexander: *The Emotions and the Will* 113; *The Senses and the Intellect* 1–2, 4, 13, 32, 47, 59
Bakhtin, M. M. 102
Ballantyne, Tony xviii
barbarism xi, xix, 67, 100–109, 111
Bataille, Georges xiii, 15–16
Baudrillard, Jean 160
Bax, Ernest Belfort 32, 44, 109, 117; as editor of *To-Day* 134; on General Gordon 105; *Socialism Its Growth and Outcome* 98–9, 103 (*see also* Morris, William)
Beaumont, Matthew 142, 155, 164
beauty: in architecture 152; arising from death and destruction 120; in battle 14, 122, 131, 169; of body 37, 119; of the hand 24; of life 70, 112–13; and love 54; madness as a result of 52; misuse of 117; as a Morrisian value xiv; in *News from Nowhere* 161; as a result of work 23, 117, 119, 127; of sacrificial violence 146; as a sign of moral purity 40; sleeping 86; socialist ideals of 167–8; and truth 41
Beer, Gillian 11
Bellamy, Edward: *Looking Backward* xvi, 114, 158
Beowulf 110, 113, 119, 127
Bevington, Louisa Sarah 134
Bevis, Matthew xiii, 6, 30
Blackwood's 5, 105
Blair, Kirstie 40
Blake, William 136
Bleak House (Dickens) 11
Bloch, Ernst 112, 161
Blunden, Edmund 169
body: actions of 1–2, 55, 82; after death 19, 59, 61, 72, 153–4; in battle xvii, xxi, 14, 30, 36, 57, 136, 144; and its boundaries 15; of Christ 14; effects of violence on the xii, 7, 9, 85, 110, 124; of Guenevere 36–44; imprisoned 32; inert 86; John Brown's 137; language and the 31, 47, 50; and mind 2, 13–14, 137, 139; needs of the 62, 113, 118; in pain 33, 47, 51–2, 60 (*see also* Scarry, Elaine); in parts 21–3, 123; and soul 17, 69; transfiguration of the 73; transformation of the 137, 141–3, 161–2; in Victorian culture xi, xvi, xxi; as a way of knowing, 14, 27–8, 148; and world 8, 11–12, 17, 34
Boos, Florence S. xiv, 32, 98, 114, 131, 144
Bourdieu, Pierre 132
Bourke, Joanna xxi, 14–16, 123, 168

Brantlinger, Patrick 54, 98–9, 135, 171
Brittain, Vera 122–3, 170–71
Brombert, Victor 55–6
Browning, Elizabeth Barrett xv; 'The Brown Rosary' 57; *Aurora Leigh* 33; 'The Romaunt of the Page' 34
Browning, Robert 34, 69, 93; 'Count Gismond' 39; *Men and Women* 33; 'My Last Duchess' 58, 79
Brunanburh, The Battle of 127. *See also* Tennyson, Alfred Lord
Buchanan, Robert [Thomas Maitland] 69, 71, 85, 101
Bullen, J. B. 31
Burne-Jones, Edward xii, 3–5, 62, 85; *The Merciful Knight* 14
Burne-Jones Georgiana 5, 102, 165
Burne-Jones, Philip 79
Butler, Judith 72

Campbell, Matthew 142
capitalism: anti- 167; colonialism as an expression of 105; in contrast to Marxism 97; destruction of 112; Empire of 108; and free trade 5; literature and art under 99; narrative of 29; overthrow of 161, 167; rise of 153; the soldier as a tool of 106; struggle against 132–3; ugliness of 112; and unjust war 162; utilitarian 16; values of 4; Victorian 136
Carlyle, Thomas 4–5, 82; 'The Early Kings of Norway' 70; and Germany 94; 'The Hero as Divinity' xvii, 77; *On Heroes* xviii, 66, 77; on heroism 82, 86; on Martin Luther 12; 'The Nibelungen Lied' 8 (*see also Nibelungelied, The*); *Past and Present* 16–17, 23, 95; 'Signs of the Times' 23; on submission to authority 71; and typography 27; on the will 82, 142
Ceadel, Martin 118
chivalry: code of 9; discourses of xi; fourteenth-century 167; General Gordon's 105; ideals of xx; knightly 7; language of 168; poetry of x, 43; tales of xv; trappings of 17; 'violent amusements' of 18
civilization: advance of 74; advanced 30; and barbarism xi, xix, 100–102, 106; British 106; capitalist 99, 111, 120; 'cramped and ignoble' 119; deadening effect of 133; destruction of 101, 103; discourse of 6; gains of 104; 'Hopes of' xvi, 108 (*see also* Morris, William); modern 101, 105, 114, 131; peace and 18, 132; Roman 97, 107–8, 113–14; Victorian 98, 113; Western 87; world of 151
Clausewitz, Carl von 15, 24, 126
Clover, Carol 86
Cobden, Richard 118, 126, 132, 162
Commonweal, The xx, 99–100, 146, 131–2, 138; account of Bloody Sunday in 160; 'The Development of Modern Society' in 108 (*see also* Morris, William); European martyrs in 148, 153; Freiligrath's poetry in 137 (*see also* Freiligrath, Ferdinand); idea of order attacked in 141; *News from Nowhere* in 156, 161; *Pilgrims and Chants* in 136; portrayal of General Gordon in 105 (*see also* Gordon, General Charles); 'Unattractive Labour' in 111 (*see also* Morris, William); Vaillant writing in 144 (*see also* Vaillant, Edouard)
Commune, Paris 14–16, 142, 158, 160
courage: acts of 67, 87; and battle 1, 20, 23, 28; communal 120; and cowardice 3, 30, 78; and eagerness 79; in the face of death 20, 92; failures of 77, 80, 82, 84; fellowship in 106; fourteenth-century 167; and heroism 27, 129; and hope 70, 91; individual 24, 65–6; the Kukuanas' 106; and loss of restraint 75; and manliness xviii, 86–8; manly 74, 91; martial 12, 77; as a Northern characteristic 68; performative 83; physical 16, 65, 158; poetic representations of 93; and truth 5; violent 84, 89; as a virtue 94, 104; women and 89–91, 95; worship of 67, 71

Crimean War, the. *See* war(s)
Crystal Age, A (Hudson) 158

Darwin, Charles 117
Darwinism, social 75, 116–17, 158
Das, Santanu 12
Dasent, George xviii, 75, 80, 87
Dawson, Graham xviii
Deane, Bradley 101–2, 104
De Beauvoir, Simone 89
degeneration xix, 69, 74, 94, 112, 118
Dentith, Simon 66–7
Dickens, Charles 11
Digby, Kenelm 18; *The Broad Stone of Honour* 5
Dixon, Richard Watson 1–3, 5, 15, 19–22
Dobell, Sydney: *England in Time of War* 3; *Sonnets on the War* 6. *See also* Smith, Alexander
Douglas, Mary 14–15, 154
Doyle, Conan 102
duel: hand-to-hand 23; war as 15, 24
Dumas, Alexandre xv
Dusky Men, the 97, 108, 114–19, 125–7

Eastern Question, the 79, 83
Eliot, George xv
Engels, Friedrich 103, 161
epic 66–8, 90, 102; Anglo-Saxon 119–20, 127; rhythms of 137
evolution: Darwinian 158 (*see also* Darwin, Charles); of history 99; Lamarckian 158 (*see also* Lamarck); and revolution 111 (*see also* revolution)

Fanon, Frantz 133, 146, 157
Fourier, Charles 108
Frantzen, Allen J. 150
freedom(s) 21, 33, 43–4, 57–8, 82; battle for 149; and behaviour 84; the cause of 1, 152; dream of 56; egalitarian 70; and equality 165; in future society 165; gender roles and 62; of hand and mind 23; idea of 5; lack of 78; manhood and 72; peace and 161; personal 80; political 65, 80; price of 57; in the sagas 71; sexual 35; violence and 51, 58, 155, 164; 'war, labour' and ix, 169; from wrong 172
Freiligrath, Ferdinand 137
Froissart, Jean: *Boys' Froissart, The* 169; combat in *Chronicles* of 45; in 'Concerning Geffray Teste Noire' 53, 55; Hundred Years' War in *Chronicles* of 167; the Peasants' Revolt in *Chronicles* of 147, 154; republication of *Chronicles* of xiv; as a source for *The Defence of Guenevere* xvii, 34; Walter Scott on xv
Fulford, William 5

Gallagher, Catherine 61
Gaskell, Elizabeth 6
Gates, Barbara T. 93
Genette, Gérard 107
Gibbon, Edward 114, 121
Gibson, James J. 13
Girard, René xiv, 149–50, 153
Glasier, John Bruce 140–41, 148
Godwin, William: *Caleb Williams* 134; *Political Justice* 155
Goode, John 71, 91, 120, 146, 148
Gordon, General Charles 105–6. *See also* Bax, Ernest Belfort; chivalry; *Commonweal, The*; Tennyson, Alfred Lord
greed xvi, 4, 19–20, 79, 83–5, 106; for gold 75, 82
Green, John Richard 147

Haggard, H. Rider xix, 102, 105, 109; *Eric Brighteyes* 85, 104; *King Solomon's Mines* 106–7, 110–11; 'A Zulu War-Dance' 106–7
Hassett, Constance 32
Hedges, Chris 168, 170
Heeley, Wilfred 17
Heir of Redclyffe, The (Yonge) 5
Helsinger, Elizabeth 62
Henderson, Andrea 46
Henderson, James Frederick 165
Henley, W. E. 6, 41
Henty, G. A. 105, 167
Herbert, Karen 32
history: 9/11 in relation to 160; accounts of violence in xii; and determinism

143; of dialectical materialism 98; end of 155, 165; of epic poetry 68; evidence of 44, 157–8; evolution of 99; of the fictionalization of violence 120; of Great Men xviii; heroic 67; Homeric writing of 100; of ideas xiii, 170; inevitabilities of xxi, 70–71; in *John Ball* 149; living 103; of manliness 72, 93; Marxist conception of 104, 111, 134; mythologizing of 146; of the Peasants' Revolt 147; poetic construction of 51, 53–5; in relation to 'The Defence of Guenevere' 36; rereading of xx; romance of xv, 129, 171; true conception of 101; of violence xvii; of the Volsung people 89; of women in warfare 128; the world's 119; of writing about violence xiii, 168–9

Hodgson, Amanda 2, 10

Holman Hunt, William xii. *See also* Pre-Raphaelites

Holzman, Michael 149, 163

hope: in action 60–61; courage and 70, 79, 95; in death 20; in destruction 102, 105, 120; in disruption xvi, 57–8; expressed in struggle 144, 162, 171; future 136, 145–6; God as an extension of 51; legacy of 153; of pleasure in rest 119; for the poor 83; of redemption 19; and strife xvi, ix–x; violence as an expression of 55, 91, 132–3, 135, 139–40

Hopkins, Gerard Manley 142

Houen, Alex 153, 168

Howitt, Mary 94

Howitt, William 94

Hudson, William 158

Hughes, Thomas 13, 88; *The Manliness of Christ* 66

Hunt, Leigh 169

hymns 137–8, 140

Hyndman, H. M. 147

Iceland xvii–xix, 87; language of 85; literature of 68, 80, 84, 86, 94; Morris's vision of 66, 70

imperialism: anti- 118; and barbarianism 102; discourses of 98, 104–5; ideologies of 100; manliness and 67; narratives of xxi; representation of xiii; and violence 65

imprisonment: as an alternative to action 33; in contrast with pain 44; in contrast with violence 56; escape from 57; of European socialists 153; Romantic concept of 55

injustice: battle against xx, 147; battle as a means of resolving 13; capitalist xix; consequences of 70; corporeal imagination in rebellion against 62; and its effects on the land xxi; government as a result of 155; present 151; relation to the Eastern Question 79; of the state 134; in Tennyson's *Maud* 144; twentieth-century 133. *See also* justice

Irigaray, Luce 90

Isandlwana 115

'Isandul'a' (Lawrence, Harding) 115

James, Simon 116

James, William: 'The Moral Equivalent of War' xv–xvi; and the 'romance of history' 129, 171. *See also* history; war(s)

Jameson, Fredric 163, 165

Janowitz, Anne 136–7

Jefferies, Richard 102–3, 158. *See also After London* (Jefferies)

Joan of Arc 35, 49

Johnson, Lionel 157

Jones, Chris 169

Jones, David 12, 165, 167, 169

Joy, George: *General Gordon's Last Stand* 105

Joynes, J. L. 134

justice: in battle 14, 125; ideas of 117; to the memory of John Ball 145; and patriotism 135; in the Peasants' Revolt 155; social xiv; without violence 131. *See also* injustice

Kaeuper, Richard W. xv, 13, 20, 26

Karlin, Daniel xiii, 33

Keats, John 41, 63

Kenworthy, John C. 158
Kingsley, Charles xvi, 4, 6, 13, 66; and Christian Socialism 83; *Hereward the Wake* 28, 104; and manliness 76; and racial purity 80; and *thumos* 76; *Two Years Ago* 5, 30; *Westward Ho!* 1, 5; *Yeast*, 17, 25
Kipling, Rudyard xiii, 102, 171; and 'hooliganism' 71; and the working-class soldier 128
Kirchhoff, Frederick 49
kisses 9, 47–50, 52, 54
Kropotkin, Peter 134

Lamarck 158. *See also* evolution
La Motte Fouqué, Friedrich 5
Lang, Andrew 109, 111
Laqueur, Thomas 86
Latham, David 132
Lawrence, T. E. 168
Laycock, Thomas 88
Lecercle, Jean-Jacques xii
Lennox, Lt. General William James 171
Lewis, C. S. 169
lies xxi, 46–7, 91; beautiful 129. *See also* truth
Livesey, Ruth xi, 120

Macaulay, Thomas Babington 103
MacCarthy, Fiona 2
MacDonald, Robert H. 126–7
Machann, Clinton 74
Mackail, J. W. xii, 3, 34
Magnússon, Eiríkr xix, 66, 94
Mallett, Paul Henri 92
manliness: adventurous 106; and ambidexterity 28; animal 74–6; barbarian 101, 104, 111; and character 142; communal 70, 76–7, 159, 161, 163; and courage xviii; evident in hands 25–6; and health 69, 71; ideas of xi, xvi, xix, 22; and identity 6, 167–8; inclusive 70, 84; meanings of ix, 65–7, 69; national 107; Northern 94, 97; parameters of 77–81, 95, 100; performative 72, 83; physical 13; and violence xix, 68; of war xv, xvi, xx; in women 84–90, 91–3

Markovits, Stefanie xiii, 6, 10
Marseillaise, the x, 119, 139
Marsh, George P. 85
Marsh, Jan 88
Marshes, the Dead 169. *See also* Tolkien, J. R. R.
martyrs, working class 145, 148, 152–3
Marx, Karl 161; and dialectical materialism 76, 124, 146, 151, 157; and historiography 101, 104, 111; and ideology 85; and the 'language of real life' 121; and progress 104; and revolution 156; and the senses 113. *See also* revolution
Maurice, C. Edmund 147
Maurice, F. D. 13
McCrae, John 124, 171
McLoughlin, Kate 170
medievalism xi, xiv, xvi, 5, 17, 45
Meier, Paul xiv, 156
Melliet, Leo 140
Meredith, George 93
Merleau-Ponty, Maurice 7, 10, 27, 45, 50
Mill, James 103
Mill, John Stuart: on barbarism and civilization 104, 108–9, 117; on character and will 82, 142; on women 87–9, 142
Millais, John Everett xii, 52
Morel, Bénédict 71
Morgan, Lewis 103
Morris, May: on *Chants for Socialists* 137; as editor and memoirist ix, xiv, xix; on *John Ball* 150; on Morris's response to Bloody Sunday 160; as recipient of Morris's letters 106
Morris, William: *The Aeneids of Virgil* 124; 'The Aims of Art' 70; 'The Blue Closet' 35; 'The Aims of Art' 70; *Chants for Socialists* xx, 136–45, 166; 'The Churches of North France' 62; 'Concerning Geffray Teste Noire' 35, 45, 52–5, 59, 86; *The Defence of Guenevere* xvii, 6, 31–63; 'The Defence of Guenevere' 35–44, 50–53, 57, 59–61; 'The Development of Modern Society' 108 (*see also Commonweal, The*); '

A Dream' 7; *A Dream of John Ball* xvi, xx, 132, 145–55, 165–6; *The Earthly Paradise* xvii, xx, 46, 68; 'Gertha's Lovers' 15, 17–22, 108; 'Golden Wings' (1856) 3, 15–16, 23, 29, 60; 'Golden Wings' (1858) 35, 52, 55, 60–61; 'A Good Knight in Prison' 35, 56–7; 'The Haystack in the Floods' 35, 45, 50–52; 'The Hollow Land' 2, 8–15, 19, 23–4, 26, 28, 168; 'The Hopes of Civilization' xvi; *The House of the Wolfings* xix, 97–129; 'In Prison' 35, 57–8; 'King Arthur's Tomb' 31, 46, 49; 'Lindenborg Pool' 11; *News from Nowhere* xvi, xx, 98–9, 116–17, 132, 135, 140, 155–166, 170; *The Pilgrims of Hope* xvi, xx, 136–7, 141–5, 150, 165–6; 'Rapunzel' 34–5, 48–50, 60; review of Browning's *Men and Women* 33–4; *The Roots of the Mountains* xix, 97–129; *Signs of Change* 134; *Sigurd the Volsung* xviii–xx, 65–95, 97, 142; 'Sir Peter Harpdon's End' 45–9; *Socialism Its Growth and Outcome* 98 (*see also* Bax, Ernest Belfort); 'Socialists at Play' ix–x, xx–xxi; 'Spellbound' 35, 46; 'Svend and his Brethren' 15, 24, 28; 'Unattractive Labour' 111 (*see also Commonweal, The*); *Völsunga Saga* xix, 81–3, 94; 'Why I am a Communist' 135; 'The Wind' 58–60

Morte Darthur (Malory): battle tales of xvi; Gawayne's trial by ladies in 42; Guenevere in 38; hands in 24, 28; injury in 51; knights in 4, 14, 37, 40; language of 110; as a source for *The Defence of Guenevere* xvii, 34; T. E. Lawrence's edition of 168 (*see also* Lawrence, T. E.)

Newbolt, Henry 126
Nibelungenlied, The xix, 8, 81, 83 (*see also* Carlyle, Thomas)
Nietzsche, Friedrich 81
Northern Antiquities (Mallet) 92

O'Brien, Tim 129
Owen, Robert 108

Owen, Wilfred 26, 167, 171
Oxford and Cambridge Magazine, The xvi–xvii, 1, 17, 32, 108; the Crimean War in 3; review of Tennyson's *Maud* in 5 (*see also* Fulford, William); T. E. Lawrence's copies from 168
Oxford Movement, the xvi

Patmore, Coventry 33
peace: absence of 34; in the barbarian gens 104; blameless 149; in *Chants for Socialists* 140; and commerce 119, 132–3; deceptive 19; false 143–4, 159; future 135–7; harvest of 124; lessons of 167; long-term negotiations for 1; Morris's vision of 131–2; movement, the nineteenth-century xi; perpetual 162; and political expediency 15; postviolent 161, 165; and reason 163–4; Ruskin on 18; Sigurd born in 75; strife and x; utopian 165; violence as a means of bringing about 98, 108, 135, 156, 168, 171–2; and war 37, 128; W. E. Aytoun on 5
Peace Society, the 4, 118–9
Peck, John x, 6, 31
Pfeiffer, Emily: 'The Fight at Rorke's Drift' 115
Pick, Daniel xvi
Pinkney, Tony xiv, 155–6
play x–xii, 102, 119–20, 128, 154; battle- 127; beautiful 18; hand- 119, 127; sword- 9; theatrical xx, 47; up! 126. *See also* work
Poe, Edgar Allan 57
Popper, Karl 163–5, 170
Pound, Ezra 169
Praz, Mario 44
Pre-Raphaelites 69
Prinsep, Val xii

Rask, Rasmus 85
'Raven, The' (Poe) 57
Reid, Julia 109
revolution: American 157; evolution and 111, 158 (*see also* evolution); failed 147; French 137, 139, 157;

historical 146; hope and xvi; Marxist 156; in *News from Nowhere* 160–62; in relation to violence xx, 99, 112, 131–6; sentiments 137–8; socialist 55
Rhodes, Cecil xix, 104–5
Ricks, Christopher 126
Rogers, James Thorold 147
Rorke's Drift 115
Rosen, David 76
Rossetti, Dante Gabriel xii, 31, 69, 71, 85; *Bocca baciata* 62; *Lady Lilith* 62; 'The Blessed Damozel' 61
Ruskin xvi–ii, 4, 70; and the grotesque 32; on manliness 70, 80; 'Of Queens' Gardens' 87, 90; *The Stones of Venice* 23, 28; 'War' 5, 18
Russell, William Howard: despatches from the Crimea xvi, 6, 11; *see also Times, The*
Rylance, Rick 4

sacrifice xx, 108, 152; Christian ideas of xvi, 145, 151; the concept of 149–50, 153; and excess xiii, 15; Girardian ideologies of 165; individual 108; and indulgence 46; myths of 146, 151; the narrative of 164; self- xi, xviii, 89, 93, 126, 150, 166–9; of the working classes 148
Saint-Simon, Henri de 108
Salmon, Nicholas 116
Sanders, Mike 138, 140
Sartre, Jean-Paul 10–12, 146
Sasso, Eleonora 3
Sassoon, Siegfried 124
Scarry, Elaine 21, 33, 51
Scheherezade 36. *See also Thousand and One Nights, The*
Scott, Walter xv, 36
Sedgwick, Eve Kosofsky 90
Serres, Michel 29
Shelley, Percy Bysshe 136
Silver, Carole 2–3, 48, 77
Sintram (Fouqué) 5
Smiles, Samuel 82, 88, 142
Smith, Alexander: *Sonnets on the War* 6. *See also* Dobell

Smith, Roger 13
Smith, W. H. 95
socialism: Bellamy's idea of xvi, 114, 158 (*see also* Bellamy, Edward); British 156; capitalism and 99; Christian 83; early struggles of 165; fin-de-siècle xi; historical development of 98; John Stuart Mill on 109; Marxist 97; Morris's campaigning for 150; Morris's commitment to xiii; Morris's conversion to xx, 83; parliamentary 170; and peace 118; propagation of 136; religious 151; in *Signs of Change* 134 (*see also* Morris, William); Victorian 140
Socialist League, the ix, xx, 99, 138, 154, 156
Socialist Society, Hammersmith 156
Sorel, Georges 145, 148–9, 157
Sørensen, Preben Meulengracht, 80
Southey, Robert xvii
Spatt, Hartley S. 81–2, 93
Spencer, Herbert 117, 162
Stephen, James Fitzjames 94
Stephens, George 94
Stewart, Garrett xii
Stewart, Susan 19
Stubbs, William 147, 154
suicide xviii, 85, 88–93, 95
Sussman, Herbert ix, 66
Swinburne, Algernon 69, 95

Tennyson, Alfred Lord xiii, 4, 30, 93, 105; 'Battle of Brunanburh' 127; 'Charge of the Light Brigade' 6, 125–6; *Idylls of the King* 7, 37, 66, 74, 83; *In Memoriam* 141; 'Mariana' 57, 60; *Maud* 1, 5–6, 10, 77, 139, 144; *The Princess* 66
Thackeray, William 6
Theweleit, Klaus 74, 78
Thomas, Edward 169
Thompson, E. P. xiv, 2, 143
Thousand and One Nights, The xv. *See also* Scheherezade
Time Machine, The (Wells) 116
Times, The 6, 11
To-Day 134, 145, 153

Tolkien, J. R. R. 169
Tosh, John xviii, 65, 107
touch: creative 25; desecrating 19; exploratory 13; the hand as an agent of 24–9; imaginary 47; Midas 4; sense of 11–12, 50; sight and 54–6; of swords, 14; transformative xvi; of violence 7–10, 15
truth 5, 16, 32, 43, 48, 22; abstract xvii, 39, 55; and beauty 41; and courage 94; and imagination 63; and lies 91; moral 38; seekers after 136; of word 18. *See also* beauty; lies
Tucker, Herbert F. 66, 71, 92
Tylor, Edward Burnett 104

ugliness 111–12, 118, 129, 164; of death 152
utopia 56, 155–6, 158, 163–5

Vaillant, Edouard 144
Valente, Joseph 84
Vaninskaya, Anna 99, 102, 146

Wagner, Richard 77
Waithe, Marcus 114, 146, 149, 152, 163
war(s): absolute 97, 107, 118, 129; against Russia 79, 82; American Civil 138; Anglo–Zulu 115; anti- 98, 111, 129; civil 99, 134, 156–7, 160–61; class 150, 154; Clausewitz on 24 (*see also* Clausewitz, Carl von); commercial 112, 132, 135; -craft 107; Crimean xi, xiii, xvi, 1, 3–6, 11, 17–18, 20–22, 29, 30–31; -dance 106; of empire 108, 143–4; epic 110; extravagance of 18–20; fellowship of 146; First World 12, 119–20, 122, 165, 167–9; as handwork 24, 26–8, 169; harvest of 124; Hundred Years' 46, 167–8; ideal 158; just 21, 172; lessons of 167; literature of ix–xvii, 3, 6, 12, 19, 167, 170; memorials 25; necessity of 125, 151; noble 98; open 17, 104, 135; organic 155; patriotic 135; and peace 128; as play 127; poets 169, 171; rhetoric of 145; role of women in 5, 32–3, 60–61, 87; as romance of history xv, 129, 171 (*see also* James, William); Ruskin on 5, 18 (*see also* Ruskin, John); and sacrifice 15–16; sounds of 142; stories of 34, 53–5, 99–100, 109; tactics of 36–7; on terror 153, 168; transformative 157; trauma of 58–9; unjust 98, 162; the work of xix, xx, 122, 126, 128 (*see also* work)
Warren, Sir Charles 160
warrior x–xi, 14, 105, 149; in battle 24, 121–3; berserker 104; -cry 20; in death 21; -epic 127; female 36, 86–7, 95; General Gordon as 105 (*see also* Gordon, General Charles); hands of a 22, 120; ideal 77; -knights xxi, 16; masculine 78; medievalist 168; Nordic 92; -society 88; the Unknown 25; the Zulu 106–7, 115
Waters, Chris 138
Wawn, Andrew xviii, 65
weapon(s) 28; hand-crafted 121; the body as 36 (*see also* body)
Wells, H. G. 116
will 71–7; revolutionary 142–3
Wilmer, Clive 69
Woolf, Virginia 128
Woolford, John 33
work: alienation from 78–9; creative 29, 70; and degeneration 116–17; hand- 21–8, 55, 112, 169; hard xv; necessary 2; and play x–xi, 119–20, 128; satisfying 113, 171; unwilling 17; violence as 149, 157, 159; war as xvi, 100, 104, 120–29, 154, 168–9; of writing 27
Wright Mills, C. 143

Yonge, Charlotte M. 5

www.ingramcontent.com/pod-product-compliance
Lightning Source LLC
Chambersburg PA
CBHW021824300426
44114CB00009BA/308